The Sales Professional

The Sales Professional

Strategies and Techniques for Managing the High-Level Sale

DAVID MERCER

KOGAN
PAGE

First published in 1988 by
Kogan Page Ltd,
120 Pentonville Rd,
London N1 9JN

Photoset in North Wales by
Derek Doyle & Associates, Mold, Clwyd
Printed and bound in Great Britain by
Billing & Sons Ltd, Worcester

British Library Cataloguing in Publication Data

Mercer, David
    The sales professional
    1. Salesmanship – Manuals
    I. Title
    658.8′5

    ISBN 1-85091-615-2

Contents

Chapter 1

Introduction

The Sales Professional

This book is a practical guide to the many activities that the sales professional may encounter in his work. A glance at the contents list will indicate just how many of these there may be. Indeed, the list of possible functions makes his role far wider ranging, and I would argue ultimately more important, than the 'job specs' of almost all other professionals, with perhaps only the management consultant approaching this breadth of skill.

It approaches all these topics from the viewpoint of the practical, pragmatic sales professional, not from the theoretical perspective of the academic. There is, quite deliberately, almost no abstract theory included; and much of that which is discussed, for the sake of completeness, is not directly relevant to what is an essentially practical job. It is based on my own experiences as a sales professional, mainly in the sales force of IBM, arguably one of the most professional in the world.

The emphasis is on providing examples of how the sales professional can realistically approach each of the various activities. Virtually all these examples have been drawn directly from my own experience; the exceptions, apart from the quotes from other authors, being authenticated examples given to me by colleagues. All of them represent the experiences, good and bad, of successful sales professionals; but not of the sales supermen beloved of most sales trainers, who are so difficult, and ultimately so demoralising, for most sales professionals to try to follow.

Much of this book is about *enjoying* 'adventurous' selling. Indeed, the working title, before it became apparent that 'professionalism' was the central concept, was 'The Adventurous Salesman'. As a result, much of it is about breaking many of the so-called 'rules' that are hung around the necks of those starting on a career in sales; and which they slavishly follow until the time that such simplistic rules are naturally forgotten in the joyful pursuit of the sale itself.

This book is therefore definitely *not* a primer for 'rookies'. It does not promise to turn the novice instantly into a world-beating sales professional. There are hundreds of books that *will* claim to offer such all-encompassing panaceas, so if these simplistic solutions are what you seek then close this book and look elsewhere. If basics are what you want, then get hold of a copy of Dale Carnegie's *How to Win Friends and Influence People*; I believe that it is still the best introduction.

If, on the other hand, you have already had some, even if limited, sales experience; and have at least begun to appreciate that every sales call is to some degree different – so that standardised techniques, learnt by rote, must inevitably offer less than optimal solutions – then read on. For this book is quite deliberately aimed at the experienced sales professional; and primarily at the sales professional who is *already* successful. It presumes that you have at least taken the first faltering, and probably painfully embarrassing steps to develop your *own* style of selling; and that you have discovered for yourself some of the self-awareness and accompanying self-confidence that is the mark of the good sales professional. Its prime objective is to help you to build on that basis of individual style; perhaps to develop some more productive and more sophisticated selling skills, as well as to extend these into new areas – but most of all to help you to develop skills that enable you best to *enjoy* the profession of selling.

The framework is largely based on the sets of philosophies and disciplines that have made IBM's sales force the most admired and feared in the computer industry; and have earned its sales professionals the reputation of being among the best, and most truly professional, in the world. It is perhaps unlikely that you will be able to deploy the massive resources or the high level of sophistication that IBM has at its command; but you *will* be able to use the very simple, common-sense sales techniques and account management skills that its sales professionals are taught – and to use them effectively.

One of the great sources of IBM's sales strength has always been its recognition that its sales professionals are individuals, each with his own unique style. IBM's sales training sets out to complement and develop that individual style – not to replace it. What I attempt to offer is essentially a 'cookbook' containing a very wide range of techniques and ideas that have worked for other sales professionals; in particular for those hundreds of IBM sales professionals I trained. I hope you will be able to select a few of these that will also be a good fit to your own style, and thus work for you too. It is possible, perhaps even likely, that the majority of the ideas will be alien to your unique needs; although I trust they will still be found interesting, not least because they may indicate how some of your competitors work!

Your main contribution to reading this book, therefore, should be that of selection. There is no way that you could walk into your next call and remember all the various sales techniques – even if they were suitable for you – let alone use them effectively. So concentrate on the few that you feel you might be comfortable with and perhaps even enjoy!

Try working those that you select into your sales campaigns, where they are suitable. Above all, critically evaluate whether they really do work for you; and, as with any technique that is suggested to you, be prepared to discard them ruthlessly if they don't 'pay for their keep'. The aim of a sales call is to make the sale, not to demonstrate technique. Don't be too greedy. If only one idea out of this whole book works for you – and it only increases your productivity by 1 per cent, then your investment will have been repaid within the next few hours of selling!

In the case of the account management skills, which are normally not taught by sales trainers, you may (if you are a typical sales professional) find rather more activities that you could (and should) implement. In which case, you may want to make a list of actions that you think you might profitably take to improve the handling of your accounts. You can then work steadily through this list, crossing off each as you implement it; until you have a very well managed set of customers and prospects. I suspect that these suggested management actions may be the most productive ideas you will get from the book. Like many such resolutions, though, they will not necessarily be easy to implement; it will be much easier to lapse into bad habits again, but it is worth persevering. As you will see from the rest of the book, after 'selling' itself, management is the central function of the sales professional.

To allow the widest selection of ideas and techniques, the book is written from the viewpoint of the more complex and sophisticated sales strategies and tactics needed to handle major accounts or industrial sales, and especially those of the high-technology industries. This is sometimes called the 'complex sale', a terminology I will follow. It also reflects my own involvement for 15 years with the various IBM sales forces. Clearly, though, many of the ideas are just as applicable, and certainly more easily applied, in less complex sales situations. But I repeat once more, it is for *you* to choose what is of value in your own specific sales environment – and, I cannot overstress, to choose what you *enjoy*.

The book also differs from most other sales training books in the weighting it gives to the various topics. It devotes less space to the basic techniques of selling, generally the staple diet of books such as this, since it assumes that by now you probably know about selling in general – and certainly know 100 per cent more about *your* selling in particular. Where it refers to basics, therefore, it merely offers a 'refresher' of a small number of key points (which often tend to get forgotten in the hurly-burly of day-to-day selling) to help you to reestablish your overall perspective; together with just a few more advanced and adventurous, perhaps even somewhat anarchic, sales techniques.

The book extends into areas such as giving presentations and demonstrations or running exhibitions, which other books do not cover in depth from the viewpoint of the sales professional; understandably so, since the junior salesmen who are their target audience are rarely called upon to perform such duties. But you, as a mature sales professional, may find that you are increasingly called upon to be an 'expert' on these more sophisticated marketing activities; these are the extensions that start to distinguish the professional from the amateur.

The other aspect of this book which is absent in most sales training books, is its emphasis on *management*; of resources, of the support team, of projects, and above all the positive account management of customers and prospects. Good professional selling has far more to do with good management than with glib talk. In many ways it is best to look on your 'territory' as your own small business.

For too long, especially in the UK, the sales professional has been greatly underrated, seen almost as unskilled, as a (just about) necessary evil, but essentially making a negative contribution to the buying process. In reality, the sales professional's contribution to this process, as the one 'consultant' who can offer the critical knowledge and skills essential to the delivery of the best solution, has now made him (in our increasingly sophisticated, high-tech world) probably the most productive member of society. A fundamental reappraisal of the sales professional's status is long overdue. Since the beginning of the 1980s the new, tougher governments *have* praised salesmanship highly; but regrettably often only in terms of their own red-in-the-tooth adversarial approaches. It has to be recognised, not least by sales professionals themselves, that their contribution can and should be wholly productive; and certainly professional by any standards.

The founder of IBM, and the creator of its legendary selling success from the early 1900s on, Thomas J Watson, had a very clear view of the position of his salesmen. As reported by Buck Rodgers (in his book, *The IBM Way*) he said:

> 'I want the IBM salesmen to be looked up to. Admired. I want their wives and children to be proud of them. I don't want their mothers to feel that they have to apologise for them when asked what their sons are doing.'

As Buck Rogers points out, 'Those were the days of the "drummer", and selling was not a respected career ...' It did soon become a very respected career within IBM. It is, however, still not recognised as such in many companies.

The book is a collection, some would say a ragbag, of ideas, philosophies and techniques. But that is exactly what a sales professional's own armoury of sales skills looks like. Indeed, this book is largely based on the very armoury that I have at some time or other personally deployed or have taught, and hence can personally recommend. As with many sales training books, it is liberally sprinkled with my own success stories, although these are on a much more 'domestic' scale than many of the superhuman achievements claimed by others. I was merely a good sales professional, not a superman (for example, I am apparently one of the few authors not to have made a million selling insurance!). But, as a result, I hope that the examples are that much more relevant to the everyday needs of ordinary sales professionals. It should be relatively easy for you to exceed my own modest achievements, and I hope you do.

However, I also describe some of my failures – unlike other sales trainers, who appear to have only ever experienced success. I think you can learn as much from failure as from success. In my experience, by far the most effective sales training comes from sharing the real experiences (good and bad) of someone who has had the time to explore the wider range of ideas, and can offer some critical appreciation of them. It is fair to say that I probably learnt more from the very varied experiences of the many sales professionals that I trained than they individually learned from me.

In addition, I have supplemented my knowledge and experience of selling with my experiences of buying. I have been fortunate in that, in addition to being a sales professional, I have from time to time held staff and general management jobs that required me to buy a variety of products and services. Being the other side of the desk was a fascinating experience for a sales professional. It was no longer a matter of understanding the buyer's mind, it was seeing with his eyes – and the results were often disturbing. It was depressing to find out just how few really good sales professionals there were around – even if it was as enlightening to see at first hand just what mistakes they made (and to realise that I had myself made similar mistakes).

Selling is an art that is mainly developed by personal experience, not an exact science that can be reduced to sterile formulae. The concepts in this 'cookbook' are best viewed as recipes created from a wide range of ingredients. For each sales campaign only a small number of recipes is needed to produce a well-balanced offering. But, as any good chef knows, the ingredients within each recipe can be almost infinitely varied to match the resources available and the customers' own tastes. The skill – and much of the pleasure – in successful selling comes from finding the right blend that leads to the sale.

Eventually, like the top-class chef, you will not need the recipes. The best, and certainly the most enjoyable selling ultimately comes naturally, although not effortlessly – long practice and sound preparation are still needed to make the 'perfect' call, and I have yet to meet a really top-class, professional salesman who has not had to struggle to perfect his style.

How to use the book

Before we start on any of the ideas on sales skills themselves let me suggest a few ideas on how to get the best out of this book. First, always assuming this is your own copy and not a borrowed one, use this as a *workbook*. Highlight the ideas that appeal to you most, make notes in the margin, and generally behave like the vandals most librarians hate. This is not a book to be handed down from generation to generation, it is a book specifically designed to help *you* to improve your sales skills.

Skim through the book at a very superficial level so that you understand the perspective. When you come to read each chapter in more detail you will then have an idea of its place in the overall 'geography'. It will help you, even on this initial skim, if you use a fluorescent highlighter to mark out the sections that you think will be most valuable – and those sections that are not relevant to your needs. Don't try to understand the material on this first run through; simply start to develop a feel for the overall picture, so that the details, later, don't take over from the whole.

Each of the chapters, and many of the sections within them, can be read independently. There is no need to read them in strict order. They are merely arranged this way for greater convenience when used for reference. Some sections, such as those on territory management and prospecting, are necessarily rather tough reads; the mundane and commonplace is the essence of both. Even if you feel that the content will be useful to you, you may find that you have to return several times before you complete them.

So, return at leisure to those sections that most interest you. Again using highlighters, and making as many notes in the margin as you find useful, carefully reread these sections – perhaps several times – until you understand them. Most important of all, try to put them in the context of your own experience and environment. Understand how you might use each technique in your day-to-day sales campaigns. If they don't work for you then ruthlessly discard them; there is no profit in adopting alien and irrelevant ideas simply because someone else found them useful. Their use has to be of benefit to *you*; and to be a natural extension of your own personal style.

Finally, plan how you will try them out in practice. Make a list of the ones that you want to try (especially of the management actions you feel you ought to implement); and steadily work through it. When you do try the new ideas, closely monitor how they work. As you try them, refine them to best match your needs; and if they don't work then throw them away.

Again at your leisure, read the other sections that you think might perhaps be relevant to future, specific sales situations. Return to them, using the book as a reference work, when you find you need them. Otherwise forget them; you will have enough on your plate adding in the few techniques that are most useful – and like any other skill you will only be able to maintain, without constant unproductive reference to the book, those that you use regularly.

Above all, continue to develop your *own* style. IBM has the reputation of employing organisation men; yet the factor that impressed me most in my years of training hundreds of successful IBM sales professionals was the great *diversity* of styles. These ranged from a few salesmen who concentrated on a very slick style with relatively low factual content, the archetypal 'glib' salesman who would instantly be recognised by the populus at large, to the great majority who had more in common with successful managers and scientists than 'hucksters' – and for whom the content was all important. All types of sales professional were equally successful. The one thing that was obvious was that after the traumatic period of training, where almost all of them were searching for the magic 'salesman' identity, each of them eventually developed his own style with which he felt comfortable; and this turned out to be the most productive, as well as the most enjoyable, for him.

The one thing this book, unlike many of its competitors, will not try to do is tell you the basics of how to sell. It will perhaps suggest some ways to help you to find your own style, and ways to extend and hone down this to make it more effective and more professional. Most of all, I repeat, it will provide a 'cookbook' of a large number of individual recipes; from which a few ingredients may be plucked for use by you to enhance a specific sales campaign, and even fewer may be chosen to complement and enhance your own overall style. If the ideas increase your productivity by a few per cent then the secondary objective of this book will have been achieved. If they help to make your job less stressful and, in particular, more enjoyable, then it will have hit its primary objective.

Terminology

What do you, or should you, call yourself? I have always thought of myself as a simple salesman; although I have been variously called a representative, a sales executive, a market executive, a sales consultant, an account manager – thank goodness I was never actually called a traveller (although that would have been accurate, where I was doing something like 80,000 miles a year). All this time, despite these misleading titles, I happily thought of myself as a salesman. When I wrote this book, I decided to differentiate the new breed of salesmen (some of whom were already called 'industrial salesmen', for obvious reasons) by adding the description 'professional', since this best described the main difference that distinguished them. But the resulting 'professional salesman' fell foul of sex discrimination; justifiably so. The term salesperson (or salespeople) is, on the other hand, clumsy; and I don't know anyone who actually describes himself or herself as a 'salesperson'.

So that left the title 'sales professional'. This seems to me almost ideally to encapsulate what I want to say. It emphasises the professional element; and it is suitably neutered! But events have overtaken me. Others have now also found the term salesman problematic (for the same sexist reasons) and are increasingly latching on to 'sales professional' as their replacement; regardless of the actual professionalism of their staff. 'Used car sales professional' is not seen as a contradiction, and 'personal computer sales professional' is becoming commonplace – where I have seen precious little professionalism on show at any level! Even so, I have decided to stand by the terminology of 'sales professional'. But please be clear about what I mean by it. In my usage, it *does* imply true professionalism.

Even then, there are some situations where 'salesman' is the only term that comfortably fits the bill; and I have left these *in situ* – my apologies, even here I really do mean 'salesperson', but just can't bring myself to destroy the language to that extent. On the other hand, I do sometimes have to refer to the group of poor unfortunates who still appear determined to live up to the popular stereotype of the 'salesman' and I cannot face dignifying this group with any other term. I make no apologies in this case, since the term is largely used here in its popular, pejorative, sense. If you can accept, and justify, the title of sales professional I suspect that you will no longer be offended by the use of the term 'salesmen' as an insult. It is a pity, however, that this has happened; and this book is intended, at least in part, to start to rectify that problem.

Chapter 2
What Makes a
Sales Professional?

There is a widely held image of what a typical salesman looks like, and of what he is. He is seen by the public at large, and often by sales professionals themselves, as a flashy dresser, an extrovert and loud talker, who could sell refrigerators to Eskimos.

This image is reinforced by the more populist sales trainers, who come across as much larger than life – theatrical rather than practical figures. They irresistibly remind me of the 'born again Christian' evangelists cast in the Elmer Gantry mode: 'Do you sincerely want to make a million?' The danger of these 'born again salesmen' is, I believe, that they set examples that are impossible for their converts to follow; and in the process demotivate them and perhaps even drive them out of selling. In the harsh reality of a wet November morning, very few sales professionals really feel like supermen; most, myself included, will happily settle for being merely good professionals.

Miller, Heiman and Tuleja make the very valid comment in their book, *Strategic Selling*, that: 'Sales is a dirty word to many people, because it has so long been linked to images of manipulation and deceit.' They then put the blame fairly and squarely where it belongs:

> 'Unfortunately, we sales professionals have only ourselves to blame for this. Many of us have perpetuated the stereotype by the way we've sold our customers. No wonder our methods turn people off – many of them *are* manipulative ... many people in sales go by the old slogan "You can't call yourself a salesman unless you can sell somebody something he doesn't really want or need." '

In my experience, however, the caricature perceived by the general public is far from the truth – at least in terms of the best (and most professional) salesmen I have met, rather than the stereotype portrayed in the media.

As mentioned in the introduction, for a number of years I was a member of IBM's sales training team, and trained hundreds of its sales professionals. These sales professionals have – with some

18

justification – the reputation of being just about the best (and most professional) in the world, yet probably less than 5 per cent bore any resemblance to the caricature described above.

Some writers appear to have a particularly clear picture of a typical sales professional. Alfred Tack, in *How to Succeed in Selling*, describes a 'selling personality' which is cheerful, strong, friendly and sincere. Alan Gillam, in *The Principles and Practice of Selling* (published on behalf of the Institute of Marketing) describes the 'tools' of selling as personality, knowledge, judgement and power of persuasion; and provides a list of the components of personality that runs to no less than 13 items.

C G A. Godley, as part of his marketing section contribution to *The Principles and Practice of Management*, summarises for me many of the more useful of these views (and avoids the gimmickry which dogs many sales trainers' lists), when he writes:

> 'It is perhaps a good start to list the attributes of a successful salesman. A short list of the most important points is given:
> Enthusiasm, the most important attribute of all, without which no selling is possible.
> Confidence in himself and his company; this soon communicates itself to the buyer.
> Persistence, a refusal to accept a blank order sheet.
> Self-discipline, the self-imposed time and motion study.
> Integrity, which builds up confidence in the buyers.
> Command of language, necessary for persuasion and communication.
> Mental and physical energy.
> Understanding the value of good personal relationships and all that this means.
> Desire to make money. The source of continuous drive.'

Even so, I am less certain that such categorisation (apart from professionalism) can be definitive. I have read these books with interest, for each contains many grains of truth. But I also approached each with a degree of scepticism when I detected that they were starting to describe a circumscribed model to which they felt I, or my customers, *had* to belong. If you detect any part of this book lapsing into such a habit you will be fully justified in immediately putting up your most critical defences!

If I had to identify any common characteristics among the hundreds of successful IBM sales professionals I would choose just two very general traits. First, they were all very capable, intelligent, experienced and well trained. Above all they knew their job; at least in terms of the product and the industries they were selling to.

In his book, *How to Master the Art of Selling*, Tom Hopkins arrives, from a very different direction, at much the same conclusion:

> 'I'm always intrigued by the variety of their backgrounds, the diversity of their personalities and the range of their interests. Yet they have many things in common, foremost of which is this quality: they are competent. They know exactly what they are doing.'

Second, and most important, they were highly motivated. They worked hard, for long hours. They believed in the products they were selling, and in the company that employed them; and, by the end of the training, in themselves. Most of all they believed in the supremacy of 'customer service'. They had no reservations about their role; it was quite simply to help the customer – and in the process they made the sale, and their enviable reputation!

With such general characteristics it is not surprising that the mix of my trainees has happily included, on the same course, an ex-member of the SAS (who had spent the period immediately prior to IBM in a very hot foxhole in the Omani desert patiently waiting to kill invading Yemenis) and a student just off an MBA (Master of Business Administration) course at the London Business School. They were equally successful, in their own individual ways; and both happily learnt from the other as much as from me.

Over the years I spent with IBM I saw thousands of calls and presentations. Surprisingly – to outsiders that is – very few of them had the slickness I have since seen in the work of other less successful sales forces. Indeed their lack of gloss would probably have made most sales trainers squirm. Yet they *were* successful; remarkably so.

How did this happen, and how did their customers still view them as super-salesmen? The simple answer was that the *content* of each call and presentation was superb; and this was what the customer saw and remembered. The content typically addressed just what the customer needed. The sales professionals had taken the trouble to find out what the true requirements were, and had taken as much trouble to address those needs – with a demonstrably effective set of solutions. The customer was, justifiably, impressed. He didn't see the less than slick style. What he saw was a clear awareness of his needs – and the empathy that came from a genuine desire to help him. The customers tended to rationalise this eventually as superb sales-manship, and it was; but it was a very long way from the conventional image of slick salesmanship! Indeed I was eventually convinced that half the reason for their success was that they were dramatically over-compensating for their shortcomings in gloss, by working themselves into the ground understanding and meeting the customer's needs!

In other words, the best sales professionals are not born to the role. They are not even fitted to the role by external trainers such as myself. Quite simply they make themselves, perhaps with some expert guidance, into the cream of their profession. Given a basic capability (which most readers of this book will surely possess) coupled with a high degree of motivation, most sales professionals can realistically aspire to reach high levels of professional performance.

Such diversity renders categorisation something of a myth but I am going to break one of my own rules immediately by expanding on some factors that *may* make some sales professionals particularly capable and highly motivated – and worthy of the description 'professional'.

Capability

The first of these groups of factors comprises some that *can* be viewed as hereditary, and to that extent (but only to that limited extent) some good sales professionals can be said to have been born to the profession. But most of the elements are the result of development; the overwhelming majority of good sales professionals *develop* their own capability.

Intelligence
It has been my perception that the most successful sales professionals are highly intelligent; and this is the main 'hereditary' ingredient of their success. They may not necessarily have demonstrated this academically, but measured by less academic standards they usually show up as very bright.

This may conflict with the conventional image, although even this would see salesmen as 'sharp' or shrewd. But a sales professional has to possess a considerable degree of intellectual prowess to undertake the detective work that is necessary to uncover prospects' true needs, and then to undertake the problem solving that leads to viable solutions. Most staff strategists undertake these mental gymnastics

21

perhaps once a year, when they prepare the annual plan; and then they talk for weeks about the intellectual challenge of it. Many sales professionals have to handle the same problems, and a similar degree of complexity, with each new sales campaign and perhaps with each new call. And they have to carry out this task thinking on their feet, at the same time as handling the call; which in itself draws on many of the intellectual skills that are required in a military campaign. Don't be afraid to think of selling as an intellectual challenge; it very definitely is.

It seems to me that most sales training concentrates on the very practical aspects of selling, with good reason. But in the process, perhaps not enough emphasis is laid on the intellectual aspects. This stops sales professionals pursuing some of the activities which might stimulate their intellectual faculties, and which might be just as valuable to their personal development as the training in the more practical aspects.

This was brought home to me by one of the best sales professionals I ever trained. His academic record was poor, having left school at 16 years old. He had doggedly clawed his way up through the IBM ranks finally to become a sales professional, but was generally regarded as not particularly intelligent, although he was, once more, seen as 'sharp'. After tutoring him for several weeks it began to dawn on me that in reality he was very bright indeed. As a result I secretly tested his abilities; and found that he *was* very intelligent indeed – probably intelligent enough to get a first on a university course. When I challenged him with these results his surprise was not at his own talents, for I rapidly became aware that he knew these as well as I did, but that I had been bright enough to discover his secret! He had been hiding it for years, because (unlike most of the population) he really wanted very much indeed to be a sales professional; and he believed, perhaps with some justification, that being seen to be intellectual would have hindered his sales career! I was able to arrange for a faster progress in his career, to use his talents, but I regret that I was never able to persuade him to take time off to enjoy the academic education that might have made him an even more rounded individual.

Experience

The second aspect of capability is experience, in its widest sense.

There is a general feeling among the populus at large that a salesman somehow deducts from the *buying* process. Often it is not even seen as a 'zero-sum game', but a *minus-sum* game (where the buyer's loss outweighs the sales professional's gain). It is interesting to note that there is a very clear distinction between the selling process and the buying process. Where most people like buying things, they actively dislike being *sold* things. They believe that the sales professional's only task is to persuade them to accept a deal that is sub-optimal; one that they would not choose if they had the full facts, and one that they are only coerced into by mesmeric sales techniques.

In reality the professional and successful salesman usually has personally to *add* value to the sale. He has to contribute his intelligence and experience to *optimising* what the customer gets. It is arguable, at least in a complex sale, that this 'tailoring' may account for the greatest part of the effectiveness of the ultimate solution; and in this situation the sales professional may contribute more to his customer's productivity than any of his own company's product designers.

In *The IBM Way* Buck Rodgers summarises IBM's position:

' ... I said the rep has to know the customer's business in order to understand his problems; he also has to know his own product line if he is going to be of any help to the customer. And he has to know what the competition has to offer ... The people in the field have to be a combination of analyst, consultant, applications specialist, technologist and salesperson – and they have to be good in every area. Too many companies think of their reps only as salespeople, their primary and perhaps only function being to persuade a prospect to buy their product. If the prospect doesn't need the product, the salesperson is expected to create an illusion of need – then get the money and run before reality settles in. That's not IBM's approach.'

Experience is generally the basic raw material that a sales professional's intelligence can work on to generate this added-value. At its crudest level it means that he does not have to reinvent the full solution from first principles in every sales campaign. The customer normally sees such experience as a valuable reassurance that he is likely to be offered a viable solution. He assumes that the sales professional has already been exposed to the same, or similar, situation and has thus previously managed to find a sound solution – which he will now offer again.

As Alan Williams says in *All About Selling*:

'It is easy to identify sales people who have complete product and applications knowledge. They have an unshakeable self-confidence that is quite apart from arrogance.'

Knowledge

As indicated in the above quote, in its most basic form 'experience' is reflected in knowledge. Alan Gillam, in *The Principle and Practice of Selling*', identifies six main areas of knowledge that a sales professional needs:

Own company	Products or services
Competition	General trade information
Human relations	The territory

This list seems to me a good starting point, since it is typical of the views that are usually put forward (indeed, Alan Gillam's book was sponsored by the Institute of Marketing). The list is, though, *not* exhaustive. For example, at one time, when my role in IBM included dealing with agents, a key element of knowledge rapidly turned out to be that of EEC law. Another time, in the medical field, I had to educate myself to become an expert on clinical haematology.

In selling, a little knowledge is a good thing and a great deal of knowledge is a *very* good thing – it may help tip the balance in your favour. Despite the popular saying, there is *no* disadvantage (let alone danger) in learning. There is also great personal satisfaction to be gained from becoming a genuine expert.

Knowledge of one's own company

It is very surprising how many sales professionals know remarkably little about their own company. Yet the company (rather than just the product) is often a large part of what their customers are buying. It is not sufficient to know only the few superficial facts included in the company handout. A sales professional needs to know far more if he is to flesh out these bare bones and give his company a recognisable and attractive character.

In IBM my most effective sales pitch (usually relaxing with a customer over a pint of beer) revolved around the principles and ethics that drove the company; these, rather than the products, were what eventually gave my pitch its edge. The anecdotes I used to illustrate them often were based on the activities of its effective founder, Thomas J Watson, during the first few decades of this century. To be effective and infect customers with my enthusiasm (and the stories often went on for an hour or more over lunch), required a significant degree of knowledge of the historical backwaters of IBM.

The more hard-nosed of the hard sellers may deride this as an unproductive soft sell. What these critics would miss, though, is that such a unique opportunity to indoctrinate prospects and customers (so intensively and yet with the full cooperation of the victim) is rarely offered to a sales professional. And it was an easy and very believable step from explaining how wonderful IBM's ethics were for me as an employee (which, incidentally, they were) to selling him on how wonderful they would be for him as a customer (which they also were).

A sound knowledge of your own company is invaluable for another reason; you need to know how best to manipulate its resources to aid your sale. The resources you so desperately need may be buried (often deliberately so) in those secret places sales professionals are supposed not to think of looking. Here you may find the experts who really can solve the customer's problems, or the admin personnel who can unblock those impossible bureaucratic bottlenecks. In IBM I used these 'hidden' resources at least as much as those more generally available; and this gave my sales an extra bite. Sometimes it pays to explore your own organisation as well as the market place.

Product (or service) knowledge
It is professional suicide for a sales professional not to have a detailed grasp of the main products or services he is selling, particularly where this is the most important quality that prospects look for in a sales professional. Market research among personal computer buyers, for example, showed that nearly 40 per cent looked for knowledge of products as the main quality of their sales professional (making it the leading requirement, just ahead of honesty!). Yet all too often sales professionals' product knowledge is woefully deficient. Try visiting your local personal computer dealer, and the chances are that you will see exactly what I mean. In that sophisticated environment it is essential for the sales professional fully to understand the complex products he is guiding his prospects through. Yet the great majority of such dealer personnel clearly do *not* understand even their major products; and they have, justifiably, now displaced used car salesmen as the pariahs of the selling profession.

This is a tragedy for such poor salesmen, and for their employers (and even more for their customers, who have nowhere to go to get the reliable advice they desperately need). It is an even greater tragedy where such knowledge is the easiest of all to come by. It is surely possible for *any* sales professional to search out all the detailed knowledge that is available on his product, even if this means going behind the glib handouts to ask his own experts what the real truth is; and eventually become an expert in his own right.

My own dealership very quickly became one of the leading suppliers of computer aided design (CAD) systems, quite simply because the customers (who had very sophisticated requirements) recognised that we knew what we were talking about. Indeed, our customers were quite barbed in their criticism of our competitors, who did *not* understand the product. It was nice that they were flattering about our expertise; but more importantly than that, they bought from us – and at prices higher then our competitors were offering.

Knowledge of competitors
My comments on knowledge of your own products and services are as applicable to knowledge of your competitors' products; although clearly it will be that much more difficult to obtain the information.

It has to be recognised that most sales are competitive, and in that situation there are bound to be at least two sides to the argument. If you are to weight the scales in your favour, you need to be almost as concerned about your competitors' offerings; for it is the comparison between the offerings that the customer will see – and decide on.

Another example from my dealer experience illustrates this. We were quoting for a network of personal computers which would eventually be worth up to £100,000. We had, in line with our customary practice, carried out a thorough survey and produced a sound system design. To our dismay, however, the local Tandy (Computer Shack) store quoted, using its own PC 'clones', at a price that was one-third less. Their offering looked sound (even to us) and they were also the existing supplier. We had been outmanoeuvred and my sales team was about to throw in the towel. I, on the other hand, hate losing *any* sale, let alone one worth £100,000; and I was fortunately able to persuade them to research a bit deeper. For the additional investment of just £10 we bought a manual describing the software that Tandy was offering, and my technical people read it from cover to cover. What this showed was that there were only three significant differences, and then only in the fine detail. *But* all three of these differences were absolutely critical in terms of the way the prospect ran his business. Armed with this information we easily won the decision, despite the price difference and apparent similarities of the overall solution. Winning a difficult battle against strong competition has a particularly sweet taste.

Human relations

I suspect that this is a slightly tendentious category of 'knowledge'; as compared with the personal experience which is the lifeblood of a sales professional. It seems to me that 'knowledge' of human relations is perhaps more properly the province of psychologists. Writers of sales training manuals are constantly developing ever more complex techniques (embroidered with ever more florid jargon) for doing unnaturally what a good sales professional does naturally! Alan Gillam does, though, stress that he sees this as much in terms of self-knowledge. Certainly my own experience of psychology left me much more aware of my own strengths and weaknesses, so perhaps a useful philosophy would be: know yourself, and then get to know your customers.

The territory

Alan Gillam *is* correct in stating that any sales professional worth his salt should know every nook and cranny of his 'patch' (his own small business); and there are a number of sections devoted to this later in this book.

General trade information

This is an area which is, I believe, very much understated in the literature. At the heart of a truly professional sales campaign must be the customer's needs, and real understanding of these is most likely to come about based on a sound knowledge of the market. Whatever your product or service you will be that much more effective if you have a sound idea of the specialised requirements of each customer. Indeed Alan Gillam, elsewhere in his book, emphasises that market research, a key source of information on the market, is one of the two critical legs of overall marketing. For the sales professional this practical knowledge leads to the understanding described in the next section. It is also a very useful 'social' knowledge. As Buck Rodgers says:

> 'It doesn't matter who the customer is; you're paying him a wonderful compliment when you demonstrate that you know something about his business – information that required research and thought. This approach is head and shoulders above the

salesperson who walks in off the streeat ...'

Conveying general knowledge of business, where IBM's market is almost universal, was considered sufficiently important that I was funded, to the tune of nearly half a million pounds, to produce a course (in conjunction with the London Business School) that taught a large part of the syllabus of the first year of the MBA (Master of Business Administration) course. It may seem that this was an example of IBM going over the top, although IBM's control on expenditure is tighter than most. It is a matter of record, though, that the 200-person sales force who were exposed to this training subsequently used this knowledge to expand their sales quite dramatically (so that the sales per head grew more than tenfold over the next five years).

Understanding
Theoretical knowledge alone is of little use to a sales professional. He is not about to prepare a learned treatise; he has instead to make intensely practical use of that knowledge.

Thus, understanding of the overall picture is more important than erudition in terms of the details. This is particularly true of market-place experience. By far the best, if not the sole, way of gaining this experience is practically – in the market place itself.

It was for this reason that the second criterion in the selection of members of the IBM field force was 'industry' experience. It was reckoned that product knowledge (even of such a sophisticated product) and sales skills could be taught; but the understanding of the customer's environment could only come from personal experience – obtained by working in that environment, typically in a management role.

This single-minded concentration on achieving understanding was also evidenced by the business education referred to in the previous section. The pinnacle of this programme was a two-week residential course at the London Business School. More than 200 key members of IBM's field force were taken (by the lecturers and professors of the school) through the 20 case studies that were the backbone of the first year MBA programme. But, as anyone who passed through this marathon will confirm, this was more akin to brainwashing (albeit in a very enjoyable way) than to conventional classroom teaching.

The course always started with the participants applying their substantial combined intelligences, and newly acquired business knowledge, to solving the intellectual problems encountered in the various case studies. That dispassionate, intellectual view was not, however, the prime objective. The goal was instead to immerse the course members so thoroughly in the different business environments that they *felt* the emotions of those involved in such situations; their experiences were as vivid as if they had worked in the real company.

They started the course typically with rather theoretical, and certainly uninvolved, comments such as: 'What can we do to solve the problems of *that* company?' By the end of the first week their reaction was intensely personal, much more typified by: 'What a mess *we* are in, how can we pull *our* company out of the mire?'

If this level of experience sounds daunting, don't worry. It clearly *is* easier if you already have the experience under your belt, or have IBM to buy it for you, but you can still make sense of the job using what I call 'instant experience' (of which IBM's business education was a highly sophisticated and expensive version). Given the right approach your experience will grow every day, with each call; and with just as much enjoyment and personal satisfaction as the IBM trainees found in their very expensive business school. This approach is described in the next section.

Understanding comes about essentially as a result of being able to link together the jigsaw pieces of detailed knowledge into an overall picture that is meaningful; and is recognisably the same perspective as that of the customer. This process has more to do with acquiring a language than learning a science. Indeed the most important aspect of it is often the vocabulary. Each trade has its own language which is subtly different from other trades. Occasionally the differences can be quite marked. Thus, in my career I have learnt at least four separate languages (as well as several dozen 'dialects'), all of which were significantly different from each other and from normal English, with several thousand words unique (or at least unique in the sense that they were used) to each of their vocabularies. In chronological order they were: physics, marketing (including the sub-language of advertising), computing (including the major sub-language of IBMese) and medicine. We took great pains to teach new entrants to IBM the special language of computing; and then took even greater pains to force them to unlearn it − so that they would use plain and understandable English with their customers!

'Instant experience'

It would be ideal if we all came to each new challenge in life complete with in-depth experience. Unfortunately, the reality is that it is bound to be new and strange, and the first requirement is survival rather than a leisurely review of all the facts.

So it is in selling. Many sales professionals have to learn totally new markets, and often new products as well. There is no easy solution to this problem; particularly where they will probably be competing against salesmen who are already experienced. Their only consolation is that such salesmen have the opposite, and frequently more intractable, problem of complacency; they know it all – forgetting that every new sales campaign must inevitably be different.

The only solution for the inexperienced is to become experienced – and fast! The most immediate need, after learning the products (which should be the easiest stage), is to learn the language of the market, together with some of the more basic knowledge. This is, I find, most generally and easily available in books. Thus, my first action on moving into a new market was always to buy a set of the basic reference books. As these often cost a hundred pounds or more, persuading my boss to pay for these usually taxed my sales skills to their limit – but they are a sound investment for any company (although surprisingly few companies actually have such a library) and are worth their weight in gold to a newcomer.

If your expenses won't stretch to these sums, then I suggest you transfer the cost to the taxpayer: use your local library. If there isn't anything suitable on the shelves then check in the catalogue; these days this is usually on microfiche and covers other branches as well, so there should be a wide selection (all conveniently arranged by subject). If the search is fruitful and you find that something useful is in print, then ask the librarian to get it for you. He or she will usually be delighted to help.

On the other hand, one great advantage cf having your own books is that you can joyfully vandalise them while you are learning – in exactly the same way that I suggest you mutilate this book. (Of course if you want to keep a pristine copy in your private library, to impress your colleagues and neighbours, then please *do* buy a second copy!) Perhaps the most important benefit of having your own copies of the most important reference material is that it means that you won't feel so impelled to take extensive notes; such note-taking is a time consuming (and often fruitless) exercise. Instead, you will always have the original material immediately to hand.

First, you should use this material to obtain a feel for the market and, in particular, an understanding of the language. Don't worry about absorbing all the details – as you gain more practical experience you will learn that most of the details are irrelevant anyway; and in your inexperience there is no way that you will be able to judge which of these make up the 10 per cent, say, that *will* be important.

The next step is to pick the brains of some tame experts, if you are lucky enough to have access to them. They may be found lurking in the hidden recesses of your own company. If not, then you will have to find them in the market (using the good offices of your local chamber of commerce, for example). Wherever you find them, treat them like gold dust because in the initial stages they may be your most valuable resource – and their goodwill is all too easy to exhaust. Don't waste their time: complete your initial background reading before you approach them, so that you are not too ignorant of the basics. Listen and learn. Most of all, 'reward' them. The best reward of all for most teachers is the flattering attention of their pupils, so make your learning (and gratitude) very obvious.

You are now ready to venture into the field. In reality, of course, it is very likely that your management will by now have discreetly insisted that you become instantly productive (after, that is, the first day's typically generous offer that you should 'take your time' – an offer which unfortunately is rarely repeated on the second day!), and will have expected to see you making calls. You can't afford to disappoint them, otherwise the honeymoon period may abruptly shorten, but I would suggest that such 'cosmetic' calls are kept very low key until the groundwork is completed, and you have at least *some* idea of what you are talking about.

The next stage is the backbone of 'instant experience'. Let your customers and prospects train you! There can be no better people to guide you through the mysteries of their trades. What is more, you will be learning, and enjoying learning, in the sales situation; which should be a natural environment for you.

Perhaps to your surprise, you may find your customers and prospects very willing to help; as long as they are approached in the right way. *Everyone* loves to talk about their job and, of course, it is flattering to be asked to. It clearly establishes the customer in an important, superior role and it just as clearly establishes you as a listener – an ideal framework for a good sales professional! Finally, it is a two-way traffic. The customer, usually, also likes to learn about his 'chosen speciality' – and you offer a new factor (a new view, if not a new product).

The best approach, perhaps, is to throw yourself on his mercy. Introduce yourself as the new, and very inexperienced, sales professional; in any case you won't be able to hide your inexperience. Tell him that you are still learning about the market. But also tell him just how *fascinating* you find it! Enthuse about it; everyone is a sucker for an enthusiast, particularly where they are probably one themselves – and most of the other salesmen have long since made their boredom obvious. Ask him for his opinions, ostensibly so that you can learn about the market – but also so that you can learn even more about him! Above all, stress that you are *not* selling, just learning.

In reality you will never be selling harder. It is a heaven-sent opportunity to get the customer to drop his guard. Most prospects automatically raise their defences as soon as they meet a salesman – and the better they think the salesman is the higher they raise their defences. The trick, always, is to find some way to duck under their defences; and what better opportunity than this? In telling you about his business he will also be telling you how to sell to him. In return you, as the attentive pupil, will automatically be transmitting all the right signals that a good sales professional should. He should remember your call with pleasure – it is the ideal environment to develop empathy.

It is such a powerful selling environment that it is arguable that you should plead such ignorance with every new prospect, even if you know more than him.

If this process of instant experience sounds too daunting let me recount my own most vivid experience. In 1978 IBM asked me to set up its Biomedical Group in the UK. Over the years I had accumulated a deal of experience in most markets but, needless to say, the one area I had *no* experience of whatsoever was the medical field and, naturally, I was more than a little nervous about the whole prospect. It was only after considerable persuasion from key members of the board, and several trips to the European headquarters for some cast-iron guarantees (IBM, to whom it was just as strange a new world, was also desperate!), that I eventually succumbed.

My first action was to obtain a couple of basic text books in clinical haematology; for the main IBM products were blood processors – although many IBM customers would reckon that IBM personnel were already well versed in extracting blood from their clientele! I sat down and read them from cover to cover, without really understanding much but this reading did allow me to start to learn the language.

Armed with this basic vocabulary I now identified, with some help, the two key consultants in the leading teaching hospitals. I then presented myself for tuition. I offered nothing other than myself as a pupil, and knowledge about a new IBM product. Rather to my surprise, since – as leading international specialists – their time was usually as scarce as dragon's teeth, they each gave me several hours, spread over a number of weeks.

These various meetings with my 'tame experts' gave me an invaluable insight into what made the market tick; and, most important, I was later able to quote them as references (and references of international repute).

I then, and only then, moved on to start my initial sales contacts. Once more I threw myself on their mercy. There really was no way that I could disguise my lack of medical knowledge from a doctor. But, once more, they were only too pleased to talk to me. Over the next few months I rapidly learned not just what was sufficient to talk the language of the trade, but even sufficient technical knowledge to be able to lead them into new lines of research. (This latter level of expertise is not normally necessary for a sales professional; but it can be very fruitful).

These initial contacts were the most productive I ever made. My first medical expert bought the first machine to come into the UK; the second took another year or so to raise the finance – but he too bought.

Before finishing with instant experience, let me stress one personal, as opposed to business, point. Too many people, especially in the UK, are nervous of change and tend to assume it will be for the worse; but it can really be fun learning new things!

Personality

This is a source of some contention among writers. Allan Gillam, for example, lists no less than 13 characteristics he considers important: enthusiasm; integrity; intelligence; courage; initiative; reliability; determination; confidence; industry; self control; courtesy; friendliness; and modesty.

Harry Turner, in *The Gentle Art of Salesmanship*, is more dramatic (and perhaps closer to the stereotype), in that he sees salesmen falling into two main camps – 'Tigers' versus 'Foxes'. Some of the characteristics of these are:

Tiger
'understands how to generate excitement'
'sells advertising'
'needs to watch his weight, his liver and overdraft'

Fox
'a high degree of technical knowledge'
'ace computer salesman'
'is a pain in the backside'

As the last comment shows, his own sympathies lie with the tigers (understandably: he was sales and marketing director selling advertising space). But he does, somewhat nostalgically, add, 'Today, the foxes outnumber the tigers. It's the way the world is going.'

I tend to be less specific in my views, and as a result incline more to Alfred Tack's simpler list of four rather general attributes:

Cheerful
Strong
Friendly
Sincere

These are, of course, very general attributes that could be applied to a large percentage of the population. My view is that, even so, they are the basics only in as much as I think any sales professional who didn't have these characteristics (together with common-sense and, most important of all, a sense of humour) would find the sheer hard grind of continuous face-to-face contact with customers unendurable. In any case, is any sales professional going to admit, even to himself, that he is the opposite of these – naturally morose, weak, unfriendly and insincere?

I will emphasise only one of these characteristics, and then only because it is conventionally supposed to be alien to the salesman's nature: that is, integrity or sincerity. Buck Rodgers, who was IBM's vice-president of marketing for 10 years, says (in *The IBM Way*):

'From the time I was a marketing rep, I established myself as dependable, especially where my customers were concerned. I did that by never making a promise I couldn't keep. It wasn't always easy. I remember rough times in the mid-sixties when we were having some difficult production problems. To guarantee a specific delivery date wasn't always possible, and often the sale hinged on that issue. It was tempting to come up with a date that would satisfy the customer, figuring that you'd dance around the problem when the disappointed customer confronted you. But I never "danced". It was more difficult to sell, but I made a special effort to be totally realistic with each customer, never misleading him about our ability to deliver. It may sound corny, but I was determined to establish the fact that my word was my bond. I could never do business any other way – and I'm lucky that I worked for a company that never attempted to put a strain on that value.'

Within the *very* broad confines of the overall attributes I think that the cult of the salesman personality is unhelpful, and even counter-productive. It can lead to a very real, if totally unnecessary, worry for many sales professionals who feel they don't fit the conventional stereotype, as propounded by the self-proclaimed pundits. I, for one, certainly didn't. More important, perhaps, was the fact that very few indeed of the many IBM sales professionals I trained fitted this simplistic stereotype; and nobody could really accuse *them* of failing to be successful.

One, perhaps surprising, finding of research is that the key element of the buyer/seller relationship is *not* necessarily that the purchaser particularly likes the sales professional; or, at least, not that alone. Research, conducted by Tack among buyers, asked the question:

'What percentage of salesmen who have called on you for 5 years or more do you:
    like very much?
    like?
    tolerate?
    dislike?
    dislike very much?'

Tack reported that 'only 6 per cent came in the first group' and went on to say, understandably, 'experienced salesmen find it hard to accept this'.

Again I quote Buck Rodgers:

'Today's salesperson has to be a lot more to the customer than a genial, back-slapping, joke-telling Willy Loman type, who drops in each season to entertain and show his wares. He's performing best when he really understands the concept of solution selling.'

Professional consultancy

If I were to summarise what I believe *is* absolutely essential, in terms of capability, I would describe it as 'professionalism'. I now extend this further to 'professionalism in consultancy'; since I believe that the consultancy aspect of a sales professional's job is often just as important as the hard-nosed ability to close.

Typically the 'professions' are supposed to have standards. Your accountant and your solicitor will proudly call themselves professionals; although any prolonged exposure to their tender mercies may convince you that they are all too often even more amoral, in the pursuit of the fast buck, than the most avaricious used-car salesman!

Consultancy is just one such profession, and is just as avaricious. One of its leading exponents advised me, early in my career, that the key task of any management consultant is to sell more management consultancy; only after that task is complete should time be made available to solve the client's problems. Even so, it does – eventually – have the honourable, if professed more than practised, aim of helping businessmen to run their businesses better. Sales professionals may, arguably, be rather more biased, for a sales professional who doesn't sell his own product is (as Alfred Tack said) working for the competition. On the other hand, anyone with extensive experience of management consultants will recognise that they too are rarely wholly unbiased. To improve his effectiveness the sales professional needs to don much of the mantle of the consultant *en route* to the goal of making the sale.

The essence of professionalism, it seems to me, is to be able to offer the customer a well-informed understanding of his problems; within which you should be able to develop a workable solution. It implies a commitment to excellence in all aspects of the sale. Despite the popular stereotype there really is no excuse for blatantly unprofessional behaviour. In general, it will lead to less personal satisfaction on your part (where knowing that you are a true professional can be very satisfying), and certainly to a reduced likelihood of an order from the customer.

In this section I will also make my only comment on dress; a subject that seems to preoccupy a number of sales trainers. Once again, I would stress it is a matter of personal preference. But, whatever your choice, it is clearly preferable that this should reinforce your image of professionalism. It is for this reason that IBM sales professionals wear dark suits and white shirts; such is still the accepted uniform of the professional. Fashions change, and no doubt some day the dark suit will be old fashioned, but not just yet.

I will similarly say very little about personal habits. Smoking appears, these days, to be seen by many non-smoking buyers as an offensive habit (even if they will politely agree to let you smoke); so if you are addicted you had better wait until you are out of the call, or at least until you are certain that the buyer smokes like a chimney as well. The only taboo I insisted on in my sales professionals was no alcohol during working hours (unless they were genuinely entertaining a customer). This was partly because alcoholism is a very real problem for many sales professionals; and losing their driving licence by being caught drinking and driving is an even bigger risk (and just as great a destroyer of sales careers). Mainly, though, it was because alcohol dulls the mind; and a sales professional needs always to be able to think on his feet. And if prospects dislike cigarette smoke being blown in their direction, they positively loathe alcohol fumes from an expansive pub lunch being breathed over them; it is certainly not conducive to the image of a professional.

One final, questioning, footnote to these comments on consultancy: do customers have problems? It is often said that it is negative for a sales professional to talk of problems; instead there should be 'opportunities'. (In IBM there was a degree of cynicism that denoted some such very tough problems, still described as opportunities, as 'insuperable opportunities'!) My own experience indicates that prospects are well aware that there are problems; what they want is a positive approach to solving the problems – not pussyfooting around them! The crime is not to describe the problems, but to be unable to solve them.

Motivation

We now move on to the second, and I believe ultimately more important, leg of the general qualities needed by a sales professional.

When it comes down to it, selling is (like any other job) largely a matter of application. The right amount of effort applied in the right areas will eventually succeed.

Enthusiasm

I believe that the key ingredient here is simply enthusiasm. The enthusiastic sales professional will naturally put in the correct effort. More important, he will naturally present the best image to his prospects.

Heinz Goldmann puts it more baldly:

'If his enthusiasm doesn't show, I know he cannot possibly be a good salesman.'

Harry Turner supports this view:

'The most successful salesmen I know are totally absorbed by their work. Leisure time and selling time blur and overlap to such a degree that nobody can see the join ... Don't be a bore ... Learn to *shimmer* with suppressed excitement.'

Enthusiasm *is* infectious. In the thousands of calls I saw in IBM enthusiasm was often the one saving grace that rescued otherwise terrible calls. It is very difficult to object to a sales professional who is, apparently, genuinely enthusiastic about his product. If he believes in it then there is every reason why you should too. If he is also enthusiastic about you and your problems it becomes almost impossible to refuse him.

Perhaps the best example of this, where I was on the receiving end as the customer, was in my PC dealership. With my background in IBM it was reasonable to assume that the pattern of our business would have at least matched the normal ratio of four IBM PCs sold for every Compaq. In reality the ratio was almost reversed. It has to be said that this was in part due to poor service and salesmanship (surprisingly) from IBM. In the main, though, it was because the Compaq salesman was an enthusiast. He visited us three to four times as frequently as his IBM counterpart; perhaps because he was always welcomed. While with us he talked to everyone. Even while waiting in reception he used to sell the receptionist on the virtues of Compaq. His enthusiasm *was* infectious, which was directly reflected in his sales figures and also, I suspect, in his enjoyment of the job.

Belief

It is, however, almost impossible to develop an infectious enthusiasm if you don't yourself believe in the product. On this point, Alfred Tack quotes Carlisle: 'Let him who would move and convince others be first moved to convince himself.'

It should not be too difficult to believe in the product, or at least in your company. Most people *do* have an overriding belief in the work they are doing – otherwise they would be forced to admit that their work was worthless. Enthusiasm in selling is merely an extension of this.

It should come about naturally, as a result of your research to find out why your company and your products are better than those of the competition; there is nothing to say that this research has to be wholly unbiased, and if you can first convince yourself then you will be able to convince others.

As Harry Turner says in his book:

'Pick a product field that genuinely interests you. Be hot for knowledge. Absorb it. Eat it. Sleep it. Live it. Above all, *show* your enthusiasm for what you're selling. If *you* don't believe it you can't expect anyone else to!'

This belief can be enhanced by the acting techniques described in later chapters, but these can only add to an existing basic belief – they can't substitute for it.

If, after the requisite heart searching, you just can't believe in your products, and particularly if you can't believe in your company, you are in the wrong job. You are doing your employer no favours simply going through the motions of selling his product; and you are doing yourself a greater disservice, both financially and in terms of job satisfaction. There are always plenty of jobs for good sales professionals – so find one with a company and products that you can believe in. Then get on with the real job of selling; and do it in an environment where you can really enjoy it.

As Heinz Goldmann puts it:

'Lack of belief in the enterprise is dangerous enough, lack of belief in the goods is disastrous, and lack of belief in the man, yourself, is deadly poison.'

The importance of this belief is evidenced by the IBM sales professionals. Their attitude is often seen as arrogant, but in truth they simply have a blazing belief in their company and their products, and they happily extend this to cover products that are *not* always the best. What is important is the belief that they very vividly transmit to their customers. This may induce some blindness to genuine objections (IBMers sometimes have considerable difficulty believing that their company might have done something wrong), but it impresses their customers immensely and is very difficult for their competitors to overcome.

The final aspect of belief is belief in your own abilities to do the job well, and (in my view) be able to help the customer. This is often described as self-confidence and is, unfortunately, all too frequently linked with the ability to persuade (in this context this usually means 'con') the customer. It is at the heart of many sales training programmes – and is the life-blood of the Elmer Gantrys of this world who only have an hour or so to change the lives of the hundreds attending their meeting.

You *do* have to have a great deal of self-confidence as a sales professional; the trainers are correct in stressing this. It is my belief, however, that this is best built slowly on the back of the real skills and knowledge that are necessary to be a good sales professional. Without the skills and knowledge the theatrically inspired self-confidence soon evaporates. It has to be admitted, however, that without the self-confidence the skills cannot be applied – but I assume that if you are reading this book, you already have that basic confidence and are not likely to run from a sales situation.

Hard work

Above all, results come from hard work. Assuming that the potential is not saturated – and it very rarely is – what comes out, in the way of sales volume, is directly proportional to what goes in, in terms of raw effort.

As Tom Hopkins puts it in *How to Master the Art of Selling*:

'I learned a long time ago that selling is the highest paid hard work – and the lowest paid easy work – that I could find.'

This is sometimes described as the 'numbers game'. In essence this says that the more effective calls you make the more business you will generate. This is generally true; if you contact twice as many prospects you should create twice as many leads, just so long as you don't fool yourself by padding out the numbers with worthless calls.

Whichever way you look at it, if you only put in two days a week of effective selling you can't operate at better than 40 per cent of your potential; where if you work a 12-hour day you may hit 150 per cent performance. It is a basic fact of life, and no amount of self-justification can hide the costs of laziness. You may take a deliberate decision to work only two days a week (and I have known some excellent sales professionals, including myself on the odd occasion, who have done just that) but you must understand what the cost is, and be prepared to pay it.

The more time that you are prepared to put in, and the better you use that time (by the self-management/time management techniques described in later chapters), the more successful you will be. I know that there is a limit to the number of calls you can book in a day, but typically (in a complex sales environment) as much as half your time will be spent in the office on paperwork. If you are prepared to put in the effort (some would say become a glutton for punishment and perhaps ultimately a workaholic) this part of your work *can* be done after office hours and the office hours used to make greater numbers of productive calls. How often do you spend a morning or afternoon (or both) in the office when you could be out making calls?

In one sales force I was involved with there were two salesmen, who eventually became known as the 'terrible twins'. They took the lead in all the sales meetings; explaining how the product range was impossible, how the marketing was bad, how the territories were wrong. When not in the sales meetings they spent their time advising their colleagues as to why they too wouldn't be able to make their sales, to the extent that eventually their colleagues felt that they even had to apologise when, despite the strictures of these two, they were successful in making sales. Finally I was forced to do a simple check (behind the sales manager's back) – which was to find out how many calls these two were making. Believe it or not, between them these two had made just three calls in two weeks! It would be nice to report that I was able to teach them to be better sales professionals, but unfortunately that was not the case. As so often happens in such extreme situations, they had spent so long blaming everything and everyone else that they just couldn't see that an average of 30 minutes a week on calls must inevitably result in an efficiency around 1 per cent (which was, as it so happens, just about their performance). Perhaps the most significant thing was that after they left, the performance of the rest of the team leapt by 150 per cent – and nobody had to apologise for making a sale any longer!

At the other end of the scale, when we came to spend close to £100,000 converting the building that was to contain our PC dealership we diligently searched the directories to discover the best possible selection of contractors. In fact the contract went to a company that was not even on our list; quite simply because their salesman walked in one evening (on his way home). Having seen our lights in the building, he had not wanted to pass up a possible sales opportunity; his sale showed that he was right!

Empathy

So far we have not really addressed the area that preoccupies most texts on salesmanship – the face-to-face selling situation.

I do not propose to add to the plethora of guidelines other tomes have laid down. By now you should have chosen those techniques that work for you, that you feel comfortable with, and that you enjoy using. To lay down a new list of rules as to how you *must* sell would be counterproductive – and presumptuous. If you feel that perhaps you could extend your techniques, or that you are simply a bit stale and need some new ideas, go to your local library and borrow some of their works; it is useful to remind oneself of the ground rules (even as others see them).

I find that perhaps less than half the books are, in the event, even worth reading. In those that I do read I find that perhaps 90 per cent is not relevant to my own needs; but I do find 10 per cent that *is* useful, and that makes the whole exercise worthwhile. I emphasise, however, that you should borrow, not buy them; not to save the expense (although that is not a bad reason) but simply because you don't want such books on your bookshelf permanently. If they remain there they will eventually have an insidious tendency to become a model for your overall selling style – and remember that you have, wisely, rejected perhaps 90 per cent of their model as irrelevant to your needs.

To put things in perspective I offer only one key guideline, an attitude of mind; empathy with the prospect. This means simply identifying with him and his problems. Do that and you will find it very difficult to fail.

Interest

The first step towards true empathy is quite simply to take an interest in the prospect and in what interests him; this will almost invariably be his business environment – people rarely discuss golf with sales professionals. Prospects love talking about themselves and their business, and will reward your rapt attention with their business.

How then do you work up an interest? The answer is that you must develop a matching interest in his or her interests. In the absence of other factors the most obvious, and productive, topic of interest thus shared is likely to be the prospect's business. Many sales professionals try desperately to find some area of social activity where they can share their prospect's interests. One sales professional who worked for me (briefly) was so obsessed by this approach that I even heard him make a pitch on such social small talk when I had just closed the order – and as a result almost lost that business again!

Sometimes this social emphasis *is* worthwhile (and some sales professionals think it well worth keeping a card index of their prospect's personal details – for example, as a nice touch, sending birthday cards), but in general it is a diversion of effort. The one interest that preoccupies most people, and especially during working hours, is the work itself. It may be fashionable for them to pretend otherwise, but watch your prospect's eyes light up when he talks about his work to an attentive audience; what is more, you will usually find that he really is interesting.

How then do you take an interest in his work, and in his business? This, I am afraid, is a problem only you can solve, although the incentive of making the sale should be enough to awaken at least some interest. For myself I am fascinated by all aspects of business; or perhaps I have very conveniently persuaded myself that I am. Almost anything the prospect does or says will be of interest to me. I, of course, have an additional motive; this book is the result of many such 'interviews'. But I am certain that you too can find some personal reason for developing the necessary interest. Business really is, in any case, fascinating. Even seeing how different companies and different managers approach the same problem is intellectually stimulating, if you choose to view it that way.

Once more, if you cannot drum up the necessary interest then change to a field where you can. As a buyer there is nothing worse for your self-respect than realising that the sales professional's eyes are glazing over with boredom; and from the sales professional's point of view, no easier way of losing the sale.

I have often been taken to task by my management, and by my colleagues, for making very long calls (often up to twice the conventionally recommended length). According to conventional precepts all calls are intended to be brief – get in and out before the prospect becomes bored. I have not, though, ever been taken to task by my prospects or customers, quite simply because they were *not* bored. I was genuinely interested – and they, and I, enjoyed the meetings.

Customer service
The next element is what you propose to offer the prospect. Clearly this will eventually hinge on the selected solution, but in the interim there is one infallible winner – customer service. The commitment to customer service (second in its trio of 'philosophies') is IBM's greatest marketing strength. This one philosophy is by itself the guiding strategy that motivates the whole company. It is not necessary to consult a published guide to determine what to do. It is sufficient merely to ask what action gives the customer the best service.

As an overall marketing objective or philosophy for a company, the theme of customer service is very powerful. In a sales situation it is unbeatable. There is no need to indulge in the Machiavellian tricks taught by many sales trainers to beat the customer. Instead, all that is needed is a positive commitment to search out what is best for the customer; and in the process you will find that this is also best for you. It simplifies the sales strategy, allowing the one acid test, which you and the customer can jointly apply: is the action best for the customer? Clearly, it also offers the best chance of real empathy developing. If you genuinely believe in the philosophy, and the customer recognises this, then you are both on the same side; the winning side!

Partnership

This commitment to customer service is best seen as a partnership between you and your customers. Ideally, it should be the sort of partnership that the customer looks for with his other professional advisers, his accountant for example. If you too see the relationship in this light you are on the way to making the sale. If the prospect also sees it this way then you are nearly there.

Too much literature on salesmanship concentrates on techniques for manipulating the customer, who is seen as the victim of the hunter's skills. I believe that this is a fundamental misunderstanding of most sales situations. Many sales techniques seem to assume that the buyer fulfils a purely passive role, an analysis that most real-life encounters with buyers will soon disprove. It is quite possible that the great majority of salesmen see their sales campaigns as zero-sum games, where their share of the deal has to be won at the expense of the buyer. It is certain that most buyers, justifiably, fear that this is the case. In my experience, though, the most productive (and certainly the most professional) sales are those where it is clear to both sides that the final deal is in *both* their interests.

It is a foolish sales professional who does not offer his customer the best deal he can make available, always assuming that there is a good profit for his own company. There may be a few salesmen who can make a living by pillaging an area and then moving on, but most sales professionals have to cultivate the same area for some time – and even if the particular customer has no future potential you can be certain that his friends, whom he will surely advise if he finds he has had a raw deal, will have!

Harry Turner, in his book, puts the same point slightly differently:

'What *success-sharing* means is working *constantly* towards closing the sale *in such a way that leaves the buyer feeling as triumphant as the seller.*'

One personal computer sales professional who worked for me had an excellent knowledge of business systems. The rest of the team were impressed, as were his prospects, with this knowledge; and the start of his sales campaigns were a joy to watch. The sales team, who were relatively inexperienced, were even more impressed with his skill in manipulating the customers. He smoothly diverted the difficult objections, and persuaded the prospects to accept simply presented solutions. He addressed the problem of price brilliantly: he was always able to offer the highest discounts, quite simply because he always artificially inflated the standard selling prices before he applied the discounts. The problem was that, after this brilliant start, his campaigns abruptly disintegrated; and his eventual success rate was abysmal.

The reason was quite simple. At the beginning of the campaign the prospects trusted him completely; he *was* very believable. Unfortunately it was inevitable that at some time during the sales campaign he was caught out. His competitors only had, for example, to point out that his prices were inflated and he was lost. When this happened the prospects invariably reacted very badly – after all, who really likes to find out that they have been conned? He, of course, immediately had to put in a realistic proposal; and his final proposals almost always offered lower prices than anyone else, as he tried to live up to his original discount offers. But he *still* lost the business because his prospects did not trust him. If you lose the trust of the prospect you have almost inevitably lost the sale, no matter how attractive you then make your offer.

Another example of the importance of trust came when I was on the receiving end; buying equipment to fit out a number of conference rooms. Having done some basic research, including physically examining the alternatives at an exhibition, I had eventually made my choice. This was the supplier who was second in the market. His products were not quite as sound as those of the market leader, but the difference was not significant and the price was 40 per cent cheaper. However, when the salesman duly arrived (and did not immediately ask for the order – his first mistake) he proceeded to tell me that they were now concentrating on another range of products. Beneath his sales pitch I could just about discern that these new products were better, and even cheaper; so his initial mistake needn't have been fatal – why should I object to paying less for better quality? The problem was that instead of spending his time persuading me of the virtues of the new equipment, he explained at length just what rubbish were these previous products. This left me with a bad taste in my mouth. The products he was rubbishing were those that only recently his company had been trying to persuade me to buy – and the ones that I had actually decided to buy (apparently making a very bad choice; I was forced to admit I had been an idiot). Thus, even though I had already made my decision, I reversed this, and ended up paying the extra 40 per cent to his competitor. I simply could not trust a company who would happily sell me a product that only a matter of days later they would admit, and indeed stress, was useless. There was surely every chance that the new range was just as defective.

With my sales professional's hat on I suspected that the simple truth was that they had switched supplier to one that offered them better terms – but the salesman needn't have made such a mess of what could still have become an opportunity. The harsh reality was that he managed to lose a guaranteed sale that I was merely waiting to hand to him.

The depressing fact is that in my experience there are far too many salesmen who would make exactly the same mistakes. Loss of trust is far worse than loss of a single sale – for it excludes you from future sales as well.

Account management
The concept of partnership leads me to the positive concept of account management. IBM always spelled out the role of its sales professionals precisely as salesmen; and I believe as such it was a necessary discipline to remind them of their prime role (as salesmen, not as representatives, travellers, consultants, marketing executives etc). Despite this welcome honesty much, if not most, of their time was actually spent marshalling the people and resources necessary to provide the 'account' with the service necessary to win, or retain, the business. Even if other sales professionals have less resources at their disposal (typically they only have their own time), it is still a useful discipline for them to 'manage' their accounts. If nothing else, it helps to put the sales role in the correct perspective; and the customer often ends up buying the 'account management' of the sales professional just as much as the product.

One of IBM's great chief executives, Frank Cary, stated:

'If I was to select one single business practice that was most important to our success in the early days, it would be that we only leased equipment. This put a discipline on the business that was excellent. It motivated IBM people and it built a great relationship of trust between the customer and the company. The customer knew he had leverage'.

Clear objectives

Before we are buried by our own altruism, and a commendable desire to provide the best professional consultancy advice and customer service to our prospects, we should remind ourselves of the whole purpose of the exercise. Remember Alfred Tack's dictum that if you don't close the sale you are working for your competition.

It is, therefore, absolutely essential that you have very clear objectives. Otherwise it is all too easy to get lost in the complexities of esoteric consultancy; and all too easy to find excuses for avoiding that most painful of duties – putting your sales ego on the line for the close!

The harsh reality which must drive the whole sale, even for a professional, is that until there has been a successful close there has been no sale – and no salesmanship.

We have already covered a considerable amount of ground, from the starting point of the rookie salesman looking for an easy set of rules to persuade his adversary into buying (a search which I suggest will be better addressed by practical experience than by any amount of sales training books), to the mature, capable, and well-motivated sales professional managing his resources to put together a package in which his account management (in partnership with the customer) may be just as important as the product itself. I believe that the real pleasure of selling lies where the sales professional's professional contribution is maximised in every respect. This book is about that professional contribution.

The personal rewards

The promise of this book is to try to make selling more enjoyable. What, then, can the adventurous sales professional expect to get out of his job?

The conventional answer to this question is money. Many sales training books revolve around the glorification of earnings (presumably in the belief that this will motivate their readers) to the extent that their public worship of greed becomes positively embarrassing. It would certainly be very offputting to any prospects (who already distrust sales professionals' motives) if they sensed this raw greed which is supposed to be the only worthwhile motivator; 'Do you sincerely want to be rich?'! In any case the figures of $100,000, or even $1 million, per annum often quoted as the earnings of correctly motivated salesmen are so far away from the norm as to be meaningless to most sales professionals.

Indeed, it would be foolish to ignore money totally as a motivator, particularly where so many salesmen are 'incented'. It is also true that good sales professionals are very highly paid, in comparison with their contemporaries in other professions. I have moved backwards and forwards between sales and staff jobs, and work on the basis that I should earn perhaps twice as much selling; and I haven't exactly been a slouch in pay for the staff jobs. The main difference, of course (where I have been a successful sales professional), comes from the commission element. But I would argue that money alone is not usually the prime motivator, and certainly not the only motivator; otherwise why should I have been willing to forsake selling periodically for jobs paying less than half the amount?

Money *is* often the focus for sales professionals because it is usually, due to the commission element, a very direct measure of their performance. And good sales professionals are, above all, results oriented. They, almost alone among their contemporaries, do not need their bosses' evaluations (often biased and often plain inaccurate) of their performance; for their performance is immediately and unequivocally written in their results.

I believe for most sales professionals it is the achievement itself that is the main spur. They want and need – even crave – success. The money is simply the most direct measure of this.

Having denigrated those who greedily promote money as the sole motivator, let me add that although it is not my main motivator I *will* be eternally grateful to those who decree that I get so well paid for doing a job I like. Sales jobs *are* financially very rewarding, and we would be foolish to persuade our paymasters that this is a mistake.

Enjoyment

For me, and I suspect for most sales professionals, enjoyment is a primary motivation. If I am to spend eight or more hours every weekday doing something, I want that time to be fun, and the results ultimately satisfying. There is no need for it to be a chore. Indeed, unlike many boring office jobs, it simply cannot be a chore; for the sales professional simply going through the motions is doomed to failure.

One of the fascinations of selling, and perhaps the one feature that makes it bearable where a comparable desk job soon lapses into tedium, is its unpredictability. Every sales campaign is different. In the same way, though, it is probably unduly simplistic to ascribe any specific pleasures to a given sales campaign, or even to a given sales professional. Each must decide for himself what he is to get out of his job. Harry Turner suggests one approach to this: 'Write down the six things [including leisure pursuits] that interest you *most* in life ... It's a start.'

For the record, though, I will list below some of the things (in addition to that inevitable money) that I have personally found most enjoyable:

The thrill of the chase

It has to be recognised that, despite all my talk of professionalism and partnership with the customer, in many ways selling at its most basic level is an aggressive act. It is a direct descendant of the role of the hunter, stalking his prey before the kill.

As such, many of the challenges and emotions of the hunt are there for the *aficionado* to savour; the adrenalin starts to pump even as you enter the meeting.

The intellectual satisfaction of sound detective work

Once through the door I have found that many of my calls have turned into feats of detection that would have done Sherlock Holmes proud. Like many sales professionals I am not really a natural listener, no matter how important I recognise this is – and such listening is at the heart of the sales professional's job. So I have compensated for this shortcoming by treating the whole process as a piece of detective work. Finding out what the prospect's real needs are and following the clues through to their logical conclusion can be as satisfying as solving a good Agatha Christie whodunit.

Customer service: helping someone

As I have said a number of times, too many people see selling purely as adversarial combat, a zero-sum game in which there are winners (the sales professionals) and losers (the buyers). This is not true of the best selling; I share Thomas J Watson's belief that *both* sides should come out ahead.

Professional pride

A pride in one's work is essential to a successful sales professional. In my days of medical sales I did not merely become well versed in my products, I became one of the world's leading authorities on apheresis and as such, was listened to by leading medical consultants in the USA and Europe, not just in the UK. I was proud of my knowledge; and my customers respected me for it.

Competition
Finally, in common with most sales professionals, I am competitive; I want to be in the top echelon of any job I do. I will always try to be first rather than second, and certainly will never settle for being second rate. For there to be winners in such competitive sales races there have also to be losers, but the best sales professionals do not come up against this problem.

IBM recognises the importance of this when it sets its targets, such that at least 80 per cent of sales professionals achieved 100 per cent on their sales targets. Thus there were always four times as many winners as losers; where in other companies, so concerned about saving commission money that they set targets too high, there may be four times as many losers as winners. Guess which sort of company has the best motivated sales force and makes the most sales!

Much of the above reflects the conventional aggressive image of the salesman. Yet I still believe that the most important motive for my success, and indeed that of IBM as well, was the almost altruistic motive embodied in the third category, that of customer service. Along with professionalism, that is what counts for the most important person in the whole sales process: the buyer.

Chapter 3
Territory Management

The difference between the rookie salesman and the experienced sales professional often starts with his basic attitude to his 'patch'. The rookie will usually look upon this as little more than a list of prospects, to whom he will need to sell the company's products, and on whom he will practise his new found skills. The professional will, on the other hand, probably take a wider view and see his territory in more complex terms, regarding it more or less as his own small business; managing it by adaptations of the techniques and procedures that small businessmen favour, as much as by any conventional sales skills. Indeed, viewing it as your own small business is, in my experience, one of the few ways of making the tedium of much of the essential admin bearable.

This was taken to its logical conclusion in IBM where the sales professional had the *sole* responsibility for his territory, and for his customers. He was personally responsible for managing IBM's resources to serve its customers best, and he alone was responsible for managing all aspects of the relationship with these customers. If there was a disagreement between him and his management (even if the manager disagreeing was the country's general manager) on policy towards one of his customers, it was his (the sales professional's) decision that carried the day. Mind you, it was a brave sales professional who actually implemented this policy!

Even without the luxury of such delegated responsibility, the sales professional will still view his territory as his own small business. As a businessman he will plan – and implement these plans – to maximise his return, his profit, from that business; and he will take satisfaction from his growing business skills, and pleasure from the deployment of these.

Many of the skills that such a sales professional requires, therefore, are far removed from the simplified sales skills that preoccupy most books on salesmanship. They reflect those of business management, where his territory is his business. It is these general business skills that much of this chapter describes.

First of all, may I make a brief diversion. The title of this chapter presumes that there *is* a territory to manage. This may not always be the case, for the concept of sales professionals being entitled to their own territory is a relatively recent one. It was only just before the First World War that John Patterson instituted the concept of territories as a fundamental aspect of the NCR sales operation; and shortly afterwards Thomas J Watson, then at NCR, took it to IBM. Prior to the time of these pioneers there had been no territories. All prospects were fair game for all salesmen; your main competitors could just as easily be from the same company as yourself.

Fortunately, since this anarchy destroys the foundations of territory management which is a key element of professional salesmanship, territories are now an established practice. Perhaps the one remaining bastion of anarchy is in shops and showrooms, where shop assistants rather than sales professionals are the rule. It is clearly very difficult to define a territory in such an environment (one can hardly give a salesman the patch between the frozen pea cabinet and the delicatessen counter!). It may be that this is one of the basic problems with the sales professionals in personal computer dealerships. They have traditionally started in showrooms, where this anarchy still exists, and have transferred the bad habits of this environment to situations where true territory management is possible (and essential).

Possibly as a result of this, in my personal computer dealership, the most common failing of the sales professionals was that of poor territory management. This was compounded at one stage by a sales manager who, reverting to type perhaps, chose to have *no* territories and let the sales professionals compete for all accounts. This ended in a fiasco where no less than three sales professionals disputed ownership of a key prospect. One had dealt with him when he first dropped in on the dealership, the next had followed up his subsequent telephone enquiry and the third had held the geographical territory on which he was located (and claimed that he had established the first contact). The inevitable outcome was that these three were so busy fighting each other that they had no time for the prospect; and we never stood a chance of winning his business. Good territory management, whatever its basis, is the start of almost all soundly based sales campaigns.

Sometimes, of course, the territory may be shared by a team; but even in this case the same principles apply – although the sales professional will need even greater diplomatic abilities to persuade his team members.

The sales plan

As with a company, the first requirement is to determine strategic and tactical plans. In theory the sales professional, as an employee, has less flexibility than the small businessman, who is the sole owner; although in reality a small businessman is likely to be just as constrained (usually by his bank manager!).

It is likely that a sales professional will have constraints applied by some form of sales plan, passed to him by his management. In the case of IBM this was a substantial document, running to 50 or more pages. It was couched in terms of the commission scheme but, nonetheless, it was a very direct statement of what IBM wanted the sales professional to do. At the beginning of every year, therefore, the wise IBM sales professional hibernated for a few days. The advice of the old hands was for the sales professional to take up to a week to digest what the sales plan meant to him personally; and then to develop his own plan to match IBM's.

On the other hand, many sales professionals are simply given directions as to where their patch lies; accompanied by the admonition, 'and we are expecting great things of you'! Even then, despite the sparse material provided by their management, the sales professionals must develop their own plans in some detail. It is just as worth *their* time to sit down for a few days and work out what they should be doing. For the business (and the territory sales professional) that fails to plan is courting disaster, and certainly is not optimising its future performance.

The company's objectives

The first step in any sales professional's planning process has to be to determine what are his company's objectives. Even if his own are very different, he still needs to determine what the company will expect of him. This is not necessarily an easy task: in the case of IBM the published, overt objectives often hide more important, unpublished, covert objectives.

But it is as well to start with the published objectives. At least these should be definitive of where the company is willing to *say* it is going. Of course, the first problem that one comes up against is that such objectives are often couched in terms of pure 'motherhood'. It is self-evident that most companies want to make a profit, but many companies feel that it is sufficient to define this as *the* objective, without appreciating that it doesn't really add to the sum of human knowledge.

If you don't have access to a written statement of company policy, you had better ask someone. Failing a sensible answer – and the chances are that your immediate management probably won't understand company policy (even if the board does) – then you will have to define your own strategy for the company.

If you want to appreciate marketing strategy in some depth, read the classic text book, *Marketing Management*, by Philip Kotler. Be prepared to find it heavy going – it's 500 pages of small print – but it offers an excellent grounding in marketing strategy.

In any case, you should assume that in many, if not most, companies, the hidden, informal objectives are more important than the published ones. One of my marketing triumphs was to develop a strategy for a subsidiary of a large privately owned group. For a number of years the group had maintained, against all sense, two companies competing in the same market place. It was clear that this luxury was about to end, as ownership passed to the son of the family, almost certainly resulting in a major reorganisation.

The group management style was such that when the two companies were amalgamated, smashed together, control would be given to the board that was currently most profitable; which at that time was *not* the subsidiary I worked for – not a very happy thought.

To rectify this situation, my strategy achieved the highest short-term profitability for my own subsidiary by the simple expedient of milking the marketing position of that company. We launched large numbers of new mini-products, which (on the back of the company's reputation) sold into the distribution channels – but not much further. The result of these product launches was to generate short-term profit (mostly from pipeline filling), but at the expense of the company's position with its retailers; a crazy decision in normal marketing terms. But (as we had gambled) there is a great deal of inertia in most industries and the bottom did not fall out of these retail channels until after the two companies had merged. Mine won the deal on the basis of these short-term profits, and buried the distribution channel problems that were then emerging under the strength of the other company; whose whole board had, as I expected, paid the price of lower profits and were no longer with the group!

I don't tell this story because it illustrates sound marketing practices, although, against the marketing odds, it did no overall harm to the group. It would have had to close one of the companies anyway – so the extra short-term profits were a bonus; and some of the new products actually proved to be winners, and were transferred to the remaining company! I tell it as an extreme example of just how powerful the hidden objectives may be; and in that case they obviously had to be *very* well hidden – only myself and the managing director knew them.

You also need to appreciate that within the company different departments have their own objectives, which may differ quite drastically from those of the board. Thus, no matter how much the board preaches the doctrine of bottom-line profitability, it is likely that the sales department will still follow their 'gut-feel' of revenue as their main target above all else. As you will obviously report to them you need to know just what drives your own management, as well as what drives the company.

For your own survival, you also need to recognise the political games that are being played (usually for the promotion stakes) all around you. I once worked for a marketing manager who had a new product in test market. We worked for a company that prided itself on its aggressive new product policy. So when our market research showed that, after an encouragingly good start, the product quickly bored consumers (who then stopped buying) and – even worse – when we found the product had a poor shelf life, this marketing manager had a major problem on his hands. He resolved it quite simply by launching the product anyway. As predicted it went like a rocket for three months, and the marketing manager made his promotion. After six months the bottom dropped out of the market (and the product went bad on the shelves) and the company lost something over £250,000 – again exactly as predicted. But (I suspect again as predicted by the marketing manager) it was his unfortunate successor who paid the price, and was fired.

I use this story to illustrate just how complex the various political objectives may be. Fortunately, politics in most companies, although almost always present, are played at a rather more mundane level. So maybe you would be just as well ignoring all but those that apply most directly to yourself; although it may still be worthwhile having a discreet appreciation of the rest, just in case they could pose problems for your own small world!

You should also be aware that a company's objectives change over time. So what you have determined, as a result of painstaking work, to be the true objectives may a few months later no longer hold true. Thus, in IBM's Biomedical Group the original key objectives had been to explore the viability of independent business units (IBUs) as a vehicle for IBM's diversification into new areas. The keynote here was caution and research; and the result was that IBM was able to use this experience to launch its personal computer – with immense success. It was only later that Biomedical Group's objectives were changed, to the more usual commercial priorities that I described earlier in this chapter. If we had not been well aware of these changes, our own policies would have been very much out of step, at one stage or the other.

The tactical requirements can also change over much shorter timespans. Thus, the third objective of Biomedical Group, even when it was operating under more normal commercial objectives, was to create favourable publicity for IBM. In some situations, this objective overrode the others, so we spent an inordinate amount of time, which was certainly unprofitable in terms of our other objectives, installing and supporting equipment donated by IBM to the Great Ormond Street Children's Hospital; simply because this was a cause IBM sincerely believed in.

After some research you may now believe you have a good feel for what the company wants, and for what its management want. So what do *you* want?

Your objectives

You would be foolish blatantly, and in particular publicly, to ignore the wishes of your management, for that could lead to major problems – no matter how good a sales professional you are. No sales manager can afford to tolerate mutiny in the ranks for long. But you would also be somewhat foolish not to inject some objectives of your own. After all it is your life, and your management cannot lay claim to own your soul.

What do you really want?

The first thing, therefore, is to sit down and decide just what you *do* want out of life. This may sound like an academic exercise, but it is important, from time to time, to put your life in perspective, and decide just what is important for you. It is worth doing, because you may decide that the priorities that society proffers as the ideal aims of successful citizens are not for you; indeed you probably *will* decide this – for these objectives are more the creation of Hollywood than of any consensus of the public at large.

For many people this would be a waste of time, for their jobs do not allow them the luxury of freedom to choose their own priorities. But you, as a sales professional, do have a certain degree of freedom to organise your own life; to optimise those aspects which appeal to you. You should take advantage of this freedom to structure your work to suit yourself, always within the constraints that still apply to sales professionals – even a sales professional is not allowed to further his charitable wishes by giving the company's product away.

Sit down and think, though, what *your* objectives are. What do you personally want out of life; in the long term and in the immediate future?

Earnings
The conventional objective of all sales professionals is supposed to be money. There is nothing wrong with being greedy in this context: after all, we are just workers succeeding in wresting a fair (or perhaps more than fair) share of the company's earnings – and that has been the aim of trade unionists and Marxists for the past century and a half. Neither is it necessarily incompatible with professionalism. Another group of highly paid individuals is also made up of professionals – accountants, solicitors, and so on. However, in this context (of setting your own objectives) you have to determine what exactly are your priorities in terms of earnings.

I suspect that the immediate answer of everyone will be; 'I want to maximise my earnings.' But in this context what you have to recognise is that there is a trade-off. The classic example is that of wanting to be promoted. If this is a higher priority for you than pure earnings, you may well choose to do things that your management favour – but which reduce your income.

So, you should determine just how much you need to earn, how much you want to earn (taking into account the 'costs' of earning it), and also how much you have to earn to keep your management happy. Indeed, it is unwise even to suggest that you would settle for less than the maximum earnings.

I employed one sales professional on a base salary of £12,000 a year, with on-target commission also of £12,000. I was dismayed when he told me that his aim in life was to earn just £15,000 a year, and would be happy when he reached this. Unfortunately this also meant that he would be happy when he achieved just 25 per cent of the sales target I had set for him; a target which I needed to achieve *my* profitability. It meant that, by the time I added on his expenses and overheads, his cost per sale was more than three times that of his more successful colleagues and, at the same time, he was wasting the potential of his patch. I explained to him, rather graphically, the facts of life. So, be careful just how honest you are with your management, if you are not quite as thrusting and greedy as they expect salesmen to be.

A more extreme, but successful, case that I knew was an ace sales professional who worked extremely hard for the first couple of months of the year to make his target; and then went on holiday for the remaining 10 months. His company were aware of this, but they needed him and tolerated his idiosyncrasies; and he lived the life he wanted to.

At the other end of the spectrum, one of my managers in an advertising agency lived only for work; he was the workaholic to end all workaholics. He worked night and day for 11 months, until he had a minor nervous breakdown; at which point the agency shipped him off (at their expense) to a Pacific island – where he spent a month in the sun recovering for his next year's stint! This did not happen just once; it was a regular yearly pattern that he and the agency were happy to operate. It was his chosen lifestyle; and it was his prerogative to make that choice, no matter how bizarre the rest of us might feel it was.

Position

After money, promotion is supposed to be the main spur of sales professionals. Indeed for the rest of the population, promotion is the only way that they can increase their earnings. It is taken for granted in our society that promotion is the aim of any sane citizen. Promotion usually awards higher salaries, even in the case of sales; your manager will claim that you can earn more than him, with your commission, but he won't be very willing for you to compare base salaries! Promotion certainly awards increased status – how many people lust after the title of 'manager'?

I beg to differ with society's priorities on this count. In particular, I beg to differ in terms of sales professionals' aspirations. A sales professional is often a rather different animal, more of an individualist, and motivated by factors that do not concern most of society. Yet he is pressured into fitting into the general mould. It was always a precept of general management that in promoting the most successful salesman to be a sales manager (the route that is chosen, almost traditionally, by most companies), 'You simultaneously gain your worst sales manager and lose your best salesman!'; but despite this generally reported management nostrum, most companies still make this mistake (as do most sales professionals).

I am not suggesting that you should not want promotion (for management is an important and fascinating job). But I would suggest that you carefully examine your motives. Is it really you, or is it your neighbours, that expect you to become a manager?

It was a decision I took fairly early in my working life. In 10 years I climbed the ladder to be a general manager, promised a seat on the board of a large multinational. I found, to my surprise, that the amount of time I was forced to spend in political manoeuvres (which were distasteful to me) made the job less satisfying than some of the lower level jobs. So I packed my bags and went as a sales professional to IBM; a choice which most would see as perverse, but which I enjoyed immensely. I had a sort of compact with IBM management that I would not ask for promotion (something I think they would, in any case, have viewed with alarm!) but that I would be allowed to choose the job that I found interesting, and wanted to do. To the great credit of IBM, I was allowed to do just that, to choose a string of fascinating jobs, for more than 15 years, until I finally chose to set up my own business. It is also to the great credit of IBM that it recognises that non-managers can be as important and valuable to it as managers. It has created a role that it calls a 'professional' for staff jobs, whose holders can have as high a status, and certainly as high a salary as managers without having to enter the role of manager.

The choice is yours. You may well choose to conform and aspire to management status. But as a sales professional you are likely to be more independent, and to have a much more interesting job. So, think carefully before you choose to conform.

If you do choose the management route this will have a considerable impact on your objectives, and on the resulting territory plans.

Satisfaction
For some of us, maybe most of us if the truth were known, the prime objective is the satisfaction of a job well done. It would be wrong to describe selling as a vocation; it is perhaps too worldly for that, and nobody would believe me if I did. But there is a significant element of vocation in the role that the sales professional eventually assumes. Certainly for such people it is the job itself that matters. For those, on the other hand, with the prime objectives of money or promotion, the sales professional's job is a way of earning these; it may even be seen as a necessary evil.

But for the true professional it is the job itself that is the reward. He takes the view that it is foolish to spend more than half one's waking time in a role that is not satisfying; and accordingly tailors his plans to maximise his satisfaction.

Having said that, there are many routes to satisfaction. Some, such as myself, obtain satisfaction from solving the customers' problems; it is an intellectual exercise as stimulating as many in academia. Others take their satisfaction from developing the personal relationships that are the essence of a sales professional's business life.

So, once more, you need to sit down and decide just what gives you the most satisfaction and pleasure, and then build that into your objectives – perhaps even as your prime objective.

How do you get what you really want?

First of all, you must produce your own set of objectives, which are suitably modified to take account of the company's objectives. It is essential to have realistic aspirations if you want the company to help you to achieve them; and it is just as essential for the company to think that your aspirations are in line with its own. Earnings and promotion are easy to handle; the company assumes that such aspirations are in its own best interests too. Those relating to aspects of job satisfaction are more difficult to present, and it may be better even to keep them as private aspirations. But to convert these objectives into reality you first of all need the backing of your management.

This is where your salesmanship once more comes into play. My most difficult sales jobs were nearly always on my own management. These were also the most important sales jobs. A prospect won over will result in an order. A manager won over could result in a year's enjoyment of the job, and might even be the start of a lifetime career.

It was always my claim, based on considerable experience and even greater observation, that the key ingredients of a sales professional's success were, in decreasing order of importance:

1. A favourable target and a good territory.
2. Hard work.
3. Luck.
4. Sales ability.

It may surprise some of you that I would rate sales ability last. It is not to say that it is unimportant; clearly it isn't. But I always believe that a sales professional should recognise that much of his performance depends on luck (he has the right product at the right time, or the wrong one at the wrong time). Above all, in terms of what the sales professional can himself control it is sheer hard work that is his main contribution.

But all of that is of less importance than ensuring, as far as you can, that you have been given a good territory and an achievable target. Once these have been set you have to get on with the job and make the best of them. But it is well worthwhile attempting to sway the odds when these crucial factors are being decided. It was amazing how the value of IBM sales professionals' territories suddenly diminished (at least according to the sales professionals) when the annual review of targets came around. There was even discussion among IBM sales professionals as to whether it was worth holding business back to the new year, so that lower targets would be the order of the day. The inevitable reward for success in IBM was an increased target – so that you had to run even harder to achieve the same success.

I was once given a new territory by IBM, as part of a national reallocation of territories. The areas were decided, scientifically, on the basis of the numbers of companies with over 1000 employees; based on a 'sales brick' analysis that IBM had bought. As an indication of the accuracy of this I was assigned five such companies, of which four did not exist and the fifth had just gone into liquidation! But, despite the naivety of the original market research on which it was based, the area did contain one of the largest factory estates in Europe.

The problem was that my management were always driving through it and coming to me with comments like: 'You have got a super patch, I have never seen so many companies suitable for computers.' What they didn't take into account was that the great majority of the companies on display were just warehouses – with head offices and factories elsewhere. So I took to driving my management the longest way to any call on my patch, describing the companies we were passing as we went: 'That's a warehouse for a company based in Birmingham; that's a small subsidiary of a firm based in the City and they are not allowed to buy for themselves; that's ...'. Eventually my management understood my problem, and I was given reasonable targets.

Succeeding

Having been given your objectives, or preferably having agreed them with your management (and most preferably having persuaded your management to agree *your* objectives), just how do you go about successfully meeting these objectives?

Earnings

The most likely, and most obvious, target you will receive as a sales professional is a quota of revenue (or some equivalent volume target), and your income will be directly based on performance against this. Clearly this concentrates the mind wonderfully!

Beat the sales plan

Normally this will not be just one simple target; but will be a collection of targets, and the earnings against these various targets may not be linearly proportional. It seems to be a requirement that a sales management team should justify its existence by producing the most complex sales plan possible! As a result almost any sales plan contains elements that will, if correctly prioritised, earn you more money than others.

The most usual example, where earnings are based on a split of base salary and commission (typically 50:50), is for commission earnings to escalate. Thus for performance below 50 per cent target, say, you will be paid relatively little and for performance above 100 per cent there will be an accelerator. Under this sort of scheme there is every reason to hold off until you can achieve at least 50 per cent.

In the case of IBM there was usually such an accelerator – so there was a high incentive to beat the 100 per cent (and an even higher incentive to get targets reduced). Regrettably, it was not possible to move business around a great deal in order to fine tune earnings, since the targets were for the whole year – although some tuning did undoubtedly happen during the couple of months around year-end.

In other companies, though, this type of scheme is run on a monthly basis. In this case there is a very strong incentive to 'clump' sales, with none in one month – to be then followed by a bumper month. If you assume that better than 100 per cent performance earns double rates, this means that by 'clumping' you could earn 50 per cent more on average, for the same performance!

In the fine print of sales plans you can usually find ways of making a lot of money. It may be that the optimal choice of products you sell, or the optimal mixture of customers (or simply just getting new customers), will earn you more money. But whatever the mix, you will need to dissect the sales plan *very* carefully, to find out exactly what mix will give you the best earnings.

So, as soon as you get your sales plan, ruthlessly analyse it to decide how you will earn most of your income during the year; and to find the 'mistakes' which may allow you to make extra money for old rope.

Optimal tactical performance

By now, always assuming that you are following the steps I am recommending, you will have decided what aspects of your company's sales plan can be best used to your own advantage. Maybe you will even have calculated exactly what sales, in what categories, you will need to make to optimise your earnings.

It remains to convert these objectives into a tactical plan; to spell out (at least to yourself, and probably *only* to yourself – you won't want your management knowing just how you are taking advantage of their carefully crafted sales plan!) how these personal targets will be achieved. It is a chore, but it is advisable to commit this plan to writing. Then, as your memory fades and you are tempted to chase other objectives (as your management will want), you can remind yourself of what the optimum tactics for you really are.

Again, I return to the analogy of the small businessman. Your equivalent of his turnover or revenue is almost the same; it is the *income* you can generate by your activities (not the sales your company will make – those are only a means to your end). His 'bottom-line profit' (which is supposed to motivate small business-men – but in reality is usually so difficult to calculate that they have to ignore it) is more difficult to extrapolate. But I suspect the nearest equivalent is your income less the *notional* effort it takes to obtain it.

This poses the question of marginal sales; much of business management theory is obsessed with marginal accounting – what extra business can *profitably* be added to the mix that the company already has. From your point of view the question reduces to: is the extra business worth the effort; does it justify all the hassle of going after it? It is a much more difficult decision to make than it might at first appear. You may justify going after it simply because you have spare time in the day to make the call. But as a result you may have to work late into the night (maybe even some weeks later) to catch up with your essential paperwork; and the extra effort this causes may be occasioned by something that produces minuscule returns. Even worse, this extra effort may mean that you are tempted to take shortcuts on one of your major projects; one of the small number that earn most of your commission.

The best technique for analysing this aspect of your work is the Pareto 80:20 rule. This is a very powerful rule of thumb that is almost universally applicable (you will find that I refer to it throughout the book). In essence it states that (in this case) 80 per cent of your commission income is likely to come from the top 20 per cent of your accounts, and from 20 per cent of your effort. On the other hand, perhaps 80 per cent of your accounts will absorb close to 80 per cent of your effort, and return just 20 per cent of your income.

It would be nice to be able to select the most productive 20 per cent and go on holiday for the remaining nine months. But that is not usually possible because it is normally not easy to see just which will be the most productive 20 per cent; and you will need far more cover in case your 'bankers' don't actually live up to your expectations.

It was Lord Leverhulme who, in a slightly different context, admitted (of the advertising for his soap empire) that he knew that half of it didn't work; the problem was that he didn't know *which* half didn't work. Even now, with all the most sophisticated tools of marketing, the position remains more or less unchanged. The sales professional has much the same problem.

I am certain that most sales professionals should be able to identify the 10 per cent of prospects which will be *unproductive*. To abandon these is a brave decision, especially when you are low on sales. I well remember when I was an IBM trainee, and had been given my first patch to develop, I spent an inordinate amount of my time on a small food wholesaler which had been foolish enough to admit that it wanted to improve its financial systems. Over seven or eight extended calls I eventually developed a 50-page proposal; which just about managed to justify the £50,000 or so I was asking them to invest in the smallest mainframe computer. I ultimately lost the order. They actually bought a new electric typewriter and a new desktop electronic calculator (this was in the days before the universal pocket calculator appeared); at a total cost of less than £1,000!

As a trainee, the whole episode was excellent experience (and I suppose I should be grateful for the valuable management time they gave up for me). The main lesson I learnt was to husband my resources, and not fritter them away on obvious losers and unproductive accounts. Such an attitude may not appeal to your management, who are greedy for any business (and are not too worried about the long hours you work); but it will help your own productivity quite significantly. If nothing else, the time you save can be very profitably used to add extra effort to the 20 per cent of key prospects that will be *highly* productive.

Match to the business
Having decided the ideal pattern of business needed to optimise your income from the sales plan, the next step is to match that profile against your customer and prospect base. You should have a

reasonable idea of what companies, or at least what sectors, will deliver business over the next year. You simply need to match this forecast (with all its flaws and inaccuracies, which you must allow for and be fully aware of) to your profile.

This will allow you (using, perhaps, some variant of the 80:20 rule) to set your customer and prospect priorities for the next year. In IBM (where even small mainframes could cost hundreds of thousands of pounds) I rarely worked to more than 10 or so accounts that I knew would deliver better than 90 per cent of my business in the next year. I didn't totally ignore the next 20 or 30 accounts, which would give me almost all the remaining 10 per cent, but they received significantly less attention. I didn't even ignore the 100+ accounts which might provide, at best, 1 to 2 per cent; like many sales professionals, I am too greedy for my own good! But I covered these marginal accounts by mass marketing activities – only getting personally involved when they actually asked to place an order. Even then, the size of the order usually made the business unproductive.

Reallocate resources
Having determined your outline account plan, you will need to reallocate your resources to match this. You may be lucky and have external resources to deploy; you may have a support team, or you may have budgets for promotional activities. These will need to be realigned to match your newly optimised plans. For example, one year I discovered that running stands at exhibitions generated less than 5 per cent of my sales, but absorbed 30 per cent of my budget and 20 per cent of my time; so I dropped them as a promotional tool. Having said that, I was forced to reinstate them the following year when I found that my customers (whose business I obtained almost exclusively from face-to-face contact) objected to not seeing us at these exhibitions; we had to return to them as a necessary image exercise. The moral of this tale is that not all apparently unproductive activities can be discarded with impunity – you must be aware of the wider implications.

In practice, most sales professionals will have as their main (probably only) resource just their own time. But that is the most valuable resource of all – and the one that is most often wasted, because sales professionals simply do not realise how valuable it is. The aspect of exhibitions that swayed me most was the 20 per cent of my time (rather than the 30 per cent of my budget) that they absorbed. When I reinstated them I carefully planned activities so that I was able to reduce this to 10 per cent of my time and less than 20 per cent of my budget – the new requirement was only to be seen, not positively to promote, and this was still attainable using cheaper stands.

Your own time is a resource that must be carefully guarded, just as your budgets should be. Because it does not appear on any account book, there is a tendency to squander it. But it has to be your, and probably your company's, main asset; and should be treated like the gold dust it represents.

In IBM, a sales professional, with all the accompanying overheads (which almost double the cost of the package he personally receives), is costed at between £70,000 and £100,000 per annum. It is assumed that he will work for 200 days a year (the remainder being taken up with holidays, training, sickness etc) and will be out of the office (on territory) for not much more than 50 per cent of this time. When out of the office it is reckoned that he can achieve a maximum rate of three to four scheduled calls a day (in reality the actual figure was probably closer to two to three). This all adds up to around 300 calls a year. The cost per call is, therefore, of the order of £300; making calls a resource that has to be *very* carefully husbanded.

Protect the future
I have stressed that it may be very productive to gear your whole account plan to the fine detail of the company's sales plan; and this may well be the most productive use of your time. But you should not totally ignore the longer term, in this single-minded pursuit of short-term goals.

Reversing my strictures of previous sections, I will state that most companies, and in my experience almost all sales professionals, suffer from marketing myopia. They are obsessed by short-term performance to the damaging exclusion of longer-term potential. This was true of the operational units within IBM, although it was carefully balanced by the staff groups, in particular at corporate headquarters, planning in detail over a time horizon that exceeded a decade – a 'luxury' that few other companies afford, and are accordingly that much less successful. In IBM the thrust of field management was always for this year's sales but many, if not most, of its sales campaigns actually spanned more than one year. So the pressure was, in effect, to close business already in the pipeline (incidentally, not a bad discipline as most sales professionals hate closing). The success of this pressure is seen in IBM's typical banana-shaped sales curve, with monthly sales steadily growing throughout the year, until the best month of all is December. Yet this is almost totally unrelated to the natural patterns of the market place.

The IBM sales curve is simply a reflection of the pressure on sales professionals to close year-end business (IBM's books close on 31 December), and the ability of those sales professionals actually to do this – in the face of all logic!

In my part of IBM this pressure was brought to a head by an ill-advised campaign for the 'three-call sell'. In the name of efficiency, field management had decided that it should be possible to sell the smaller systems using no more than three calls, spread over less than three months. This was despite the realities of the market place, and the result was a great deal of unproductive thrashing around, and a steadily deteriorating morale. My own analysis at the time suggested that less than 5 per cent of the business fell into this category; where more than 70 per cent took over six months (with an extended call pattern). At that time I was running IBM's business school, through which passed most of its best sales professionals, so I was able effectively to counter these simplistic views of field management. The following year (having returned to longer, more realistic time horizons) the morale of the whole sales force was dramatically better, and productivity correspondingly improved (indeed sales almost tripled).

So, while attending to the short-term targets, you must also invest in the future. In practice this need not divert too much resource, since it should be largely complementary to your other work. If it isn't, you should seriously consider whether the company has its priorities correct (and estimate how long *it* can afford to ignore its longer-term future before harsh commercial realities, and maybe liquidation, catch up with it). Probably most of your long-term business will come from your key accounts (both by direct sales, and indirectly by references), so nurturing them should not be a problem – since this will at the same time generate much of your short-term business.

This is the time to stress that in dissecting the sales plan you *must* get your analysis correct. Read the fine print carefully, otherwise you may still find yourself backing a loser. For one thing, management teams rarely want to give away money, so they build in clawback clauses. And even management themselves, if their brainchild has the usual degree of complexity, probably don't understand the inter-action of all the clauses!

Position

We now come to the second category of objectives, or aspirations. If position or status is important to you then you need to plan to succeed.

The Sales Professional

At a most basic level, most sales professionals at least want to be seen as successful. IBM even used this desire to graft on another set of targets. Its qualification targets for the Hundred Per Cent Club (in theory for those who achieved 100 per cent of their sales targets) were, at least in detail, often quite different from those that drove the commission scheme. The award was worth less than £1000 (and even then in kind – three days at a convention in a foreign holiday resort), but it still represented a more powerful incentive than the commission. I once traded £2000-worth of commission for a minor qualification that was keeping me out of the Club. It was simply more than a sales professional could bear to miss being one of IBM's highly visible successful sales professionals.

For the more ambitious, though, there is the drive for promotion. To achieve this, you will have to decide just where you ought to be going during the current year. You will have to decide what training you need, or at least what training you think your management will be suitably impressed with. You will also have to decide what commission you are willing to sacrifice to help your management to achieve their objectives. I was never more feted (and subsequently promoted) by my management than when I closed the order that got me into the Hundred Per Cent Club, but I was not feted for my personal success, rather I was feted for the fact that this order also put the branch into the Club.

You also have to decide what 'social' events you need to invest in. Within IBM there was a pub, fortunately quite near our branch, which was frequented by senior sales management; and it was fascinating how many ambitious sales professionals also found it a very convivial hostelry – and how many of these eventually managed to obtain promotion!

Political activities

If you are very determined, then you may choose to indulge in the political games that enliven (or bedevil, according to your viewpoint) most offices. It has been my observation that such political machinations are usually successful; even the most inept of practitioners seems to be able to satisfy the wishes of his masters. I do not, however, intend to turn this book into a primer on office politics; in any case, if that is your bent you will probably already know far more about the techniques than I do!

I will just mention one caveat for those who have not yet learnt some of the more painful lessons. Politics is a subtle and often unpredictable game, and you should be aware of the downside risks – and guard against them.

Satisfaction

Even if satisfaction and general enjoyment of your job is not your highest priority, you should still positively plan to get these from your work. I have stated that this book is just as much about getting enjoyment out of selling; whatever your ambitions, you would be foolish to miss the real pleasure and satisfaction that can be had.

In any case, getting pleasure and satisfaction actually helps you to do it better. Customers appreciate a sales professional who enjoys what he is doing; and they trust him. Conversely, customers will shun a sour salesman.

I personally got much of my own satisfaction from getting to know my customers' businesses in depth, and from solving their complex problems. As a result, this was the slant that I gave my work. Perhaps fortunately, this was also the area where most of the business came from, and it was a 'technique' that was very effective. I don't know how I would have coped if this hadn't been required but, then, that was why I chose the job in the first place.

A good job well done

Perhaps the greatest satisfaction of all comes from knowing that you have done a good job. Almost everyone wants to do a good job (even if many don't succeed). What aspects of the job you consider most worth doing well is, of course, a purely individual choice. I once worked for a manager who had, for various odd reasons, apparently been friendly with the heads of the Genovese family when they were the most feared godfathers in the Cosa Nostra. His experience was, surprisingly, that they had just about the highest developed moral sense of any group he knew. The problem, for the rest of society, was simply that the Cosa Nostra's morality was some distance removed from that adopted by the remainder of us. Even the Cosa Nostra wanted to do a good job – and the Genovese family clearly displayed their satisfaction, reportedly over a quiet Saturday tea, as they discussed who they had dropped in Long Island Sound that week!

Integrity

Perhaps the one aspect of character that impresses customers most is integrity and, paradoxically, it is the one element wholly missing in the stereotype. On a personal basis it is also (perhaps surprisingly to those who still believe in the stereotype) a prerequisite for some, maybe most, sales professionals.

At its most basic level, you have to have some belief in what you are selling. If you don't, it is likely that you will make a poor job of it, and would perform much better with a product you *could* believe in – so why are you hanging around in the wrong job? The basic question which you should ask yourself is: can I believe enough in this year's sales plan to be able to sell it to my customers? It's a question that not enough sales professionals ask themselves. Mostly, of course, the answer will be yes; but occasionally it will be no – and a sales professional has to come to terms with that.

Even if the answer is yes, it is still worth determining how you can implement the sales plan in a way that protects your integrity. *You* have to believe; if you are to persuade your customer to believe. As Buck Rodgers says in *The IBM Way*: ' ... I was determined to establish that my word was my bond. I could never do business any other way ...'

Outside activities

Even for the most dedicated sales professional, there will be other things to life beyond selling. If nothing else, it is difficult to make a sales call at midnight, although not impossible. The support work, such as proposal writing, can absorb as many hours as you want to make available. But it is sound practice to have hobbies or interests that are a complete change; no matter how much you love selling, it is a stressful occupation that demands that you rest when not working.

So, you will have outside activities. These may run from onerous responsibilities, such as being a local councillor, to simply being with your family. For most sales professionals, it is all too easy to neglect their families; it is *not* simple to maintain good family relationships where long hours and stress take their toll. But it clearly is essential that the family gets its fair share of your time – they will, you hope, be with you long after the company is just a dim memory.

Thus, any comprehensive sales plan you make has to take full account of these outside activities. If you have to attend a local council meeting you cannot plan to be 300 miles away at that time. If you plan to spend a reasonable amount of time with your family, you can't plan to work an 85-hour week. You simply have to choose your priorities, and then put them into practice.

Defining the territory

Once you have defined the objectives of your 'business', the prioritised mix of company and personal objectives, you will need to define your market. Any business has to decide unequivocally where its market lies, so that it can allocate and concentrate its resources on its core business. In the same way you will need to define your territory, your particular market, carefully. You may feel that this is self evident; your company will already have told you. But the picture is more complex. As we will see, you may wish to define the key elements of your territory (so that you can optimise your use of resources) by factors other than geography, which is the most usual basis for definition.

Geographical definition
Most territories are based on a geographical patch ranging from a whole country to a single postal district. Whatever the size, no sales professional is *ever* happy by being limited to a territory, however large!

Physical location
The physical boundaries of your territory may seem obvious, always assuming that it is a geographic patch. But they are still well worth examining in some detail. Indeed, it is essential if (as is quite likely) you have part of a town or city, to draw up the borderlines very carefully on a large-scale street map; which you will, in any case, need for planning your call schedules.

Territories are often divided along main roads, so it is important that you know what numbers are on your side of the road. There is nothing quite so frustrating as getting excited over what is obviously a banker of a prospect, only to discover it is on the wrong side of a dividing road. Nothing so frustrating, that is, except finding this out when you have just spent six months closing the business – and it goes to a colleague, who is very grateful for your help!

Yet I have met very few sales professionals who rigorously check what is their territory. I found it quite astonishing, as a personal computer dealer, to walk into the sales office with a hot prospect for a territory salesman, only to find (too often) that nobody knew exactly whose territory it was on. Of course this has advantages for the more adventurous sales professional. After a while a new sales professional joined us, and each new prospect was rapidly claimed. It took the other sales professionals more than three months to realise that if nobody else immediately claimed the prospect, the new sales professional would; by which time he was, justifiably, doing twice the business that they were (half of it from the borders of their own territories!). Needless to say, by that time all the sales professionals had developed a very acute perception of their geography.

It can also work in the other direction. There may be nooks and crannies on your territory, which look as if they naturally belong to someone else. So it is well worth spending an evening tracing the *exact* borders. I found this out when I had half of the NW10 district of London. I am no slouch when it comes to laying claim to territory, but I was somewhat embarrassed when my manager found a part of my territory that I didn't even know existed. At the time I was making noises about the lack of potential (well, the annual review of targets was under way!) and he set out to prove me wrong. One edge of the territory was defined by a railway line, and where it crossed a main road it divided into two. I had stopped at the first railway bridge, but nestling between the two bridges (and still on my territory) were two office buildings. My manager gleefully reported that they were a key part of a large corporation, and they wanted to purchase a system. He was even more gleeful a couple of months later, when he waved goodbye and went to be sales director of that organisation; all on the back of his one sale! So the effort of tracing the exact boundary can be very worthwhile.

Potential
Having established that you haven't overlooked any important parts of your empire, the next (and most important) step is to decide what parts of the territory have the most potential. This may be immediately evident, in the form of large factory estates, shopping centres or office complexes. But it may also require considerable research in terms of searching the various lists and directories to determine where individual large prospects are located. Such a search is still advisable even if you are convinced you know where the business must be; hot prospects have the unfortunate habit of choosing to be in the wrong places. And, of course, nothing can beat walking, or more probably driving, every street of your patch; particularly as this is the only way of finding the new businesses that are just moving in – who must normally be some of your hottest prospects.

Once these decisions have been taken, you will be in a position to plot those areas of highest potential on your map(s), to give the true shape of your territory (large areas of housing or farmland may provide pretty patches of colour on the map, but they won't pay your salary).

Resource and time
Against this potential you will also need to determine what resource will be required to tap it, and what is actually available. If you have the whole of the UK, it is much easier to support a customer who is just five miles down the road than one who is 500 miles away. On the other hand, one of my biggest markets was Scotland (which was up to 500 miles away); market potential should always override other considerations.

You will need to plan how you can best dispose your resources. Where will you obtain local technical support and demonstration facilities? The location of key reference sites may also be central to the development of your territory.

The limitations on this may not be immediately obvious. Thus, one reason why Scotland turned out to be such a good market was logistical. From where I lived, on the outskirts of London, I could be in almost any of the major centres of Scotland in less than two hours by air. On the other hand, large sections of England were three to four hours away; including, paradoxically, just the other side of London, which (before the days of the M25) was a nightmare to cross. Some parts of Wales were more than six hours away, and might take two days for a single call. Needless to say these were not well covered, and I even paid for one hot prospect to visit *me*.

The traffic patterns can mean that physical distances are much less important than travelling times, and it is the latter that you must allow for in your plans (drawing 'contours' of equal travelling time). IBM found this out to its cost when it relocated its headquarters from London to Portsmouth; an eminently sensible decision in terms of costs and environment. Unfortunately, it found that its key personnel were still having to spend large amounts of time in London, accompanied by even larger amounts of travelling time (since public transport connections were poor). Even worse, it was discovered that they had to consider a 'mortality' budget; since, with such extensive car mileage taking place, they were losing one or two key managers killed or maimed in traffic accidents every year. Such budgets are normally only allowed for on major construction projects (and even then they are not exactly publicised).

In order to manage your resource plan, you will need at least to know how much you cost per hour. Alan Gillam suggests that you base your costing on the following factors: salary; commission;

bonuses; direct expenses; and indirect expenses. I would also add overheads (although Alan Gillam may include these in 'indirect expenses'). Such overheads cover the cost of your support staff and management.

If you bother to do this calculation (and too few sales professionals make the effort) you will probably be surprised at how much you actually cost per hour. In my experience, such knowledge certainly sharpens your drive for productivity. It will, in particular, put in perspective the costs of marginal business on the fringes of your patch.

Annual calls available

Once you have a feel for the territory you can carry out perhaps the most important calculation, which is quite simply how many calls you will be able to make (typically over a year). It is a calculation that relatively few sales professionals make. Its importance is not in the knowledge itself, but in subsequently tracking your own performance; in monitoring whether your call rate is too low, you need to know just what *is* too low.

The basic element of measure will probably be the day. If you were to make calls all day, just how many (on average, for your whole territory) could you make? This needs to be an honest measure. For many sales professionals, myself included, it may be difficult to book more than two (or perhaps three) calls a day (where it cannot be accurately predicted exactly how long they will last and, hence, you have to allow a full morning or afternoon for each). On the other hand, even here it should be possible to supplement this by *ad hoc* or cold calls, to at least double the rate; and these extra calls must be allowed for in your plans. Of course, there are retail salesmen who can easily achieve rates of 10 times this level. Only you can forecast what is an achievable call rate; it depends on so many factors, including typical call length, flexibility of customers, travelling time, reporting procedures etc.

Of course, this rate assumes an *ideal* sales day, and this almost never happens. Many sales professionals have to spend a great deal of time preparing for calls, supporting customers and writing proposals. In IBM it was realistically recognised by management that sales professionals spent at least 50 per cent of their time at their desks in the branch office, although this fact was not publicised to the sales professionals themselves, who were instead exhorted to spend every second *out* of the office.

You also have to allow for holidays, training etc. Again in IBM, it was assumed (again without publicity) that a sales professional (or any member of staff) would be available for just 200 days a year. So by the time 50 per cent was needed for office work, and the possible total was only 200 days, the effective time available was reduced to just 100 days a year of face-to-face selling. At perhaps two calls a day (which was my target when I was covering the whole of the UK, with typically 50+ miles between each call) this gave just 200 possible calls a year. It is sobering when most sales professionals first come face-to-face with their true figures. It makes them much more aware of how important *each* call is. They realise that they cannot afford to miss any, or to do anything less than optimise their performance in each call they make.

The key to this self-knowledge is quite simply the basic calculation that shows just how many calls are available.

Designing a call schedule

The first practical application of all this planning will be the call schedule. You could, of course, make calls at random; many sales professionals do just that – and wonder why they spend so much time travelling and so little in front of the customer.

Call frequency

The first decision is not when to call, but how often. Many sales professionals are demand-driven; they call when asked. There certainly is a logic to this. You do not want to make too many unnecessary calls, and you certainly don't want to refuse to make a call because the prospect has exceeded his quota. But even so, it is advantageous to prioritise your accounts and budget to allow them the number of calls that their importance deserves, and demands.

Whatever your approach, you will start with a list of your prospects (or categories of prospect) which will need to be annotated with the amount of business you expect from each, preferably taking into account the chance of obtaining that business. Against the grand total of all this business you can set the number of calls which you have calculated you can make each year. This calculation shows exactly how much business is needed to justify *each* call. Thus, if your total business is forecast at £1.2 million (after allowing for a suitable 'conversion' rate – essentially the average of all the percentage forecast success rates) and you can make 300 calls a year, each such call should be 'worth' £4000.

Against each account, therefore, you can determine how many

calls they justify. Extending the above example, if you have a prospect potentially worth £40,000 (and with a 50 per cent forecast chance of achieving this), he would justify five calls; and your call schedule would reflect this.

Instead of forecast sales you could, more subjectively, simply give each prospect (or category) a weighting of importance; from 1 to 10 (with 10 as the most important). Then you apply the same calculation as before.

Having completed all these forecasts and calculations, you should be in a position to develop your overall call schedule. But before you do, it is worth looking at the call rates. How many prospects justify only one call, and how many of them do you really think you will close in that one call? It is a salutary check and graphically illustrates how marginal many prospects are. Without this simple check, however, many sales professionals still make these calls – to the detriment of their more important prospects.

Walk pattern

The next step, traditionally, is to plan what is the most efficient pattern of calls; the walk pattern. This is clearly most relevant for very routine calling – and is most highly developed in selling to retail outlets. But it is still worth considering its implications for more complex situations, where perhaps it might be better titled the 'drive pattern'.

Grid

The simplest and most frequently used pattern is that based on a grid. Nothing could be simpler. You simply group your calls in the same area into a day's work, and start there; moving on to the next block when the first is completed at the end of the day. Thus, you move

1	2	3	4	5
6	7	8	9	10
11	12	13	14	15
16	17	18	19	20

Figure 3.1

steadily through all the blocks until all the prospects are covered –
then the whole process starts over again.

A modification, illustrated in Figure 3.1, is a true grid – in which
all the columns in a row are completed, before moving on to the next
row. The advantage of this approach is that you are regularly (once a
week) relatively close (no more than three sections away) to any part
of your territory. This means that you will find it easier to schedule in
more frequent calls on important customers; or to schedule call-
backs against earlier calls.

Segments
If the more important customers are concentrated in one core area, a
city centre for example, an alternative choice is to divide the territory
into segments radiating from the centre (see Figure 3.2). This means
that each day's calls will include some portion of the core and be
close to all parts of that core, so that key prospects can easily be
called on within 24 hours.

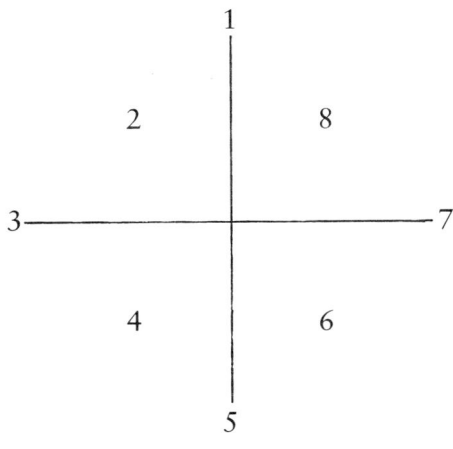

Figure 3.2

Starting points
Having chosen your block or segment for the day, it is next necessary
to decide where to *start* within the block. This is a matter of some
debate, and may be of some consequence when calling on retail
outlets, but for sales professionals it is usually only a matter of
personal preference. If you get up early, and want to be home early,
you will start at the furthest end of the territory and work back
towards home. If you are a late riser you will do the reverse. If you

want to have lunch at home (or at the office) you will start near the middle and work back home for lunch. The choice is yours, depending on your sleeping and eating arrangements.

Timing
A side issue is how long a working day you intend to observe. Most sales professionals tend to start making calls no earlier than 9.30 am and finish by 4.30 pm. But Alfred Tack quotes research on buyers:

> 'Significantly, almost one in twenty began to see salesmen at eight-thirty'
> 'over one in five could be interviewed at sixteen-thirty and slightly more at seventeen hundred.'

This shows that it is quite possible for most sales professionals to start an hour earlier and finish an hour later. This could add an extra two hours to the working day; perhaps as much as a 40 per cent increase, if a two-hour lunch is allowed for. But, once more, the choice is yours.

Ad hoc customer support
All the above planning work is designed to produce a scheduled day's work, with every minute productively allocated. The problem, of course, is that life is not so simple. Many sales professionals spend long hours sitting, in solitary boredom, in their cars, as appointments finish long before the end of the generous 'buffer' that has to be allowed between calls so that they are not cut off in mid-flow).

Many sales professionals write their reports in this time. I, however, mainly used this dead time for *ad hoc* calls. There was usually a customer nearby, so I dropped in 'on spec'. Most pundits will claim, with considerable justification, that you should *never* visit customers or prospects without a deliberate plan of campaign. In terms of scheduled calls I would agree wholeheartedly with this philosophy; and would go even further to state that you must set a target for some positive *action* that you will agree in that call.

However, my strictures do not apply to 'bonus' calls. If you keep yourself well informed on customer progress you can always justify a 'free' call. They are almost certain to have some problem since you last called (and, if they haven't, then simply check that they *haven't* had any problems). You can use the opportunity to apologise in person for the problems, and to check that they have been properly sorted out. You can take the opportunity to offer excellent, personal service which will always stand you in good stead with the customer – if nothing else you are very obviously showing an interest (which it appears surprisingly few sales professionals do!).

In addition, most importantly, you can also check if there is any business in the offing. By frequently appearing in accounts on this *ad hoc* basis (prospects as well as customers, although these require more skill in justifying such calls), I was normally able to beat my competitors to the draw for most of the major business on my patch – and the first sales professional in stands a good chance of setting the ground rules for everyone else, which is a decided advantage.

It is by no means certain that your prime contact will be available, but that may offer an excellent opportunity to bypass him and see another influencer/decision-maker, although this will require some tact and sensitivity. If all else fails, you can talk to the operational staff or the receptionist; it is still customer service. Most sales professionals neglect these lesser players, but that is probably a mistake. In most companies even the views of these lesser players are taken into account. They may not carry much weight but they can tip the balance – and if they veto you that may be the kiss of death. I, as the buyer, have several times had to choose the supplier who ran second on my list, simply because the operational staff wouldn't work with the sales professional from the preferred supplier. And talking to these otherwise neglected personnel can often give you a unique access to the 'grapevine'.

The other alternative is to spend the time making some cold calls. Again it's free – and if you can 'take it or leave it', cold calling comes much easier (especially in short bursts) and is correspondingly more successful.

Industry

A territory split which is used much less frequently than geography is that by industry. But this can be a very powerful choice. For many years IBM split its main business by industry; this had the great benefit that the sales professionals dedicated to each industry were steeped in the knowledge and folklore of that industry, although at the price of having a wider geographical spread of their territories.

If, as is likely, your management have not chosen to give you an industry-based territory, then there is markedly less benefit in trying to apply such a split within your territory.

Industry knowledge

If, however, your territory contains collections of specialised industries it may be worth putting in the effort to get to know these industries, so that you can sell more effectively to them. Of course, if you already have some knowledge of a specific industry you have a head start – and should consider putting rather more effort into these prospects (since your knowledge should make you more productive in these areas).

It is essentially a balance between cost and returns. Will the extra effort – in terms of learning these industries – be made worthwhile by sufficient quantities of extra sales? It is a calculation that only you can make – but it *is* worth making.

In IBM Biomedical Group I believed that there was an opening for our equipment in the area of general clinical haematology. This was not an area that IBM had explored elsewhere in the world. As a result it required something like six months of educating myself (at the same time as selling to the existing markets) and then a further year establishing our place in the market. In the end it *was* worthwhile, since some 80 per cent business eventually came from this sector. But, in making that 18-month investment, I had to recognise that there was a degree of risk – it might not have paid off as well as expected (although before making the investment I had conducted research to make certain I wasn't on to a total loser).

Product

It is also beneficial to look at your territory in terms of what products it will be capable of absorbing. There is little point in looking to sell services designed for stockbrokers in a small country town, or farm equipment in the City. Within most product ranges there is an element of specialisation, so you must determine what products will do best on your particular territory.

This analysis is necessary because to understand the products in sufficient depth to be deemed an expert may be time consuming, and you may not have the personal resource to apply this to all products in the range.

When I launched IBM's first micro (the little-known IBM 5110) I already knew it was doomed to be a failure by IBM standards. I knew that no IBM sales professionals would waste their time selling a micro when they could use that time to sell a mainframe; it was not an efficient use of their time. But I carefully worked out the only possible strategy: only if he could sell nothing else was a sales professional, just before walking out of the door, to offer the 5110. If there was any interest, then he could call in a specialist.

The product still didn't sell, since even to take this step required the sales professionals to educate themselves to know the 5110, and they understandably still preferred to dedicate their valuable resources to learning about the much more profitable mainframes – and an excellent product languished unproffered, even in those accounts that might have wanted it.

References

Another factor which might colour what you sell on your patch (in terms of product applications, industries etc) will be the references you have on the territory, or have access to. If you have some good references you again stand a better chance in these areas; and it is worth putting more effort into them.

Defining the customer and prospect set

Having decided the shape of your overall territory, and the key factors that will determine your overall sales approach, you now need to look at the individual customers and prospects, since each of these will, to a greater or lesser extent, require individual attention.

This is the stage at which (if you haven't already done so) you will build your customer and prospect database, with a card for each. Indeed, you should have completed this work earlier since it is needed for the work on the overall territory; but it is essential now, for you must categorise your customer/prospect set – and develop account plans for each category (or for each customer or prospect).

Customers

Without any doubt, the most important split on almost all territories is that between customers and prospects. Customers are almost universally more productive than prospects; and indeed more productive than many sales professionals allow for. What is more, assuming that you have offered good customer service, they are already tied to you; competitors will have to justify breaking these links before they can even begin their selling process. In such customers you already have an existing base on which it is natural to build. You don't have to sell over the psychological barrier caused by them not wanting to bring in new ideas (justifiably so because new installations often *are* painful).

Yet many, if not most, sales professionals devote disproportionately less time to existing customers. They spend their time touting for new business, when common-sense should tell them to spend at least adequate time defending, and growing, their customer base.

This problem was particularly evident in the personal computer market. All the research showed that the one group who were almost guaranteed to buy a system were the group that had bought a system within the past year; and these had to be customers of someone. On the other hand cold prospects were unlikely to show a better than 10 or 20 per cent chance of buying a system. Yet the sales professionals still sadly neglected their customers and the industry had an appalling reputation of poor service to customers. Paradoxically, though, this made it more difficult for sales professionals to win competitive business. The customers had invested enormous effort in learning how to make the relationship with their existing supplier work; even though they were still on the receiving end of appallingly bad service. They simply could not face starting all over again with a new supplier: better the devil you know!

So the first priority must be to allocate resources to your *customer* set. Having said that, you must also differentiate between customers, according to what they are worth to you. Some will be 'bankers' and will bring in a large part of the easy 80 per cent of your business – you must cosset these investments. Some, on the other hand, will be totally unproductive, demanding resource for little return – in these cases your plan must be to contain the 'bleeding'. It is only in exceptional circumstances that you can afford to amputate such a bad customer – if you do, there will be a danger that the rest of your customers may see it as failure to provide support.

'A' prospects

You should know your customers well enough to be able to predict their sales performance. But the real skill comes in being able to separate the sheep from the goats among the prospects. You need to decide which are the 10 per cent or so of prospects who will bring in 50+ per cent of the new business. This is partly a function of their size (in terms of potential business) and partly of their probability of closing. These are the prospects that should take first cut of the resources left after the planned support of your customers.

'B' prospects

Similarly, you will have to determine the 50 per cent or so of the remaining prospects who will bring in the remaining 50 per cent of new business. It will need careful planning and a ruthless determination to control resource exposures, to ration out the small amount of resource remaining after you have allocated to customers and 'A' prospects.

Determining which are A and B prospects is unfortunately a matter of experience; it is a skill you learn. There are no easy guidelines, although obviously size of company is a good indicator. You will, though, learn the types of company that are more likely to be productive prospects. I myself looked at all the facts I had unearthed about my prospects and, as best as I can describe it, I simply felt that some of them had the 'smell' of business.

There were so many different factors involved, that I can't describe how I developed this 'nose' for the most productive accounts, except that it was a matter of experience built up over time (this represented weeks on a particular territory, rather than years). An example from my time of running a territory in London will illustrate the importance of this. On examining the prospect list, which fortunately was comprehensive, covering all business of any size on my patch, I identified six key accounts (my A list), a further 12 likely prospects (my B list) and something like 100 other runners. As it was early in my career I still chased *all* of these aggressively, although I was not able to devote much time beyond the initial cold calling on the 100 – and, as I was selling mainframe computers, it was very obvious that very few of these were in my market. At the end of the year I had closed or was about to close five out of the six A prospects. Of the B prospects I had closed none, but four were lined up to be closed within a few months. Of the remaining 100 prospects just one was in line for closing in the next year. My nose had been remarkably accurate. You too will be able to use this skill (whatever it comprises) to concentrate your resources productively.

Losers

All others have to be treated as outcasts. No matter how much they plead, you have to be ruthless and refuse to fritter away resource on unproductive areas. I learnt this lesson very early in life, working (just 15 years old) as a bar waiter, where a substantial part of my income came from tips. I earned, on average, twice as much as my colleagues. The key to my success was quite simply that I only served those customers that experience had told me would be good tippers. If they didn't look like tippers they didn't get served by me; I always managed to be too busy with my 'bankers'. They had to use one of the other waiters and waste their time instead of mine! Of course you may be wrong – everyone makes mistakes – and what you have previously considered a loser may still turn out to be a winner; in this special (if unlikely) case you *will* have to provide resource quickly.

The main danger is that you are persuaded that you were wrong, and you allocate some of your precious resource, only to find that they are 'tyre-kickers' after all – happy for you to spend considerable time talking to them, indeed demanding this, but never really likely to buy (despite their loud promises). So you must be ruthless and insist they *prove* their good intentions. It sounds the reverse of good salesmanship, but at times good salesmanship is as much about managing your own scarce resources as it is about winning friends and influencing people.

Husbanding your resources, for the 20 per cent of accounts that will bring in 80 per cent of your business, is a critical aspect of territory and account planning. It is one of the management aspects of professional salesmanship that many sales professionals find most difficult to implement. They more naturally 'shoot from the hip', rushing to the account that immediately demands attention without considering the long-term implications. Planning is essential to the sales professional; and is often the activity that distinguishes him from his less professional juniors.

IBM often resolved this problem by inundating their sales professionals with business. It liked to grow its sales force more slowly than it grew the business. As a result the sales professionals almost always had more business than they could handle (at least in the good years). Thus, to be most successful, the sales professionals had to allocate their resources very carefully. They had positively to select the accounts they were going to support. The best selling sales professional was the one who was more skilful (or more lucky) in choosing his key accounts, rather than the one who was most skilled in selling to them. Territory and account management were far more important than conventional selling skills.

Key characteristics
Even when you have got your customer and prospect sets sorted out, you still have not finished work on your territory plans, although (if you are a typical sales professional) you may be raring to go out and do some real selling. But, as in all businesses, time spent on productive planning (as opposed to bureaucratic form filling) always returns the investment in it many times over. The great majority of sales professionals almost certainly spend far too little time planning ahead (and far too much time 'fire-fighting' the inevitable consequences!).

The next task is to categorise your accounts; to marshal them into groups that share some common characteristics. In this way you can plan campaigns that share common resources, the most obvious of these being specialised seminars (for example, based on specific industries) or demonstrations.

Defining the product

You may think that your company has said all that there is to say about the products; and your company will be *sure* it has. But it is always worth spending some time working out what the products mean to your customers and yourself, since this may be rather different from what they mean to your company. In IBM Biomedical Group, for example, our best-selling UK product line was totally different from the best-seller in the USA, and different again from the best-seller in Germany. This was largely a result of how each country chose to develop their particular markets, rather than any inherent technical differences.

Optimal product mix

If you have a large product set, it may be just as important to allocate your resources between products (or product sets) as it is within your prospect sets. I will not elaborate, but you may need to decide your A and B products, together with the losers, in exactly the same way as you do with your prospect set.

Unique selling proposition

What you really need, though, is not a product but a unique selling proposition (USP), or a series of them. This is what you will present to your customers. It is the subject of endless soul-searching in advertising agencies: the USP is at the heart of most television commercials (whether it is British Airways somewhat tendentiously claiming to be 'the world's favourite airline' or Burger-King studiously explaining how they 'flame-grill (broil) their burgers').

If your company hasn't already explained the USP to you (to your satisfaction), you will be well advised to develop one or more for yourself. In any case, you should be aware of the fact that in professional selling (as opposed to televised mass consumer goods) the USP may well differ, depending on which prospect you are selling to.

John Fenton describes an interesting process he evolved, which involves the whole sales force in a day-long exercise. In the morning anything up to 20 flipcharts (along the walls) are filled with reasons why customers buy from you. The reasons they buy are provided by the salesmen, not management. After an initial embarrassed silence, followed by the more predictable ideas, the useful in-depth contributions begin to flow. In the afternoon the process is repeated, with another set of flipcharts covered by the reasons why customers buy from your competitors. Finally the two sets are compared, and only those that are unique to you are allowed to remain as the USPs. According to John Fenton, this process helps to focus on the USPs; it also helps to provide invaluable product training for the sales force.

Feature/benefits

Vast tracts of most books on salesmanship are devoted to feature/benefit arguments. Alfred Tack takes these arguments to their logical conclusion when he suggests: 'As many (key) sentences should be evolved as there are benefits.' His thesis, which has admirable logic, is that to remember the benefits rather than the features you should commit to memory a list of sentences, one for each key benefit, which you can introduce 'naturally' into the conversation.

There is some advantage in looking at your products in terms of benefits rather than features; anyone who has looked for a personal computer to solve his business problems will have realised just how irrelevant are all the features (a 10 megahertz 80286-processor with zero wait states complemented by a micro-channel making full use of OS/2) trotted out by almost all dealer salesmen. But though I applaud the attempt to stop salesmen selling features, I regret that, in the context of professional selling, I remain a sceptic. My quarrel is with a style of selling that requires the sales professional to enter a call with a list of benefits.

Certainly you must be aware of the benefits, and must go through the process of compiling a list so that you understand what each of the features can mean. The importance of the fast personal computer processor illustrated earlier, for example, is that it means that, 'the user doesn't have to waste his time sitting in front of a blank screen waiting for the answers to his questions to come back'. But, in professional selling, I do not believe you should be over-aware of these benefits, waiting to pounce with the glib benefit statement. My criticism is that such an approach distracts the sales professional from establishing just exactly what are the prospect's needs and wants. Only when you have established these can you think about what specific benefits you can offer to meet these needs and wants.

Indeed, the real benefits for a given prospect may not even appear on your list. For a number of months I sold one item of high-tech medical equipment to hospital consultants, on the basis of the very real benefits it offered for treating their patients. I eventually realised, after a couple of years, that in reality one of the main reasons such consultants purchased the equipment was that it demonstrated their professional status; it showed that they were leading-edge clinicians. It was not even necessary that they used it on their patients – and some didn't! It was only necessary that they had it. I was not so insensitive that I then changed my sales pitch to tell consultants that they could ignore their patients (they were quite capable of taking that decision for themselves!); but I did very successfully, if also very discreetly, emphasise the element of status.

Perhaps a more important disadvantage of having a list of benefits to hand is that you feel almost honour-bound to beat the prospect about the ears with it, particularly when you have spent long hours developing and honing the list. But once you have determined those few benefits that mean something to the prospect, *shut up*! Any additional benefits, no matter how much you love them, can only distract (and dilute your more important messages). They will confuse and may offer controversy without adding anything to the call.

During the 'dummy' calls at the core of IBM sales training, one of the standard tests that the instructors introduced was quite simply to agree, quite early in the call, that the benefits already put forward were enough to win the business. It was illuminating for us as instructors, and for the trainees (who never repeated the mistake) just how many of them effectively told *us* to shut up so that they could continue reading off their list of benefits, when they should have been asking us to sign the order!

Support
One of the features that is very important to buyers of complex products, but is often relatively neglected by many sales professionals, is that of support. For example, market research showed that it was the most important selection factor of all in the personal computer market (mentioned by more than 50 per cent of buyers). It was even more important to them when they had the equipment, with nearly 60 per cent choosing this as the prime area where their suppliers could improve (nearly 10 times that of any other requirement). It is also the area where you can make a personal contribution; most of the evidence as to what support will be available will come from your own performance. If you are professional, then you should look (at least) as if you might provide professional support. But you must make certain that you live up to this when you get the order!

Plan targets

It is inevitable that the major objectives imposed by your company, by its management in the sales plan, will be performance targets; typically enshrined in numbers – sales volume, sales revenue and (not often enough) profit. Making these numbers is, of course, critical to your career – and often to your income.

So, in outline at the beginning of the year and in detail as you go through the year, as a matter of survival you need to be able to forecast where the business is coming from.

Forecasting

The classic, and I believe still the best, way of forecasting is to run through your active customer and prospect list to determine for each the size of the potential business, together with the odds of doing that business during the period, however long that might be. The size of the potential business should generally be relatively easy to quantify; if you are forecasting it as a potential 'win', you should at least know what it is worth (even if you are not yet certain exactly how you are going to win it). Much more difficult than most sales professionals will admit to themselves is forecasting the *real* chance of winning the business, and of winning it in the period in question. The forecast is for the specific period, and even if you were actually to win it in the period after that under discussion, forecasting it in the target period would still be inaccurate.

The period must be matched to the pattern of the business. It is pointless having a weekly reporting period if you are selling airliners on timescales which may exceed five years. But in general, the shorter the time period you choose (within sensible limits) the better you will control your customers and prospects – and your selling. Maybe your company will choose your reporting period for you, although too many have reporting procedures that are lax, which is bad for the company and probably just as bad for you. In this case, you must manage yourself, and set up your own reporting periods. In practice, though, almost every sales professional needs good, close management – and thinks he doesn't.

Most important, and most difficult, is attaining an acceptable level of honesty (with your management and with yourself); of balancing pessimism against natural optimism. In my experience sales professionals, myself included, vacillate between the two extremes. At one end, you are naturally nervous of promising management that you can definitely deliver the goods. If you don't make it, your management will not consider how aggressive were the targeted actions that these promises required; they will just note that you have failed to deliver the goods. As such it is always worth being slightly pessimistic and underestimating what you can achieve. The hero is the one who beats his forecasts, although the laurels should more fairly go to the one who hits the target exactly – over-achieving also means that your forecasts are inaccurate. If you forecast 50 units and hit 60 units you will be praised far more than if you forecast 100 units and hit 90 units.

The problem is that you cannot be *too* pessimistic, since your management will then (fairly) think you are crying wolf, and will put unacceptable pressures on you to overperform. So you need to be realistic, erring somewhat on the side of pessimism.

In practice, at the other extreme, the main problem of many sales professionals (rather surprisingly so, particularly of the inexperienced) is undue optimism; making a rod for their own backs when they fail to deliver. This is perhaps understandable where to succeed in the job they must be optimists, inexorably chasing the order until it is won. But the sales professional needs to have a sound appreciation of his true potential. If nothing else, it is a waste of time to continue chasing an order if it is obvious it is already lost. Persistence is a sound virtue for a sales professional – but only just as far as the point beyond which it costs him precious resource.

So it behoves a sales professional to develop an ability to forecast realistically what his business potential really is. If he has such a realistic appreciation he can optimise his use of resources and amaze his masters by his accuracy of forecasting!

Bankers

The easiest part of any forecast should be to deal with the 'bankers', those accounts that you know will soon complete the formality of signing the order. If you are wise you will still not have told your management that these are bankers, for mistakes can still happen (and management view the loss of bankers as a particularly heinous sin), but *you* should know they are committed.

Even then forecasting exactly *when* they will sign is not necessarily that easy. Paradoxically it is somewhat more difficult to control if they have already told you they will be giving you the order. They have, as far as they are concerned, already given you the order and see their formal signature as a petty administrative detail, failing to appreciate that it is *all* to you.

For this reason in IBM we discouraged letters of intent, unless there were very good political reasons for seeking them. A letter of intent is not a legally binding document and your customer can walk away from it without penalty (and many do so). Worst of all, it takes the pressure off him: every time you ask for a formal order he can reasonably retort that you have already got the letter of intent.

In any case, bankers not infrequently turn sour. Your contact, who assures you that the business is yours, may not be the decision-maker; and despite his earnest wishes, the business may eventually go elsewhere. Even worse, your contact may be playing games with you – so that you don't rock his boat.

In the early 1980s I worked in an advisory capacity with the IBM team trying to sell a large mainframe to a health board. Some six or seven years previously the team had been in the same position, and had been promised the business by the DP manager. Unfortunately that earlier business went to Honeywell, and the DP manager apologised profusely that he had been overruled. On the latest campaign, the same DP manager was once more promising that IBM had the business. I, being a professional cynic on such matters, enquired of the team what the DP manager's superiors thought, only to be told that they did not deal with his superiors, since the DP manager was the key to the sale and he was in their pocket – the team weren't going to rock the boat. I was not surprised, therefore, when once more the business was lost (this time to DEC); with the DP manager yet again apologising profusely. I don't know whether the DP manager was playing games, or whether he genuinely misjudged his influence. But whichever, making the mistake once was bad enough. To repeat it was grossly unprofessional.

I repeat, though, that bankers are still the easiest to predict, and should form the core of your forecast.

Probables versus possibles

Looking at sales professionals' forecasts it has been my experience that 'probables' and 'possibles' fall into three main groups. Those accounts labelled as 80 per cent chance of closing can (if the salesman is a professional) usually be counted as genuine probables. Sales professionals may tend to be unduly optimistic, but an 80+ per cent confidence level is usually indicative of a good chance of success.

Between 50 and 80 per cent, in my book, has to be counted as only a possible, although most sales professionals would want to count it as a probable. My experience is that if the sales professional doesn't feel happy enough to put it at 80 per cent (or possibly 70 per cent –

the psychological breakpoint does vary with individual sales professionals), there is still a lot of work to be done.

Below 50 per cent, however, are usually not the possibles that most sales professionals would like to think they are, but are more normally 'likely losers'. The main question I asked of this category was: is it worth putting any more resource into these? In my own group forecasts, which were aggregates of the individual sales professionals, I only included any business with a better than 50 per cent chance. I totally excluded anything below this level; if it came in it was a nice bonus, but I made certain I was not dependent on it.

In submitting my aggregated forecasts I simply added up the potential business (or at least that with a better than 50 per cent chance), multiplied by the per centage chance of getting it. But then I always divided this total by at least two, even for a strong sales team; and I was usually right! With the best will in the world, the best forecasting and genuine realism, sales professionals still seem to be optimistic by a factor of two. To be fair, much of the discrepancy was a matter of timing; the optimism was that it would be closed in the period in question (the business *was* eventually closed, but not necessarily in that period). With inexperienced sales teams the optimism can boost sales forecasts by a factor of three or four, which can prove a disaster in terms of attempting to allocate resources.

This optimism of inexperience can be just as much a function of inexperience of new products and new markets as of general inexperience in selling. Towards the end of my time in IBM Biomedical Group I went back to look at my earlier forecasts. They were about 80 per cent accurate in terms of the final outcome, but less than 50 per cent accurate in terms of timing. Some of my B prospects (the 50 to 80 per cent category) eventually came in nearly three years after I had first forecast them!

Documentation

This leads me to an important area, that of documentation. I have attended a number of meetings where the salesmen have been allowed to report verbally (typically with forecasts written on a flipchart). I have been singularly unimpressed, since it has been fairly obvious that the salesmen present were giving all of 30 seconds thought to their forecasts!

I believe that there has to be a discipline of fully documenting these forecasts. At the very least this material should show the forecast business for each account, together with the potential of closing it in each of the periods forecast (and the forecast should cover at least three periods ahead – separately identified).

I have always found that it is also useful to include a summary of the progress to date on each account; usually verbally, but also as a series of 'tick-boxes' showing, for example, whether a particular category of action has been undertaken (for example, a proposal submitted). This helps to clarify your thoughts and explain the bare figures to your management.

Reviews

The other advantage of documentation is that it can be used for subsequent reviews. It is something that sales professionals as a rule hate, for the inevitable question is, 'Why did you lose that business?' But it is a useful process, if management are fair and recognise the successes as well as the failures. It is even more important that, whatever management do, you undertake such a review for your own benefit. You can learn a great deal from an honest appraisal of what went wrong and right with your forecasts.

A basic problem is that the worst, the least professional salesmen, want to delude themselves. It takes a degree of strength, and even courage, to be able to confront the truth about your performance, particularly where it is a poor performance.

This is most evident in what I would describe best as 'incremental forecasting blindness', which occurs in poor sales teams. Having provided their forecast for the period (say four weeks), at the end of the first week if they have made few sales they will claim that the missing business will all come in the remaining three weeks. Similarly, even at the end of three weeks, this claim will be extended so that all the missing business will be promised for the last week. At its most ludicrous extreme I have had a sales team that had achieved less than 30 per cent of its forecast in the previous four weeks, confidently claim that they would make the remaining 70 per cent of the month's forecast in the last two days! Needless to say, they didn't.

The basic flaw here is an obsession with the forecast itself. Clearly, even salesmen as poor as this would not normally forecast, in the first place, a weekly strike rate of up to four times the average; but the insidious incremental creep deludes such salesmen into thinking that they can suddenly increase their productivity by very large amounts.

Another sign of inexperience or poor judgement is that of 'reverse confidence'. I first noticed this with a colleague who was consistently failing to make forecast. An analysis of his forecast (percentage) chance of winning showed an interesting trend, which was the reverse of normal. Those accounts where he had made very few calls (often only one) were shown as having a high degree of confidence of closing. But as the number of calls increased and the point of closing approached, the degree of confidence decreased; until the great majority of those about to close showed (justifiably as it turned out) a less than 50 per cent chance. This delusion caused him major problems because it hid the true pattern. It also meant that he concentrated his resources on the earlier stage of opening the sales campaign and was not devoting enough of his resources to the critical job of closing. Once we had redirected his resources towards closing, his performance improved dramatically.

Setting personal targets

The ultimate end of any strategy must be to achieve the performance objectives discussed in the previous section. But such performance is the result of a whole series of other actions and check-points, that can also be tracked.

In the first instance, though, your targets should include your personal versions of the performance targets you report to the management. As I stated earlier, if you are wise, you will offer management slightly pessimistic forecasts. But you should set *yourself* much tougher targets; your aim is to over-perform, since this is where the best money usually lies – and where the main accolades certainly do.

In the various companies I have worked for there have typically been up to four different sets of forecasts. The basic forecast was the one that we realistically and honestly believed was the most accurate we could achieve. Based on this, we produced a more pessimistic version that was used for the financial projections forwarded to the international headquarters (or the shareholders) – companies want to over-perform just as much as sales professionals do. A slightly optimistic forecast (again based on the realistic figures) was provided to the production management; optimistic so that we could be sure that the necessary capacity was available. Finally, a *very* optimistic forecast was passed to the sales team as their target!

Companies appear to assume, with some justification, that their sales professionals will be unduly optimistic in their projections, and extra cover is accordingly needed. As I have already mentioned, the rule of thumb for short-term forecasts in IBM was that you allowed a 100 per cent extra cover. The margins applied were significantly less on the annual figures, but even so, there was an elaborate process whereby the targets were upgraded as they were passed down the line. Thus, the country set itself a smaller target than it set for the regions, which in turn set higher targets for their branches, which finally set even higher aggregate targets for their sales professionals. All their reserves were needed (it was believed) to ensure that all management could achieve 100 per cent.

From a personal point of view, therefore, you need to set yourself higher targets than are set *for* you. Another important aspect is that you should set *earlier* targets. It almost inevitably takes longer to close business than you originally expected. So aim earlier, and you may still make the original estimate!

Call targets

The basic building block of any sales campaign has to be its calls. Generally speaking a number of calls are needed to get the business; and it is certainly true that the more calls you make (not on the same customer though!), the more business you will get. This is often described as the 'numbers game'.

Thus, for every 1000 mailshots you send out you will obtain a certain percentage of returns which justify your calling personally; and telesales and cold calling will also generate proportional results. From these subsequent calls a proportion will turn into serious prospects, some of whom will progress to demonstrations and proposals. Out of these serious prospects a proportion will place orders, and a proportion (hopefully a good proportion) will place those orders with you rather than with your competitors.

At each stage, therefore, there is a conversion ratio. It is clearly the sales professional's personal skills (backed by sound account management) that ensure that this conversion ratio is as high as it can be. Converting a good prospect into a customer requires all the skills a sales professional possesses (as does converting a reply-paid card from a mailshot into a prospect). But providing the raw material to feed into the 'machine' that eventually converts it into business, is just sheer hard work. The more mailshots you send out, the more teleselling you do and the more cold calls you make, the greater the raw material for the conversion process. The eventual outcome is almost directly proportional to the numbers that are fed in. There will be a slight effect due to the best prospects inevitably being fed into the mill first – but generally the results are directly proportional.

To be certain that you *are* feeding in the correct number of prospects (that you are sending out enough mailshots etc) and are achieving the correct conversion ratios, you must monitor the progress. This means that you must log all your calls and track just how many you are making in each category. Once more it is the sort of chore that all sales professionals hate, but only when you have this information can you really exert (self) control.

It is easy to underestimate the number of calls needed to get the business. Miller, Heiman and Tuleja report, for example:

' ... a recent survey done by a national association of sales executives ... concluded that 80 percent of the new sales in this country [the US] are made by 10 percent of the sales representatives − and that they close their sales only after making five or more calls on the client.'

Activity targets
You also need to set specific targets for all your other main activities. For example, if you plan to run seminars, you must set yourself hard and fast targets for how many to run, and when. I found that I ran less than one-third of the seminars that my initial plans called for. This was despite the fact that seminars were a critical part of my prospect generation process; the pressures of other work simply swamped them.

So you must set hard targets for all activities, and make certain you achieve them.

Resource targets
As well as knowing what results you are achieving, you should know how much these are costing you in terms of the resources (personal and external) you are putting in. If you have already spent most of your promotional budget on achieving 25 per cent of your sales targets, you may have real problems. So you need to track your expenditure of resources as assiduously as you track your results.

Key milestones
In the same way that you have to undertake a number of calls and other activities to achieve your business targets, your prospects will also have to undertake a number of activities (attending seminars, demonstrations, holding review meetings, board meetings etc). It is sometimes worth tracking these 'milestones' as well, although they are more difficult to monitor, and by now you may feel that 99 per cent of your time is taken up with paperwork!

Reviews

Once more, all these targets are meaningless unless you monitor your actual progress against them. Only by knowing the deviations or variations can you maintain control. It is always easier to take control decisions based on deviations against target, than on absolute figures which are not measured against anything.

These reviews are, however, more difficult to achieve. They will not be forced on you by management. Instead you will have to motivate yourself to make the time available, when the daily pressures will militate against this. But, once more, planning will increase your productivity out of all proportion to the time spent on it; but only if progress is regularly reviewed and control rigorously exercised to achieve the plan.

Win/loss reviews

One special form of review which is applicable to larger accounts is that immediately following the close. Hopefully this is a 'win' review, at which the lessons which can be learnt are discussed (and preferably documented) by the team involved. In some respects a 'loss' review can be even more useful, although it is obviously less welcome to the sales professionals involved. Many lessons can be learnt, which are often *not* learnt otherwise, by working out just exactly what went wrong.

So after each win or loss, sit down, perhaps in the car on your way to the next call (although perhaps that may be a bit too early – you need to be able to distance yourself from your personal feelings), and quite deliberately and logically think through the campaign, to work out what you did wrong, and what you did right. It is important to keep a positive perspective – it is no use just putting on sackcloth and ashes, you have to make use of the lessons you have learnt.

Scheduling personal resources

As I have mentioned before, sales professionals tend to undervalue their most important asset – themselves. It is just as important to schedule yourself and your time as it is your promotional budget.

Miller, Heiman and Tuleja make the telling point that:

'Most top salespeople, in fact, spend somewhere between five and 15 percent of their total working time actually engaged in face-to-face selling.'

Time management

There are plenty of books written about how to improve the management of your time. Unfortunately these are normally written from the viewpoint of the deskbound manager and are not particularly relevant to sales professionals, although some of their techniques can be modified to work.

William Davis echoes many salesmen's views when he suggests that the best approach is to eliminate unnecessary activities: 'Meetings are the biggest timewasters ... Paperwork is another chore that salesmen detest.'

I think this is, unfortunately, rather simplistic. Perhaps the best advice I can offer is regularly to plan what you need to do, and when you will do it. To be fair, so does William Davis: 'But the most effective method is, quite simply, to plan your day, week or month.' The skeleton will always be provided by your scheduled sales activities – these have to come first – and building a productive call schedule must be your best route to good time management (no matter what the more esoteric theories say). Having such a skeleton should help you to impose the necessary disciplines on the rest of your work, although the uncertainties of, for example, how long calls will last, also offer too many excuses for avoiding unloved tasks.

Probably the main discipline is regularly to prepare a list of 'things to do'. It is just as important to prioritise them, so that you concentrate on those that matter most. Finally, it makes it much easier to control if this list is short and is rewritten regularly. I used to spend valuable time ploughing through pages of such lists with most items crossed off, until I worked out that it was actually more productive to rewrite them, cutting out all the completed projects.

There are sophisticated techniques for dealing with the paperwork, but my simple advice would be to deal with the essentials immediately. A paper backlog is one thing that soon swamps any sales professional.

There are two exceptions to this. First, *all* customer requirements must be dealt with even faster (if you *can* get faster than immediate; and you will find that you can!). This is not just a matter of good customer service, although that is, in itself, full justification; it is that customer requirements and problems seem to grow exponentially the longer you leave them. It has always been my policy to pile the resource in immediately to solve the problem, and as result I have never had any significant resource exposures. But I have seen others, either taking their time or trying to limit resources, steadily sinking into a morass of ever increasing demands on resources. If the customer sees you responding immediately, he will be tolerant and undemanding. If he thinks you are dragging your feet he will try to take you to the cleaners and will normally succeed. So don't just respond immediately, make certain that the customer *knows* that this is what you are doing.

The other exception is *ad hoc* paperwork demanded by your own head office staff. My heretical advice on this score is quite simply to file this until you get the 'final demand'; most times the requirements will simply go away before then. I knew one sales professional who had a drawer in his desk dedicated to head office memos. When he received one he would briefly look at it to be sure that he would not be offending anyone really important, then he would put it in this drawer. Only when he received threatening memos with real bite would he look in his drawer for the original material. This way he reckoned he could successfully avoid replying to 80 per cent of the memos!

If you really are keen on time management I would recommend that for a couple of weeks you maintain a diary of everything you do, by half-hour time segments. When you analyse this you will probably find the results fascinating. For one thing you will realise just how little of your time is directly used on productive work; and, thus, how important it is to control the administrative workload, which is much of what time management aims to do.

Training

One aspect of personal planning that is usually neglected (but in IBM was rightly considered important enough to be included in the annual review of each employee's performance) is a training plan. As you will see in Chapter 7, regular on-going training is an essential part of a sales professional's personal preparation. This starts with a positive plan including it as a key part of the year's activities.

Planning without bureaucracy

Most of this chaper has been extolling paperwork, which is anathema to most sales professionals. Indeed paperwork for its own sake, which it often is in bureaucracies, *should* be shunned like the plague.

Nevertheless, I have seen whole sales forces actually becoming enamoured of paperwork, simply because it removed from them the onerous duty of coming head-to-head with prospects. I remember looking out on the car park of one such sales force, dismayed to see it full of salesmen's cars. The salesmen themselves were spending hours composing a single letter. Anything was preferable to having to face the demoralising experience of being turned down by a prospect.

Given a choice of paperwork or selling there should be no contest. Selling must always win. You can generate good business even with poor, or non-existent, paperwork. You certainly can't generate any real business without calling. So one final comment. You must monitor the amount of paperwork (and other bureaucratic pursuits) you are indulging in. A sales professional can never be a bureaucrat without losing his professional status as a salesman.

Having made these important caveats against bureaucracy, this chapter has in reality been about the virtues of planning. But such planning must be based on a hefty dose of common-sense, not bureaucracy.

I return to the analogy of the small businessmen. Such 'entrepreneurs' find bureaucracy an anathema; justifiably so, as they cannot afford the luxurious overheads of a bureaucracy. Neither can you, as a sales professional. Running your own small business, you need to keep it very lean and mean. Good planning should help you to do this. If you use common-sense in your planning, such planning will allow you to maximise the time you can spend on face-to-face contact; giving the most time to your most productive activity, and the one you should enjoy most, selling.

Chapter 4

Prospecting

The basic building blocks of any territory have to be, along with customers, the prospects. Generally speaking, whatever conversion ratios you achieve, the more prospects you feed in, the more business you will get out; and, within limits, your new business will be directly proportional to the numbers of new prospects.

Miller, Heiman and Tuleja stress its importance in their list of priorities, by putting it second only to closing; and ahead of what they call 'covering the bases' (which covers everything else between becoming a prospect and closing). They positively recommend: 'Every time you close something, prospect or qualify something else.'

Building the prospect profile

On the other hand there are grades of prospect. Not all businesses will want, or even have a need for, your products or services. Some will clearly be a total waste of time; there is no point in selling a CAD package to solicitors. But some will be possibles, and a few will be a close match to what you have to offer; 'hot' prospects. To take the necessary resourcing decisions, you will first have to decide what factors determine who is a prospect. You will need to build profiles of the likely, and the ideal, prospect.

From history

The easiest and most usual way of building this profile is simply to learn from the past. You will know who you have previously been successful in selling to, and it is a reasonable (and the usual) assumption that you should be able to extend this success to similar prospects. This can lead to quite a sophisticated profile.

Thus, in IBM Biomedical Group, it was clear very early on that our blood processing machines would be bought by haematologists (the hospital consultants specialising in analysing and treating blood disorders). After a while, it became clear that within this overall group the main buyers were those who saw themselves as 'clinical' haematologists (particularly concerned with the treatment aspect, rather than with the analysis which preoccupies most haematologists). Furthermore, the hottest prospects were young (typically under 30), and (as I eventually found out) they tended to have been trained in just a handful of teaching hospitals. This profile allowed me to concentrate my efforts on less than 100 prospects (although I never abandoned the other 1000, I only contacted them with mass marketing). Perhaps even more important, it caused me to concentrate special effort on penetrating those few teaching hospitals, so that I could use them as very powerful reference sells.

The one thing to be aware of using this approach is that it can tend to limit your horizons. Just because you haven't been successful selling to a certain category of prospects in the past, you are not necessarily precluded from their business in the future. You may just have been unlucky in your choice of prospects, or the market and/or your product may have changed since you last tried.

This was true in IBM Biomedical. Our (UK) research had quickly shown that haematologists were the main market. Yet the advice from the USA, where they had already been selling for five years, was that blood banks (the same as blood transfusion units in the UK) were the prime target. If we had blindly followed that experience we would have decimated our potential.

The message here is that you must always keep your eyes open for new business; as soon as you put your blinkers on you inevitably limit your sales potential.

From the market
The best and most comprehensive profile is to be obtained from the market itself. This may be derived from history, but ideally it should also include a deliberate attempt to investigate all the areas where your products might be used – before you discard categories to concentrate on your core business. This investigation can be in the form of actual calls, or it can be simply by reading about the customers you might want to sell to.

For example, it's obvious that solicitors won't need CAD packages, but it might seem that they could need standard accounting packages. Only by reading (and talking to experts) will you find that, in fact, they have special accounting needs that can't be met by standard packages.

From the product
Of course your product itself will largely determine the profile. If you are selling mainframe computers (costing hundreds of thousands of pounds) you probably won't waste much time on small businesses turning over less than half a million a year. But surprisingly, few sales

professionals take the dispassionate view of their products that is necessary to determine where they can best market them. The rose-tinted spectacles need to be discarded before you build your prospect profiles. Maybe some borderline prospects *might* order if you are at your persuasive best; but can you afford the time and is it the best use of your resources?

By your 'nose'

In practice all these factors come into play, as you will probably select your prime targets almost intuitively, applying your historical knowledge of the market and of your products. I always likened this to finding that hot prospects have the right 'smell'. As I looked down a list of prospects, with their vital statistics, my nose twitched with anticipation at some of them; and my nose was rarely wrong – these *were* usually the best generators of business.

Selecting the databases

The basis for all sound prospecting has to be a good database. This is an erudite term for a commonsense device. It does not have to be computerised; the simplest list of prospects is still a database of sorts. Using the term database, though, does allow a wider range of devices to be considered; and I will accordingly use it in its widest sense. I repeat, do not assume it must be sophisticated; as with most things, the simpler you can keep it the better.

You should start to build your database of prospects as soon as possible; its size and accuracy will be reflected in your business. What is more, you must continually maintain, update and extend your database as you have access to new information.

You should be aware of the limitations of databases that are available from published sources. These are an indispensable foundation for your own database in the absence of better information, but they typically represent partial information (there are large gaps in their coverage), they are out-of-date (typically at least two years old) and they are not designed specifically to meet your needs. Ultimately, the most valuable part of the database will be that which you add from your own personal observation. In the meantime you will be forced to use other resources, but be aware of their shortcomings.

Existing customers

The one database which should, however, be comprehensive and accurate is that of your existing customers. In any case this will usually be the source of your most valuable business and should always be your highest priority. As such you will need formally to document these customers as assiduously as you, or the database suppliers, document your prospects. Too many sales professionals believe they 'know' their customers; and, accordingly, do not maintain good records of them. This is a dangerous view when their business is so important.

You can *never* assume that your records are complete. On taking over one IBM territory I looked down my prospect listings and, as usual, my nose twitched over a handful of them; over one in particular, which I believed had all the signs of being a hot prospect. Surprisingly, I found it quite easy to get in to see the DP manager, and (having asked all the usual questions about his existing computer) I spent a good hour introducing him to IBM. He listened attentively and then, at the end of the call, added the crushing comment: 'But obviously nobody has told you we are already an IBM customer!' Even worse, he went on to describe, in graphic detail, all the problems he had recently experienced with his IBM equipment. He didn't have an IBM mainframe (my questioning had revealed that at the beginning of the interview), but had a room full of IBM data preparation equipment. Being (as I later found out) a customer who liked to manipulate salesmen, he had carefully omitted to tell me about this. Of course, nobody from IBM had attended to the problems he had experienced and, worst of all, he gleefully finished by pointing out that, as a result, they were just about to switch to Honeywell!

I did, eventually, rescue that account but I could have avoided considerable aggravation if I had only known the real score beforehand. It took nearly two months to get back to where I should have started in the first place and it highlighted for me just how important it is to maintain such records rigorously.

Directories
The basis for your lists is likely to be one or more directories (preferably as many as you can lay your hands on). The scope of these range from the comprehensive 'Yellow Pages', to very detailed directories of small groups. As a personal computer dealer specialising in CAD, one of our most productive lists was that of all qualified architects.

National directories
These are the most obvious starting point. They are well known to most sales professionals, so I will not elaborate to any great extent.

As I have already said, 'Yellow Pages' is the most comprehensive. It also selects your local prospects, but otherwise it is almost totally unselective and provides no information apart from name, address, phone number and the category of business (although some more information may be deduced from the display adverts). The worst problem is that every business, no matter how small, is included. You may find yourself spending an inordinate amount of time on the phone, researching which few (of the many) ought to be on your own list.

The national business directories, of which 'Kompass' and 'Dun & Bradstreet' are probably the best known, lurch too far in the opposite direction. They give plenty of information, but their coverage is limited to the larger companies, and they may not cover all the businesses that you want to contact. In their national editions companies tend to be grouped alphabetically; this is certainly the case with 'Dun & Bradstreet', but 'Kompass' does to a certain extent group regionally. Perhaps more useful are the regional editions which, for example, 'Kompass' produces. These do group the businesses by local areas; and being a tenth of the size are a lot cheaper to buy, and easier to carry around. It is well worth buying these. Even if they don't cover all the prospects, they *will* cover the major prospects; and in some depth.

Local directories
These are more difficult to find, but the local Chamber of Commerce, public library or town hall may be able to provide quite comprehensive lists, and these are likely to be more up-to-date than other such lists. They are well worth finding, to provide additional material for your database.

Trade (industry) directories
If you decide to specialise in a certain industry, because your product or your own expertise points to this (or your territory is full of such businesses), trade directories will be a vital source of prospect lists. Most industries seem to justify trade directories. If you can't find one for your industry, ask your local library to track one down — although if you find one you will almost certainly need to purchase your own copy. You will eventually find it an invaluable reference book, with information about the industry as well as the lists of prospects.

Mailing houses

A more specialised source of listings is that offered by mailing houses, but this is one that is normally not available to individual sales professionals, since they will not usually consider providing a list of less than 5,000 to 10,000 prospects.

There are a few general lists covering all businesses, for example, you can buy such lists covering both 'Yellow Pages' and the 'Dun & Bradstreet' directory. But normally they cover special fields, and this is where they come into their own.

Such a mailing house should be able to offer a comprehensive list. These houses spend large sums of money keeping their lists up-to-date, and they may represent the only source of genuinely up-to-date lists. But they are expensive (costing up to several hundreds of pounds per thousand names). A bigger drawback is that they will normally not make the list available to you, but will insist that they handle the mailing for you. This is understandable, since they earn their living by their lists and they accordingly don't want anyone else to have a copy – an unscrupulous customer might just try to sell it to other mailing houses. But from your point of view, this has a number of disadvantages. Of course, the cost will be higher, since they will have to handle all aspects of the mailing. You will also have no control over the mailing.

A few mailing houses will provide you with labels, so that you can undertake your own work, but they will still insist that you only use it once (and will bury dummy addresses in it, so that they can check if you use it again).

The best mailing houses will offer personalised mailings; 'type-written' letters personally addressed to individuals. These are the best to buy (but also the most expensive), since they come closest to what you would do with your own mailings. Beware the lists (typically the more general lists) that do not have a named addressee. Such 'Dear Sir/Madam' letters may have significantly less impact.

The best use of these mailing houses is in the more specialised areas. I *have* used more general lists, with variable results. But I have found the higher quality, more specialised lists much more effective. For example, I successfully used the lists of the leading medical mailing house as a means of rapidly building up my list of prospects to include a wider range of medical disciplines, outside the core disciplines where I built up my own list.

Going walkabout

Nothing, though, can beat your own research, obtained by driving up and down every road on your patch and visiting every business premise (although even then you will still miss some, hidden out of sight in back gardens). This is just a matter of developing a faculty of curiosity. As you travel around your patch on your normal business, simply explore all the various back roads and add the prospects you find to your database.

The great advantage of this information is that it is up-to-date. In particular, it will be your only source of information on new companies starting up, and on those moving to your area. These are likely to be particularly hot prospects, since they will be in the market for many products and services, and will have no existing suppliers.

Local centres of business

Local factory estates, shopping and office centres (or business centres) are clearly particularly important, since they represent concentrations of business that are easy to monitor. In these compact areas you should be able to monitor almost all comings and goings, and be ready to pounce on any new arrivals.

Using the receptionist

A special person in all your local prospecting has to be the receptionist, who is is likely to be the best source of the initial information you will obtain about the company. Fortunately, receptionists are talkative people; they are often chosen for their social skills and then given almost nobody to talk to. So a friendly interest on your part will probably obtain a full history of the company, and access to its innermost secrets. Receptionists are a much underrated asset of a sales professional.

Reading the press

An important source of information on your prospects will be the press. In particular, most local press runs articles on firms in their area, and on new arrivals to the district. Trade press can also provide useful information on prospects if you are specialising in certain industries. In all these areas you will also obtain as much, if not more, information from the advertisements.

One particularly useful source of information is the job advertisements (as well as the 'appointments' section of the editorial). One suggestion (made by John Fenton) that I have not tried myself, but which sounds eminently sensible, is to make a note of any key appointments (buyers, for example), and four to six weeks later check up to find who has been appointed. Then you write to the new appointee, congratulating him and offering your services, at a time when he is building up his own list of suppliers.

Contacts

The most productive leads of all often come from your customers; not only will they have already been qualified as hot prospects, but your customer will probably have begun your selling job for you.

Smith and Dick, in *Getting Sales*, quantify this:

'Referrals are usually more productive than leads. You are four to six times more likely to close a sale on a good referral than you are to close a walk-in lead.'

They also list five 'good reasons' for this:

'You have an introduction to the prospect.
You know something about the prospect.
The word may already have got around.
Your customer can introduce you.
You can cross-refer with non-competitors'.

A number of other pundits also suggest that you develop contacts with other (non-competitive) sales professionals, and 'swap' prospects with them. This sounds a good idea, but I was never on a single territory long enough to develop these sorts of contacts, so I can't report my personal experiences.

Building contacts, and in particular building a set of 'opinion leaders' or 'trend setters', is much underrated by sales professionals. But personal recommendation is a very important part of the buying process. For example, according to market research, nearly 40 per cent of personal computer buyers had found out about their supplier by personal recommendation; and nearly 20 per cent from their previous business dealings. So less than half had been introduced to the supplier by the 'normal' sales processes. Indeed, only just over 10 per cent had learned about it from a sales professional (and a meagre 2 per cent from a mailing). It is, therefore, critical that you nurture your contacts, so that they will spread the good word about you. If the above statistics apply in other markets, you will be about four times as productive concentrating on making your existing contacts very happy as going out looking for new prospects; but that shouldn't stop you doing both!

Your service department
One much neglected source of prospect information will be your own service engineers. In their calls on your customers they will learn of other prospects, and will probably be more likely to mix with other companies' engineers, again learning of more prospects. So it is well worthwhile occasionally buying a beer or two for your support team; it will usually pay sound dividends.

In my personal computer dealership, at one stage my head engineer was so good at finding such leads, and my sales professionals so dilatory at following them up, that I actually gave him two such plum accounts to run himself. The sales professionals rapidly learned not to ignore these leads when they saw how much commission he was earning (which otherwise would have gone to them).

Associations

One way of building personal contacts is to join one or more of the various associations that relate to your customers.

Chambers of Commerce
The most obvious organisation to join is the local Chamber of Commerce. These are of somewhat variable quality, but they certainly offer the opportunity for building contacts.

Industry associations
These are more problematic in terms of building contacts, because very few of your local prospects will attend the meetings (apart from conferences and exhibitions, which can be a good source of contacts). Even so, you may be able to obtain some leads; and the membership lists alone may well be worth your joining fee.

Social associations
These are more controversial. Certainly joining the Round Table and the Rotarians will allow you to mix with many of your prospects on a social level, without any problems of ethics. Whether you should join organisations such as the Masons, however, is a much more personal decision. Many businessmen swear that such organisations generate their bedrock business, but I have my doubts. The decision is yours, but the investment to find out how productive a source of prospects they represent is a high one.

Building the working database

If you have followed my advice in the preceding sections, you will, by now, be inundated by prospects! The problem should no longer be generating prospects (although this should remain an on-going process), but should be managing your prospect list to optimise its productivity.

Selection
The first task, therefore, is that of selection. You must prune your list ruthlessly to get it down to manageable proportions. The danger is, otherwise, that the good prospects will be lost, swamped by the flood of second-rate.

It takes real discipline to relegate large numbers of prospects to the archive file (or to the waste-basket). But if you don't do this, once and for all, you will be forever ploughing through the dross to find the gems you want to pursue; and *en route* you will stop and wonder if, after all, you should pursue some of the borderline cases. Such thoughts are a dangerous waste of your valuable time.

Prioritisation
Throughout the last chapter I stressed the virtues of prioritisation, and the 80:20 rule applies just as much here. In sorting your database, you should structure the information in ways that will allow you to prioritise the prospects. The classical approach is an 'ABC analysis' in which the data is sorted by increasing (or more usefully, in this context, by decreasing) value. This is often applied to sales data and is a very powerful device, in that it concentrates your attention on the accounts that really matter. But you will also need to be able to sort quickly by a range of other factors, including the likely date of business and the chance of getting it. All of this says that you will probably need to use cards (or a computer equivalent).

The prospect record

The heart of any prospect tracking system is the record keeping system. So it is worth taking some time to design or obtain the one that is best for you.

There are many forms of records, from very sophisticated computerised systems down to the simplest address book. Indeed, my most valuable records were often in my diary, where I made cryptic notes alongside appointments (and when I could not find contact names elsewhere, I almost invariably found them in this diary). To allow you to rearrange the database proper, however, I believe it is best to use some form of loose-leaf system (or the computer equivalent). The classic systems are based on the use of cards, and the ones I have used most effectively were based on A4 (letter) sized cards, held in four-ring binders. Again, though, there are a number of proprietary systems, as well as the infinite variety you can design to meet your exact requirements. The choice is yours, to meet your needs.

Clearly, you will need space for the demographic data: address (including postcode, which usually provides the best reference for sorting geographically), telephone number, contact names (and positions), industry type etc. Then there will be the most important numeric facts (when you have these available): turnover, number of employees, size of potential business (and, more subjectively, the percentage chance of getting it), likely date of order etc. John Fenton suggests that you also record the best time to call (as well as suggested call frequency). He goes further, to suggest that you ask the prospect himself to give you his preferred call time – a very sensible suggestion, which many sales professionals ignore and then wonder why they have difficulty getting to see their prospects.

There is much descriptive material that can be added: management structure, products and production processes etc. Some record systems would have you describe all of these by putting ticks in boxes but, although they are a useful *aide-mémoire*, I doubt that such rigid techniques will be really viable for many sales professionals – the complexity of their customer information will normally not be suited to such simple solutions (although the method may be more suitable for retail salesmen with large numbers of very similar accounts). In general, my own experience is that large expanses of blank paper (or card) are the best medium for recording descriptions of prospects. But you *must* record these descriptions (there is the inevitable pressure to do it later, which never happens); not least so that someone handling the account in you absence (on holiday, for example) won't destroy all your good work. I must admit that most of my accounts were, in practice, brought up-to-date just before I went on holiday.

Then there needs to be ample space for recording details of the calls themselves. Once more, there are sophisticated (typically box-filling) techniques available, but again my experience suggests that the most useful format for the sales professional is blank paper. Again, however, this call information must be kept up-to-date. I (in common with many sales professionals) was not the world's best record keeper and I found a number of times (to my great embarrassment) that I had forgotten a crucial piece of information about a call and had (inevitably) not recorded it; so I had to go back, cap in hand, and ask again – which did nothing to create confidence. Perhaps, even worse, there might have been data that I did not even realise I had forgotten! I thus learnt the lesson the hard way: a sales professional *must* keep good records, no matter how much of a chore it is.

For customers (and the larger prospects), where the amount of paperwork can mount up, I maintained a separate file (or folder) for each account, to hold all this material which could rapidly build up and swamp any other system.

As I said earlier, there are a number of pre-printed systems, which can, however, be expensive. If the company does not already subscribe to a standard system, I favour drawing up my own to match my exact needs. I then have them printed on thin A4 sized cards, at the local instant print shop. This is not unduly expensive, but if cost is a problem, simple photocopies will do almost as well.

There are virtues in maintaining simpler systems; perhaps in parallel with the main system, although that does begin to pose problems of duplication of effort. But the only *essential* requirement of any record system is, I repeat, that it must be maintained regularly. In particular, calls must be written up *immediately* you have made them, or preferably (since it makes certain you do document them) in the call itself – there is nothing to stop you writing your notes directly on to the record card (removed from its binder) instead of a pad. I cannot overstress the importance of maintaining up to the minute records (even if they are barely legible notes made in the call); otherwise such a record system will be an expensive waste of time.

In one particularly badly organised (and badly performing) sales force, I arranged to receive copies of all leads when they came in. A couple of months later, I carried out an exercise to determine what had happened to these leads, as I wanted to find out which was the more productive vehicle from the two magazines we had used. I was shocked to discover that something like one-third of the leads could not be accounted for; nobody knew what had happened to them! Perhaps these had been poor leads, but maybe they were good ones that had simply gone missing among the atrocious records that these sales professionals kept. If that was the case, they might have increased their performance by up to 50 per cent for very little effort – just by keeping adequate records.

Computerised records

In theory, computerised records ought to be the answer to a sales professional's prayer. By now most sales professionals should be adept at using a personal computer (as a word-processor, if nothing else), so entering the data should be as easy as putting it on a manual system. The great theoretical benefit is that once the data is on the system you can ask the computer to sort and analyse your records by any criteria you choose. This should allow you the best possible control of your accounts, immediately printing out a list of the prime prospects for any new product (or at least that is how the computer vendors would have you see them).

In practice, computer systems are as yet less flexible. You can't update the record in the car immediately after the call; although genuinely portable machines are now becoming available, they are expensive and it is inordinately difficult to enter data with them balanced on your lap (despite all that the advertisements say). You certainly can't enter the record while in the call without distracting the prospect's attention. Even back at the office, computers seem to introduce a barrier between the sales professional and the record.

I have to admit that, even though I am very computer literate, I have always used cards in preference to computer systems. I have spent some considerable effort, a number of times, trying to set up a viable computerised system, but it has always lapsed. Even the advantage of being able to report on the basis of many different criteria is not particularly helpful, where you normally only want the simplest of analyses (by turnover being just about the most sophisticated analysis asked for). At present, I believe that computer systems have not yet proved themselves; so my advice is to concentrate on developing a good manual system.

Mailings

So far you have had to plough through a number of sections largely devoted to administration, which is the bane of most sales professionals' lives. Even I wouldn't claim that you are likely to get much fun out of this paperwork. But I strongly believe that, despite it being such a chore, this planning is one of the keys to professional selling, and I therefore make no apology for the space devoted to it.

Now, however, we can start on the first section where contact with the prospect enters into the picture, even if it is by the indirect medium of mailings. I actually found some satisfaction in shipping out hundreds of mailings, even when I had to do the work myself.

This was not least because I knew that perhaps one in 30 of them would come back again, as a live prospect. The more I put out, the more future business I was lining up; and the more satisfied I was.

Mass mailing
One effective way of generating numbers of prospects is to undertake mass mailings. This represents the shotgun, or even blunderbuss, approach. By covering large numbers of the target audience it is hoped that proportionately large numbers of prospects will be unearthed. The normal response rate for such mailings is often claimed to be as much as 1 or 2 per cent, but I have experienced rates as low as 0.3 per cent. On the other hand, mailing to specialised markets with a particularly powerful message, I have reached almost 10 per cent. Whatever part of this very wide range your own mailing falls into, you will still have to distribute large numbers to obtain even reasonable numbers of prospects. It is a numbers game with a vengeance – as long as your budget can afford it.

Before conducting any mailing, however, you have to be clear what your specific objectives are. Most mailings are designed to produce immediate sales leads, enquiries. Even then you may want to make this route more clearly defined, and decide to set your specific objective as attracting people to a free seminar, or to 'buy' enquiries by offering a free sample. There are many ways of achieving results; but it is important, before you go further, that you know *exactly* what you wish to achieve.

For quite a long period, in IBM Biomedical Group, my main mailing was deliberately designed as a 'sleeper'. It was a quarterly medical journal of some international repute. Discreetly, but very clearly, it gave my address and telephone number; so that, when the prospect came to make his decision (which could be any time over a five-year period), this information was instantly available on his bookshelf and he would contact me before thinking of anyone else. It was a relatively long term investment, which many sales professionals would not consider, but it worked. But in this context the moral is that, right or wrong (or just plain idiosyncratic), I had a very clear objective.

The offer
The basis for a mailing has to be an offer. This may be simply a statement of your products or services, or it can be a specific promotion. You need to be very clear what your real offer is; for you will want your prospects, on the receiving end, to be equally clear

about what you are saying to them.

The offer, in this context, should be the most powerful that you have in your armoury. It should also be just about the simplest. Your material will arrive on your prospect's desk at the same time as half a dozen other pieces of flotsam and jetsam; just when he wants to get on with more important things. Your message has just a very few seconds to grab his attention, otherwise it will be consigned to the waste-basket along with the rest of the rubbish he receives.

If it is to succeed in this murderously competitive environment, it is imperative that you refine the initial message down to its barest and most powerful form. It has to be immediate: there will simply not be time for a complex argument to grab the necessary attention. It is not difficult to find a simple sales message – you do it all the time in your sales calls. The difficulty is in resisting the temptation to load your mailings with all the goodies in your kitbag. I have several times been seduced by the idea of putting in more sales points. But even as few as three or four major sales messages seem to cause confusion, and the response rate drops (to the 0.3 per cent quoted earlier). The much quoted acronym, KISS (keep it simple, stupid) is nowhere more applicable than in mailings.

Finally, there must be a clear action associated with the message. This may be just the suggestion (but a strong one) that the recipient should return the reply-paid card; or it may be a stronger action, telling the recipient to be prepared for your telephone call. Mailings are rarely conducted as educational devices. They are used to create action, so make certain that your own does.

The letter

It is, of course, quite possible to send out a mailing without any letter; many, perhaps most, mailings simply comprise such unaccompanied 'flyers'. But most mailings sent out by sales professionals, even mass mailings, usually include a letter; often because this is needed to tailor the mailing to their own needs – the enclosed flyers will be standard company issue, complete with the head office address. In any case, the evidence suggests that enclosing a letter improves the response rate; and enclosing a personalised letter improves it significantly (otherwise the Reader's Digest wouldn't spend a fortune doing so).

Market research among personal computer buyers shows that between 60 and 80 per cent of them will read a letter addressed to them by name (the range being due to how much the letter looks as if it is typed, at the top end, or obviously word-processed, at the lower end), where less than 40 per cent will read one addressed to them by title, and only just over 20 per cent where it is addressed to the company. Personalisation can, according to this evidence, improve the performance by a factor of four!

On the other hand, the letter has to be at least as well written as any of the enclosures, since it is probably the first (and maybe the only) thing that the prospect will read. As such, once more, the message it contains must be well thought out; powerful and simple.

There is some controversy as to what is the best form of letter. Some would swear by short letters, enlivened by catchy headlines and full of highlighting and underlining. Others feel that this smacks of gimmickry, and prefer long letters which encapsulate the whole message on one page (or even on several pages – without any enclosed flyers).

I believe that, in the absence of firm evidence, you should choose which style suits you, the subject matter and your prospects. Clearly, a simple price promotion (still one of the most powerful ways of getting a prospect's attention) will benefit from the shorter, more punchy style; where the more 'serious' nature of a technical brief on a sophisticated new product might be better suited to the longer format.

Any format should, however, be written in a style that is easy for the reader to understand; with the minimum of jargon, for example. It should be laid out so that it is easy to read; with short paragraphs, indented if necessary, and with headings if it is a long letter – and with plenty of white space to break up the slabs of verbiage into easily digestible morsels. Try to look at it from the reader's point of view: if you were the reader would it grab your attention?

Howard Dana Shaw (one of the greatest US authorities on writing mail order letters) produced, 'Six Checking Points for Writing That Gets People to Do Things':

'1. Be Natural Instead of Literary [don't be pompous].
2. Simplify Your Sentences [keep them short].
3. Write in Pictures [make the prospect see what you want].
4. Make Things Move [give it a sense of direction].
5. Use Personal Pronouns [you are 'I' not 'the writer'].
6. Don't Inflate [don't use too many superlatives].'

Whichever format, whatever style you choose, you must be sure to make the message that it conveys powerful and simple.

The one point that most commentators seem to agree on is that the areas at the top and bottom receive the most attention from the recipient. At the top the best way to use this is to try to encapsulate your overall message in a punchy headline (in capitals and underlined, to grab attention), and then make your hottest offer immediately, in the first paragraph (instead of the bland courtesies that start most letters). The best way to use the bottom area of attention is a 'PS' (a postscript). This is a particularly useful device for gaining attention; it seems to be just about the best read part of most letters!

Inserts

Again, there is an almost infinite variety of material that can be put into a mailing. The only rule appears to be, once more, to keep it simple, and in line with the message of the letter. If there are conflicting messages between the letter and the inserts, or between different inserts, this will just confuse the reader. The current approach from a number of consumer goods companies, for example, seems to be to inundate the reader with half a dozen different items which each compete for attention. I know that such companies research these matters diligently, so there must be method in this apparent madness; maybe some people like spending time puzzling out what the mailing is about. But an overworked businessman hasn't the time; so no matter how well presented – and such material is excellently presented, it goes straight into the waste-basket. Simplicity pays dividends.

If you have too many messages, then save the material for the next mailing. The most effective mailing campaigns are those with a number of separate mailings. Like most advertising the effect is cumulative, and it can take a number of mailings before the recipients become aware of your existence. One of the problems in running such mailing campaigns (apart from the cost of the multiple mailings) is finding enough material to justify a fresh approach each time. Be grateful, therefore, if you have material for more than one mailing, and don't waste it all in one confusing mass.

One point to be aware of is the weight of inserts. If you are not careful they will push you into more expensive postal charges. I was persuaded to pay £50 more to have one insert printed on a higher quality card. The real cost, though, turned out to be the extra 7p for each mailing which, on a total mailing of 10,000, added up to £700 – for a very minor improvement in quality!

I have received a few mailings which are the exception to the rule, grabbing my attention despite the fact that they contained a number of items. In these cases, though, all of the items clearly related to the overall message. The most memorable, for example, comprised a folder containing a letter, a catalogue, a price list, a special offer and a free pen (of good quality). All of this material was tied into the same message (the heart of it was the mail order catalogue for stationery supplies) and, most importantly, the whole had been carefully *designed* as one package.

This last example highlights one point about inserts; you will almost certainly need professional help with them. What is more, if they are elaborate items (some material comes complete with 'pop-ups' and cut-outs), they can cost a lot of money. You will have to calculate whether the expected returns will really justify the price. My medical journals, for example, cost £4 each (costing me £16,000 a year for my prime 1000 prospects); this is not a commitment you enter into lightly – far better to keep it simple.

Using agencies

If you are getting into the area of sophisticated mailings, you will almost certainly need to hire a specialised agency to do the design work for you. I have used both advertising agencies and mailing houses to produce such work; and both have produced well-designed material.

For a sales professional, though, it is quite a difficult process choosing an agency and, unless you are planning vast mailings, most agencies will probably not be interested in your business. As already mentioned, it is expensive to employ such people: mine (which was very carefully chosen to offer the best value) seemed to charge a basic £2000 for just *starting* work on any item. It is also difficult for a sales professional to know exactly what to look for in such an agency.

My advice is to keep it simple so that you don't need an agency and then, if you are absolutely forced to produce material that needs design work, to use a reputable mailing house. The bigger reference libraries will usually have a copy of *The Direct Mail Handbook*, published by Gower Press, or *Benn's Direct Mail Yearbook*. Either of these will list the mailing houses that cover the areas or industries that interest you.

To illustrate the effectiveness of a good mailing campaign, I will quote that of Reliance Life, as reported in the *Dartnell Sales Promotion Handbook*:

'To stimulate replies the letter offered the inducement of a genuine leather memorandum book with the prospect's name imprinted in gold. If he sent in the card, the company made up the memorandum book and sent it, with the reply-paid card [on which he had indicated which of seven basic insurance needs he was interested in] to the salesman who submitted his name [where each salesman provided 25 to 100 names for the mass mailing]. The salesman then delivered the books as the opening wedge for his interview ... One year's operation of the prospecting plan ... cost $30,000, but produced 16,700 inquiries – 6,200 more inquiries at half the cost [compared with the previous programme of newspaper coupons].'

Reply-paid cards

If you want to improve your chances of generating a response, you should include a reply-paid card (or a Freepost card – the effect is the same from the point of view of the prospect). As also reported in the *Dartnell Sales Promotion Handbook*:

'The cheapest way to get inquiries for a product service is the postpaid reply card. An offer to send some helpful booklet, or to send some article of use, to a list of prospects has been known to produce as high as 37 percent replies at a cost of less than 54 cents each. Returns of five percent to ten percent on reply paid cards of this kind are common.'

My own experience has been less dramatic, but the writers do add the caveat (where free gifts are frequently used to stimulate such high return rates):

'Such inquiries, however, are usually of questionable sales value because they result from a desire to get something for nothing ... Sending inquiries of this sort to salesmen soon disgusts them.'

You will have to obtain a licence from your local head post office (in fact the Freepost is the easiest to obtain and has no special disadvantages, so I normally used this). You will, of course, need to have this card printed (on thin card, of a weight and size approved by the postal service), with the boxes you want ticked, or the questions you want answered, on the reverse. Again, you must design even these questions so that they are attention grabbing and easy to answer – they are just as much part of your selling package.

I found that I obtained significantly better results (by a factor of three or four) if I personalised the reply-paid card (in addition to personalising the covering letter). In other words, the prospect's name and address were already filled in on the card (usually by means of a computer generated, or word-processed, self-adhesive label), so that he didn't have to fill in this information. Whether it was because it reduced the prospect's effort (he only had to add a couple of ticks and toss it into the out-tray), or whether it was seen by him as representing greater commitment on our part, I don't know; but it worked.

Best of all is to send a personalised reply form, together with a ready *stamped* envelope (using a normal first class stamp – not a reply-paid cover). The better returns this generates are presumably because it is seen as being more personal and more committed, but it ups the cost dramatically – you have to pay for all the stamps, even on the 90 per cent that are still not returned.

Timing

When you send your mailings can influence their impact. Clearly, they will have to be integrated with your overall campaign. On the other hand, the lead time needed should not be underestimated. From the date of despatch of your original letter it may take between two and four weeks to obtain the bulk of replies (and a few may, in my experience, still be drifting back many months later). If you are (as is frequently the case) using a seminar as the 'bait', the prospects will need to get this in their diaries (so something over two weeks needs to be added for this); and the net lead time from the mailing to the first seminar will probably become at least six weeks. Add to this the preparation time (which will include the printing of, at least, the special reply card), which may take around a month, and you will have to start to implement such a mailing perhaps three months in advance of the seminar.

There are some times of year when it is traditionally supposed to be unproductive to mail. The summer months, of July and August, when prospects are supposed to be on holiday (or thinking of nothing else) are one; as is December (when your letter will be lost in the deluge of Christmas mail). The message is simply that you must choose your time carefully; and plan it well in advance; to close year-end business, you often have to start active planning in the first quarter.

Even the day of the week the mailing is sent can have an impact. The *Dartnell Sales Promotion Handbook*, for example, reports:

'Care should be taken, they say, to avoid reaching a businessman's desk on Monday, or any day following a holiday, when there is

119

likely to be a large accumulation of letters needing attention ... the best day is Tuesday, and Wednesday is next best.'

Individual mailings

Most likely, you will not be personally involved in mass mailings, although they may be run, on your behalf, by a staff department – in which case you had better understand such mailings, so that you can monitor their activities (and ensure that they don't destroy your prospect base!). More likely you will undertake small–scale individual mailings, and these are probably the most productive of all.

Tailoring

With small numbers it is possible to tailor mailings (often, in this case, just a highly specific letter, with no inserts – except the inevitable reply-paid card) to match the prospect's requirements closely. With mass mailings you are limited by needing to be all things to all men, and this blunts the impact of such mailings. With smaller, specialised mailings you can hone the material down until it has a real cutting edge; cutting through to exactly what the prospect wants.

Typically, such mailings are based on industries or professions. We ran different seminars on accounting (software) packages for company financial officers then for chartered accountants; and the mailing campaigns that featured each of these had quite different slants, even though the software package was the same. Similarly, mailings to different functions within a company need to be tailored; what you will want to say to the buyer will probably be quite different from your message to the production manager. The beauty of small mailings is that you *can* tailor them easily to achieve the right note. Once more, the time spent in honing the message will be amply rewarded; and with a word-processor it is very easy to tailor even a quite long, more general message for specific subsets of prospects.

Personalisation

In the section on mass mailings, I stressed how important personalisation is (including the reply-paid card). It is possible to personalise even more in small mailings (using the word-processor to add in extra, personalised details, or even adding these, in your own hand, as a PS). Make the most of the benefits that modern technology offers you in such mailings.

Advertising

It is unlikely that most salesmen, even sales professionals, will be called upon to deal with advertising. It is, though, *just* possible that you may come into contact with it; and for those aspiring to be a sales manager, it could offer a useful element of knowledge. So, for the sake of completeness, it is included here. The coverage is, however, necessarily brief. For more detail I refer you, once more, to Kotler's book, *Marketing Management* (in preference to the more glib popular books on advertising).

The pitfalls
First of all, you should be aware of some of the problems. Not the least of these is that advertising is not a game for amateurs; and you are bound to be one. Your first, and major, contribution will be to minimise your interference: shut up! As a sales professional it will have been necessary for you to develop a degree of myopia. Your horizons are, necessarily, limited to those of your customers and prospects. Unfortunately, the perspective of marketing in general, and of advertising in particular, has to be that much wider. It is quite removed from that of face-to-face sales. It is normally not worth the investment of your time and energy to develop this new perspective and learn the specific skills of advertising, so leave it to the experts.

I have often seen sales management in action, where they have (probably foolishly) been involved in advertising decisions. The result has almost inevitably been that they have, due to their inexperience, made a negative contribution. Almost everyone and, in my experience, especially sales professionals, has strong views as to what advertising they like. What they forget is that the advertising is not designed for them. It is irrelevant whether a middle-aged, middle-class sales professional likes a video for a pop record; what matters is whether its teenage buyers are influenced.

My success in advertising was probably mainly due to being able to view the material from the point of view of the customers (as you view your sales messages from the point of view of your prospects). It was irrelevant what I, or even the rest of the advertising industry, thought of its creative appeal. As much of the advertising was aimed down market, I was actually alarmed if any of the industry critics liked it – it was not designed for them.

Another important factor for success is not being swayed by boredom with the campaigns. By the time any commercial first appears on television, those involved will have seen it 20 or 30 times.

It is very easy for them to think that, a few weeks later, everyone is as bored with it as they. What they forget is that (if the media experts have got it right) the viewing audience will on average have seen it around five or six times.

I am proud of having put in motion the work that led to one of the UK's longest running commercials, that for Condor pipe tobacco. The research that went into the planning was impeccable, as was the advertising that resulted. But, for me, the laurels must go to subsequent managers who have resisted the temptation to remove a winner, just because they were bored with it. More than two *decades* later, it is still going strong – giving the lie to those who rush to remove a successful campaign for something new.

Advertising skills

The message put out by advertising has to be even simpler (and more powerful) than any message in a sales call. On television it has just a few seconds, in the press even less as the page is turned, and there is no second chance. The message must grab the viewer or reader immediately. It has to be simple, powerful, brief and in the language of the target audience; which is why advertising agencies employ highly skilled copywriters to create these messages.

Converting this message into essentially visual form (most advertising, with the notable exception of radio, is primarily visual) takes all the skills of the artists and television producers that also populate these agencies. The amateur does not stand a chance.

The first time I went on to a small sound stage, to see one of my commercials being shot, was an enlightening experience. The door I entered faced the brilliantly lit set, where a solitary young mother was rehearsing with her baby. As I slowly turned to look at the rest of the studio I became aware of a sea of faces. A typical crew can run to 20 or more personnel. This is not just featherbedding. It is essential to have experts on hand to handle *any* problem without delay, as the simplest shoot can cost tens of thousands of pounds a day.

The other, less publicised skill is that of buying the 'media' on which the message will be run. Unlike a sales call, which is immediate in scoring a success or failure, advertising depends upon the cumulative effect of multiple messages. In media (especially television) terms it hinges on two measures. The first of these is coverage. Clearly, any promotional campaign tries to make its message available to the largest number of potential buyers. This does not necessarily mean that it should be seen by everyone: the ideal media campaign would be seen by the target audience and nobody else (why pay for those who won't buy?). But the higher percentage coverage of even this target audience, the more expensive it gets. It is a matter of exponentially reducing returns.

There is a similar effect in terms of zeroing in on a specific target audience. The smaller the target audience the more expensive, per head, it becomes to cover them. Eventually the cost of producing the advertisement itself becomes the dominant factor, almost regardless of the numbers of recipients. It is very difficult to run *any* effective campaign (even one limited to the trade press) for less than £20,000.

One reason for this is the second of the key media measures, that of opportunities to see (OTS). This measures the number of times the average viewer (or reader) is exposed to the message. Again, this is where advertising is most different from a sales call. The cumulative effect is what counts. Thus, as a rule of thumb, it is reckoned that, to reach a reasonable minimum level of impact, an OTS of at least five is required (needing, perhaps, as many as 20 individual advertising spots to achieve this average).

This is probably the second biggest area for mistakes by sales professionals involved in advertising (the first being their assumed knowledge of what is the right message!). They do not realise that a single advertisement has little power – unless, perhaps, it is in a key reference book which will be referred to many times. They therefore grossly underestimate the number of insertions which will be needed to produce significant results.

Overall, then, 'buying media' is a specialist skill and, without expert assistance, it is all too easy to make expensive mistakes.

Using an agency

My advice is to employ professionals. The problem for the small advertiser is that this is not, at first glance, any easier than doing it yourself.

The traditional approach, where (as a large advertiser) you have an appropriation of several million pounds burning a hole in your pocket, is to ask several agencies to present, which they will be delighted to do, with the prospect of large billings to come. Unfortunately, if you are the typical small spender you will find that most agencies will not even want to talk to you, since they couldn't recover their overheads on your business.

There are numbers of small agencies, but even they will expect you to spend more than £50,000 per year (of which at least £20,000 will go directly to them as service charges). Even then it was my experience that there was a cover charge of £2000+ for every piece of work such small agencies produced for me.

If you still believe you can afford an agency, then how do you select one? There are directories listing such agencies (the most generally available being the *Advertisers Annual*, published by British Media Publications), but I suspect that they will not be particularly meaningful to you; they weren't to me, and I had worked in the industry. Your safest bet is to find someone you know who has had personal experience of such an agency. If you don't know anyone who can provide such advice, look through the adverts that are similar to those you would like to place, and select a small number that impress you. Then phone the advertisers and find out who the agency is (and what these advertisers think of them).

Having selected an agency, you must establish exactly what are their charges. Examine these carefully, not because the agency is likely to cheat you, but because the apparently innocuous small charges rapidly accumulate to large sums. Be certain you know what you are letting yourself in for.

The agency will want a briefing, so *very* carefully collect your thoughts (well in advance of the meeting) and *document* them so that there can be no confusion as to what you want. Agencies love open briefs which allow full rein to their artistic talents, but their clients are not always as happy with the results.

Thereafter, you will need to monitor the agency's work to ensure it meets your brief. This may not necessarily be an easy process, where their creativity takes over. I briefed one well-known agency to produce a commercial for a baby product, where the research showed that the advertising had to exude a bright, clean image. The new agency creative team excitedly presented a concept which revolved around a grubby Italian 'earth mother' in a dirty slum setting. Perhaps not unexpectedly, I rejected this approach, but was astounded when the agency proved to be so enamoured of it that they produced a test commercial (at their own, substantial, cost). I rejected this too. As by now I was becoming worried by the single-minded dedication of the creative team, I sat in on all the casting sessions, rejecting all the plump Italianate models for an 'English Rose'. At the shooting itself, for the first time ever, I insisted on looking through the lens on every set-up, just to be certain there were no strange women lurking in the background of the shot. Even then I lost out. Despite the specific direction in the script, for high-key lighting, the creative team had persuaded the director to turn the aperture down a couple of clicks. The end result was my 'English Rose' swimming in a sea of murkiness which was almost indistinguishable from a Naples slum! I had to write off a fortune in shooting costs and we eventually recut a commercial from footage of previous commercials. The moral is that a creative team with the bit between their teeth can be almost unstoppable.

The agency will first present their ideas to you as 'roughs'. These will be visuals: a sketch of what the ad will look like or, in the case of a commercial, a storyboard – a series of cartoons illustrating the various scenes. Accompanying these will be the copywriter's 'copy', the words that will accompany the visuals. This is the stage at which you need to voice any reservations and discuss any changes you may want; after all you *are* the client and you will be footing the bills. But remember my earlier strictures. You are an amateur and, unless you disagree very strongly indeed, you should leave the major decisions to the experts. You should, though, check the fine details, particularly on the product, on which you should be as much of an expert as anyone in the agency. (For example, one of my colleagues failed to notice that an advertisement for Shift oven cleaner had dropped the rather critical 'F'.)

Once you reach the artwork stage any changes will be expensive; so you must really *hate* anything you want altered. Even changing a few words may mean relaying the whole ad, with totally new typesetting at a cost of hundreds of pounds. I once presented artwork to my director for approval. The artwork was a photograph which, to achieve the specific effect we wanted, had needed extensive retouching. My director idly noted his thoughts (in blue biro) on the artwork itself; and all those hundreds of pounds of retouching had to be repeated. Again, I emphasise, leave it to the experts; but monitor, very carefully, what they are doing with your money.

Do-it-yourself
With all these expenses, you may be tempted to do your own advertising: *don't*! Even so, just occasionally this may be forced on you. A valued customer may insist that you place an ad in a trade directory or local press, to demonstrate your support for him. Clearly you won't be able to hire an agency just for this.

Fortunately, the need here will not be for results; just for lowest cost. So draw up a rough idea of what you want, and get your local instant-print shop to set it and paste it up (with suitable illustrations from material you have around). By all means make certain that the quality will not offend the customer – but don't worry overly about the message (indeed, in view of its purpose, use it as pure flattery towards the customer!).

Beware, though, the hidden costs. Many journals (and, in particular, the national press) require the ad to be provided as a block, ready to print. This can cost hundreds of pounds. Even if you already have such a block, the chances are that it will be the wrong size for the chosen newspaper. Gestures of support can sometimes be expensive. Fortunately, these days, most journals just ask for 'camera-ready' material; so you can simply send the artwork that has been created.

Best of all, avoid advertising like the plague; leave it to the experts.

Exhibitions

I am tempted to offer the same advice about exhibitions, because at times they can be a real pain! But many prospects expect to find their suppliers at such venues. For example, market research showed that just under 30 per cent of personal computer buyers expected to find their suppliers at exhibitions. Thus, sales professionals are likely to be exposed to them, and will even occasionally become involved in organising a stand – so the next section puts forward some hints.

As always, the first step should be to determine just what you want to achieve. John Fenton, in *How to Sell Against Competition*, has a long and interesting section on exhibitions, but he assumes that your only intention in attending will be to maximise your impact.

This may be true of many situations but, in practice, your own ambitions may not be as grandiose. You may have to match the standard of the majority of your competitors, but their offerings probably will not be that lavish. You may even just need to be there as a courtesy to your customers. Obviously, the objectives in these situations will be very different – so it is worthwhile spending some time on these (and, once more, documenting them).

Selection
Every exhibition organiser thinks his offering is fantastic, but very few of them really are, so you will need to select those which you *must* attend. Clearly, the organisers should be able to provide you with statistics of attendances at previous events. But you should, above all, use your own judgement (and that of your customers): how well attended was last year's show in terms of visitors and, more important, of exhibitors like yourself? The exhibitor list for the upcoming show is a good starting point. It will give the best flavour of that show. Is it a major event, or one for also-rans? If the main vendors in your industry are not attending, then ask yourself why.

Having been persuaded of the virtues of a given show, the next step is to book the space you require. You should carefully work out what size (and shape) you need. Just how much space will your equipment require if it is to be seen at its best?

The easiest approach I found was to draw up a scale plan on squared paper. After some experience you will know almost intuitively what size you need, but in the first instance it is worth thinking the matter through in some detail. The most common mistake is to take too small a space, forgetting that you have to handle the crowds gathered around your demonstrations (and still have space for other visitors to circulate). On the other hand, too large a stand is as big a problem. If your stand looks empty in relation to the more crowded (smaller) stands of your competitors, visitors will be nervous of approaching it. They will wonder why it is not popular, and they will feel more exposed to unwanted attention.

The main requirement, whatever the chosen size and shape, is to obtain the best location. As John Fenton stresses, the three main priorities are, 'Position, position and position', echoing the well-known dictum about the location of retail outlets. The best positions are typically along the central aisles, as close as possible to the larger, more spectacular stands. Avoid sites around the perimeter and close to the refreshment areas; unfortunately, visitors to exhibitions differentiate very clearly between business and pleasure.

Make certain that you know what the real traffic flows will be. I remember manning one stand, at an international exhibition in the Sorbonne in Paris, where the stand had been carefully (and expensively) chosen to be at the foot of the main stairs, only to discover that the organisers had just as carefully rerouted everyone up other staircases, and the stand was isolated! Whatever your choice, book early; the best sites go to those who snap them up first.

Stand design

John Fenton insists that you must use a professional stand designer; understandably, as he is looking for the maximum impact. In line with my strictures on the use of professionals in advertising, I am tempted to agree; an unprofessional stand can look very shabby, and can do more harm than good. If you have a major stand design on your hands (and are going to spend thousands of pounds on it), then you must use a professional.

On a lesser scale, it is possible to use one of the many modular stand systems that are available. If you buy a set of such material, it will be possible to take it to a number of exhibitions, which will help to recover the cost – even the simplest set is likely to cost several thousand pounds. Take some time choosing which system you are going to use; you may have to live with its problems for some time. In addition to deciding how good it looks, you will need to decide how easy it will be to use; how easily it can be carried around the country and assembled.

The costs do not stop with the stand system. This will only provide the framework for the graphics and photo blow-ups that will form the backdrop to your display. You will need a designer (although not necessarily a specialist stand designer) to produce these. Again, it can be expensive, the cost seeming to grow exponentially with the size of the material. The massive photo blow-ups covering the whole back walls of stands are impressive, but hideously expensive. They might not even be productive.

One IBM group, with which I worked, spent a small fortune on a colour blow-up to cover the whole back wall of their stand at the Royal Show, the largest agricultural show in the UK. It showed a hillside covered with a crop of corn and colourfully dappled with poppies and other wild flowers. It was a beautiful picture. Unfortunately, all that the farmers attending the show could see was a good crop ruined by *weeds* (poppies are pretty for town dwellers, but an expensive mistake for a farmer – and, in that case, for IBM!).

As John Fenton states, whatever your objectives you will want your exhibit to stand out from the general throng. This requires some artistic ability, another reason for using professionals; but even then things can go wrong. I well remember one IBM stand which was very tastefully decorated in discreet beiges and light browns – I spent a fair amount of time being pestered by punters wanting to know where the IBM stand was! Loud colours can be in bad taste but, properly handled, they can also command attention. One of the simplest, cheapest and best means of highlighting a rather dreary stand is to use at least twice the amount of lighting that everyone else does. The stand will be a (somewhat hot) pool of light, standing out from its competitors, for very little cost.

The stand may have to accommodate a range of uses. Usually it will have a demonstration area. If it doesn't you may be in trouble; visitors expect to see something happening. Often it will have a 'hospitality' area; usually a few seats around a coffee table, where you can sit down in a bit more comfort with your prospects. Sometimes the hospitality area can be the main focus of the stand, with lavish hospitality available to visitors. John Fenton suggests that, if this is the case, then the hospitality suite proper should be away from the general stand (and by invitation only), so that resources are not wasted on tyre-kickers.

One particularly attractive feature on a stand is a 'theatre' where the audience can sit down and watch a professional presentation (and demonstration – as long as you have closed circuit television). This is a great attraction; if nothing else, visitors are grateful for the chance to sit down. It can be a very effective way of showing your wares to large numbers of people. But it *is* expensive, since it uses up a large amount of (expensive) space. It may also need to be enclosed, to provide the correct lighting conditions, and that will be *very* expensive.

The techniques of demonstration are the subject of Chapter 9, but in the specific context of exhibitions it is worth noting that you can demonstrate to twice as many visitors if the equipment is at shoulder height, rather than the more normal waist height. With personal computers, most exhibitors show equipment at desk level, which means that only about 10 people can peer over each other's shoulders to see what you are doing. Lifted to shoulder height, the equipment is just as easy to use, but up to 20 people can see it (only having to look between the heads of the people in front of them).

Whatever your design, you should check that there are no physical or psychological barriers to stop visitors approaching the stand. Ideally they should see it merely as an extension of the gangway, and naturally drift into the demonstration area. I have, though, seen many stands where elaborate confections of staircases, linking different levels, deter visitors (unless they are *so* intrigued that they want to explore); and cost a fortune to build. Just as bad, however, are choke points (often caused by a narrow entry) where visitors have to run the gauntlet of the waiting salesmen – and too often the visitor chooses not to!

Your plan will also need to make provision for services. If nothing else you will need cupboards, which are cheaper than a purpose-built store-room, for your supplies (and for your personal items, equipment covers etc). Almost everyone tends to underestimate the amount of cupboard space needed; and as a result spends many minutes trudging to the car park to retrieve material 'stored' in car boots, leaving the stand undermanned. You will also need enough power (and lighting) points, which will have to be specifically ordered, as well as water/drainage etc, if needed. Unless the show is very short, you will also need a telephone.

John Fenton suggests that there should be no telephones, except one for emergencies. He has a point. In the case of very busy stands, visitors will not be pleased to be kept waiting while a member of the stand staff publicly chats on the telephone. But even on these stands a phone (discreetly hidden behind the scenes) is needed, to contact the various support units (simply to ask for more supplies, or to track down the answer to a complex question). On very slow moving stands a telephone, on the main part of the stand, can be a life-saver. In the long hours between punters (which happens where the show is associated with a convention; the stand is inundated at lunch and coffee breaks, but deserted at other times) you can call your customers and prospects, using your time productively and avoiding going quietly mad.

Budgets

Establishing budgets for an exhibition stand requires a considerable amount of experience and shouldn't be undertaken lightly. To give you some idea of the complexity, however, I list below some of the possible cost headings that John Fenton includes in *How to Sell Against Competition*. It captures most of the items you will have to fund:

Space
Design
Furniture & Fittings
   functional
   protective
   decoration
Services
   communications
   insurance
Staff
   salaries
   outside demonstrators
     hostesses
     Interpreters
   expenses
Promotion
   advertising & PR
   literature
   other giveaways
   catalogue entry

Exhibits
   main items
   sign writing
Publicity display equipment
Stand transport
   packing
Construction
Misc
   entertainment
   clerical aids
   security
   safety
   cleaning
   waste disposal
   utilities
   repairs
   consumables

Manning

The worst problem facing almost any stand organiser is manning it. It takes a disproportionate amount of your time, particularly where the people you want have already experienced the 'joys' of manning such a stand. Even when they have been coerced into attending, the problem doesn't stop; for there are always other attractions (and almost anything is preferable to, and less tiring than, manning an exhibition stand).

Resource plan

The first requirement, then, is to produce a plan of the people resources you need day by day, since there will be some days, especially the first, when the exhibition will be busier. The second is to persuade those departments, typically the field force, to release enough personnel to meet these needs. Third is to make those departments live up to their promises when the day comes. In practice you may find that less than half the personnel turn up without chasing (and even with chasing you will be lucky to get three-quarters); so you will be advised to practice some fairly hefty over-budgeting.

The critical requirement is that you have sufficient cover to handle all prospects at all times, although you will inevitably be stretched somewhat thin during the worst rushes. This means that everyone involved must be aware of the schedule (including the hour by hour, or preferably half-hour, schedule each day) and must stick to it – otherwise you will find (conscientious) staff who have had no meal breaks, and who will be less likely to man your next stand.

I ran a very sophisticated IBM exhibition (called, appropriately, 'EXHIBIT'). It ran for six weeks in the UK (although it toured Europe for three years, carried on no less than 22 container lorries) and cost £1.5 million for the UK's first six weeks alone – overall the cost must have been near to £50 million, making it one of the most expensive exhibitions ever.

In the first six weeks in the UK, just under 100,000 people passed through it. It was spectacular, but, true to form, the greatest problem was finding our staff. During any one day we needed 70 staff, with a complex two-shift system to cover the manning from 9.30 am to 10.30 pm, seven days a week. Of these, at least 50 needed to be trained IBMers, to man the 20+ separate exhibits. Recognising the inevitable problems (where, because of the training needed, these staff were at the exhibition for at least one whole week, and preferably for two) we concentrated on using trainees – at that time,

IBM had nearly 200. Even so, we needed two admin staff dedicated (for a total of nearly three months) to finding, and then ensuring they attended, the 300 man-weeks of effort needed. Even then, we typically had to run with just 30 IBMers, making up the difference with specially trained temps.

As the above example indicates, it is possible to use temps for some jobs; we essentially used them for the routine admin jobs. But you will be *forced* (by union agreements) to use special contractor labour for certain aspects of stand building, if you are not using a modular system; so be warned.

Enquiry processing
One special resource you will need to plan for will be how enquiries will be processed. It is assumed that the exhibition *will* generate leads and enquiries, otherwise why attend it? But all too often these leads get lost. It is necessary to set up a rigorous procedure for collecting the leads, using special cards and ensuring that these are handed in immediately and taken away – or safely locked up – every evening.

More important, and more difficult, is ensuring that these leads get passed on to the relevant sales professionals – and (believe it or not) that they deal with them. For some unknown reason, many sales forces seem to view with considerable suspicion, almost distaste, leads generated by anything other than their own fair hands. I believe that this is crass stupidity, since it only takes a few moments to check how good a lead it is (whatever its source); and there are very few sales professionals with too many *good* leads. But many sales professionals still ignore these externally generated leads, which wastes potential and considerably annoys those prospects who are expecting to be contacted. So your lead handling plan must be effective.

In the case of 'EXHIBIT', which was mainly attended by the general public (rather than prospects), we recognised that the normal enquiry processing system was unworkable. The evidence was that enquiries, even from specific prospect events, were not handled well – and in many cases were not handled at all. Our solution was that every enquiry was handled on site, with a complicated escalation, which saw the IBM staff on the stands handling most enquiries, backed up by their six supervisors (and ultimately by myself) on the more complex questions. If someone wanted to buy a personal computer we gave them a list of the dealers and explained how they should contact them. We didn't have any serious enquiries for large mainframes but, again, I would have dealt personally with these. In this way, every single enquiry was dealt with on site, and we knew that there would be no unanswered queries floating around. This was, though, an unusual case, normally you will judge the success of the whole venture in terms of the *good* leads you can pass on to your sales force.

Briefing
It is essential that everyone involved should understand exactly what is happening and what their own role should be. This means that everyone should be fully briefed. For 'EXHIBIT' all personnel were given two days' specific training. While this was justifiable for personnel who were to spend one or two weeks at the exhibition, it clearly would be an unnecessary luxury for most two- or three-day shows. Even so, there should be a briefing of all those attending, taking as long as is necessary (typically an hour or so).

It is also advisable to have a short (15-minute) briefing before the start of every day, to share the lessons learnt the previous day.

The briefing should also cover aspects other than the most obvious and most important duties of dealing with prospects. Not least is that it should emphasise that the housekeeping must be good; the stand should be kept clean, the literature replenished. I have attended exhibitions overseas (in Iron Curtain countries) where there were permanent stand cleaners – and it did make a pleasant change not having to wade around in a sea of discarded coffee cups and cigarette ends. But in normal practice, the stand staff should be capable of handling their own housekeeping during the lulls (although, in your preparations, you must remember to book full stand cleaning overnight). It is important, however, that you don't just tell them, but that you also regularly monitor what is happening.

Stand staff should be advised to take the opportunity to update themselves on the competition (who will also be exhibiting). At the same time they should be warned to keep competition away from your own stand. A useful technique is to ask for the prospect's business card. This is a quick way of dissuading competitors and, in any case, it is an easy way of getting a prospect's (legible) name and address, usually together with an indication of what the company does.

The real threat of competitors is not that they will learn about your equipment; they will soon do that without your help – my tame customers passed on full details of any new competitive product within a matter of days of its announcement. It is that they will mingle with your prospects, and later pick them off.

If nothing else they will be absorbing your precious resources at the expense of your prospects. At one extreme, I have seen sales professionals ignoring genuine prospects, who were impatiently waiting for assistance, to talk at length with competitors' staff (who were *very* good listeners). At the other extreme, I have had competitors entering into discussions, on *my* stand, to make sales pitches for their own products – but not for very long!

Competitors *are* a problem when prospects are around, but when the stand was quiet I found it no real imposition to talk to them. They will learn, by hook or by crook, what you have got; so make a virtue of necessity and invite them on to the stand. In practice, I learnt as much from them as they did from me, and was able to justify a return visit to *their* stand (when I got my money's worth). It also offers an opportunity for some psychological warfare. I always preferred my competitors to be over-confident, so I took the opportunity to complain at length about how *badly* we were doing; it made a change from the obviously inflated claims of outstanding sales successes that most sales professionals purvey to their competitors (who always immediately discount them).

Sales techniques

So far I have discussed the role (perhaps unlikely for most sales professionals) of running a stand. A much more likely role is that of being one of the sales professionals called on to man the stand, although after reading much of what I have just written, you may have already decided that you will avoid such a duty like the plague.

In many respects, taking a 'call' on an exhibition stand follows many of the rules of an ordinary call. It has, though, a number of special characteristics.

The introduction is very different. The prospect has voluntarily come to you: be in no doubt about it, the great majority of prospects would never venture on to an exhibition stand unless they were interested. This gives you an immediate advantage – but you will still have to hook him.

Many writers frown on the conventional opening, 'Can I help you?', since it allows (and the critics would say encourages) the prospect to say 'No,' or more politely 'No, I'm just looking.' My own feeling is that this is not really a major disadvantage. Always assuming that you have a busy stand, it is better that you don't annoy a diffident prospect, and get on with selling to someone who really wants it. Perhaps, though, you could use the more positive, '*How* can I help you?' John Fenton goes so far as to suggest that stand staff should wear badges saying this; and it *is* important that you do wear some form of badge showing that you are one of the stand personnel (preferably with your name on it as well). It is frustrating, as a prospect, not to know who can help you.

Some other writers suggest that you should start on an even more positive note, going straight into a pitch on the major benefits of what you are showing. As you might expect, I believe this falls into the trap of selling benefits without the slightest idea of what the prospect wants. Perhaps a less blinkered approach, which still capitalises on the demonstrated interest of the prospect, might be to ask, 'What particularly interests you?'

Whatever the opening, the 'call' itself will almost inevitably be short. The prospect will have other stands to see and you will want to talk to other prospects. So you must move rapidly to qualify the prospect and then to persuade him to allow a positive follow-on action; some form of call (merely sending literature, for example, is usually a waste of time and of your expensive literature). It is an excellent opportunity to practise your qualifying and closing skills, for most of the prospects will be the 'property' of other sales professionals – and that lends a touch of ruthlessness (or simply take it or leave it) that can add bite to your close.

This does, however, highlight one aspect that makes such calls difficult and potentially boring. The prospects you unearth will almost all have to be passed on to other sales professionals, as it is unlikely that you will be able to close an order on the stand, which takes away much of the motivation of the 'sale'. To maintain your sanity and impress your management, you need something to pep you up, some target to go after. I am intensely competitive (as are most sales professionals) so I used to motivate myself simply by setting the target of booking more leads (as measured by the number of cards filled in) than anyone else.

Whatever techniques you use, it is inevitably a very tiring job. Just standing on your feet all day is debilitating (ask any shop assistant), and having to cope with a steady procession of prospects, most of whom will not be yours, and all of whom follow much the same course of questions, can be mind-blowing. Be prepared to get some rest when you can, especially in the evening. Nobody ever made a good job of manning a stand while coping with a king-size hangover!

Promotions

Promotional activity is probably most often related to those mass consumer goods which are not normally the province of the sales professional; every packet of detergent seems to scream 'money off' or 'free plastic daffodil'. But such activity, usually in a rather quieter form, does have a place in professional selling.

It essentially serves two main roles, both of which are largely indirect in their application. Despite sales professionals' presumptions, most promotional activities are anything but direct – most of those on consumer goods are designed to buy more shelf space, which *does* produce more sales. The first, which this section will concentrate on, is to generate the initial interest in your product. The second is to provide an additional incentive to close, bringing forward the time when the customer will sign the order (possibly swinging it from a competitor to yourself). The latter aspect is normally a function of pricing, and is discussed in Chapter 6.

Reverting to the initial objective of attracting attention, these promotions typically run in association with mailings (and occasionally as part of advertising campaigns). They have, though, to bear some relationship to the product. The IBM Supplies Division did an excellent line in promotional give-aways. There was much competition within IBM to obtain the items of desk furniture (all carefully embossed with the IBM logo, and the telephone number where you could order the supplies). I suspect that customers were just as appreciative, and I believe that (probably) those give-aways brought in more than enough extra business to cover the cost; although it was an act of faith – as is most mass marketing.

In the area of mainframes, however, IBM's promotions were often tied in with sponsorship. It sponsored major exhibitions, and ran a private view for its customers and prospects, which offered an ideal social occasion to close business.

Whatever the promotion, you must (once more) very carefully define your objectives. Is it simply to keep your name on the prospects' desks or is it to bring together prospects in a social setting? Too often the promotion consists of simply dumping a supply of nondescript diaries on sales professionals' desks. (Incidentally, if you must send out diaries, send them out well in advance; I have seen sales professionals eventually sending them out in January in the rather vain hope that their business contacts would not by then have acquired a diary!)

Telesales

After the rather impersonal mailshot, the most important prospecting device is the telephone; this is, to a degree at least, personal and interactive. Its great advantage, of course, is the speed with which calls can be made. It is quite realistic, even in professional sales, for 50 calls to be made in a day (compared with, say, 300 calls in a *year* face-to-face). It is thus a very efficient way of contacting large numbers of prospects.

The clear disadvantages are that it is considerably more difficult to be persuasive as a disembodied voice, and it is a very different technique which many, perhaps most, sales professionals hate! For most of us there is nothing worse than being faced with a cold telephone, and the chilling knowledge that we need to make half a dozen appointments.

But the telephone sell is an effective tool. As a means of making mass contacts, it is significantly more successful than mailings. It is generally reckoned to be something like 10 times as productive. Of course, it depends on what you have to offer and what you will settle for (the hit rate will be much higher if you are only asking someone to attend a free seminar). But it is possible to achieve a 10 per cent hit rate, even in terms of appointments; making perhaps three new appointments from half a day's work.

The right environment
Teleselling is tough, and it is (in some peculiar way) unnatural for many sales professionals who make superb face-to-face calls. It is normally difficult enough in ideal circumstances, but it is almost impossible in a general sales office, with all the distractions it offers.

The first requirement, therefore, is to find the right environment; one which makes teleselling as pleasant as possible. It needs to be a quiet place, ideally a separate office so that you won't be interrupted and your telephone conversations will not be drowned out. You should be relaxed and at ease, in a comfortable chair, with a large expanse of clear desk for your notes and other essentials. Ideally, the surroundings should be both cheerful and relaxing. I have always put more effort into fitting out and decorating my telesales rooms than any other. A bright, cheerful atmosphere really does make teleselling that much easier.

Finally, but not least, you need a good telephone; one that is comfortable to hold and to which you can listen easily. Most important, the customer needs to hear you, so the mouthpiece should work well; many of the trendier looking telephones have mouth-pieces which are not angled towards your mouth, and muffle your voice.

It was so difficult to find the right telephone (even for normal use) that IBM UK ran a special investigation just to find the best product.

It turned out that, at least for IBM's needs, the best telephone was an outdated model (at least in terms of trendiness) from the 1970s. It had just been discontinued, but IBM managed to buy up 2000 sets that British Telecom had lying in a warehouse! The most modern products are not always the best.

Everything to hand

The right environment should also contain everything that you will need. You should have your reference material beside you; you won't normally need it, but it will give you a feeling of security to have it available. You should have your notes, your crib-sheets, your directories; everything to hand. Nothing is worse for your productivity than to have an excuse (such as going to find some materials) to justify breaking off calling; and once the rhythm is broken it usually proves hard to start again.

Timing

It is important to make your calls at the time when most prospects will be at their desks. For obvious reasons, the most productive times are from 10.00 to 12.00 in the morning and 2.00 until 4.00 in the afternoon. It *is* possible to contact some prospects at other times (and for contacting existing prospects and customers such times may even be preferable), but the success rate in terms of making productive calls goes down dramatically when less people are at their desks; that is bad for morale, and it is difficult enough to maintain the momentum when you have everything going for you.

If you are going to try for the whole two-hour slot, it is also important to take a deliberate break, say quarter of an hour, in the middle. It is very easy to start to get stale and about an hour is the maximum most sales professionals can manage at a stretch. Perhaps the best advice, for you as a sales professional, is to limit your telesales activity to one-hour slots; then get on with something completely different. You will, however, still have to put in the necessary hours (but spread over a number of days) if you are to win the numbers game.

You cannot continue productive teleselling if you get tired. So, as soon as fatigue really sets in, give up and start again another day.

Attitude of mind

Almost the prime determinant of success in teleselling will be your attitude of mind. If you believe you will be successful, you probably will. Needless to say, it is not always that simple; otherwise teleselling would be the most popular pursuit of sales professionals.

Teleselling does tend to exaggerate swings in mood, to which many sales professionals are prone. It was most obvious in my days selling to retailers. If the first three calls were good, then I was unstoppable for the day. If, on the other hand, they were poor, I found it very difficult to pick myself up. With teleselling you need to will yourself into the right mood. If you can't, then get on with something else – but don't use this as an excuse for avoiding teleselling. I had one sales professional who simply refused to telesell, with the result that his prospect list was very much smaller than any of his colleagues (as were his sales).

To a certain extent it is necessary to adopt a 'take it or leave it' attitude to teleselling; the exact reverse of the normal sales attitude. However good you are at teleselling, you will still experience far more rejections than acceptances, and this can destroy your morale if you take them too seriously. For this reason it is probably better to undertake teleselling when you need it least – when you have plenty of business – because then you will be most able to face it. In addition there is the lead time to take into account, and that says this new business will probably start to come on stream just when your current bonanza runs out.

It helps if you can work with colleagues as a team, supporting each other. The extra competitiveness gives an additional bite to calls that otherwise could easily become stale. Also, sharing the stresses – joking about the oddballs you get through to (and even a dramatic rejection can be hilarious if shared) – makes the load easier to bear.

One key to teleselling is very rapid qualification and closing. If the prospect doesn't want to see you, then thank him courteously and move on. Only in the very rare instances, when you sense there is still potential, should you try to persuade him to change his mind. This advice is the reverse of that normally offered; most writers give long examples of how you can win over unwilling prospects. My experience is that this is a waste of time. Better move on; try them again some time a few months later, when they may be more receptive. Teleselling is a numbers game, and there are plenty of other fish in the sea.

Similarly, where you *can* close, do so immediately. Your only objective is to get the appointment. Any other information you provide may work against you in the time before you meet the prospect. He will think over your various messages, and may decide he doesn't like them; in which case you will have a hard job convincing him or, even worse, he may call and cancel the appointment. So be content with an appointment – that is all you need.

I learnt the value of brevity (something I do not naturally possess) as a political candidate. Canvassing door-to-door has some of the characteristics of teleselling. Your aim in knocking on voters doors is simple: it is merely to 'show the flag'. Voters fall into three categories. The first are your convinced supporters. These are a delight to meet and one could spend hours talking to them (and many candidates do), but that would be a total waste of time. They are already going to vote for you, so the key technique is politely (but ruthlessly) to move on to the next call. The next group is the most important, the 'floating' voters. Even here, though, the requirement is to present them with a smiling face, demonstrably taking a personal interest in them, and rapidly move on! Floating voters rarely want to indulge in long arguments, although they do appreciate the candidate calling; but they appreciate it even more if his call is brief. The third group are your committed opponents, who will be delighted to argue with you, but again will be a total waste of time.

The key to canvassing, whatever the category of voter, is to move on fast. If you spend valuable minutes discussing politics with any single voter, you will not have time to cover other voters. The essence is the polite goodbye. Much of the same is true of teleselling. It is more productive to make 30 calls, with a 10 per cent conversion rate (that is with three converted into appointments), than to take three times as long to make 10 calls, with an impressively doubled conversion ratio (but giving only two appointments, and then probably prospects that will be harder to take further). It really is a numbers game.

Getting past the secretary

The first rule of teleselling is that you must get through to the correct person. It is little use making a superb call on someone who is not a relevant decision-maker or influencer. So the first and usually simplest part of the job is to find out who you should be contacting. It is normally surprisingly easy. The receptionists and secretaries will go out of their way to help; they only see their 'guard-dog' role, of saving management from being pestered by uninvited callers, quite specifically in terms of their *own* manager. The difficulty will be in asking unambiguous questions, and in finding the key people who can point you to the real decision-makers. If you simply ask, 'Who buys the computers?', you are inviting the answer, 'the buying department', which is usually incorrect. You will need to rephrase it, for example, as, 'Which director is responsible for deciding your computer strategy?'; and even that will probably need further explanation, reducing eventually perhaps to, 'Which of them is the most interested in computers?' The effort is usually well worthwhile and you will finally obtain the information you need.

I knew one college lecturer who phoned the British Shoe Corporation for some rather obscure information. He was passed from person to person, with nobody knowing the answers, until he eventually ended up with one manager who turned out to be a fount of information. The lecturer was delighted and spent nearly an hour pumping him for all the data he needed. At the end of the call he decided he had better ask who his contact was, in case he needed to speak to him again. He was astounded to discover that it was Charles Clore, who was then one of the richest men in England (personally owning a number of retail chains as well as the British Shoe Corporation)! Yet he had been happy to answer genuine questions, and his staff had been happy to pass on the caller to him. I am certain the lecturer would never have dreamt of calling Charles Clore direct – and would never have been allowed near him on the basis of such a direct call.

Using the telephone for such research work can be very productive.

Creating the excuse
I found that the first and best (as well as easiest) technique for getting past the secretary was 'authority'. (In a rather indirect way that was what worked in the case of Charles Clore: the lecturer simply had a very valid reason, the authority, for being put through.) You just sound as if you have the absolute right to speak to him. The best approach is to be brief, but pressing: 'John Smith, please.' It always helps to use the prospect's first name. If the secretary is doing her job conscientiously, she will ask who you are (although given sufficient authority in your voice, many allow you through without even that check). Again, your answer should be brief, but with authority, 'David Mercer'; once more, with first name and without any elaboration.

By this time even the toughest secretary will be in something of a quandary. She risks offending a possible important contact if she probes too much, as your authority seems to imply that you have a compelling reason to be put through. Most secretaries will give up at this stage. A few, though, may go on to ask, 'From what company?', and in reply you simply give your company, again with no further explanation. Normal callers, who have a genuine reason to contact a manager, do not expect to have to undergo a third degree. It is only the sales professional who loses his nerve, and starts to explain his reasons for calling, who falls at this hurdle.

Some secretaries may persist or (more likely) their manager may ask for more explanation. It is at this stage that you need the valid excuse. The easiest is to refer to a mailing you have sent: 'I would like to discuss my letter of xxx' (again on an unspecified subject – unless you are pursued further). You don't even have to have sent such a letter, although it is a good idea to link with real mailings for maximum impact; few managers can remember all the mail they receive, and anyway it could easily have been lost in the post. Alternatively, you might use the excuse that you want to talk about a new product that will be important to the development of his business.

Best of all, though, is to use a reference (if you can find a source): 'Harry Jones suggested I speak to him.' In any case you can often *create* an internal reference. If you get through to the director and he (or even his secretary) suggests you talk to a subordinate, then the opening should (quite legitimately!) be: 'Charles Grey (the director) suggested I should talk to you!' This is almost guaranteed to throw the fear of god into any underling. They will not know what your relationship is with the director, and cannot afford to challenge you!

There are other gimmicks. John Fenton suggests, for example, making all sales professionals 'Directors', since prospects will take calls from directors. But I believe this can rebound dangerously at a later stage. I never referred to *any* title, it was only my 'authority' that conveyed the impression that I was someone of importance – and I very rarely had any difficulty in talking on equal terms with any director, even those of multinationals.

The sales pitch

Once the barriers are down and you are face-to-face (or at least ear-to-ear) with the prospect, is the time when you have to make the most of your selling skills. You have just a few seconds to persuade him, by voice alone, to allow you to continue talking.

A first routine check should be: 'Is that Mr Smith?' This establishes that you are talking to the right person; there is nothing quite so embarrassing in this situation as talking to the wrong person, and using the wrong name! It also starts the call positively, with the prospect saying, 'Yes.'

Many pundits suggest that you then follow with a courtesy question such as, 'Have you a moment to speak on the phone?', or 'Is it convenient for you to speak on the phone now?' I think these are, just about, acceptable approaches although, I suspect, unnecessary (the chances are that if he didn't have the time he wouldn't be talking to you). The one approach, as a buyer myself, which immediately caused me to put up all my defences was: 'Thank you for giving me your time.' I immediately knew I was about to be the victim of a sales pitch, and I wasn't about to *give* the caller an order!

That part is easy. The next element represents the critical moment. You have to attract his attention with a simple, but powerful message. KISS (keep it simple, stupid) once more is the best advice.

Alfred Tack describes an approach he calls 'the hinge':

'There should, wherever possible, be a hinge on which to hang your approach. This can be a letter which you or your company have written, an advertisement, a new product – a special claim you can make for your product – or a reference from a friend or business associate.'

He illustrates four examples of this:

'Have you a moment to speak on the phone?' [as a lead in, followed by]
LETTER HINGE 'Did you receive my letter?'
or REFERENCE HINGE 'We haven't met, but x suggested I contact you'
or QUESTION HINGE 'Have you heard of us?'
or QUICK APPROACH 'I would like to take just 10 minutes of your time to tell you about xxx, would … or … be more convenient for me to call?'

The one critical aspect of the message is that it must be *relevant*. If you have something that immediately interests a prospect he will listen, where he will not have time for a general statement. My telesales team barely achieved a 3 to 5 per cent success rate when calling about personal computing in general, but they hit at least 10 per cent when calling architects specifically about CAD.

The secret is to find the right 'hot-button' to turn on your prospect in the first few seconds of the call. That requires you to have the maximum information about him, to know his type of business, and to convert that into a sales message. In other words, you have to be a sales professional.

The script

Teleselling is the one time when it is advisable to use a script, at least for the first few key sentences. It is important to get these exactly right.

In the case of full-time telesales personnel, the whole call is typically (and usually best) based on a script. They are not usually product experts, so the script has to be used to keep them on the straight and narrow. This is, undoubtedly, quite acceptable to prospects who usually appreciate the fact that they are talking to 'administrative' staff. One of the worst problems I encountered with a telesales team came when they tried to behave like sales professionals. Although they were better than average telesales personnel, they were still not up to the calibre of sales professionals. The result was that we experienced prospects thinking that we had poor sales professionals (rather than excellent admin staff) and, accordingly giving us *less* appointments.

These scripts are developed to a fine art in the big telesales agencies (which you might consider as an alternative, albeit an expensive one, to carrying out the work yourself). In the ultimate they can comprise 'programs', sometimes even run on personal computers, but anyway with 'branching' questions depending on the prospects' answers. Such elaborate scripts require considerable expertise to produce, however, and agencies maintain teams of scriptwriters to develop them.

You will not need such elaborate resources, however. Once you are over the first few scripted statements and questions you will be into a normal call.

Follow-up

It is always advisable to confirm a telephone appointment immediately in writing. This is courteous, and it also ensures that the prospect will put the appointment in his diary. It is sometimes even worth checking with his secretary before starting out on the call. This is particularly important when he is coming to you, for a seminar for example, where there will typically be up to a 50 per cent drop out rate.

For this follow-up 'admin' work you can safely use your admin staff; your secretary, for example, if you are fortunate enough to have one. Indeed, the more people you can persuade to telesell for you, the more productive you will be.

Repeat calls

Just because you were unsuccessful previously is no reason not to repeat the trawl after a few months lying fallow. You should find that the response rate is just as good as your first canvass, from prospects that previously turned you down. Their situations will have changed. They may now be in the market for your product, or they may just feel more amenable. This time, though, the calls will be much less resource consuming because you already have all the preparatory research material to hand – it *always* pays dividends to make, and keep, good records.

Cold calls

For the masochists among you there is a theory that, in the case of those prospects where your 'nose' tells you that there should be business but you simply cannot get through on the telephone, it might still be worth making a cold call. Maybe this alternative approach will work; but don't count on the business.

Events

If you haven't already run events, as an excuse for mailings or telesales, it is worth running them as a 'catch all' to bring in those prospects who won't allow a face-to-face call. Events are much easier to sell. The prospect feels less threatened. He will be in company, where he can't be mugged by an aggressive sales professional. Seminars also represent neutral ground. The prospect doesn't have to admit formally that he is a potential buyer, he can legitimately pretend he is just there to learn.

Best of all, though, the telesales message is much simpler and correspondingly easier to get across. This is particularly important where you are using specialist telesales personnel. I found that they were three or four times more successful in obtaining recruits for a seminar than they were in obtaining face-to-face appointments, although the inevitable 50 per cent drop out rate diluted this advantage.

Using specialist telesales staff

You are fortunate indeed if you have access to good telesales staff. They can be worth their weight in gold if you use them well. It takes a considerable degree of mental toughness to withstand almost constant rejection for four hours a day (which is their typical productive working time). At the same time they still need the sensitivity to catch the nuances of the prospects' replies. So the best telesales staff are very rare, special and valuable people, especially for you.

Brief and teach

The first requirement is that you give them a good brief. This will require some preparation on your part. You will need to brief them on what is important to *them* (not to you, or even to the prospect). You should develop the script that they will work to; it is unrealistic to expect that they will be able to do this for themselves.

The overall brief needs, however, to be as thorough as possible, so that they don't feel too exposed when a prospect diverts from the script. I gave my telesales teams at least a day's training on any new application package or event that I was expecting them to sell. Most of this went over their heads, but in the process they began to understand the 'language', and felt more comfortable talking to prospects in that language.

In addition, I always sat in on the calls for the first day or so. Every hour we had a review of how well the script was going, and agreed changes to it, to make it more productive and easier for them to use. That way the script matched their style as well as mine.

Pamper and motivate

Above all, pamper your telesales staff. Generally, they face a (literally) thankless task. The prospects yell at them, but sales professionals only see them to complain about appointments that have gone awry. The prime, and quite bitter complaint I received from my telesales staff was simply that nobody told them how their prospects turned out; and, like any other sales professional, they were desperate to see their leads turn into business (even though they weren't paid commission on them).

So be prepared to spend a little time reporting back, telling your telesales staff just what a good job they have done and crediting them with at least part of your success. This way you will ensure that when they work for you they will really put in their top-notch effort. You will also find that, mysteriously, you get more appointments than your colleagues. This will in part be due to the more positive attitude with which they will approach your prospects, but it will also come from the telesales team stealing time from your colleagues to give to you. Everyone wants to spend most time on the jobs that are most rewarding.

Answering the telephone

One aspect of teleselling that is often overlooked is when the prospect (or customer) calls you. These calls are even more important, since they represent genuine interest. As a result, it is important that they are particularly well handled.

I am certain that you will handle yourself well during such inbound calls. But, as always, make certain that you document the contact well, so that you can follow it up. I have lost track of the number of times I have heard a sales professional asking around to see if anyone has found the scrap of paper on which he noted a key conversation. To be truthful, I have had more than my fair share of such messages lost in all the rubbish that accumulates on my desk. It is essential that you document (albeit in somewhat more brief form) telephone calls as well as face-to-face calls; for the same good reasons.

The biggest problem, though, will almost certainly be with the system that handles calls before they reach you, or when you are out. Very few companies are really efficient at handling telephone calls. Try phoning in (to 'yourself') occasionally, as if you were a prospect, and see how your telephonists and secretaries (and message centres) handle the call. You may possibly be shocked by how badly the call is dealt with, which may explain why your prospects are somewhat antagonistic by the time they have reached you. If you can, persuade your company to train all these personnel formally in good telephone manners; your prospects will have as many, if not more, contacts with them as with you.

One key problem is what happens when you are out (and, as a sales professional, you should be out a lot). Who answers the phone for you? I fought hard (and ultimately successfully) for my own secretary to deal with my calls when I was out, but whoever handles your calls, make certain that they have a pad (of photocopies if necessary) with a list of the main information that you want recorded. They probably still won't fill it in, but at least you have done your best.

Above all, let everyone know where you are. You can be certain that the worst crises will erupt when nobody knows where you are. The customer will get steadily more irascible if nobody can help him, while your management will become more and more convinced that your handling of the account is a disaster. Avoid such pitfalls, simply by ensuring you are contactable.

Cold calling

This is generally second only to teleselling as the average sales professional's least favourite pursuit; and on a cold, wet, windy, winter's day it easily becomes almost everyone's least favourite. In fact, it shares perhaps many more of the characteristics of teleselling than it does of conventional calling.

Miller, Heiman and Tuleja comment:

> 'We've only met two kinds of sales representative in all our years in the business; those who say they hate to prospect, and those who don't admit the truth and say they like it.'

Limited objectives

Of these similarities with teleselling, perhaps the most important is that of setting limited objectives. The typical aim, once more, is only to book an appointment. To set out deliberately to do more than this on a cold call risks a number of problems. Such an ambition will, first of all, limit the number of calls where you are allowed in at all. Even in those calls where you actually get your foot in the door it will be in imminent danger of being chopped off. You have no time-slot reserved, so the prospect may at any moment be called away to deal with something else, just when you are in the middle of your pitch. What is more, you will not be properly prepared, and neither will the prospect. So resist the temptation and, like a telephone call, keep it simple – restricted to making a further appointment, when you will reveal all.

As it is a face-to-face call, however, you will have *some* leeway. You can, justifiably (but briefly), ask him what will be his special interests when you attend the appointment; but let him do the talking and resist the temptation to start a hard sell. You are in just as much danger of preempting your subsequent call as you would be on the telephone.

So, as in any canvass, aim to get in and out quickly. It is still very much a numbers game. The more calls you make, the more appointments you should achieve.

Research

On the other hand, you should not ignore the opportunity to conduct some research. You can learn a lot about how a business works just by looking at the outside of its premises. Are they big? Are they well maintained? Are they workshops or offices? You can learn even more by looking around you as you are taken through the offices or workshops. Most of all, as mentioned earlier, you can learn from all the people you meet, particularly the receptionist. And of course, all this research should be immediately documented.

Targets and incentives

But it is still a bloody awful job. So you will need to motivate yourself to make the numbers. You will need to set yourself very clear targets. Perhaps you will decide that you won't stop calling (and get back into your lovely warm car) until you have made 20 calls or, better still, until you have made two appointments – better because it is more positive (and you finish your calling on a high, an appointment, which is always good for morale).

Best of all, prospect with your colleagues as a team: blitz the area. If it's your patch, set up some incentives – a bottle of champagne for the sales professional booking the most appointments for you. You will find the competition, and comradeship, makes cold calling much more bearable.

Even if you can't arrange such a team blitz, it is worth sharing the load with a fellow sales professional; and, indeed, worth going into the calls together. It may seem counter-productive, having two sales professionals holding hands in the same call, but it seems to boost morale enormously, and success in cold calling has a lot to do with morale. In addition, surprisingly, prospects seem more willing to see two sales professionals than one. Perhaps they are flattered by the attention, or perhaps they just feel less threatened. In any case, it has been my experience that teams of two do not lose dramatically on coverage (they don't cover as many calls as two sales professionals separately, but they do cover more than one alone), and their conversion ratio is significantly better. Most important, the sales professionals end up less demoralised; indeed they usually enjoy the experience – and, as this book is about enjoying selling, there is no reason why you shouldn't enjoy even cold calling!

Sales enquiries

Most writers ignore this category, perhaps because there is something almost shameful about business which has come about by accident. Even so, a sizeable part of many sales professionals' cold business will come from such unexpected enquiries. Of course, the enquiries don't really come to the company without there being some reason behind them; the prospects may have seen the advertising, they may have received a mailing (but not bothered to return the card), or (best of all) they may be a referral from a satisfied customer. Whatever the reason, they have not materialised out of thin air; they are the reward for some marketing virtue.

To the sales professional, however, they are unsolicited; bluebirds. That might take some of the gloss off the business when you close it (the critics among the other sales professionals are almost sure to remind you of it) but if you can stand the comments, which are often sour grapes, I don't see why you shouldn't revel in the opportunity. It represents potential business, and is likely to be more productive than most prospects that you have, with great effort, persuaded to talk to you. A bluebird actually *wants* to talk to you, and that must be worth something.

The only action you need take is to respond, but do it *immediately*. As Alan Williams says, in *All About Selling*:

'There is only one way to deal with a sales enquiry – urgently. And there is only one person who can do the job – the salesman! That must seem like a rather obvious statement, but the fact is many sales people are so indifferent to sales enquiries that they respond in a manner most likely to minimise the chances of success.'

That is my experience too. My advice is simply to be the exception: respond rapidly and win the business.

Lead handling

Tracking such leads (or any leads) to make sure they are properly handled is essential for a well-managed sales department, and for a sales professional. The system used by the BSMD division of Kodak, as reported in the *Dartnell Sales Promotion Handbook*, seems to me to be very comprehensive.

Every enquirer is immediately replied to by personal letter or form letter and those requesting literature are immediately sent this by first class mail. Requests for a representative to get in touch receive priority handling and are processed the day they are received. Where information is required immediately the district sales manager is notified by telephone.

To track all of this, a four-part enquiry form is produced. One part goes to the district sales manager and one part to the computer. The sales professional receives two parts, one of which he must return, describing the action taken, within 30 days. Every two months the sales professional gets a printout of his resulting prospects, and has to report progress (by ticking boxes on this and returning it).

I like this system. First, it imposes clear deadlines on handling enquiries, where the worst problem is almost always that sales professionals are tardy in replying. Second, it clearly tracks what is happening, so that a sales professional cannot say (particularly to himself), 'I've never seen that', which I found was frequently the excuse used. Finally, it stimulates a sales professional to follow up, which reduces the second biggest problem, where sales professionals forget and let leads go cold.

Whatever your own system, and I doubt it will be as complex as that of Eastman Kodak, it is important that you track your leads, particularly if you are in the enviable position of having numbers of them.

Analysis

Whichever forms of prospecting you eventually subscribe to, they will represent a considerable effort for (sometimes) variable results. It is important, therefore, that you analyse the results against the input.

Test marketing

Before even committing all your resource, it is worth conducting a test market. This is a good old marketing device that limits your exposure until you are certain you are on to a winner. It simply means, for example, that you send your mailing to a proportion of your target audience. This could be a small percentage (say 10 per cent) or, better, a small (but statistically significant) absolute number. To achieve reasonably accurate results you only need about 500 in this sample. To satisfy the exact criterion of market researchers the size of this sample should be carefully calculated, and it should be truly random.

In my days as a member of the Market Research Society I duly impressed my management with the sophisticated statistics I was using. But I also learnt, much more pragmatically, that it was possible to get almost as good results from much less sophisticated methods. In practice it is quite sufficient to take every tenth name (say), or even those in a certain area if you know it isn't grossly untypical. If the outcome is positive, *then* you commit your resource to the full mailing.

If you want to be really sophisticated, you can even send different letters to different samples, to compare their performance and choose the most effective – but make certain that you can tell apart their reply-paid cards. On the other hand, don't get carried away with this market research. You can spend all your time on it and, fascinating as it is, it is the real prospecting that will pay your salary.

One word of warning, though, don't be overawed by the results; don't let your own judgement be drowned in statistics. I once ran a test market for a pipe tobacco in the Tyne-Tees television area. Doubling the advertising apparently reduced the sales! This was, of course, not impossible, but all my other research showed that it was very unlikely. I still went ahead and doubled the advertising nationally, with all my fingers crossed, as were those of my directors – to take a gamble on that scale you need a board which is just as brave as you are. Sales *did*, in fact, increase by 10 per cent, which was enough to earn the company an extra £1 million a year – and me a promotion.

If you do have the misfortune to come into contact with market researchers, don't be overawed by their jargon. Just ask them what their damn statistics mean. Interpreting all that garbage is their job and they are failing in that job if they can't make the results intelligible to you. Beware of their pyrotechnics. The results, in terms that you understand, are all that matter.

Post-analysis

In addition, it is always worth analysing exactly what was the outcome of each of your campaigns. How many leads, and at what cost, did each generate? More important, how much business did they eventually produce?

With this information you will be well placed to run the most effective campaigns in the future.

Chapter 5

The Call

The subject of this chapter is expanded by some other writers (perhaps even by most others) to fill a whole book. Arguably they are right to do so, for it represents the basic essence of the sales professional's job, and of his skills. A sales professional might be less productive if he fails to meet the challenges described in the other chapters of this book, but he will be a sales professional in name only if he fails to handle his calls well. The call is still crucial to the role of the sales professional and to his enjoyment of it.

Having made these comments, however, this chapter will be somewhat *less* detailed and shorter than most of the others in this book. The reason for this is that it is the one chapter that should be almost purely a 'refresher'; you should know most of it already, and will probably be well practised (if not expert) in most of the techniques. I include a few extra ideas, but these are peripheral to the central task.

I stressed in the introduction that I had no intention of telling you how to sell. That is a skill that you will have developed by practical experience. By now you should have grown your own style, that you can wear comfortably. It would be presumptuous of me to instruct you in how to change that style, and unproductive for you to listen. So, unlike books which contain long lists of things you *must* do in a call, this chapter contains no *mandatory* lessons. You can safely ignore all of the suggestions, and still be just as good a sales professional as you are now.

Indeed, I have argued, as has Buck Rodgers, that only one thing is necessary to conduct perfect marketing. This is a 'philosophy'; in the case of sales professionals an 'attitude of mind'. This philosophy is quite simply: customer service. If you use it as your touchstone in selling in general, and for handling calls in particular, you can't go wrong.

If you want to read a book specifically on selling style, the one book that encapsulates the concept of customer service is Dale Carnegie's *How to Win Friends and Influence People*. I only discovered this work while researching for this book. Of course, like most sales professionals, I knew about it; but I had arrogantly dismissed it as 'populist'. It *is* very out of date in its examples, but the lessons it contains are still unbeatable in terms of coming face-to-face with customers and prospects.

For those of you who haven't yet found this gem, some of its major points (in selling terms) are:

'*Fundamental Techniques In Handling People*
Principle 1 – Don't criticise, condemn or complain.
Principle 2 – Give honest and sincere appreciation.
Principle 3 – Arouse in the other person an eager want.

Six Ways To Make People Like You
Principle 1 – Become genuinely interested in people.
Principle 2 – Smile.
Principle 3 – Remember that a person's name is to that person the sweetest and most important sound in the language.
Principle 4 – Be a good listener. Encourage others to talk about themselves.
Principle 5 – Talk in terms of the other person's interests.
Principle 6 – Make the other person feel important – and do it sincerely.

Win People To Your Way Of Thinking
Principle 1 – The only way to get the best of an argument is to avoid it.
Principle 2 – Show respect for the other person's opinions. Never say "You're wrong".
Principle 3 – If you are wrong, admit it quickly and emphatically.
Principle 4 – Begin in a friendly way.
Principle 5 – Get the other person saying "Yes, yes" immediately.
Principle 6 – Let the other person do a great deal of the talking
Principle 7 – Let the other person feel that the idea is his or hers.
Principle 8 – Try honestly to see things from the other person's point of view.
Principle 9 – Be sympathetic with the other person's ideas and desires.
Principle 10 – Appeal to the nobler motives.
Principle 11 – Dramatize your ideas.
Principle 12 – Throw down a challenge.

If you haven't come across the book before, you will still recognise many of the ideas; these, albeit uncredited, have been the staple diet of many later sales trainers. If you want to pursue them, I repeat that you can't do better than read the original (see bibliography).

There is, though, no one perfect style. Despite what many trainers would have you believe, there is no guaranteed golden path to success. To illustrate just some of the divergences of style that are possible, I include below Tony Adams' views on the two extremes of selling *he* experienced (from his book *The Secret of Successful Selling*). In the first of these he lists the eight lessons he learnt from door-to-door selling of encyclopaedias:

1. Make the calls.
2. Never sell on the doorstep.
3. Control the interview [eye-to-eye contact – never side by side].
4. Get agreement.
5. Get the order form out early.
6. Don't oversell.
7. Break down the price.
8. Get the order signed now.

In the second, on the other hand, he lists a very different four lessons he learnt from selling capital goods (refrigeration equipment):

1. Pre-planning and utilization of time.
2. Always selling to the decision-maker.
3. Always selling the real benefit, filling the need.
4. It was essential to get buyer's trust, never oversell, never lie and always keep a promise.

Most recently, one part of IBM has described its selling cycle as simply:

Find the need
Sell the solution
Satisfy the need

I would not presume to give my own rules; it would only add to the confusion. The objective of this current chapter is simply to provide a refresher on the key points; and, most important, to re-establish a perspective. It is all too easy as a sales professional to lapse into bad habits that are not an essential part of your selling style. It is, accordingly, a useful exercise to stand back and review what you are doing. *Don't* be worried that what you see is nothing like the ideal style purveyed by most pundits: in terms of how *you* sell, as opposed to how *they* sell (and would have you also sell), they cannot know what they are talking about. But, all the same, check if there are any aspects of your style that might be improved.

Preparing for the call

Once more, much of this chapter will emphasise the management, or more basically the admin, aspects of the job. Not because this is the essence of the call (clearly it is just about the least important aspect), but simply because it is the area where (in my experience) most sales professionals could *improve* their overall performance.

In *The IBM Way*, Buck Rodgers says unequivocally: 'I've never known a successful salesperson who doesn't do his homework before he calls on a customer.'

Developing the call plan

The most critical requirement of planning any call is to determine exactly *why* you are making it. What, exactly, do you want to come out of the meeting?

Campaign objectives
It may seem self-evident that the campaign objective is to make the sale. But *what* sale? No matter how clear-cut the initial requirements may seem, there is nearly always some room for debate; and, indeed, very few prospects have a definitive view of their real needs. It is sensible, therefore, to think through just what the desired end result really is likely to be and, more important, how you will attain it.

For example, Buck Rodgers stresses:

'When I'm asked "What products does IBM sell?" I answer "IBM doesn't sell products. It sells solutions." The answer may sound kind of flip, but its meaning is quite serious. People buy products for what they can do, not for what they are. They buy products to solve problems.'

Alternatively, Miller, Heiman and Tuleja stress:

'The objective of a good sales strategy is to get yourself in the *right place* with the *right people* at the *right time* so that you can tactically make the right presentation. The only way to accomplish that objective is to do your homework first: to log that desk time that so many people in sales resent, so that once you get into the actual selling event, you're certain to have everything you need to make the most effective presentation.'

Campaign plan

These objectives should lead to a plan for the whole campaign. Calls are inevitably free-form and fluid, so such a campaign plan will (almost by definition) be wrong in detail. Events will never develop exactly as you would wish, but you still need to provide a positive framework within which you can control the overall campaign. The details may change and sometimes the whole strategy may need to be abandoned, but at least you will be following a consistent course and will better control where you will be going.

The alternative, of no strategy at all, would mean that you would go into each call with no clearly defined idea of why you are there, other than a gut-feel that you want the order. From my experience as a buyer, that is exactly what the majority of salesmen really do. Very few salesmen indeed came into a meeting (or even left it) with a crisp idea of what was to be achieved. I was generally left with the feeling that, once I had *independently* decided what I wanted to do, I could place an order with them.

On the other hand, there were just a few that clearly set out to win my business. They pinned me down, they pursued me, and generally made me aware that they wanted my business. I found that I had considerable difficulty turning these sales professionals down, even when their offering was inferior to that of their competitors. Quite simply, I felt that they were interested in my business and in me. It is flattering for a buyer to feel that a sales professional wants his business, yet many salesmen appear to think that a buyer will feel threatened by such an outright approach.

I believe that John Fenton has the right idea, when he suggests that the most important question you can ask is: 'What do we need to do to get your business?' That is a *very* powerful question.

Timescales

One key aspect of your plan should be a projection of the various timescales. It is important that you pace yourself. If you throw everything into the first call of what will be a long campaign, you risk not having any sales messages to develop in later calls – and risk confusing the prospect with too many separate messages in that first call. On the other hand, you can't afford for the campaign to close unexpectedly with half your sales messages undelivered.

You will need to plan not just what to say and do, but *when*.

First call objectives

All of the above is a preamble to what is really important in terms of any one call: what are the specific objectives of that call? As you will have gathered, I believe that few salesmen really have such clear objectives. I myself learnt the lesson (as usual the hard way) early in my career. As a manager (not a sales professional) I was *en route* to a major customer, accompanied by my boss, John Cahill (now managing director of BTR, one of the larger multinationals). We spent the journey discussing the customer in some detail, for he was important to our business. Just as we were arriving at the customer, John asked me: 'Why are we here?' To my great embarrassment, I realised I didn't know! After the call, in which I did eventually find some objectives, John explained to me (in graphic detail) that nobody should ever go into a call without knowing *exactly* why he was there. It was a lesson I never forgot.

You must decide exactly what are your call objectives. Those objectives should normally be derived from your overall campaign plan, and should further that overall campaign. When I first started making calls I took the job very seriously, reviewing the objectives of upcoming calls over a number of days and making copious notes. I regret that more recently I have tended to finalise my objectives in the car on the way to the call, as do many other sales professionals (if, that is, they actually decide to choose some objectives).

I have found that with my considerable selling experience, this somewhat skimpy preparation is now generally sufficient, but this rather laid-back approach does embody at least one major gamble. If, on the way to the call, I realise that my objectives call for some additional back-up (for example, in the form of extra technical information or references) that I don't already have with me, the call is blown. I have to make a wasted or, at best, crippled call. So, before key calls I prepare fully and some time in advance, although I should do this for more calls. But even my skimped review of objectives in the car was a positive move; at least I had some objectives, where most sales professionals appear to have none at all.

John Fenton swears by extensive checklists. He believes you should go into every call with a prepared checklist, ready to tick off the items as you go along. He says, with justification, that this will ensure you cover *all* the points. I must admit that I have several times needed to call back to expand on points I had overlooked – and found the experience somewhat embarrassing. Even now, I believe it is an excellent discipline to *prepare* such a checklist, since it ensures that you think through all the implications of the call you are about to make.

Where I diverge from John Fenton is in his insistence that the checklist must be completed in the call. I believe that, at least for a sales professional, the prime task in the call is to listen and to follow where the prospect leads. A rigid checklist can induce a sales professional to adopt a blinkered approach that will not allow him to follow (or even recognise) critical responses from the prospect.

In any case, I soon found that my long checklist was really only a psychological prop, equivalent to the theatre prompter. Once I had developed the confidence in my performance, I found I didn't need these elaborate checklists, although I did still find it useful to have the objectives of the call listed. Checklists are a useful prop for the inexperienced, just so long as they don't actually use them!

References

One key piece of back-up you will need for a call is a set of relevant references. These are the most powerful supporting devices that you can field in a call. To be really effective, the references you use should be directly relevant to the prospect's business, and to his needs.

A successful sales professional will usually keep a library of references. He will develop his own (obtaining their formal permission to use them as references), and he will cajole his colleagues into letting him use theirs. As a result, he will be able to select the ones that most closely meet his prospect's needs. Too many sales professionals use the company's one or two standard references, regardless of how relevant to the prospect these are; on the basis that if it is good enough for ICI it must be good enough for anyone else, even if he is only a struggling insurance broker!

John Fenton suggests that you should have actual reference letters (testimonials in other words), not just a verbal reference. These might be a nice touch in the less sophisticated markets, but for many sales professionals (and their prospects) I suspect that they might be somewhat redolent of the double-glazing sale, with its list of satisfied customers. Worse, such testimonial letters are specific about what the reference liked or found useful, and this severely limits what you can say. A verbal reference, on the other hand, can be elaborated to include those aspects most relevant to the prospect's needs.

The opening

In some respects, the opening is the most critical part of any call. The first few minutes set the tone for all that follows. The impact of those first few moments has been most extensively documented in the context of job interviews, where it is reckoned that the decision is usually made within the first three or four minutes, the remaining time being used to justify that decision. The sales call is not as clear-cut as this, but those first few minutes are still critical.

The opening is also, in my experience, the most difficult part of the call. You are required to move very fast, to set the tone, but you are still not fully at ease. I always wished I could have entered the call about five minutes after it started, when it became fun!

Social niceties

It seems to be expected of sales professionals (at least by themselves) that they should start every call with a bouquet of social niceties. They talk about the weather, about sport, about television, about almost anything but business. If you really would feel uncomfortable about starting a call without these social niceties, then by all means employ them; the prospects have come to expect them, and anything that puts you at your ease early in the call is worthwhile. But do, as soon as possible, get down to business.

I had one sales professional whose calls consisted purely of social niceties, deliberately so; he believed that prospects gave their business to nice guys and refused to waste his time on inessentials such as the technicalities of our products. I even once found him avidly diverting a prospect with a long conversation about golf, just when I had closed that prospect and wanted him to sign the order. Needless to say, that sales professional was one of the nicest guys I have worked with – and the least successful!

Alfred Tack refers to these introductory niceties as the chat gap, and he, too, stresses that the best sales professionals aim to minimise this unproductive gap. Heinz Goldmann is rather more brutal: 'A salesman is not a travelling storyteller or a wandering minstrel. Buffoonery is not salesmanship.' IBM is more straightforward, it now sometimes characterises the opening as 'earning the right'.

Getting down to business

There is often no real need for anything but the briefest of social niceties, although you must still follow the social conventions and, for example, wait for the prospect to invite you to sit down. But the one thing that you are certain you and the prospect have in common is not golf, or a love of television soap-operas: it is his *business*. The one justification for you being there, and hopefully not wasting the prospect's time, is again his business. So the sooner you get down to business the better for all concerned.

Alfred Tack makes the astute observation, 'never attempt to sell under adverse conditions', though he adds, 'but be sure the conditions are adverse – don't jump to conclusions'.

For Tack, the specific context of these 'adverse conditions' is where a sales professional finds that a call is about to take place standing in a corridor, or in any other unsuitable location. But the comments apply just as well in any circumstances. If the prospect, for whatever reason, won't be able to give you the necessary attention, politely close the call ('to allow him to concentrate on the urgent matters at hand') and make another appointment.

I once had to make *four* calls on one prospect before he was in the right frame of mind, but I did eventually get his undivided attention. It would be pleasant to recount that I then made a big sale, but unfortunately we agreed that he didn't need my product! On the other hand, he did direct me to a colleague who became one of my best customers, so perhaps the effort was finally rewarded.

Getting attention

Alfred Tack stresses that the most important task is gaining the prospect's attention. He suggests six specific rules:

1. Never sell under adverse conditions.
2. Don't gabble; always speak slowly so that the buyer can hear every word.
3. Keep the CHAT GAP as short as possible.
4. Make certain that you have worked out the best possible opening sentence, based on:
   a) factual opening
   b) question opening
   c) reference opening
   d) sales aid opening
   e) demonstration opening.

5. When calling back, make sure that you get attention by using any of the standard openings, or a LINK opening.
6. Always remember, the objective of the opening is to obtain the undivided attention of the buyer.

I prefer to view this introduction more simply as 'justifying the call'. The prospect needs to know why you are there, so tell him. Hopefully, this will grab his attention; if it doesn't you have an uphill battle on your hands. Above all, you need to let him know that you want his business, and what that means. Best of all finish this part of the call with John Fenton's question: 'What do we need to do to get the business?'

Agreeing objectives

The logical extension to this question is to *agree* with the prospect exactly what you need to do in the call. It is normal in a stand-up presentation to show your audience an agenda so that they know where you will be taking them, but I have rarely come across any equivalent in a call. On the few occasions where I have, that call has usually gone very well; the sales professional has remained in control and I have been propelled inexorably towards signing the order. If you are confident of your standing in the call it *is* a powerful technique, although it can be something of a gamble in a first call, where the objectives may change considerably as the call progresses.

Questioning

In my opinion, the one selling skill that differentiates the most professional and most successful salesmen is that of questioning. It is the reverse of what the stereotype would have you believe. The stereotype would not let his victim get a word in edgeways, let alone positively question him. Yet questioning lies at the centre of the professional sales call, and the success of the outcome is largely dependent on how successful that questioning is.

As Buck Rodgers says in *The IBM Way*:

> 'An IBM marketing rep's success depends totally on his ability to understand a prospect's business so well that he can identify and analyze its problems and then come up with a solution that makes sense to the customer. Don't be surprised if that solution involves an IBM system, but it doesn't always.'

As a result, the one skill I concentrated on teaching my IBM trainees was how to question. It is an art that few, apart from sales professionals, share. It is also, in my experience, one of the joys of selling. Achieving a successful conclusion to your call is a particularly satisfying experience.

The right attitude

Once more, the key to success is largely the right attitude. It is very difficult, if not impossible, to question a prospect successfully if you are merely deploying another sales technique and are not genuinely interested in his answers, as is the case with some of the 'pseudo-questions' that are part of many feature/benefit approaches. You must want to know the answer and, as in truth the sale may depend on it, you have every reason to be eager for the answer.

The most positive attitude comes simply from being interested in his business, and in him. It is crucial to selling success, and in particular to questioning. Genuine interest and enthusiasm conveys itself to the prospect, making questioning much easier and more natural. Such interest is not just academic, however, for it achieves a much better understanding of the customer and his business and, hence, where every bit of potential for the product lies.

At the same time you have to develop a fascination for the prospect as an individual. In practice, once more, this is not a fascination with him as a social animal; you need to be fascinated by what he does. This may be difficult to achieve when you are talking to the tenth admin clerk who is enthusing about his precious paperwork, but even then the thought that his support will help you to get the order should perk you up. Fortunately, most managers (but not all) *do* have interesting jobs (and ones very directly linked to your order), so it is not unduly difficult to build up an interest; and, most importantly, *show* it.

Indeed, one of the most important features of your questioning is that you should show interest. Questioning then has the dual benefits of unearthing the points that you will develop into your most powerful sales messages, and building rapport – and it is often the latter that is the greater benefit.

Relaxed selling

One of Alfred Tack's main messages is that a sales professional sells best when he is relaxed. After six years' experience of selling he was still a bad salesman. At that point he met a Frenchman named Simon whose sales abilities impressed him immensely. In particular, the whole thrust of Tack's career was changed by Simon's statement about his style, that he and most salesmen 'would improve if they *stopped* selling'.

Based on this thought Tack now redefines selling as, 'the gentle art of giving other people your own way'.

More immediately, Tack and his brother then proceeded to

develop what he calls 'relaxed selling', because 'a tense buyer never buys'. As a result he pays significant attention to relaxation techniques.

His thoughts on this subject are particularly relevant to questioning, since this is the time when it is easiest to achieve a relaxed rapport with the prospect. The prospect relaxes and so do you, the conversation starts to flow naturally, and the call starts to be the fun that it should always be.

Structuring the call

Even so, you shouldn't relax so much that you lose control of the call. Above all, don't lose sight of your objectives; which is why it is useful to have them on your notepad, in front of you.

There are many different structures suggested as to how sales professionals should handle a call. Of these, perhaps the best known is AIDA: attention, interest, desire, action.

There are many other similar acronyms. Interestingly, Alfred Tack (who quotes AIDA) discounts such sales formulae: 'After many years of teaching and research we know that separate steps no longer apply.' He does add: 'Nevertheless, a salesman must have guidelines if his presentation is not to lose impact.' So he produces his own acronym, ABC: attention, benefits, close.

Of all the suggestions, I suspect that his is the best, but only because it is the simplest. Best of all don't follow acronyms, follow your own judgement and the logic of the call itself.

My own faith in acronyms was somewhat shaken in the mid-1970s when IBM's new information system, called 'Branch Utilisation of Common Knowledge', soon earned itself the (somewhat justified) reputation of passing the BUCK. However, even that was preferable to the previous name (which was changed at the last minute, very expensively, as much of the material had already been printed) of 'Field Utilisation of Common Knowledge'.

Qualifying

Two questions you need to ask very early in the call, of yourself rather than the prospect, are: 'Will this prospect generate worthwhile business? Is this call itself worthwhile?'

Qualification is a central feature of prospect management, and accordingly of the questioning process. Too many sales professionals ask the question, 'What business might there be?', but not the question '*Is* there business realistically available?', or the even more difficult question, 'Will this business be worthwhile?'

Enthusiasm is a great virtue for a sales professional, but so is discretion. Knowing where best to apply that enthusiasm is the basis of productive selling. Thus, questioning needs to be positively used to separate the sheep from the goats; to decide just which prospects to pursue. Any unnecessary resource devoted to prospects who will fail to deliver the goods is wasted. The sooner you identify them, and discreetly unload them, the better you can utilise you resources on more productive accounts. It is important to recognise the losers, and as soon as possible, as well as the winners.

Miller, Heiman and Tuleja's view is that:

'The reason that up to 35 percent of the prospective business in most people's Sales Funnels [their analogy for the numbers game] at any given time is poor is that these sales representatives lack a dynamic, field-tested, process for analysing their customers needs.'

Qualification was one of the keys to IBM's sales success. As a company it always had too few sales professionals, so they were overloaded with work and, in particular, with prospects. The only way they could function at all was by very rigorously sorting out the most productive prospects and ruthlessly discarding the less productive ones. I have attended calls with IBM sales professionals on prospects which other companies' salesmen would have given their eye teeth for, for just the chance of a contact. Yet the IBM sales professional deliberately dropped the business; not because he couldn't eventually close it, but because it would be relatively difficult to close and he could use the same resource to close two or three times the amount of business elsewhere.

If you are similarly lucky, and have been given a rich territory (or, more likely, developed one), the main question should be: could I bring in more business by putting in this effort elsewhere? It is a very difficult decision for a sales professional to make, but only if he ruthlessly qualifies his prospects and manages his resources to concentrate them on the most productive accounts will he maximise his sales. The greatest sales success usually comes not from sales persuasion but from resource management, and expert qualification is at the heart of this.

As Tom Hopkins, in *How to Master the Art of Selling*, says (of most sales professionals, who do not qualify):

'Their problem is that they try to close the wrong people too often and too hard. In other words, they don't fail to close, they fail to qualify ... Champions know better. They know that qualification is the key to high production ... The primary difference is that your sales are 500 percent greater with qualified leads than they are with the non-qualified type.'

Qualify your objectives
It is, of course, just as important to qualify your *objectives* when you do identify a potential winner. The 'campaign objectives' with which you enter the first call are inevitably based on guesswork. The sooner you get these objectives exactly right, the sooner (and more likely) you are to get the business.

This can actually be a very difficult task, particularly where the potential business could be large. This is one reason why it is advisable for the most senior marketing management not to be *too* personally involved in individual sales; the amount of personal commitment required of a sales professional (whatever his level in the organisation) is so high that it can easily warp his judgement.

Questioning techniques
I will break my vow not to promote specific techniques, in this one area. Questioning is so important to the sales professional that I believe it cannot be overstressed.

Open questions
The most important and productive questions are the open ones, which allow the prospect to ramble on about his needs. They also seem to be the most difficult for a sales professional to ask, perhaps because they are not so obviously leading directly to the sale, or maybe because the sales professional feels less in control. But they are the key to unlocking the prospect's tongue. If the conversation proceeds with very short replies (and particularly just 'yes' or 'no') from the prospect, you are probably not using enough open questions and may be missing his real needs.

The more open the question the better. I found that the most powerful question in my armoury was 'Why?', often closely followed by 'How?'; the most powerful combination of all being in the 'trial close' (described later in this chapter) where the question of 'Why (won't you sign the order yet)?' is followed by 'How can we resolve that?' In practice, open questions come naturally if you are genuinely interested in finding out what makes the prospect's business tick. I found that using open questions was usually the most relaxing and enjoyable part of any call.

Even if sales professionals do ask the correct open questions, they often undermine the progress by stopping the prospect in mid-flow. The natural accompaniment to an open question is *silence*. John Fenton summed it up succinctly in his book, when he said:

'Whenever you ask a question (especially closing) SHUT UP. After 6-7 seconds of silence REPEAT QUESTION. Silence is very effective. Don't let him off the hook because you are embarrassed by the silence.'

In the specific area of closing, Tom Hopkins makes a similar point: 'Whenever you ask a closing question shut up. The first person to speak loses.'

Silence is probably one of the most underused of selling devices. It is, though, a surprisingly aggressive technique, and you should not make it *too* obvious – it is best just to look very thoughtful. It requires a great deal of courage to use, particularly for a sales professional who is supposed to be all mouth. But it is effective. The prospect will eventually feel *obliged* to talk, and usually (at least in my experience) what he then says is especially enlightening (since he too will have had time to consider).

Reflective questions
This is sometimes thought of as a separate category of open questions. These are questions, typically open questions, which are used to develop or clarify what has been discovered by the initial questions. They are designed to reflect on what has been said and give it some consideration or further thought.

Closed questions
These questions, typically requiring the answer 'yes' or 'no', have (justifiably) received a bad press. But it is still necessary to use them quite extensively to clarify points. The problem only comes when they are used instead of open questions.

Directive questions
These are a form of closed (or partially closed) questions which are designed to steer the conversation in the direction you wish it to go. Typical examples are: 'If you could …', 'Do you …', 'Would you …'

Agreement
By far the most important closed questions (and arguably the most

important questions of all) are those where you check for agreement. As the call progresses, it is imperative that you establish whether or not you are taking the prospect with you; or is he, as is all too often the case, politely acting out the role of audience to your orator?

In the same context, you can (and should) ask questions to establish the prospect's attitude. As Miller, Heiman and Tuleja say:

> 'Questions about attitude are always appropriate; they should never be regarded as prying. Because they help you to probe beyond the product to each individual Buyer's Wins [his real buying wants].'

Listening

The necessary corollary of questioning is listening. This is not the passive act of hearing. It is the very positive act of listening; of interpreting and understanding what you hear.

Two-thirds listening

It is conventionally reckoned that a good sales professional should should spend two-thirds of his time listening and only one-third talking; again the reverse of the stereotype. This is probably the ideal ratio to aim for, although the particular ratio will vary with the specific conditions.

What is important is how you use that time. I had one sales professional who was a superb listener; his prospects loved to talk to him. But he was never able productively to use the information he was given and he eventually gave up selling. It is the *quality* of the listening (which has much to do with how you analyse what you hear) that is as important as the quantity; a factor that most sales training pundits overlook.

For example, I probably spent about two-thirds of the time talking, and only one-third listening; a fault which I well knew, but which was not fatal because I used my listening time very well. I gained more insight from that one-third than some others did from their two-thirds. As the call progressed, I pondered over everything the prospect said, analysing it and building a cohesive picture. If I couldn't make sense of the picture I was not afraid to question until I could – in which case I *did* spend most of my time listening.

Let him sell to you

The best technique, once you have developed the necessary level of skill, is to let the prospect sell to you. Let him persuade you to take the order! It sounds like a fairy-tale but it can sometimes be achieved. If you really are in full rapport with the prospect, you can carefully ask him what *he* wants, and (with skill) guide him to what *you* want. It is, as Tack said, 'the gentle art of giving other people your own way'.

This is a technique that I increasingly came to use, as my confidence grew. At first I was afraid to lose control; afraid that the prospect would choose a lesser solution than my hard sell would win for me. But I found that this didn't happen. If anything, the prospects persuaded themselves to go for more than I would have set as my own highest target. Indeed, one very sophisticated technique I used was to try apparently to persuade them to reduce their ambitions. Needless to say, they resisted this and even escalated the size of their orders; and, of course, I eventually let them have their way!

Forget your objectives
One prerequisite for effective listening is that you must be prepared (temporarily) to put aside your objectives, if you are to understand all the nuances of the prospect's replies. He (fortunately) doesn't know what your objectives are, and will accordingly tell you what he believes is important. You ignore his comments at your peril, no matter how far removed from your own objectives – and, in fact, *particularly* if they are far from your objectives.

Taking notes
I always take notes in a call, but only after asking permission. There is, however, a peculiar reluctance on the part of some sales professionals to take notes. Perhaps they believe that their prospects will object. All I can say is that I have *never* had a prospect refuse; and I can't see why they would – after all, you can still remember what has been said. On the other hand, using a tape recorder in a call does seem to be objectionable to many prospects and, anyway it can take an inordinate length of time to decipher after the call.

When I first started I took copious notes, not wishing to miss a word. But I found that in practice I never consulted these, and writing so extensively actually distracted me from analysing what was happening in the call. I soon discovered that it was only the critical elements, which I abstracted when reviewing the call later, that were really important – the rest was a morass of detail. Now I rely almost exclusively on my memory, until I make the key notes after I have left the call. I do, though, still make some notes of the central points, of the facts and agreements that really count, just in case I forget them before I make my review notes.

I still do, however, go through the motions of apparently making notes, even though I really don't need most of them. I believe that prospects expect it and feel that I am not taking them seriously enough if I don't record their words for posterity. You don't just need to be interested in your prospects; you have to make them well aware of your interest.

Understanding

As indicated in the previous section, hearing, and even listening, is not enough. The key to the professional sale is understanding. This is a process to which the main contribution must, of course, be what the prospect says; although this will include what he said in a number of previous meetings as well as in the current one. But it will also include all the other evidence you have unearthed. Put it all together and, hopefully, you will be able to complete the jigsaw.

Understanding is, therefore, a cumulative process that may span *several* calls. It is, I believe, a fundamental skill of the sales professional. Yet it is almost totally ignored by other writers, who concentrate on the single call and the instant reaction – and do not allow for the *sequence* of calls which typically lead to the sale.

One writer who does appreciate the need for understanding is Alan Williams:

> 'Very often the buyer will not be absolutely clear about his needs. Of course he knows he has a problem, otherwise he wouldn't be discussing the matter. However, that doesn't mean to say he knows precisely what the problem is. The salesman who can specifically identify it for him, and also come up with the most effective and imaginative solution, must surely be well ahead of his competitors.'

Analyse what you hear

As mentioned previously, it is the quality of your listening, not just the quantity, that is critical. Analysis is central to this quality. Ideally this analysis takes place as the call progresses. But this takes a great deal of effort, even when listening, and may divert your attention to such an extent that you miss critical facts. This has happened to me several times; and I have had the embarrassing task of asking a prospect to repeat a whole section of his comments. Analysis is almost impossible when you are talking – another good reason for listening instead. The best compromise is to take copious notes (unless you have an excellent memory) and analyse what you have heard after the meeting.

At leisure, therefore, you can (and should) analyse what was said. I normally carried out this post-analysis in the car on the way back to the office. The matter was fresh in my mind, although (while driving) I obviously had to rely only on my memory rather than the notes. I then completed my analysis and made my final summary (review) notes when I was at my desk. I also, at that time, finished my report with a draft plan of action for the next call, including all the questions I now wished I had asked in the call just completed!

These belated questions can and should be asked at the next meeting. You will find that the prospect will be flattered that you have taken his business (and him) seriously enough to ponder over what was said last time. He is used to a startling degree of indifference from most sales professionals; just *asking* questions that show your grasp of previous meetings will impress him, and build that essential rapport.

In practice, missing questions usually does not prove fatal, just so long as you *do* ask them at the next meeting. If, however, the business is lost before that next meeting you will have to grin and bear it, and live to fight another day. But do learn from your mistakes.

Hidden motives

Perhaps the main reason for such analysis is to establish hidden motives. Maybe these motives are hidden by accident: you didn't ask the correct question, or didn't listen well enough to the answer. I found that my post-analyses showed that almost all my calls contained some omissions (fortunately normally only minor ones); selling strength lies in *always* rectifying these on the next call.

Often, though, the prospect *wanted* to hide these motives. Sometimes I was being called in merely to provide the nominal respectability of having a second supplier, where the decision had really already been taken. This was particularly obvious where I received an 'invitation to tender', which many sales professionals would enthuse about, but which I normally perused with a somewhat jaundiced eye. Many, if not most, of these documents were clearly written with a specific product in mind; tendering was a necessary admin procedure but was unrelated to the decision, which had as good as been taken already. (This reached its ludicrous extreme when I received a solemn request to tender for an 'IBM 2997 Cell Separator', which only I could supply!)

In these cases it was important to appreciate the facts; otherwise, I could have wasted considerable resources chasing business that was already lost – as many sales professionals do. Indeed, a number of times I *was* fooled this way.

A particular problem in the personal computer business is that some prospects will happily promise you the business, until you have put in considerable effort to work out the correct solution for them. Then they will simply put your proposed configuration out for tender to other (cheaper) vendors. Unfortunately, it is often very difficult to unmask such fraudsters before it is too late. There is, however, no reason to repeat the error, as I have known some sales professionals do.

In other, more important, cases (which could be won) the prospect was simply diffident about putting his real views forward. He felt himself at a disadvantage (an amateur against experts), or just distrusted sales professionals (with good cause). Whatever the reason, it is clearly important to find out what the prospect truly thinks. This is, perhaps, most evident among those prospects who firmly claim that price is all; superficially, at least, an eminently defensible position. But I have usually discovered that there are far more complex motives involved.

One of my personal computer sales professionals was desperate because one potential £40,000 sale was as good as lost to a competitive bid of £30,000 for a system that was adequate, although ours was better. A couple of calls, and some in-depth analyses, revealed that the prospect's business revolved around two crucial factors. The first, and most important, was (unusually as a main business factor) the high quality of his data processing. The second was the accuracy of his laboratory equipment; he had just spent nearly £500,000 to buy the best analyser for a task that was only run once a week. I deduced, correctly, that he would never choose a computer solution that was anything less than the best and, in these circumstances, the £10,000 difference was (in his terms) almost trivial.

Missed targets
One simple but important question to be asked in any post-analysis is: did I achieve everything I had planned? If the answer is 'no' (and it usually is), then you need to ask: why, and were the omissions important? Every situation is fluid, and objectives can rapidly change.

The detective mystery
I like to think of my sales campaigns as akin to a good detective story. Instead of a whodunit, though, the mystery here is: what needs

to be done? I find it a stimulating intellectual challenge, a very good motive in itself for spending time on the analysis – and the winning of the business is a bonus.

Putting together your analysis should be much like detective work; painstakingly sifting all the clues, not neglecting even the smallest pieces of evidence, to build the overall picture that makes sense of the jigsaw. Often this will be an extended process, covering a number of calls, and a careful on-going analysis is essential to link them together. Many of my IBM campaigns ran over two to three years, with dozens of calls. Bringing all this material together was an intellectual challenge that I found very stimulating – which is one of the pleasures I find in professional selling.

Body language
There has been much written about this subject, mainly populist and simplistic, but it is true that the body language in a call is as eloquent as the words and, indeed, often swamps the words. You can to an extent disguise your words, but it is very difficult to camouflage the true meaning of your body postures. You can make all the correct noises of wanting to help the prospect, but if a stiff, tense body posture says otherwise he probably won't believe you.

The only solution I have found is to *live* what you say. This is where enjoying a call pays dividends. You actually *have* to be interested in what the prospect says, and enthusiastic about it, if you want your body language to convince the prospect of this. In my experience, any attempt to falsify body language (no matter how carefully implemented) looks unnatural, and just makes the prospect wary.

Perhaps the most important part of the body, in this context, is the eyes. Eye contact is a critical part of any call, and you cannot afford to miss it by spending too much time looking at your notes.

Relationship
The essence of body language is to develop a positive relationship with your prospect. For a while in IBM this 'partnership' was seen to be best achieved by finding some pretext to sit on the same side of the desk as the prospect, so that the sales professional was physically, as well as metaphorically, on the same side as the prospect. It was a noble thought, but utterly impractical in use. The gymnastics necessary to share the constricted space behind the desk were sometimes hilarious to watch; and, if nothing else, it destroyed the all-important eye contact. But the idea that you are 'spiritually' (if not

physically) on the same side of the desk is a powerful concept, well worth cultivating. It also makes the calls that much easier to enjoy, for both you and the prospect.

Disagreement

One aspect of body language you have to be particularly careful to control is that of disagreement. In many calls there will come a time when you disagree, sometimes strongly, with what the prospect says; but you must be careful not to show this too obviously. When you feel the phrase, 'with the greatest respect ...' about to overcome you, relax and discreetly ignore the comment – and save the sale.

Boredom

Worst of all is boredom. There is nothing quite so demoralising for a prospect than to feel he is boring a sales professional to whom he might give an order. It is an unforgivable insult by the sales professional, no matter how unintentional it is. Fortunately, few sales professionals actually make their boredom obvious, even in body language, but just occasionally they do so unintentionally. If they have had a rough night before this can sometimes show (typically by an occasional yawn; ever so discreet, but never quite discreet enough). The prospect may be forgiven for interpreting this as boredom, particularly as it is usually accompanied by a distinct lack of concentration on the matters at hand. The moral is: if you have got to make a particularly important call, think twice about carousing too much and too long the night before.

Visual aids

At one level, visual aids are the psychological prop of the inex-perienced and poor sales professionals. When I began my sales career I used to enter calls with a large briefcase crammed full with brochures. The theory was that if I ever got into trouble, I only had to sort through this briefcase to find the answer, although how I could have found anything in front of the prospect out of all that material, I don't know. In practice, I never used this material at all, and at the end of my first year this was reduced to just one or two brochures, specifically selected as relevant to that call; and yet I found I still didn't use even these!

Some sales professionals, however, swear by them. For example, in his book Tom Hopkins goes as far as to say:

'... we find that people who make the greatest use of

company-provided visual aids are the top producers. The ones who make the least use of them are the sellers in the cellar, the bottom boys, the ones who never make quota and change jobs most often.'

There is some justification in what he says, in terms of the less skilled sales professionals, although even then, I think his position is somewhat extreme. I personally believe that in many respects, almost the exact reverse is true in the complex sales that are the province of the professional salesman.

Brochures
Many poor sales professionals are forever thrusting brochures on their prospects. Indeed, in the case of personal computer dealers, the topics that their junior salesmen feel capable of handling seem inextricably linked to the brochures they have in stock. I have gone into a dealership to try to buy a word-processing package and come out clutching brochures on a spreadsheet, simply because that was all the salesman had available and, consequently, all he felt able to talk about!

In reality, brochures are at best a mixed blessing, and are often counter-productive when used in a call. Brochures are inevitably written for a general audience, not for the very specific needs of your prospect. Even very good brochures, and there are very few of these, are usually alien to the specific messages emerging in a call. To abdicate to them responsibility for at least part of the call, as do many salesmen who thrust a brochure at the prospect, is to admit defeat.

Some brochures (even then very carefully selected) are useful to sprinkle around at events, and to send out in mailings. But the occasions you can profitably use them in calls are very limited. The one area where I can see brochures being of particular use is the very specialised one of 'catalogue' selling. As part of this type of sale, you need to allow the prospect to choose between different alternatives, and a good visual explanation of these alternatives will be a great help. Even at a very sophisticated (professional sales) level, though, it has its place. The one brochure I swore by in IBM was actually a loose-leaf book full of examples of all the reports that the various programs were capable of producing. The prospect could thus see exactly what he would be getting.

In more general usage, brochures may contain the best photographs of the product (if that is important), or good diagrams of how it works. In which case, my advice is to clip out these useful elements and mount them in a 'flogging book'; a book with transparent leaves into which can be inserted A4, letter-size illustrations.

There are a number of serious problems, in terms of using brochures in a call. The first is that prospects naturally expect to be able to pick them up and look at them; and once a prospect starts reading it, or thumbing through its pages, you have lost control of the call – the brochure has taken over. This is one reason why I suggest using the flogging book instead; prospects do not seem to expect to be able to take the same liberties with this.

The second problem is that even excellent illustrations are almost inevitably associated with long paragraphs of description; which tempt the prospect into reading them (wasting time and again losing control) – another reason for just clipping out the relevant parts (excluding the text, for example) of the diagram and using it in a flogging book.

The third problem is that a brochure (particularly an interesting one) allows the prospect to divert his attention. As a buyer, I have often been grateful for the offer of an interesting brochure, as it allowed me to occupy myself while the boring salesman droned on interminably.

Relevance
The fourth problem of brochures is that they are not usually relevant. Their writers have inevitably needed to hit a wide, very general target. They have to be all things to all people, whereas you need to be quite specific with your prospect.

Indeed, the crucial requirement of any visual aid in a call is that it should be directly relevant. Salesmen are far too often seduced by the superficial attraction of very expensive visual aids into using them where they are not needed. As a personal computer dealer, I was often recommended to provide each of our sales professionals with the ultimate in visual aids, a laptop personal computer which they could carry into every call. This would have allowed them to demonstrate products immediately. We steadfastly resisted this temptation, even though it would clearly have shown the expertise of our sales professionals. Once again, the problem was that the demonstration would have taken over from the call.

Nothing, not even the best visual aid, should be allowed to get in the way of the call itself.

Samples

I suppose there are products where actually putting a sample in the hands of the customer is important to the sale. Certainly, buyers of furniture may want to see samples of the fabrics. Even in computing, my prospects found sample reports useful. But in general, the product itself doesn't add a great deal to the call; although, if it fits into your pocket or briefcase, there is no harm in taking it with you. But beware, the call may once more turn into a demonstration. If that is what you want, and have prepared for (see Chapter 9), then that is fine. But it does mean that you are no longer following the rules of a good call, and are losing its special benefits.

Leaving material

There is just one rule: *don't*! Companies burden their sales professionals down with brochures in great numbers, and their sales professionals feel honour-bound to use them (even if their management don't insist that they use them) to justify the high cost of their production. So, just as they are getting up to leave the call, these sales professionals press on the prospect a wadge of material, usually with the words: 'I am sure you will find something in there that you will like.' In so doing they have lost control of not just the call but probably the whole sales campaign.

In the weeks between the sales professional's relatively short visits, the prospect will be able to peruse these brochures and put his own interpretation to them, without the distraction of the sales professional's explanation of them. Are they as glossily produced and as easy to read as those of the competitors? Are all the main points more or less identical? Does your product have the 10 extra features that your competitor has built in? These features may be irrelevant, but by opting for 'trial by brochure' you have agreed to accept the judgement.

There are arguably two exceptions to this rule. The first is where the prospect is not currently in the market, but might be in the future. Leaving a well-produced catalogue of what you offer might mean that your name would be available to him (in his files) when he does finally decide to order. But better still, mail him the catalogue later (at a time when he might be better placed to order) and keep on mailing him regularly (even if it is only every six months).

The second exception might be where a prospect wants to show his colleagues what you are offering. Here, the preferable answer is: 'I'd love to come and talk to them.' If this is impossible, then there might be some justification for leaving a brochure for him to show them. It has to be an excellent brochure; well written and produced, simple and to the point (the specific point you are selling). Furthermore, you should *teach* him how to use it on his colleagues. Finally, you should be sure that he is 100 per cent enthusiastic about your product and is willing, and able, to answer his colleagues' objections.

On further thought, there *is* only one rule: *don't leave material with the prospect*!

The 'pencil sell'

I have been somewhat scathing about the use of visual aids in general (apart from the flogging book); perhaps unfairly so – I *have* seen a few sales professionals use them well, but they were in a small minority. But one type of visual aid *is*, I believe, one of the most powerful but underused sales devices available. It is also the simplest. It only relies on the use of a pencil and a pad of paper (the one on which you are, in any case, making notes).

If you really do need a visual, draw it yourself! This will inevitably mean that the visual is very simple, but that is exactly what it should be. It will not be cluttered up with irrelevancies; it should just be a powerful, very specific visualisation of what you are talking about. Clearly, such visuals will be restricted to diagrams or lists. Listing the benefits in this way is a very powerful way of consolidating them in your prospect's mind.

Mind you, you must know your way around any diagrams you intend to draw. However, that is just as true of any visual aid. Inexperienced sales professionals may feel that they will be protected by the self-explanatory nature of brochures, but in reality these lead such sales professionals further and further out of their depth.

The other, particularly powerful, effect of a pencil sell is that it involves the prospect. He watches, and can often be persuaded to participate in, the production of the visual. Even better, he has to lean forward and work alongside you; both *sharing* the same piece of working paper. It is a superb way to establish rapport. There is no need to draw upside down (as some sales professionals do); it is difficult, and it doesn't allow you to get alongside the prospect.

As you may have gathered, I believe that the pencil sell by itself redeems all the shortcomings of other visual aids. One specific pencil sell is worth a thousand general brochures, and might even help you to win the business.

Agreeing 'milestones'

As the call progresses, it is imperative that you constantly seek for agreement. Make certain that the prospect really *does* agree with what you are saying. I have known a number of prospects who would nod in agreement (out of politeness, or just by habit) even if they hadn't the vaguest idea what I was saying – so specifically ask if they agree.

At critical points, 'milestones' where one or more of your objectives has (you think) been achieved, summarise what the position is and very clearly ask for agreement. This will ensure that your call progresses in a controlled manner. It will also ensure that the prospect gets into the habit of agreeing with you, and will do the same when you come to the close!

Types of buyer

There is almost a cottage industry providing categories (or, more honestly, pigeon-holes) for buyers. Alan Gillam describes seven types:

The Brusque Business Like Buyer The Dictatorial Buyer
The Hesitant Buyer The Overfamiliar Buyer
The Busy Buyer The Uncommunicative Buyer
The Hostile Buyer

After quoting Jung's division of people into three categories (thinking, feeling and intuitive) Alfred Tack even manages no less than 18 categories, spread over two groups:

MANAGING DIRECTORS
 Self Effacing Self Denigrating
 Strong Man Kindly & Friendly
 Short & Sharp Sharpshooter
DIFFICULT BUYERS
 Talkative Buyer Too Friendly Buyer
 The Buyer Who is The Bluffer
  Scared of Buying Taciturn Buyer
 Stubborn Buyer Busy Buyer
 Mr Pompous Mr Shy
 Sarcastic Buyer Old & Experienced
 Young

I prefer not to pigeon-hole. At any one time, in any one call, I have just one buyer and I concentrate on finding out what makes him as a unique individual (not a pigeon-hole) tick.

Objection handling

It seems to me that many writers, having spent most of the first half of their books on features/benefits, fill the second half with handling objections. They, and many sales professionals, appear to be obsessed with objections.

In fairness, it should be pointed out that much of sales training originated in the field of selling to retail outlets, where the one-call sell (and then perhaps only a 15-minute call) was a matter of sheer survival. In these specific circumstances effective objection handling is important; there is no time for the niceties, or the sale is lost. But professional selling is a rather different game, often extending over several calls, and certainly using calls in a much more complex manner.

I should also point out that my own views would be considered idiosyncratic by most sales trainers. You must, as always, decide for yourself with what styles and techniques you are comfortable and productive.

I would agree with Alan Williams when he says, in *All About Selling*, that:

> 'It is unfortunate that the term "sales objection" has somehow crept into the selling vocabulary without being identified as the negative expression it really is, responsible for much self-inflicted, irrational anxiety for many salesmen. There is seldom such a thing as a sales objection! ... It should be welcomed as a clear indication of the buyer's interest and involvement! ... The sales objection should always be seen for what it really is — a plea for more information.'

Tom Hopkins makes a similar comment:

> 'Objections are the rungs of the ladder to sales success ... you'll learn to love objections — because they announce buying intention and point the way to closing the sale.'

Alfred Tack also comments that 'Salesmen are sometimes given the advice: Welcome objections, they prove the buyer is interested and wants more information.' However, he goes on to shoot down this advice: 'They obviously do not differentiate between MAJOR objections and INFORMATION-SEEKING objections.'

He also says: 'The best technique ... is not to let the objection arise.' *This* is the approach I would back. I never handled objections, because I never had any. If I had gone looking for them no doubt I could have found them. But I never looked, because my sales style was essentially positive. Even using the term 'objections', I believe, puts a sales professional in the wrong frame of mind. It immediately relegates the whole sales call to an adversarial game of verbal tennis, instead of concentrating on helping the prospect. I believe that he should be on the same side of the net as the prospect; this automatically makes verbal tennis impossible.

It was noticeable that inexperienced IBM trainees delighted in smashing back any objection that I (as an instructor, entitled to think in terms of objections!) fed them. Much of the conventional training in objection handling is designed to slow down these retaliatory reflexes. In such matters I believe it is preferable to be a pacifist and refuse to fight in the first place.

This is why, despite Tack's condemnation, I favour the approach of welcoming objections; after all, you really have no alternative! If you positively welcome them, you will be in the right frame of mind to handle them, whereas if you immediately go on the defensive, or even worse on the attack, the objection has severely weakened your sales position.

Information seeking
The fact is that, in my experience, most of the 'objections' that sales professionals fight are nothing more than innocent questions. Most buyers, once you have established a good rapport with them, have no reason to score points off you. On the other hand, as a buyer you can easily detect which are the weakest points of almost any sales professional's offering, quite simply by noting which of your innocent questions provokes a barrage of response – such overkill almost always hides weakness. Buyers are interested in what they are buying, and will ask many questions, not a few of them difficult and complex. But that is good, because it shows they are still interested.

If you positively welcome these questions (not objections), you will build towards a successful conclusion to your sales call. If, on the other hand, you mistakenly deal with them as objections, you risk alienating the prospect. It is difficult to maintain a positive approach of partnership while wielding the very aggressive techniques of objection handling.

In his book, Alan Williams supports this approach:

'The satisfactory rebuttal of sales objections does not demand a quick-footed liar, it requires a knowledgeable person who has immediate access to the truth. Salespeople who have complete fluency in their product and its applications virtually welcome sales objections for it presents them with an additional opportunity to demonstrate their knowledge and skill and thus strengthen their case for securing the order.'

Building the sale

There are, though, what Tack calls '*major* objections'. These are the problems the prospect faces you with which may stop the sale. Once more, however, I believe that adopting a posture of objection handling is counter-productive. After all, solving the problems which stand in the way of the sale is the sales professional's job. Highlighting just some of these for special treatment as objections can unbalance the whole sales campaign. The best philosophy for handling *all* the problems of the sale is to deal with these in partnership with the prospect. The best question is: 'How can *we* solve this?' Objections are no different: you (and, most importantly, *he*) still need to think in terms of *we*; as soon as you start to think of how *I* can handle *his* objection that partnership is in danger.

The greatest danger of special treatment is that you can all too easily get into the game of objection tennis, with arguments being tossed backwards and forwards until a winner emerges. As described earlier, the inexperienced tend joyfully to smash the service (objection) back, and destroy their opponent's argument. There is (as all the pundits would agree) no easier way of annoying the prospect and losing his business. The trained sales professional may, however, gently lob the objection back, but with deadly topspin. It is teaching such deadly but inoffensive-looking returns that forms the staple diet of much sales training.

My own view is that no matter how well, or how apparently inoffensively, you enter into such a game there can still only be one winner: the prospect. He can win despite you, or he can win in partnership *with* you. I always chose to play the latter, doubles, game!

As Miller, Heiman and Tuleja point out: '*Serving the customer's best interest is ultimately the best way of serving your own.*'

In this scenario, an objection is deliberately only recognised as a question, so that it can be redirected in the form: 'How can we solve this so that you (the prospect) can still obtain the best solution?' The buyer has just as much incentive as you to work for the best solution.

Although I disagree with many of the pundits on the basic attitude to adopt, there are a few ground rules for making the handling of 'objections' an easier process, where I would be in agreement with most sales trainers. Alfred Tack, once more, best sums up the most important of these:

1. Don't interrupt.
2. When dealt with do not return to it later.
3. Sometimes wise to repeat it to ensure understanding.
4. THE APPARENT-AGREEMENT TECHNIQUE.
   'I can understand your thinking at this stage ...' [but only showing understanding NOT agreement – simply to relax buyer].

I would go somewhat further on the first rule. Certainly you must not interrupt the prospect's exposition of an 'objection'. But I believe that you must be not just neutral, but positive. I always made it clear that I accepted the comment, took it seriously and indeed was sympathetic. You must very clearly show that you want to help the prospect, although this does not mean that you necessarily agree with him.

The most violent disagreements I have seen have come about simply because the salesman refused to *register* the prospect's objection; the prospect became steadily angrier as he tried to make the salesman recognise that the objection even existed. Remember that we all get angry when we aren't taken seriously.

Tack's second rule is sound. If you have successfully resolved an objection then to return to it is merely to ask for the whole issue to be reopened.

The third rule is a particularly valuable one. Repeating the prospect's statement, where this is not merely a question designed to elicit more information from you, has a number of benefits. In the first instance, it checks that you understand what he really wants to say. Many 'objections' arise from genuine misunderstandings by the prospect, and repeating his comment (in more logical form) will often lead him to answer his own objection. Even more 'objections' result from the sales professional's misunderstanding an innocent comment on the part of the prospect; obviously, a restatement will clear these up immediately. Second, the restatement allows you to slow the pace, stopping you from reacting too quickly and giving you valuable time to think. Third, it shows that you have really registered the comment and take it seriously.

This naturally leads on to the fourth rule, which is where I start to diverge from Tack. This is where I believe you should *genuinely* want to understand the problem. You must certainly accept what the prospect has said, although even he would not necessarily expect you automatically to agree with it (and, indeed, there is no need to go that far). Tack uses the technique to relax the prospect. I would do the same, but would extend this positively to build sympathetic rapport.

All of these rules are in truth only techniques for putting you in the right posture to handle the 'objection'. As you will have gathered, I believe that just as important is to adopt the right, sympathetic attitude to search jointly for a solution. I do not, therefore, believe it is even necessary to look on such comments as objections.

As already mentioned, almost all the sales trainers would disagree with this view. If you want a real refresher on detailed objection handling techniques, then almost any of the more popular books will give a good summary of these. It is the one set of techniques that most commentators are agreed on! But, once more, I would stress that it is *your* decision. As an experienced sales professional, you will by now have handled many such situations. What did you do to resolve them successfully? Did you resort to techniques such as the pundits recommend, or did you work out the solution with the customer as part of the overall campaign? I suspect that, if you have been selling for some time, you will probably remember objections (which you consciously handled as 'objections') as very rare events indeed.

Pseudo-objections

The tomes on objection handling techniques identify many different classes of objection and offer suitable techniques to deal with each. I, rather more simplistically, only recognise one further category of 'pseudo-objections'. Most of these hinge around the fact that the prospect just doesn't want to show his hand or take the decision yet.

The most typical 'objection' of this category involves simply delaying the decision (classically described as a 'stall'), putting off the evil moment. There is always a problem in closing (as we will see later in this chapter), but this should not be seen as a separate objection. The answer is just to carry out an effective close. To involve special objection handling techniques is to risk confusing this essentially simple situation.

The most worrying objections, to which you must remain sensitive, are those hidden ones, where the prospect in reality favours another solution (from a competitor). Here the objection must be correctly identified as a symptom only, and the true underlying problem addressed. Again, the correct context is the overall campaign, not the specific objection.

Then there is the trivial objection, for which the best technique is simply to ignore it; it is the one situation where a sales professional can ignore the prospect. Finally, there is the old standby of the price objection, which I will leave to the chapter on pricing.

In all the discussion of the various techniques I hope my basic message has not got lost. I refuse to recognise an objection; I only see an opportunity to develop the sale, in partnership with the prospect.

Using references

My earlier comments about building a list of references indicated just how important I considered references to be. Correctly used, they can swing the whole sale. More than any other factor they can show your prospect that yours is the *safe* solution; and that is probably the prime (if undeclared) objective of most buyers. But, despite their importance, in my experience (as a buyer) remarkably few sales professionals ever use references (unless specifically asked for them). This is a waste for, although use of references requires more effort on the part of the sales professional, the results are often dramatically better. Every one of the campaigns I won against the odds made good and significant use of references.

Most references will be simply dropped into the conversation, in a form of commercial name dropping. It reassures the prospect if you intimate that you have just been talking to the board of Shell International (even if they have thrown you out on your ear – although you probably won't stress that aspect!). Some use of references will be prompted by specific queries, to which the easiest and most effective answer is to describe exactly how someone else dealt with the problem. Some references will be quite deliberately introduced to add authority to specific claims. Just a few will be deliberately introduced as an integral part of your sales campaign; where you would expect and encourage the prospect actually to contact these references for reassurance.

Obviously, in the last case you must be sure that these references are sound. But even those lightly dropped into the conversation have to be genuine; the prospect may challenge you to prove what you say. I saw one sales training company lose the business of a number of companies (to whom they were making a presentation at a group meeting) when their salesman dropped into his pitch the 'fact' that he was also working with IBM. Needless to say, with my background, I was interested enough to follow this up with some questions. The salesman retreated in some disarray; it was obvious that his connection with IBM was somewhat tenuous, and his company lost the business at that point.

All references are good
On the other hand, even though buyers may be convinced that sound references show that the proposition is safe, in my experience an expert sales professional can use almost *any* customer as a good reference. Clearly, the ideal choice for a reference will be a customer whose use of your products is directly relevant to the prospect's needs and who is also one of your guaranteed, 'trained' references. You can be certain, in these circumstances, that the reference will work well.

But, even if this ideal is not attainable, you can still use other references; although you should be aware that you are gambling with the sale (and should ensure that it is a calculated gamble). The reason that you can usually afford to take this gamble is that most customers hate to admit, to anyone, that they have taken the wrong decision. Almost whatever they think of your product, they will usually tell your prospect on a reference visit (or making a telephone call) that your products are the best available: would they ever admit that they had bought anything less than the best? Regardless of the reality, they will generally describe your offerings in glowing terms.

One of my largest accounts was in deep trouble; indeed it was claiming something in excess of £200,000 from IBM for failing to deliver the working product it had paid for. Yet, throughout this period, I still took my colleague's prospects into the account, as one of our prime reference sells; and, for each of these, the customer praised IBM to the heavens – then, after they had left, he once more beat me up about his problems!

Sometimes there is no choice. On several occasions I have been forced to take my prospects on visits to customers who were completely unknown quantities, simply because they were the only customers using the specialised applications the prospects were interested in – and relevance takes priority over all other factors in a reference. Yet on none of these occasions did I find the customers anything other than embarrassingly enthusiastic; although, at least once, I overheard the customer (discreetly out of the prospect's earshot) heavily bending the ear of his account sales professional, who was accompanying us, about all the problems he was having!

Reference visits

The prospect may be satisfied with the mention of a reference, or he may accept (as both John Fenton and Tom Hopkins separately suggest) the evidence of a testimonial letter from the reference customer. But if the reference forms an integral part of your sales campaign, you will probably want to use the opportunity more positively. The prospect may be happy with a telephone conversation with the customer (or that may be all he is willing to do), but such telephone reference calls are somewhat dangerous. Without the visual signals, it is too easy to misunderstand what is being said.

Ideally, you will want to take your prospect on a visit to your most suitable (and, hopefully, also your best) reference site. The one caveat is that you must make certain that it really is a *relevant* reference. Many companies, and many more sales professionals if they use references at all, subscribe to a standard (usually relatively short) list; all of whom are supposed to be equally applicable to all prospects.

Prepare the ground

If you are wise, you will put in some preparatory work for the visit. If the reference is one of your customers, this will be easy. It will also be very productive. There is, in my experience, no better way of selling to the *reference customer* than using him as a reference. It very firmly establishes you and he as being allies, and it forces him to concentrate on all the good points of your products – these may be sales messages which you may have been trying to get across to him for months (and now he has to learn them by heart!).

My reference customers typically bought at least twice as much as my other customers. In part this was undoubtedly due to the fact that they were also my best customers; but at least half of this extra business was, I am convinced (based on circumstantial evidence), due to the reference activities. This was true even when it was my colleagues' prospects who were visiting, so there is a direct benefit even in such 'altruism', and a good sales story to offer to your colleagues who are less enthusiastic to let you use their references.

You will need to train your customer in what is expected of him. He will undoubtedly be very willing; being chosen as a reference is very flattering. But he will certainly want to know what he should do – and you will definitely want to tell him what to do! It is important to plan a reference visit as carefully as a visit to your own works, even to the extent of rehearsing the event – if this is possible.

If the prospect does not belong to to you all of this preparation becomes more difficult, but it should still be possible (and indeed is courteous) to have a brief preliminary meeting with the reference, preferably accompanied by your colleague, whose customer it is.

The end result of this groundwork should be a reference customer lined up to make a far harder sell than *you* would ever dare make. I well remember a dinner in Paris attended by a dozen of my leading UK prospects, and also by my reference customer. It was still a reference sell: you don't always have to meet at the customer's premises, and multiple prospects can be involved. The reference was in fact one of the leading UK medical consultants, of deservedly high international reputation. It was the first such reference meeting I had arranged in the medical field and, as the dinner drew to its close, I was startled to hear him whisper in my ear: 'Have I covered all the points you wanted me to bring out?' I would never, before that, have dared to brief anyone of his stature, but he, better than I, recognised the reality and (as he definitely would have said nothing that was untrue) the validity of the situation.

Accompany the prospect
No matter how much you trust the reference customer, you *must* go with the prospect on any reference visits. You need to be present in the (admittedly unlikely) event that any 'fire-fighting' is needed. I have had more problems with prospects upsetting customers than the other way around. On one memorable occasion the prospect turned up drunk and generously insulted everyone from a leading medical consultant to the doorman – now that situation did take some skill to handle!

In any case, accompanying a prospect to a reference allows you to use the most productive sales situation you are likely to come across. If you do not take advantage of this you are abdicating your skills as a sales professional. I believe in extracting the maximum opportunity from such visits, by driving the prospect there myself. It is courteous and it saves him all the hassle of finding the customer's premises. Best of all, though, it allows you unrestricted and uninterrupted access to him for the time in the car. As this can easily run into a number of hours, it may represent the longest time you ever have alone (and undistracted) with him. Indeed, I believe that a reference visit can often be the factor that clinches the sale.

Leave well alone
Once in the reference call, however, the most productive technique is to merge with the wallpaper, and shut up. The customer will quite be capable of saying everything himself, especially if you have briefed

him well. Anything that you add will merely be gilding the lily (and won't be believed by the prospect anyway). So resist the temptation, unless the customer overlooks a particularly important point; at which stage you should very discreetly prompt him – but still let him make even that point.

With my best references I did participate; but in exactly the reverse way that most sales professionals would. I played *down* the various claims. The customer would inevitably be praising IBM to high heaven (even when this was grossly unjustified), where I would be apparently attempting to minimise these claims. I found it best to praise the customer himself for the achievements he was ascribing to IBM: 'It was his contribution that really made the difference.'

This ploy had a number of distinct advantages. Not least, it prepared the prospect to make the maximum personal contribution when (having placed the order) he came to undertake his own installation. It was, of course, immensely flattering to the reference customer (part of the sale to him that I ran in parallel). Most beneficial of all, it stimulated the reference to even greater heights of praise about IBM, and the prospect still believed him not me. From the prospect's point of view it established the credibility of the customer's claims (if I was holding him back, the stories couldn't be a set-up), and it firmly established me as an 'honest broker'. Thereafter, the prospect would start to trust me – the very few salesmen who have their prospects' trust are the *really* successful sales professionals.

Negative selling (to stimulate the prospect's own judgement) can be a very powerful device, as you will see in Chapter 6.

Reward the reference
Once the visit is over, it is courteous and productive to reward the reference customer for the work he has put in. Sometimes this can take the form of a suitable gift. Sometimes, if very discreetly handled (and fully justified), it can be cash. But the most powerful reward of all is simply to thank him and tell him how successful the visit was. It is even worth following up when the prospect orders; simply to let the reference know just how successful the visit was.

The close

The close is, at the same time, the simplest and the most difficult of sales techniques. It is the simplest because all the work should have already been done. It should almost be a formality; all you have to do is ask for the order which, if the groundwork has been correctly completed, the prospect will quite naturally give you – after all, he is there as much to buy as you are to sell. It is a natural part of any sales (or buying) campaign. Indeed, it is the only essential part of such a campaign. You can close a sale (or a purchase, if you are looking at it from the other side of the fence) without any preliminary work. But, no matter how much preliminary work is undertaken, if you never ask for the order you cannot claim to have conducted a complete sales campaign.

Only if you haven't put in all the necessary work to win the order will the close be difficult; and then it will be better closed as a 'trial close' (see later in this section). Having said that, a close will not always be successful; indeed, the odds of the numbers game say that most sales professionals will be unsuccessful more often than they will be successful.

Selling direct to individual retail outlets (as a trainee, early in my career) I quite naturally closed several hundred times a day, since I made up to 30 calls a day, and sold up to 20 separate lines in each (closing each of these in a matter of seconds). In these circumstances closing did not assume the monumental proportions it appears to have in some professional sales; the only trick was in closing positively, so that the size of the order was maximised. But I had no hang-ups about asking for the business; it was a perfectly natural part of the call as I, and the customer (or prospect) went though my product list.

The difficulty for many sales professionals is introduced by the psychology of the situation. Salesmen are naturally results oriented, and only one result counts: winning the order. The effort (involving perhaps months of work) is all to be decided on a single word: yes or no. It is much easier in the environment where the investment of effort has just been two or three minutes, for example selling to retailers, and the next 'sale' is also only two to three minutes away (for the first sales professional it may be as many months before his next prospect closes).

The sales professional's whole reputation rests on the one word; at least until his next close. It is often said that a sales professional's reputation is only as good as his last order. I was once marketing manager with a biscuit manufacturer, where the managing director and myself met daily to review the orders received in the post from the salesmen. I remember one salesman who stood out from the rest. Every day, for months on end, he was constantly up with the leaders; consistently outselling his colleagues. The day came when, for whatever reason, his sales slumped and he came last. For the next four days he was consistently bottom of the list. By the fifth day the managing director was seriously asking whether we should get rid of him. I had to remind him that this was the salesman who had previously outsold everyone else. But it was only the salesman's return to form the following day that saved his job. Memories can be *very* short in the sales game.

The result is that most sales professionals approach the close with trepidation, and many with something akin to panic. As Alfred Tack says:

'The average salesman so rarely asks for a decision. This is due to timidity or fear.'
'Every buyer knows why salesmen are employed. Yet possibly as many as 30 percent of all orders are lost because salesmen will not ask the direct question, "May I have the order?" '

The normal close, therefore, is one not described by any of the pundits; it is the 'default close'. The prospect (rather than the sales professional) eventually *gives* the order to the sales professional. If Tack is to be believed, and my own experience (both as a sales manager and particularly as a buyer) supports his evidence, it is normally the *prospect* who closes; and it is he who is, therefore, totally in control during the critical phase of finalising the order.

Alfred Tack points out: 'Probably because salesmen are usually optimists, they believe time after time in promises made by industrial or retail buyers.'

It should be a natural process. As Tack says, every buyer is well aware that the sales professional is going to ask for the order (although the above evidence suggests that the buyers are somewhat optimistic in this view!). The buyer will not have been entertaining the sales professional for so long purely as a social duty; the buyer, just as much as the seller, is dependent on the order being placed. Yet sales professionals still fudge the issue.

At its most ludicrous extreme, many sales professionals prefer to ask for an order in a letter rather than face-to-face. Once more, as Alfred Tack says: 'Many salesmen, asked to submit quotations, lose orders because they substitute the GPO [the mail] for themselves.'

A number of sales professionals in my personal computer dealership did exactly that. After putting in considerable (and commendable) effort, the final stage of their campaigns was often represented by a mailed proposal (their rather loose description of a two-page letter) or quotation. On the other hand, in IBM if I was asked for a quotation I typically used this to justify at least *two* face-to-face calls. In the first I sat down with the prospect to discuss my draft version; and got his agreement to the final version (and, in the process, completed much of the work of the formal close). In the second I presented him with the final version – and asked for the order.

Closing techniques

As a result of this fear, a whole range of techniques have been proposed to help the sales professional to ask for the order: psychological props to underpin the natural process. The list that Alfred Tack gives is typical and, it seems to me, succinctly covers the main categories:

> THE ALTERNATIVE CLOSE [this was the standby in my days of selling to retailers: 'Will 20 cases of baked beans be sufficient, or should we increase that to 30 cases?']
>
> THE SUMMARY CLOSE [having listed everything that has been done you can justifiably say: 'Well, I guess all that remains is to sign the order.']
>
> THE FEAR CLOSE ['Our stocks are getting low, and I wouldn't want you to have to wait for your order, so can we get it signed now?']
>
> THE VERBAL PROOF CLOSE [using a good story, for example a good reference sell, to lead to: 'Does that convince you that you should order?']
>
> THE ISOLATION CLOSE [having listed the outstanding objections, you ask: 'If I am able to answer each of these points to your complete satisfaction then can I assume we are in business?' This is sometimes referred to as the 'half-nelson close', because it is a powerful but very aggressive close]
>
> THE MINOR POINT CLOSE ['Shall we make the order out for red or blue?']
>
> THE CONCESSION CLOSE ['I'll add an extra five per cent discount if you order now.']

John Fenton also adds the 'trial use close'; making the assumption that the prospect won't bother to return the equipment when the invoice arrives at the end of the trial period, Interestingly, his research showed that:

> '74 per cent of successful salesmen preferred the "Alternative

Choice" close.

In selling to retail 64 per cent preferred the "Order Form" close.'

It is clear, therefore, that most sales professionals use the 'alternative close'; that is on the few occasions when they get around to a positive close, and don't succumb to the 'default close'. I am not surprised by this result, since the 'alternative close' is the easiest to use, and often follows most naturally out of the preceding discussion. It is not too difficult to change the informative question you are about to ask from, 'Would you want the larger model?', into the closing, 'Do you want the larger model?'; to be followed by the even more positive, 'When do you want us to deliver?'

The assumptive (joint) close

My favourite technique was simply to let the close develop naturally. I 'assumed' right from the beginning of the call, and indeed from the beginning of the whole campaign, that the prospect would want to place an order (a reasonable assumption); and that it would be placed with me (which was less obvious, and stretched credulity somewhat until I had won the sale). I further made the assumption that both the prospect and I wanted me to win the order; circumstances might, of course, force him to place the order elsewhere but that would be an unfortunate aberration. The close, therefore, was *shared*; it was a joint effort between myself and the prospect (almost as if making the 'default close' work in my favour, by initiating and controlling it). The typical wording became: 'How do *we* now go about getting the order signed?'; 'we' in this context being very clearly the prospect as well as myself, making it a joint responsibility and a shared 'win'.

Alfred Tack quotes one saying that supports this view: 'There is an old selling tag: A GOOD SALE CLOSES ITSELF.'

The progressive (incremental) close

This also highlights one aspect of many professional sales: there is not one *single* close, but a steady progression through a series of increasingly committed intermediate closes. This was especially evident in selling to the UK National Health Service. I frequently persuaded my prospects in a matter of a few weeks that they definitely wanted my equipment and were committed to buying it (which would, normally, represent the classic close), but it then took many months (often years) to get the budget allocated and the official order raised.

The Sales Professional

The close here becomes the agreement to each of a series of steps that will eventually lead to the order. Each close, though, has to be as rigorously pursued as that which *will* result in the order. Each must be *clearly* agreed, and each must be accompanied by an action plan leading to the next step.

It also means that you must constantly guard against what your competition is up to. John Fenton suggests that you watch the visitors' book (and make your own entry indecipherable)!

This long drawn-out process obviously has disadvantages; not the least being that there are that many more opportunities to lose, although there are also that many more opportunities to recover. Unlike the eventual order, each of these steps is by no means final. For many sales professionals who have difficulty facing one close, it will be death by a thousand closes! It does, however, have the major advantage that it is an incremental process. Each decision escalates the commitment; but the prospect only has to make a number of small decisions, rather than one big one. This makes the process easier for you to control, as the decision develops its own momentum. The final close is just as small and as easy to achieve as any of the intermediate steps.

It is also an ideal vehicle for the assumptive (joint) close. Indeed, it almost forces you into this mode; since, with so many steps, it is almost impossible not to work alongside the prospect. The *routine* question becomes: 'What do *we* need to do now?'

The best example I know which clearly shows the power of the progressive or incremental close is from the arena of politics, rather than from industry; but, then, politicians now have to be very good salesmen (albeit of the old school, where their product is so dubious!). It is the price that the UK (Thatcher) government eventually persuaded its electorate to pay for the Falklands War.

The eventual cost was several billions of pounds (personally costing each UK taxpayer several hundreds of pounds), together with nearly 1000 lives. Yet it was fought for the benefit of only a couple of thousand Falkland Islanders, the population of a very small British village, who could have been resettled in great comfort (not to say great luxury) at a much lower cost than the £5 million (and one life) that was the actual cost for *each* of these families. The much quoted 'matter of principle' was proved to be somewhat worthless when, just a few months later, the UK government happily ceded Hong Kong to the (much stronger) Chinese government.

Put like this (and I will admit it is a deliberately simplified, even biased, picture to help me to make my point) there would have been no way that the UK electorate would have approved such a cost (I doubt that even the Falkland Islanders would have agreed). Indeed, at the start of the war, opinion polls showed that the voters were almost unanimous that they would not agree to the loss of a *single* life – let alone approaching 1000. But the sales job was handled brilliantly.

The government's sales campaign was based on a large number of *incremental* decisions that gently moved public opinion along from one end of the spectrum to the other. The decision was never put to the electorate in terms of one big decision, as to whether they wanted to pay the horrendous costs that finally emerged. Instead, they were presented with lots of little decisions, many of them developing during the long weeks it took for the task force, initially presented as only a show of force, to reach the islands; by which time the logic of the landings had become – by incremental steps – inexorable.

It was, I believe, one of the most brilliant sales campaigns ever (even the competitors, the other UK political parties, were won over!); particularly so when compared with those of the US government (classically that of Vietnam) – although the US government has less control over the media (where the UK government's handling, indeed total control, of 'public relations' was an outstanding example of just what can be achieved by inspired censorship). It was, perhaps, a macabre example of the 'incremental' technique, but it does vividly demonstrate the real power it holds.

John Fenton says: 'Ask for AN order on every call.' This is, though, a slightly different process: looking for small orders (which may not always be available to the sales professional) to get the prospect into the habit of doing business with you.

The trial close
Just about the most powerful sales technique I know is the 'trial close' (described by John Fenton as the 'pre-close'). It simply comprises a conventional close of any type (but most normally an assumptive one, probably as part of a progressive pattern) put at the *earliest* possible time you believe that a close might be possible; or even earlier, as most sales professionals are unduly pessimistic about how easy it is to close. It is then repeated at discreet intervals over succeeding calls, until it is finally successful.

As it is, in essence, a repetitive close it needs to be more subtle and discreet, of the 'What do we need to do?' type. John Fenton's powerful question, 'What do we need to do to get your business?' can almost be classified as a trial close during the opening of the call!

As Tom Hopkins puts it:

'A Champion is closing most of the time. He's constantly trying test closes, and he'll go into his final closing sequence anytime he sniffs the sweet smell of success ... the great ones usually close after their fifth attempt.'

One of its main benefits *is* its trial nature. It is not the life-or-death final close. The chances are that the answer will be 'no', but the doors will not be closed. The downside risk is, thus, minimal. As such, it appears to be much easier for sales professionals to use. In my experience, they do not have the same reluctance as they have over the final close; simply because the trial close usually is *not* final – it is that much less important. The psychological effort, the sheer courage, is much less; and the effect of a 'no' is not shattering to the ego (since it is expected).

Not a negligible benefit is that its use means that the final close, when a trial close actually results in an order, comes earlier in the campaign; close to the earliest possible moment. This has benefits for the flow of business but, more important, it minimises the time that the business is at risk. (If Alfred Tack is right, at least 30 per cent of business goes to competitors because the close is not early enough, or is missing altogether.)

Conventionally, you are supposed to be on the lookout for the buying signals, which are said to come in the form of a change in posture, or increased enthusiasm, or special interest, or even a spate of objections – or, surely most nebulous of all, a look in the eyes! Sometimes it is obvious when the prospect wants to buy, not least because he says so, but I have never seen much of these signals; perhaps because I have never waited that long. For I believe, if the sales professional wants to close at the earliest (and safest) moment, the stimulus is likely to come from him rather than the prospect; and this is where the trial close is so helpful.

But, for me, the invaluable benefit came when (as in most such trials, by definition) it resulted in a 'no'. I could then proceed boldly (but discreetly) to ask the question: 'Why?' For a sales professional, this combination of trial close and question is the most powerful analytical tool I know. The answer has to be (with very few exceptions indeed) a do-it-yourself guide to closing the business. The prospect is put on the spot, and typically has to give a completely honest answer; stating what he thinks would be the best actions needed to win. I have never yet found a prospect who lied, or was even evasive in answer to this question, where otherwise I have chased many a prospect for hours to find out exactly what was happening.

Getting out of the call

Having got the order: *run*. Run as fast as you can. There is always a temptation to hang around and talk some more: *don't*. There is only one way you can go from the peak of success, and that is down. If you really try hard you might even be able to persuade the prospect to cancel the order!

It is amazing how many sales professionals throw in additional sales points after the order is closed. I must plead guilty myself: I have found myself, to my horror, doing exactly this on several occasions (although, fortunately, I have never done it so badly that I have lost the order).

Thank the buyer, and *leave*.

The killer instinct

Making the successful close is often seen as the key skill that the best sales professionals have. As you have seen, it is almost more of an attitude than a skill, and is sometimes described as 'going for the jugular' or 'the killer instinct'. John Fenton defines this (somewhat defensively) as:

> 'This means the determination to succeed; even against the odds. It means emphasising positives not negatives. It requires confidence (you're the expert – with a USP) and determination.'

I think he is trying to play down the aggressive nature of the job. It is true, as I have emphasised a number of times, that much of selling should be about developing a partnership with the prospect. But there has to be a degree of courage and of ruthlessness to risk that partnership in order to win the business. Without the close (with all its risks) there has been no selling, and John Fenton is right to say:

> 'If you don't close you are working for the competition.'

Be yourself

The one danger of all sales training courses and books is that they attempt to make you a different person; the sales trainers would say a more successful one, but I have my doubts. I believe that successful selling comes mainly from harnessing the talents you already possess; directing them into ways that enable you to help the customer better. There is no need to change yourself dramatically; indeed that would probably be counter-productive – and 'born-again' salesmen are often walking time bombs.

This is particularly true where you are already a successful sales professional. That is a rare skill, so don't endanger it by taking any of the techniques discussed in this chapter too seriously. If they suit your style, and you're not already using them, they may be worth a try; we can all improve our performance. But if they don't fit, or aren't productive, discard them ruthlessly. Only if you are comfortable and relaxed, self-confident in your style, will you be able to gain the maximum enjoyment and the 'high' that results from a successful call.

Chapter 6
Advanced Sales Techniques

The professional salesman is likely to come into contact with a 'complex sale'. This is a sale where there are a number of individuals involved in the buying decision, and the sales campaign extends over a number of calls.

Miller, Heiman and Tuleja define it as: 'one in which several people must give their approval before the sale can take place.' They then expand this comment:

'In a complex sale, you have short-term and long-term objectives. In the short term, you must close as many individual deals as you possibly can, and as quickly as possible. In the long term, you want to maintain healthy relations with the customers signing the deals, so they'll be willing to make further purchases in the months and years to come. It would be great if these two objectives always coincided, but you know that they don't.'

Thus, in many ways this environment is very different from that of the single-call sale, which is the staple diet of many (if not most) sales trainers. This chapter explores some of the more advanced techniques that may be applicable to these complex sales. Once more, though, I would emphasise that you should look at these techniques with a sense of realism, if not cynicism. It is for you to decide which of these may, or (more probably) may not, be suitable for your own special needs.

The techniques are sophisticated and, used correctly, can be very powerful. But most of them depend on turning almost upside down the conventional views of what selling is or should be about. As such, it is arguable that they are very idiosyncratic, so it will be that much more difficult to find a specific match to your own needs. Do not be afraid to reject *all* of them; most salesmen do, and aren't failures as a result.

The techniques are often deceptively simple but this simplicity comes from extensive practice, in much the same way that world class athletes make their achievements look easy only because they have been practising for long hours every day for years. Apparent simplicity often hides very real skill, and it certainly does here.

The Sales Professional

What is more, the techniques generally assume that you are already an expert in the basic techniques reviewed in the last chapter. They are *not* for the inexperienced, let alone for the new salesman. Even if you *are* expert, before using them on an important prospect I would suggest you rehearse them thoroughly, not least because you really do need to be sure that they fit your style.

One final caveat: in using some of these techniques you run the risk of being badly misunderstood by your colleagues and (much more importantly) by your management. As the techniques are often the reverse of the normal, you run the real risk of being viewed as a poor salesman who doesn't even know the basics. Several of the techniques even ask you to become an 'anti-salesman', and this is an image that can stick. It is an image that (as I will show) your customers and prospects will love; but, by its perversity in terms of conventional stereotypes, one that may be difficult for other salesmen to accept – and your sales management may well also fall into this category.

The lack of understanding is the more marked where the salesman is less experienced. Most of the salesmen in my personal computer dealership were *very* inexperienced, and were still operating in 'showroom mode' (far removed from the professional selling that is the subject of this book). As a result, I carefully explained (as I made calls with them) that I didn't want them to try to copy my style – for most of them such an attempt would have been a disaster. Even so, they naïvely registered my idiosyncratic selling style as that of a poor salesman, despite my undoubted sales successes. They eventually rationalised the problem by deciding that I must have been giving very large, hidden discounts. Needless to say, that was not the case, but their persistent disbelief illustrates the potential misunderstanding you may have to face.

If you do decide to use any of these techniques, I would suggest that you make a great point of telling everyone so; and emphasise just how *sophisticated* these techniques are. By all means try the ideas on your prospects in secret; you won't want to advertise widely your conversion to a new technique which you subsequently find you can't handle! But before you use them in front of your colleagues (and, especially, in front of your management) make certain that you *have* publicised this new and very sophisticated style.

I well remember one call with my branch manager, after which he lectured me: 'You should not slump in your chair, and you should not call a managing director by his first name.' I discreetly pointed out to him that I *had* just persuaded the managing director to place an order three months early, before he had received formal approval from his company's US parent – an action which put his job at risk. In return all I had been able to offer was a vague suggestion that IBM would be grateful (my branch manger was there to add some weight to this rather nebulous claim). It was also the order that was needed to get me and the branch into the Hundred Per Cent Club. It was a classic sale; I had walked on water to win it – and all that my branch manager had noticed was that my shoes were wet!

Some of these advanced techniques have been described by others, but a number of them are (as far as I am aware) the result of my own development. In part, the latter group were suggested by observations (as a long-time marketeer and market researcher) of what customers wanted. In part they were derived from the strengths I observed in the approaches adopted by systems engineers (IBM's technical consultants who supported the salesmen, whom I also taught).

I always taught the systems engineers that they were IBM's most powerful salesmen; justifiably so. The salesman, before he could even start his main sell, had to break down the barriers raised by his prospects: everyone knew that the salesman, coming from a sales force with such a formidable reputation, was bound to sell them something *they* didn't want, so the defences were raised every time he hove into view. When the salesman walked out of the door and the systems engineer walked in, however, the prospect would greet him like a long-lost brother. This was someone he *could* trust; an expert whose only role was to help the prospect. The systems engineer then proceeded to say exactly the same as the salesman. But he was gratefully believed and the sale was made, although formalities required that the order was still placed with the salesman.

The real stimulus for these techniques came, though, from the opening up of the IBM Biomedical Group. It was an exploratory venture and for the first few months my role was largely as a researcher. Subsequently, as the group became established, the role was extended to 'consultant', where the PR element was still more important than the commercial aspects. Even so, I found that this low-key approach was immensely successful; in truth it made me even more successful than I had been with my hard sell. The picture was consolidated by the fact that for much of the time I was up against (head-to-head) just about the best conventional salesman I have ever come across. He was superb. His techniques were near perfect; his skills and personality could not have been faulted. Yet I managed to achieve a 90 per cent win rate against even this paragon, which persuaded me of the real power inherent in the techniques I had been (often almost unwittingly) using.

The other, and for me, just as important benefit is that these techniques are normally more fun to use. Generally requiring a much more laid-back approach, they allow you more time, in a more relaxed environment, to obtain the most enjoyment and satisfaction out of each sales campaign.

Decision-makers and influencers

Perhaps the most obvious difference of the complex sale is the multiplicity of buyers involved. It is no longer sufficient to persuade just one buyer. Instead you have to convince a whole gaggle of individuals, all with different (often contradictory) requirements.

Identifying the buyers

The first problem this poses is quite simply that of identifying who are the various buyers. This is not an easy task. It is no longer a matter of looking for the door helpfully labelled 'buyer'. The buyers involved in the complex sale can range from the chief executive to members of the typing pool.

As Miller, Heiman and Tuleja put it, in *Strategic Selling*:

'Because most sales-training programs emphasise tactical rather than strategic skills, even very good salespeople sometimes find themselves cut out of a sale at the last minute because they failed to locate or cover all the real decision makers for their specific sale. Unfortunately, most trainers pay little attention to this initial task of identification. They assume that salespeople already know whose approvals are necessary.'

The convention is to split these buyers into 'decision-makers' and 'influencers'; with the clear implication that the small group of decision-makers should be the prime target, although influencers should not be neglected. I agree that this is a useful distinction, in that it correctly focuses the salesman's attention on the key decision-makers, and forces him to contact these; where too many salesmen are bogged down among the influencers.

It was certainly true, in the personal computer market, that dealer salesmen rarely contacted more than one person in their prospect (even in the larger corporations). He was usually a buyer in the purchasing department and was usually only an influencer. The real decisions were taken elsewhere, untroubled by the attentions of salesman; although, where the only sales message was price, the lack of face-to-face contact with the decision-maker was not really a critical factor!

The problem with this two-way split is that both decision-makers and influencers are very general categories; in my experience, too general (and too confined within the sales perspective) to help you best to zero in on the exact decision structure. In their book, *Strategic Selling*, Miller, Heiman and Tuleja seem (at least to me) to offer a much better, if at times much more complex, structure. They identify four buying influences, of which the first three relate to the more conventional structure: economic buying influence; user buying influence; and technical buying influence.

The first category, the economic buyer, is the ultimate decision-maker. He is a single entity, usually a single person (but it may be a group, such as a board). He holds the purse strings and *must* approve the decision:

'The Economic Buyer is the person who gives *final* approval to buy your product or service. The role of this Buying Influence is *to release the dollars to buy.*'
'His focus is "Bottom line and impact on organization" and he asks "What kind of return will we get on this investment?" '

Clearly this buyer is the most important in the whole structure:

'Almost by definition you don't find people who give final approval far down on the corporate ladder.'
'If you don't identify the source of funds – and do it *early in the selling cycle* – you run the risk of handing the ball to the competition.'

But it would be a serious mistake to assume that a price sell is the key to this buyer:

'The focus is never price per se, but *price performance.*'

They also suggest a starting point to find this ultimate decision-maker:

'… useful to ask the question "At what level in my own organization would such a decision have to be made?" … it will start you looking at the right corporate level.'

The user buyers are the people who will use whatever you are offering. In the more conventional model they would lie uncomfortably between decision-makers and influencers. A virtue of the more complex model is that it allows the salesman to handle this important group most effectively:

> 'The role of the User Buyer is filled by someone who will actually use (or supervise the use of) your product or service. The role of the User Buyer is *to make judgments about the impact of that product or service on the job to be done.*'
> 'Because the focus of User Buyers is how a sale will affect *their* jobs, their reactions to sales proposals, and their predictions about performance, tend to be subjective.'
> 'They ask "How will your product or service work *for me?*" '

Technical buyers are the true influencers of the simpler model, but with a powerful veto power which could still be fatal for your sale. They vet the specification for technical conformity. Paradoxically, in many complex sales situations (certainly in the case of computers of any sort) the purchasing department falls into this category:

> 'The Technical Buyers' role is to *screen out.* They're gate-keepers.'
> 'Their focus is "Product per se" and they ask "Does it meet specifications?" They only make recommendations, and can't say "yes"; but they can say "no" (and often do!).'

Miller, Heiman and Tuleja make the important point that these categories are not a function of the titles on the doors; they are a result of specific relationships to the 'purchase'. Even more important, these authors emphasise the fact that the structure is not fixed. The relationships change for different purchases, and people move from one category to another. In particular, they stress that the role of economic buyer can vary, depending on five main influences:

1. DOLLAR AMOUNT [the more the product costs the higher up the ladder the decision will be taken].
2. BUSINESS CONDITIONS [in times of hardship, when money is tighter, again the decision will be taken higher up the ladder].
3. EXPERIENCE WITH YOU AND YOUR FIRM [if you are a long-standing supplier who is known to be trustworthy, the

decision can be safely delegated to lower management].
4. EXPERIENCE WITH YOUR PRODUCT OR SERVICE [a similar rule applies to the product itself].
5. POTENTIAL ORGANIZATIONAL IMPACT [a change that will have a direct impact on the organisation in general automatically escalates the decision to the higher levels].

I have always found a classification of this type most helpful (and a natural reflection of the customer's business). The driving force for most sales comes from the group of users, moderated by their technical advisers, with the final decision approved by the board. My only reservation is that, in common with all 'pigeon-holing' systems, it is too restricting; even where the pigeon-holes are close to reality (which those of many other such systems are not).

In my experience, the decision-making process is normally deeply embedded in the 'user' process. The users have a great deal of delegated power. In many cases, although the final decision may have to be approved by higher authority, this is in reality only a veto power (any board that saddles its user departments with an unwelcome choice is asking for trouble). On the other hand, often the most important (if not the heaviest) 'users' are the higher authorities themselves. In terms of computers, for example, the chief executive is often the main proponent and the main beneficiary of the 'management information system'. He then becomes the most important user (by far), and his involvement in the decision-making process becomes very much more direct than simply being the holder of the purse strings.

There is only one solution to these complexities, and that is *not* to offer ever more complicated sets of pigeon-holes. It is quite simply to approach each new sale afresh, determined to find out what the relationships are in this case. Further, each contact should be approached as an individual, not as a pigeon-hole. That way you will never make the fatal mistake of dismissively treating a decision-maker as merely a second-class influencer.

'What are *his* needs and wants?' is the most important question, not, 'What category does he fall into?' The categories only become important when you discover that one individual favours a competitive solution, and you cannot win him over. Then it is important to understand the relationships, the categories, so that you can handle (and neutralise) him in the context of the overall organisation.

Even then, the relationships can be much more complex than the simple categorisations imply. A very highly motivated user (or even influencer) can sometimes outvote (or at least out-veto, which has the same effect from your point of view) an uninvolved economic buyer.

Perhaps the most useful aspect of the three categories is that they provide a helpful (if often arbitrary) framework to start your investigations. It *is* likely that the different categories will have different perspectives. Miller, Heiman and Tuleja provide what is, for me, the definitive picture of the various needs (quoted earlier in this section).

But you must be sensitive to the slightest divergence from these pigeon-holes. If the managing director really does want to know about the bits and bytes of your computer you must accommodate him, even if he is manifestly failing to behave as a managing director should. The categorisation, though, should ensure that you can check that he really does want this.

The one thing that you must be certain of is that you have identified and sold to *all* the decision-makers and influencers. In one of my most important, and most competitive, UK sales some of the key decision-makers were located in the USA, which made selling to them difficult but not impossible. Their contribution eventually decided the sale in my favour, mainly swayed by my colleagues in the USA and supported by some horrendously expensive transatlantic phone calls. My own answer to locating *all* the key personnel was usually to undertake extensive surveys (described in the next chapter). These allowed me to contact the widest cross-section of prospect personnel; and I used the opportunity to question everyone in depth to find out what were the true relationships between the main players – and to check that I hadn't missed any of them.

John Fenton suggests a useful ploy, which is to ask: 'By the way do you have a copy of your purchasing cycle plan handy?' Almost certainly the buyer won't even have heard of such a thing, but his interest will be aroused, and it allows you to question him for the information you want (preferably using a copy of such a document, mocked up as necessary, from your own company). This will allow you to establish the other personnel in the buying cycle, and will justify your getting permission to call on them.

Miller, Heiman and Tuleja's contribution to this search is to identify a fourth category of buying influence: the 'coach'. I deliberately left this out of the earlier list, because it is quite far removed from the more traditional approaches. It is, however, a powerful concept. In essence, it says that you should identify one or more contacts who can (and are willing to) guide you through the complexities of the sale. Using the sporting analogy, they can 'coach' you:

'The role of a coach is to *guide you in the sale* by giving you the information you need to manage it to a close that guarantees you not only the order, but satisfied customers and repeat business as well. Your Coach can help you identify and meet the people who are filling the other Buying Influence roles ... and can help you assess the buying situation so that you're most effectively positioned with each one. To close any Complex Sale, you should develop *at least* one Coach.'

'The first three Buying Influences already exist. They're waiting to be identified, and you just have to find out where. Your coach, on the other hand, has to be not only *found* but *developed* ... The Coach's role is one that you, in effect, create.'

'[He] can be found in the buying organization, in your own organization, outside both.'

His focus is "YOUR SUCCESS WITH THIS PROPOSAL", and he asks: "How can we pull this off?" '

They put forward three criteria for a good coach:

1. You have credibility with that person.
   'By definition ... a good place to find potential Coaches is among your own satisfied customers ... This person's past experience is that you can be *trusted*. That's what credibility means.'
2. The coach has credibility with the buying organization.
   'Because credibility with the buying organization is so important, you'll often find good Coaches within the organization itself ... A Technical or User Buyer who's on your side can serve as an excellent Coach. The best of all scenarios is to turn the Economic Buyer into a Coach.'
3. The coach wants you to succeed.
   ' ... this person sees that it's in his or her own *self interest* for the buying organization to accept your solution.'

The reason that I have quoted this coach concept at some length is that it succinctly summarises a range of techniques that I have also found particularly useful.

As I described in Chapter 2, my first task in moving into a new market was to identify and 'recruit' the best advisers. In the first instance this was to obtain the best advice and guidance, but their role soon became as guides to where the business lay (and to how I should approach it); they were thus coaches. To these I gradually added the key personnel in customers and prospects, until I had an extensive list of coaches even if I didn't categorise them as such (for that was long before I read Miller, Heiman and Tuleja's book), to cover every eventuality.

Miller, Heiman and Tuleja comment:

> ' ... test that person's potential usefulness by asking him or her for Coaching. Seldom will a Coach refuse to give you the assistance you require. In fact our data indicate that most people welcome the opportunity to do Coaching.'

I would echo these sentiments, although the very direct appeal to 'coach me', as suggested, is a very American approach – which would perhaps need to be toned down considerably in other less flamboyant cultures.

Building alliances

My own description of such coaches would be that they were valued 'allies', although of a very general (if powerful) nature.

In any customer or prospect, I always set out to build the maximum number of 'alliances'. This was not a cynical, political process, as some pundits would suggest. It was a natural extension of the sales process. As part of the process of achieving the necessary rapport with my contacts and establishing a 'partnership' with them, I had to move into a posture of working alongside them; more as a colleague than as a representative of a supplier. I thought of such contacts as allies, and cultivated these alliances by involving them in my work (particularly as references – a crucial device for building alliances), as well as being involved in their activities. I also made certain that, wherever possible, I made a regular contribution to their work independent of the sales campaigns.

Such alliances should not be confused with political alliances, where you and your contact(s) take on the rest of the prospect's management. Such political alliances are sometimes necessary, but they must be handled with the utmost care; they can (and often do) backfire spectacularly. My sales team, in the personal computer dealership, lost one major sale because they became closely identified (as political allies) with the consultant who was supposed to be selecting the system, but who was soundly beaten in an internal political battle – and, along with him, we lost the business.

In the case of IBM Biomedical Group, a particularly powerful alliance was that with the national experts in the Scientific and Technical branch of the DHSS. Charged with ensuring that the National Health Service had the best possible equipment and service, these experts much appreciated the significant effort I put in to ensure that our own offering was close to their ideal. As result they aided our sales activities, albeit very discreetly.

One added bonus was that many of these allies eventually became personal friends. There was nothing forced about this. It was not just expedient; I did not simulate friendship, as many salesmen seem to think necessary, because it helped my sales. It was simply a natural extension of enjoying each other's company, and it made selling even more pleasant.

Overcoming blocks

In the ideal situation you will have easy access to all the decision-makers and influencers, and will be able to build alliances with some of them. Just occasionally, though, you will come up against a block. Most typically, the lead contact will want to control the whole campaign himself, and to achieve this will effectively deny you access to any of the other key players, especially those above him. This is perhaps understandable; such campaigns can get very political, to the extent that they could pose a threat to the position of your contact.

The easiest, if very glib, answer is: 'Well, I wouldn't have started there!' Indeed, it is true that the higher your initial contact the better. This initial contact can always be, justifiably, contacted once more. If he is at the top of the tree that opens up the whole of the organisation to you. On the other hand, if you start at grassroots level (as do most salesmen) it is often very difficult to fight your way up to the top.

It is often claimed that the level of initial contact sets a ceiling on how high you can go. Alan Williams, for example, says:

'In general terms, the point of initial sales contact automatically becomes the "hierarchical ceiling" beneath which the salesman's subsequent negotiations will take place. He can easily move down, but not up.'

In practice, if you have the confidence, it is not too difficult to start near the top; it is simply a matter of expecting to deal at that level. If you believe you should (and will) be welcomed at board level, most times you will be. Whatever the true situation in your case, it still makes good sense to start as high as you can. It obviates many (if not all) the problems with 'blocking' – and nothing makes an underling more attentive than the knowledge that you have been sent to him by his boss (or better still by his managing director).

But what if you *haven't* been able to start at the top? Miller, Heiman and Tuleja suggest you find some powerful reason (they suggest 'knowledge', which is what top management, with its focus on strategy, is most interested in) to justify going to more senior management – *jointly with the blocker*, who has to feel that he, too, will benefit by bringing this 'knowledge' to his superiors. This is the ideal situation, but it is not easy to use, and is not always an option that is available.

A more pragmatic approach is to use a time when the blocker is out of the office, and then contact his manager, although you should be aware that in so doing you are in serious danger of alienating the blocker. If you must use this approach, it is best to find a real 'emergency' that must be handled immediately.

Another very practical approach is to use your own management. It is quite reasonable to say that your manager would like to come and meet the prospect; and, as a matter of courtesy, he would naturally expect to meet your contact's manager. This is a very difficult ploy for the contact to avoid, as protocol demands that he agrees. If he still refuses then you are in trouble and will have to switch to a more direct approach; with nothing to lose you might as well 'put the boot in' and, with a bit of luck, the blocker will have been moved by the start of your next sales campaign.

If your company has a top-heavy management structure you might be able to bring in several more levels of management, gradually upping the stakes (and the levels) within your prospect's management.

Another possibility is to use a reference to provide you with an introduction to a higher level. Often your own directors will have contacts in common with your prospect; the 'old boy network' can be very useful.

However, the block may just not be movable and you may judge it necessary to get round it at all costs. In this case, you need to screw up your courage and do whatever dastardly deeds are necessary. The call when the blocker is out of the office is probably the best starter. You do, however, have to be prepared to accept the possibly dire consequences of alienating the blocker; so make sure you have nothing to lose.

Miller, Heiman and Tuleja realistically comment that:

'Whenever you make a sale *in spite of* a key player's disapproval, you're perceived as playing Win-Lose with that person ... since *any buyer ignored is a threat.*'

Politics and bribery

I have only one rule: *don't!*

Major purchases often become the focus of political activities by the various managers involved. As a result you may be tempted, or even invited by one of the participants, to back one or other of the sides. But such involvement in company politics is dangerous, no matter how skilful you are. As an outsider you will not have the intimate political knowledge necessary to be certain of backing the winner. Even if you *are* on the winning side you may find that you are expendable; part of the price that the winning side is ready to pay for a suitable peace (and who better to blame than an outsider?). Much better to stay outside the struggles, treating all in the same friendly way, while stressing that your integrity bars you from interfering in internal company affairs. Most companies will respect your integrity far more than your political support, which they will ultimately distrust – just who will you support *next* time?

Very few UK (or US) salesmen become involved in bribery, even in the least risky forms; but it does exist, and is the normal form of business in some countries. It is fortunate that it doesn't normally intrude on your selling; bribery can be very dangerous indeed, as some recipients of prison sentences have found to their cost.

In theory, at least, it is an offence to buy a borough councillor a pint of beer if you are in the process of selling to his council (although it is not an offence to make such an offer to a Member of Parliament – but, then, they wrote the law!). Even if your adventure is not strictly illegal, you can be certain that if you are caught in the act of 'buying business' you will be instantly dismissed. Those companies who would be happy to use almost any, no matter how dubious, route to obtaining the order will still offload anyone who might destroy their remaining shreds of reputation with the taint of bribery. Respectable companies will have you out of the door for just thinking about it.

What if you are asked for a bribe? Take it to your manager *immediately*; you are not paid to take such risks (and neither, probably, is he – so the problem will possibly ricochet around the company for some time). What if, on the other hand, you think your competitors are involved in bribery? The safest answer, in almost all cases, is to ignore it. In my experience, most times when it looks as if you are the butt of underhand competitive tactics, it turns out to be just yourself being unduly sensitive to quite innocent events; and any ill-thought-out reaction, let alone an over-reaction, would be disastrous. Besides which, if there *is* bribery involved it will be so well covered up that you would need the resources of Interpol to prove anything. So forget it, and concentrate on winning the campaign proper.

If, however, things start getting out of hand, John Fenton suggests you (or your MD) make a call on the prospect's chief executive. You should use this opportunity to present a watertight case for your product. This should invite the question from him, 'Why haven't I seen this?', hopefully followed by, 'What on earth is going on?'; to which your eloquent answer can be a rather ingenuous, 'I don't know, it's a mystery to me too!' Then let the subsequent blood-letting be a private matter and put your own effort into the sale.

In practice, such situations are very much a rarity. I have only ever come across two borderline cases. One was where the buyer had been invited, all expenses paid (and with his wife), to a conference in Switzerland. It was *very* borderline and could have been quite innocent. In the other case I was facing a DP manager who I did suspect might have been made an offer. To my astonishment, he suddenly blurted out: 'You think I have been offered a bribe, don't you?' My immediate response was: 'Of course not! No reputable company would ever make such an offer. It would put their whole reputation at risk, and it would undermine your trust – since it would prove they had no integrity. And you, yourself, wouldn't fall for such a bribe even if a salesman made one against his company policy. You wouldn't want to put your job on the line; particularly where you would have no guarantee of a pay-off. It would be much safer for the salesman to string you along, and then not pay. You couldn't complain, and he wouldn't need to risk his company's reputation or his job!' I won the sale; I suspect not least on the basis of that reply – I just wish I had been similarly inspired at other times.

Competitive selling

Complex sales allow more scope and more time for sophisticated competitive activity. The professional salesman will, therefore, find himself spending much of his time defending his position against competitive offensives.

On the other hand, the professional salesman least of all can afford to knock his competition. It is a very unproductive pastime. As Alan Williams says:

'Clearly, slandering one's rivals is not only discourteous, but also implies elements of fear, envy, dishonour etc, which will not gain you the admiration of the potential buyer. It can only destroy your own credibility.'

Barring the competition

It is, thus, a sound (if possibly risky) investment to try to lock out your competitors very early in the sale.

John Fenton describes how Douglas McGregor conducted an interesting experiment:

'He arranged for a set of ideas to be communicated to a sample of people. Then a couple of days later a different person communicated an entirely different, and contradictory, set of ideas to the same people. The research showed that up to 80 per cent of the sample happily changed their ideas to the new set.

In a parallel group, though, the person conveying the initial set of information WARNED the group that someone else would later try to get them to change their minds. In this case only 20 per cent of the sample would accept the second set of ideas in preference to the first.'

The first, and critical, step is to be there before your competitors. It is very difficult to 'bar' a sitting tenant.

Once there, my own approach was subtly (but legitimately and safely) to undermine the integrity of my competitors. In an early call, usually my first long call, I explained the *problems* in some detail. This was a gamble that flew in the face of conventional sales wisdom. It is traditionally held that the sales pitch must always be positive; and problems are taboo. Most salesmen, therefore, will not even admit that problems exist. Their conventional answer to the question, 'Will there be any problems?', is quite simply, 'Of course not!'

The reality is that some problems must almost inevitably be inherent in the current prospect situation, otherwise he wouldn't be listening to your suggestions for changes. The prospect will be well aware of the problems and will respect the fact that you too are aware of them, as long as you approach the situation sensitively.

What is more, almost any solution proposed will also have its own (usually obvious) problems. Complex sales almost invariably lead to complex installations; the chances of the project going perfectly, without any hiccups, is very low. The more experienced users will already be aware of this, and the inexperienced ones will soon recognise it.

In my own calls I quite deliberately highlighted these problems, particularly those of the installation to come. It was a powerful and very fast way of building rapport and trust; I reeked of integrity – even the most naive prospect recognised me as the anti-salesman (the best mantle, or disguise, any salesman can assume!). But it was a gamble. I had not just to describe the problems (if I had stopped there I *would* have killed the sale stone dead); but, in the same call, I had also to show the prospect that there were solutions to these problems – and that I (and, by implication, I alone) had these solutions.

It was a very sophisticated and difficult sell, but it was the hinge of many of my campaigns. It was difficult, and a risk, because it needed a long call to cover all the points (problems and solutions). In particular, it needed a great deal of fast thinking (and experience) to be able to suggest possible solutions to problems as they emerged, for the problems have to be the specific problems of the prospect, not generalised ones that can be predicted in advance.

The real justification for the gamble was quite simply the effect that it had on my competition. It was an incredibly powerful means of crippling, and even barring, my competitors before the campaign even opened. Having been exposed to the problems in some detail and having also been shown that solutions were possible, the prospect was suitably prepared to meet the salesmen of my competitors. When he asked *them* if there were any problems he was almost guaranteed the obligatory response of, 'Of course not!' But now he knew better. If he was kind he might pursue them further; asking specific questions based on the problems I had already identified for him. The usual response from a salesman thrown this lifeline was to go on the defensive, with ever growing panic as he got further and further out of his depth. If the prospect didn't have the time or inclination, he would write him off immediately as a glib salesman.

For me the gamble *always* worked. I never failed to win that first call. The calls were long, but the fascination of the prospects, who seemed never to have come across an honest salesman before, allowed me to expand the normal time limits set aside for such calls. I always got a positive message across; and I usually locked the door against my competitors.

If you can carry it off, it is a *very* powerful technique. It can also be great fun when, as often happens, the prospect relays back to you the misfortunes of your competitors who have fallen into the trap!

Anti-salesmanship

The seeds of anti-salesmanship are evident in the previous technique, but in its extension it becomes probably the most controversial technique described in this chapter. Its use is foreshadowed by much of the work of the few writers who set out to describe complex sales situations. In particular, Miller, Heiman and Tuleja describe the now popular 'win-win' strategy, where, for successful long-term business (the essence of complex selling) both the salesman *and* the prospect have to win. The conventional stereotype would have only the salesman winning, at the expense of the prospect (who, by definition, must lose). The anti-salesmanship technique simply extends this apparent reversal of the salesman's role, to establish this as a very positive and distinctive competitive position.

As described earlier, the research very clearly shows that customers (particularly for complex sales) desperately want expert support from a salesman they can trust. But they believe, with considerable justification, that the reality is that they will most likely receive poor, inexpert (and very biased) advice from a totally untrustworthy charlatan. Personal computer buyers, for example, were shown by market research to rate too much hard sell aggression as the most offputting quality of a salesman; 30 per cent of buyers giving this factor as their favourite hate, almost half as many again as for any other failing.

Clearly, in marketing terms, the 'market position' I wanted to be in (the image I wanted to convey) was just where those prospects wanted to see me; with the positive qualities they wanted. The conventional hard sell position occupied by most salesmen was diametrically opposed to this ideal. So, the short-term device I deliberately adopted, very specifically (*and very obviously*) to highlight my own position as being close to the ideal, was to be an anti-salesman. I was in effect establishing my position as exactly opposite to that of the conventional salesman; and, almost by definition, this immediately placed me in the 'ideal' position that I sought.

It is not too difficult for me to become the anti-salesman. I am tubby and balding; and one of my favourite (and most powerful) throwaway lines was, 'How could anyone take me seriously as a slick salesman, with my figure!', subtly reinforcing the image of my competitors as *smooth* (and, by association, untrustworthy) operators. In addition, as a balance to the very professional ('expert consultant') image I presented, I used to include anecdotes about my 'incompetence' as a salesman, typically adding the comment, 'I will never make the grade as a real salesman. It's fortunate that in this job I can concentrate on helping customers, and forget about all the sophisticated techniques of selling!' I even used to let slip honest 'snippets' about problems with the equipment; very carefully, though, explaining how they had been solved. By implication I suggested that my competitors had similar, or worse, problems which they didn't talk about – probably because they hadn't resolved them. I accompanied these 'indiscretions' with the disclaimer: 'Of course, if I were a good salesman I wouldn't tell you this, but I believe that honesty is the best policy.'

Most of all, though, I deliberately displayed my admiration for the sales skills of the individual salesmen competing against me. My most 'vicious' competitive campaign was reserved for the best salesman ever lined up against me. During the social chit-chat, I would confess my admiration (which was genuine) for his sales techniques. I would carefully explain to the prospect exactly how the techniques worked, and suggest that the prospect watch them the next time this salesman called. As a result, that salesman walked into calls where nobody listened to his pitch, but instead watched his techniques. All they saw was his smooth objection handling ('That must have been the apparent agreement technique') and his closing ('My god, that was a clever alternative close'). Of course, these prospects did not admire his style; they hated it – it was the epitome of salesmanship (a term of abuse for them)! That salesman must have wondered what was happening: the harder he practised his skills, the more he lost their confidence.

I backed up my 'admiration' by explaining that he was such a good salesman, much better than me, that: 'If I didn't have a machine that was *much* better than his, the proverbial better mouse-trap, with his sales skills he would walk all over me!' (This was not strictly accurate, since the machines were not dramatically different in performance and his was significantly cheaper.)

The final benefit of anti-salesmanship is that it is a very distinctive trade-mark. Before a prospect can place an order with you, he has to *remember* you. If you are indistinguishable from the morass of other salesmen, he may have some difficulty matching you to your product. It is essential, therefore, that very early in the sales campaign you establish a clear and distinctive identity.

Prospects often link you to unusual things you have said or done: 'That's the salesman who described his product as the better mouse-trap', or even (for one successful salesman I employed), 'That's the salesman with the pink glasses'. I achieved (very useful) notoriety at one of my earliest exhibitions by accidentally and very publicly covering myself with blood from a burst transfusion bag. One of my customers still used this story (to great effect) when he introduced me to one of his contacts some five years later!

Being an anti-salesman is in itself *very* distinctive. It is highly unlikely that any prospect or customer will ever have difficulty in remembering who you are, or even in remembering the details of what you said. Anti-salesmanship is memorable. As it is just about the ultimate in laid-back approaches, it can also be highly enjoyable.

Knowing your competitors personally
As the example in the previous section shows, it is a great advantage to know your individual competitor's salesmen in some detail. I always went out of my way to meet them at exhibitions, so that I could evaluate them and predict how they would behave in a call. In return I carefully presented my anti-salesman image. Competitors will, very usefully, fall into the trap of underestimating such an approach – and a competitor who underestimates you is weakened accordingly. I discreetly supplemented this picture with information gleaned from my customers; finding out how my competitors actually sold. The guise I often used was that of trying to learn lessons about salesmanship; in the process also subtly continuing my attack on these competitors as 'salesmen'.

Based on this knowledge, you can tailor your specific campaigns to capitalise on the weaknesses (and neutralise the strengths) of these competitors. I had one competitor where a very weak (indeed abysmal) salesman was backed by a strong manager, who the salesman (foolishly for him and fortunately for me) chose to keep out of his accounts. When it was obvious that this competitor was likely to be involved, I deliberately did this salesman a 'favour' by suggesting to the prospect that he contacted him personally. That salesman was as grateful to me as I was to him (he *never* won any of this business off me); and, as I expected, he very carefully kept his manager, who *was* a threat, at bay. Because I knew that this salesman posed no threat whatsoever, I even deliberately introduced him into prospects where I felt that they showed signs of wanting a choice.

Be careful, though. Providing your own competition can rebound if that competition is not as weak as you think; but, if you handle it with skill, 'running' your own competitor can be a useful way of minimising competitive pressures.

'Hi-jacking' the specification

One particularly effective way of winning the sale is to make sure that the specification only applies to your own product. Again, this means that you have to be in and influencing the prospect before anyone else. Once you are in, and have quickly established your relationship with the prospect, the first help you should offer is to assist him in writing the specification. Prospects are usually only too happy to have this offer of help (unless they have been taken for a ride with this technique before!). Producing the specification is often a real pain for a prospect because he simply does not know enough about the products. So he should welcome your attention.

Having got his support, you must make a good job of the specification. Ideally, it will be based on a mini-survey and, allowing for some amendments designed to favour your product, it should be the best specification possible to match his needs. The whole of this process, regardless of what the specification finally says, is an ideal opportunity to establish your presence and demonstrate your support very early in the campaign; well in advance of your competitors. It will build excellent rapport and partnership; to the extent that, if you do a good job on the specification, the competition may never be invited in. Preemption always beats competition.

The covert skill of this operation lies in producing a specification that favours you. It is easy to produce a specification out of a hat that is only applicable to your product: 'It is a critical requirement that remote sites should only need one concentrator, which should be capable of handling 17 terminals.' Maybe this matches your own strengths, but unfortunately ignores the reality that: 'There is just one remote site, and that is served by a van not a data network.' Even the most naïve prospect can usually see through such a trick, particularly if he has seen no survey to back it up.

In general, as soon as a salesman launches into a pitch about the absolute necessity of having some obscure feature you can be fairly certain that is the only product advantage he has! With *very* naïve prospects it may sometimes be possible to run a more subtle version of this 'scam'. But, even here, it is always possible that a disgruntled competitor (from whom you *can't* hide the truth) will the blow the whistle. That competitor will probably not get the sale (no prospect likes being told he is an idiot), but neither will you (prospects like even less being *made* an idiot!).

Clearly, if you are not to miss an opportunity, the specification should be written to favour your own solution. But this has to be subtly done and backed by a full justification; the overall specification has to be sound and obviously in the prospect's best interests. The acid test should be what will happen if a competitor points out your 'unfair bias'. Will the customer recognise that you have tampered with the evidence, or will he think it is just sour grapes on the part of your competitor?

If you think the prospect might see through your machinations, modify your approach until you are confident that the specification appears (at least to the prospect) whiter than white. There is always time to win a sale based on a fair specification (that's your job), but if you are not careful a fake specification can lose you the business before you've begun.

Even with these caveats, it is still very easy to write a transparently fair specification that still gives you a significant edge – enough to win you the sale. So get in early, and win the sale early.

The quiet call

Salesmen do not *have* to be showmen, although I admit that I am – and revel in the theatricality of the call. Despite my own predilections, the most successful call is often the quietest, low-key one.

Negative selling

This is, I must admit, a deliberately controversial title, to link with anti-salesmanship. As such, it is somewhat misleading, if memorable; you should never indulge in true negative selling. On the other hand, you can extend the anti-salesmanship approach to other parts of your sales pitch. More accurately, it is deliberate underselling. Once more, however, it requires considerable skill to succeed.

It is essential to get across the sales messages just as clearly as before, but with much of the normal sales hyperbole removed. This is a difficult role to play, because the one thing you must *not* remove is your enthusiasm. It is best described as an honest approach. You should describe the product, for example, truthfully (more or less); warts and all. If you are confident enough about the situation, you can even appear to be diffident about the benefits the prospect might find; let *him* tell you what they are.

This last comment highlights the secret of the technique. It is to get the prospect to make the sales points to you; the reverse of the normal approach. If you have carefully chosen and presented your sales messages so that they obviously meet the prospect's exact needs you don't need fanfares. The prospect will soon enough recognise them as major benefits and, indeed, will probably recognise them more easily if he doesn't have to disentangle them from the hype of the oversell. It is a relatively easy matter then (if you have the skill) to lead the prospect into telling you the benefits. Every benefit that a prospect 'works out for himself' and proudly describes to you is worth a number of benefits presented by you to him. It ensures that he believes the message and is committed to it (after all, it is *his* idea). It also allows you genuinely to enthuse, without any risk of being accused of an oversell, about his idea!

Genuine honesty

Perhaps the most difficult technique, though, is genuine honesty. It hits hardest when you have to turn down business. As Miller, Heiman and Tuleja say:

> 'One of the hardest decisions you have to make as a sales representative is the decision *not* to close a sale, even though it's possible to do so.'

Heinz Goldmann reinforces this:

> 'Selling is the art of "how to win" customers; not how to overpower them. If the salesman should discover in the course of negotiation that his offer can be of no benefit to the customer, he should not press it, even if the customer is well disposed towards him.'

Such a decision may be necessary because you don't want to jeopardise a customer's other business, or it may be because you are targeting major long-term business from a prospect, and again don't want to jeopardise it for dubious short-term gains.

In any case, taking business that is not justified (either because the prospect doesn't actually need the product, or because your own product doesn't really meet his needs) will very quickly wreck any worthwhile reputation that you may have built up. It will lose you that prospect for an indefinite period. Worse, though, it will also lose you his many contacts who, you can be sure, will be told all about your sins. Much as you will build a sizeable proportion of your business by word-of-mouth references from your satisfied customers, you can lose it even faster by 'dishonest' selling. On top of that, you will spend long hours, which you could profitably spend elsewhere, trying to sort out all the problems that you will have landed on the prospect.

Despite all that the sales trainers say, or imply, honesty really is the best policy!

The pregnant pause
In the quiet call, a most effective technique is the long pause. It is also one of the most difficult (particularly for the more theatrical of us). It allows you and (more importantly) the prospect to relax and gather your thoughts. A call doesn't have to be all vacuous talk. Some of it can be very productive thought.

The late run
One effective technique I saw used by some Burroughs salesmen was to change the ground rules very late in a very competitive (usually price competitive) game. They would spend virtually all the campaign standing aloof from the price haggling that everyone else was involved in. They would stress that they would not offer a cheap solution, but only the best solution: 'Our reputation would not allow us to do otherwise.' They would, therefore, spend the sale (very productively) selling the virtues of their 'ideal' solution – although at the same time they would be discreetly honing it down to the leanest possible, so that it was very competitive, apart from price. Because of the high price, the competitors would see Burroughs as a non-runner, and would concentrate on destroying the other competitors.

However, just before the decision (typically as little as two hours before), the Burroughs salesman would suddenly jump in with a new price. This would be marginally below the the lowest priced (viable) offering from its competitors, and they would add the comment: 'We have decided that your business is so important to us that we are prepared to subsidise it.' The prospects were nearly always bowled over by this approach. It made them feel ten feet tall; they had beaten down the Burroughs price, and got the 'ideal' machine. The competitors had been wrong-footed. In the accompanying euphoria, Burroughs were often able to clinch a deal that, if it had been examined competitively, might not have been justifiable! In my early days as a salesman I certainly lost at least one sale to such tactics.

Win-win
Throughout this book I have stressed the need for partnership with

the customer and prospect. Miller, Heiman and Tuleja have encapsulated this in the concept of win-win:

> 'Those of us who have prospered by using Strategic Selling [the name of their technique and their book] know that good selling is never an adversarial game in which Buyers' Losses are our Wins, but are in which Buyers' Losses are our Losses too, and their Wins always serve our self-interest as well as theirs. We understand that only by enlisting our buyers as *partners* in mutually supportive joint ventures can we hope to achieve mutual satisfaction over time.'

They conceptualise this philosophy in terms of the win-win matrix, shown in Figure 6.1.

SELLER (I)

	I WIN YOU WIN	I LOSE YOU WIN
BUYER (YOU)		
	I WIN YOU LOSE	I LOSE YOU LOSE

Figure 6.1

In practice, this is something of a gimmick since their comments show that all of the remaining quadrants tend to be unstable, and degenerate into the lose-lose situation. Even the lose-win situation degenerates, since it sets up unrealistic expectations for the future. They stress if you do use this tactic: ' ... *let the buyer know it* ... the most serious mistake you can make in playing Lose-Win is failing to tell your Buyers that they're getting a special deal.'

On the other hand, the concept of win-win is very powerful, and the only real alternative, of lose-lose, serves to highlight this. Partnership, or win-win, is what you must always be looking for.

Pricing

The one element of competition that, more than any other, seems to give salesmen sleepless nights is pricing. What price will win the deal, but still make my company the most profit? If you price even slightly too high you may lose everything; and, for many salesmen, the nagging thought is that the sale might be lost for just a few pennies. But if you price too low your company is losing profit and the whole deal may not be worthwhile. If you don't have to worry about profit (and many companies are remarkably secretive about even their gross margins, let alone their net profits) then your company may well have the wrong sales plan – and you should worry about its long-term financial viability!

This nervousness about price, and particularly the fear of losing because of a 'few pennies', can be a major factor in very large capital projects. On a big civil engineering project, such as BTR was involved in supplying for example, the competitive teams may have spent long months (even years) of their lives and hundreds of thousands of pounds preparing their tenders. All of this effort, with the financial and emotional investments, depends on one decision; and on one price! There is, therefore, an almost inevitable move to shave the price – to make certain of winning. Unfortunately, *all* the vendors do the same, and the only winner is the buyer, who almost invariably gets a bargain; unless, as too often happens, the deal drives the supplier into bankruptcy.

In his book on negotiation Gary Karass reinforces the importance of the psychological aspects:

'The sales person is in a terrible position in negotiation – *because he thinks he is*. The buyer always has a lot more clout – *because he thinks the buyer has more clout* ... Your job conditions you to go into negotiations in a negative frame of mind. Your job, most of the time, brings you criticism and complaints – about your products, your prices – and compliments, about your competitors. Your job brainwashes you.'

There are, therefore, many markets where prices are very keen (sometimes suicidally so). The personal computer market is just one such market, having been moved in the direction of suicidally unprofitable price-cutting by its dealers (most of whom know no other sales technique). Whatever the reason, the end result is that in these markets the salesman must be very aware of the price.

Some buyers will take advantage of this situation, and Gary Karass identifies three particularly interesting ploys to watch out for:

> 'One of the more seductive and successful [buyers' tactics] is the *bogey* ... I love your product ... but the price is $100,000 and I only have $80,000 ... [or] the budget ... says 92 cents per pound.'
> 'Another seductive buyer tactic: the *Krunch* ... You've go to do better than that ... [or] You're close.'
> 'The next tactic is a non-selective one ... *Take it or leave it.*'

It is not an easy situation in which to win against the odds, especially where the key buying criterion is so simple; it would be foolish to pretend otherwise. Indeed, the first answer to this dilemma (offered by other pundits as well as myself) is that of: 'I wouldn't have started from here!' There is clearly no way that you could persuade a whole market to stop this sort of self-immolation and push the general level of prices up. But within the market it is still possible to build a 'monopoly' situation which removes you from the worst head-to-head competition.

Much of modern marketing is aimed at doing just this. The unique selling proposition (USP) is intended to establish your product with a unique quality and, hence, with a monopoly. If the prospect decides that your USP is essential, he simply can't buy it elsewhere. Coca Cola has spent vast sums in advertising, trying to persuade its teenage prospects that it alone is the 'real thing'. If they believe this, as many do, and decide it is the one key buying criterion, then they will not buy another brand no matter how low its price.

Your initial effort must, therefore, be directed to building that USP, and that monopoly. For more than half a century, in a very competitive market where discounting was endemic, IBM *never* offered a discount to anyone. But the IBM brand was so strong, and IBM had so successfully persuaded the market that it really *was* different, that most prospects still bought its products.

It is somewhat more difficult to adopt this rather high-handed approach in a very price competitive market where all the products are similar. Even so, it may be quite possible to build a highly specific USP (or set of USPs) for an individual sale. In my personal computer dealership, we established the USP that we (and we alone) had the expertise necessary to support the particularly complex CAD systems, and sold successfully despite offering minimal discounts. In practice, even in competitive markets it is not too difficult to find a USP for a specific prospect, since all the other salesmen will be conducting 'box sells' based only on price – and the salesman who puts in the effort to find out exactly what the prospect really wants has usually found his USP.

One further advantage of hi-jacking the specification (discussed earlier in this chapter) is that the specification can be carefully positioned at a 'price-break' that favours you. I had this tactic used very effectively against one of my salesmen by a Tandy salesman. He persuaded the prospect that he needed just two more workstations, which pushed us just over a break-point. His price went up by just £5000 and ours by £15,000!

If you too examine your offerings compared to the competition, you may also be able to find a similar (apparently innocent) move that will give you a distinct price advantage; but be prepared for your competitors to fight back with a similar response – as we did, successfully, against Tandy (but I still admire the original Tandy move).

It is often recommended that you emphasise the *whole* package that you are selling, to put the price in perspective and to reduce its impact – and, even there, the pundits suggest that you should talk about the differences in price rather than the absolute prices. For many years IBM didn't talk at all about price, but only about 'price performance', which allowed a much greater leeway for the salesman to inflate the 'performance', and hence relatively deflate the price.

However, if price *has* been established as the deciding factor, I suspect that this is merely spitting into the wind. You must *persuade* the buyer to look at other factors. To encourage this, I deliberately refused to let my PC salesmen offer discounts above 10 per cent. Discounts over this level were not barred, since this would have been suicidal in a market where the typical discounts exceeded 30 per cent (and some went as high as 45 per cent), but the salesman was told to explain that, 'In view of the seriousness of the potential trade-offs' (in itself an anti-discounting sales point), 'my senior management have to examine all the impacts on the solution being offered.'

Ideally, any discussion of discounts was deliberately postponed until after the 'survey' stage; the quite reasonable excuse being that we couldn't discount until we knew what was needed – although we also hoped that in the process we would find our USP! Indeed, the idea was that any discounts would only be discussed at the formal presentation of the proposed solution. At that meeting, which we called a 'systems review meeting' (and which was also attended by our technical experts, to emphasise the consultancy aspects), a flipchart would be produced listing the requirements. In answer to the prospect's request for a discount, he would be asked which requirements he wanted to drop, thus making him very aware of the trade-offs. In practice, by this stage most prospects had forgotten all about discounts and were concentrating on more important matters; which was exactly what we wanted.

I regret to say, however, that this postponement of discounting offers (so that it could, in effect, be fought on ground of our choosing) was beyond the grasp of many of my dealer salesmen, who were used to responding immediately to price demands and who simply couldn't face the stress of postponing them. On the occasions when the technique was used, however, it worked well; and it should not be beyond the capacity of most professional salesmen.

Indeed, the main virtue IBM found in refusing to offer discounts (in the good old days) was that paradoxically it gave a major *selling* advantage, as well as the more obvious profit advantage. As an IBM salesman, I could simply sweep aside any requests for discounts with a simple 'no'. I could then get on with the real job of selling; that of finding out what the prospect wanted, and building a solution to match that. My competitors, on the other hand, spent most of their time in calls haggling over exactly what discount they would offer. Thus, when the order came to be placed, I was able to offer a solution where they were only able to offer a discount.

In reality, pricing is rarely the major factor in most sales, even in very price competitive markets. It is usually only the salesmen who make it so. The first question any salesman should ask, before he decides what level of discount he should offer, is quite simply: does he need to offer *any* discount? In most markets, if the salesman has done his job (and is working in partnership with his prospect), discounts should be the exception rather than the rule.

One aid to this is to have a printed price list, so that when a customer asks for a price you can work it out together. Such is the awe in which the printed word is held that few customers will challenge such printed price lists. Even better, use a computer to 'configure' the price – everyone knows that computers can't be wrong!

Gary Karass says quite simply: 'The printed price list, standard terms and conditions ... published procedures and policies – all these have the power of LEGITIMACY, for you to use.'

If price is still important, though, you need a good feel for what the competitive prices will be. In part this will come from (often bitter) experience, from the wins and (more likely) the losses you have had against them previously. But in some sales it may be possible to use your 'coach' (your inside adviser) to find out exactly what is being offered. Knowledge here can be worth a lot; as long as you aren't a victim of the 'late run'.

Pricing has become such a complex (and emotional) issue that whole books have been written about 'negotiation'. If you want to review the techniques in depth then read one of these; I can't do the subject justice in one small section. But, once more, take the advice these books offer with a healthy dose of cynicism – and make certain that the techniques fit you well.

The salesman as actor

Every salesman has to be an actor, at least to some degree. One guaranteed way to lose the business, for example, is to show your true feelings when the customer complains; and very few salesmen are foolish enough to fall into that trap. A salesman has still to be a bundle of joy even when he is soaking wet, and just about to catch flu. A salesman has to play a part, just as much as an actor. Conventional sales training would have you learn a range of techniques, in much the way that an amateur thespian learns his lines; carefully following the stage directions: 'Smile when you ask the prospect to repeat his objection.'

But there are other, much more sophisticated schools of acting, which also have the great advantage for the salesman that they do not require a slavish adherence to an arbitrary script, since the most powerful sales messages are actually built into the structure itself.

The Stanislavsky method

Constantin Stanislavsky was the founder of the Moscow Arts Theatre; an unpromising start for someone who I would propose as one of the patron saints of professional salesmanship! He did, however, develop the 'Method' school of acting; most eloquently described in his own work, *The Actor Prepares*, and most extensively promoted in the West by the Actors' Studio of New York.

Stanislavsky was scathing about the previous script-based acting (and by analogy, many of the rote-learned sales techniques):

' ... clichés will fill up every empty spot in a role, which is not already solid with living feeling.'
' ... never allow yourself externally to portray anything that you have not inwardly experienced ...'

Instead, he insisted that the actor must *live* the part he was playing:

> 'In our art you must live the part every moment you are playing it, and every time.'
>
> ' ... the very best that can happen is to have the actor completely carried away by the play. Then regardless of his own will he lives the part, not noticing *how* he feels, not thinking about *what* he does, and it all moves of its own accord, subconsciously and intuitively.'

The importance of this, at first glance, apparently obscure analogy for salesmen is that it indicates how he can best get 'inside' his part. He has to create, and then live, the part of the ideal salesman; as the *prospect* would wish to see it.

By now you will have a good idea of what I think the typical prospect wants. But you must draw your own conclusions, based partly on your specific prospect set, partly on the character of your company and what it sells, but mainly on what you feel you could be comfortable with. You must already have something approaching this persona; every morning as you leave to start your selling you almost certainly put on the role (albeit unconsciously). What you now need to do, following the 'Stanislavsky' school of salesmanship, is to develop that role to fill out the part as it really should be; in the prospect's (audience's) eyes.

The first stage of that personal development is to develop some self-awareness and understanding of what you currently are. Stanislavsky emphasised this step: 'If you only knew how important is the *process of self-study*!'

You will probably find that your sales self is an amalgam of various elements. It will be based on your own 'private' personality (but typically will not just be that alone). It will, no doubt, also incorporate elements of the styles of the role models you chose; the salesmen you admired when you started your sales career. Finally, and probably damagingly, it will contain elements of the various stereotypes that are bandied around by the media and (in a rather different form) by the sales trainers.

If you compare this with your fleshed out image of the 'ideal' salesman your prospects want, I suspect you will find that there are major discrepancies. If nothing else I imagine most of the stereotypes will need to be abandoned! You then have to set to and build yourself into that role. You have to start to 'live' it. While you are in the call ('on stage'), at least, you must believe in the part. Stanislavsky says:

'Truth on the stage is whatever we can believe in with sincerity, whether in ourselves or in our colleagues. Truth cannot be separated from *belief*, nor *belief* from truth.'

It sounds a horrendously difficult exercise, particularly for a salesman who has had no acting experience and who last went to the theatre 10 years ago. In reality it is not too difficult, because the role calls for only *one* dimension to count, and that (once again) can be summarised as customer service. The salesman that the prospect wants to see (and the one who is successful) subjugates everything to that one driving force.

Once again, there is only one acid test of any action by the character you create, and that is: is this action in the best interest of the prospect? Of course, there are related dimensions: genuine interest in the prospect and his business, genuine sympathy for his problems and rapport with him personally, a genuine desire to be honest and trustworthy – but, above all, a burning desire to help.

Clearly, this character is much larger than life; and prospects would be very unsettled if they ever met a salesman who actually behaved in this extreme manner. But such caricatures are a useful starting point for the role, before you tone down the model to match your own personality. Once more, it is *you* who has to feel comfortable with the part.

The big advantage of this approach is that very soon you will come to *believe* in the role. This means that even your reactions will always be consistent with the ideal; something that is almost impossible to simulate otherwise. The consistency of the role also makes selling that much easier. You won't have to keep thinking whether you should now use the apparent agreement technique; you will just agree naturally. And these natural responses will give a great deal of power to your performance.

Alienation
If you have managed to fight your way through the 'Stanislavsky' school of salesmanship, there can be one further, even more sophisticated stage; again based on acting techniques. This is 'alienation' which was developed by Bertolt Brecht.

The problem with the 'Method', in the theatre and in the sale, is that it becomes too easy to produce a very rich characterisation. The role, in developing a life of its own, acquires a great many 'natural' characteristics. In the theatre these can easily get in the way: the actor becomes so involved in lighting his cigarette 'in character' that the theme and pace of the play can get lost. The same can be true in a call: in empathising with the prospect you can lose sight of the real reason you are there – to make the sale.

'Alienation' starts with the role already fully developed by the 'Method'. It then asks the actor to refine that naturalistic role down to its essential characteristics, to abstract the key elements that can be simply (and very powerfully) communicated to the audience. It asks the actor, while playing the natural role, to be able to stand outside himself and direct his performance to highlight those abstracted essences.

A similar technique can be used in selling. While naturally following the 'Method'-derived role (so that your reactions are still sound) you should try to stand back and (within the overall framework imposed by the 'part') simplify your presentation. This should enable you to make your sales messages easier for the prospect to follow, and correspondingly more powerful. It also should allow these sales messages to be more than unguarded reactions; to be controlled responses which inexorably propel the prospect towards closing. This constant self-criticism, self-direction, imposed on the role means that your performance can be optimised for each prospect and, to a certain extent, for each call.

Again, it sounds difficult, and in truth very few actors have the skills necessary fully to project the most complex aspects of 'alienation' as Bertolt Brecht would have wished them. But for a salesman, put crudely, it simply means that he shouldn't get totally carried away with empathy for the prospect. He still needs to remember his campaign objectives – and make the sale.

Be yourself

You may well decide that these esoteric schools of acting are totally irrelevant to your own needs. If you feel this way your decision will be right. I stressed at the beginning of this book that you should aim to pick up only a few of the 'recipes' it contains, choosing just the very few that are suitable for *you*. It is likely, therefore, that you will want to follow your own existing approach, without risking the damage that a flirtation with the 'Method' might cause. The important thing is that *you* must feel comfortable (and productive) with what you are doing. So feel free to forget Stanislavsky and Brecht; but please don't forget customer service!

Chapter 7
Account Management

Much of sales training stresses the aggressive skills necessary to break into a new prospect's business. The challenge is to overcome the prospect's natural resistance, and get a foot in the door. Most of this sales training appears to assume that, once this sale has been made, the matter ends there. The bottle of champagne is opened, and the salesman moves on to accost the next prospect on his list.

The reality is that the typical sales professional will generate the major part of his business from *existing* customers. Of course, he must not ignore prospects; they provide extra business in the short term and, more important, they grow his customer base to increase his overall business in the longer term. On average, though, the business coming from such prospects will bring in less revenue than that from customers; and especially from the most important 20 per cent that will bring in 80 per cent of the revenue. Prospects are, perhaps, best viewed as an investment – albeit a necessary investment, and one that will normally pay for itself.

For the sales professional, therefore, the most productive area of improvement will be that of account management, handling the business of existing customers; an area that is largely ignored by most conventional sales training.

In *The IBM Way*, Buck Rodgers gives the secret of IBM's success:

'No magic formula or guarded secret keeps customers "married" to IBM long after their equipment is installed and their check deposited. It's just that IBM approaches the customer, *after* the sale, with the same interest and attention as when he was the prospect to be courted.'

The skills of account management are, indeed, quite different from those of prospecting; and far removed from the cardboard skills that many sales trainers purvey. The essence of the role is management (of resources and people), and the essence of the contact is partnership (even more so than that with prospects). One great advantage of developing account management skills is that this will also improve your overall selling skills.

For many years IBM's business was based on renting equipment (as opposed to selling it outright), which meant that the customer could switch to a competitor's product almost at a moment's notice; leaving the sales professional to take a commensurate *debit* in his commission for the business lost. Frank Cary, one of IBM's great chief executives, commented:

> 'If I was to select one single business practice that was most important to our success in the early days, it would be that we only leased equipment. This put a discipline on the business that was excellent. It motivated IBM people and it built a great relationship of trust between the customer and the company. The customer knew he had leverage.'

Keeping the account

The basic requirement will be that you keep the account. But this is not just a passive act. If you rest on your laurels, as many sales professionals do, you will all too soon lose them; your competitors won't stop their activities simply because you won that sale. A wise sales professional will almost redouble his efforts, and certainly redirect them, when he has created a customer. For the repeat business from a customer will be far more productive than any from his prospects. If nothing else there should be a close to 100 per cent chance of winning it if you manage the account well, where you will be lucky to win 20 to 30 per cent of prospects. Furthermore, the repeat business from the average customer will probably be larger than that from the average prospect; their needs will have been developed further and with them the level of business you can expect.

Customer satisfaction

The one critical measure of sales performance here will be customer satisfaction. A satisfied customer will rarely look elsewhere. Why should he gamble on an unknown quantity when his existing supplier (you) is providing a perfectly satisfactory service? He can happily get on with more important things.

IBM had no doubts about the importance of customer satisfaction. It was the prime responsibility of every sales professional. But, even so, IBM conducted surveys of its customers twice a year, to check their overall satisfaction with IBM's offerings. IBM senior management watched these surveys with avid attention, to check that satisfaction was being maintained. If there was as much as a 2 per cent reduction in the ratings (which were typically in the 80 to 90 per cent range) alarm bells started to ring, and at a 5 per cent 'slump' heads could be expected to roll.

Buck Rodgers describes how he saw it at the grassroots level:

'IBMers are not Pollyannas or altruists; they're pragmatists – realists who know which side their bread is buttered on. They know they'll be out of work if there are no customers. They also know that although their ambitions may be boundless, there's a limit to the number of customers they can acquire. So while they work very hard to get new customers, they work even harder to hold on to the ones they have. Someone once said I behaved as if every IBM customer were on the verge of leaving, and that I'd do anything to keep them from bolting. There's a bit of truth in that.'

Miller, Heiman and Tuleja put it succinctly:

' ... the "lucky" sales professionals understand that long-term success means keeping all of your customers not just sold but *satisfied*.'

For most sales professionals there can be no more important activity than ensuring that the customer is kept happy; whatever that entails.

Maintaining contact
It may seem obvious that you should maintain contact, and regular contact at that, with your customers; but, in my experience, it is not self-evident to many (probably most) sales professionals. Most of the sales professionals who have successfully sold me their products have taken the order and then disappeared without trace. I would estimate that less than 20 per cent of sales professionals ever returned; and less than 5 per cent regularly maintained contact.

Regular contact is essential to maintain rapport; to maintain the partnership. It is also (as we will see later) very productive in terms of growing the account.

Buck Rodgers says:

'Successful salespeople understand the importance of long-term customer connections. The size of their paycheck is determined to a large extent by their ability to develop sound, lasting relationships with enough customers. For the best of them, it's easy enough. They are respectful and thoughtful and go out of their way to be helpful.'

The Sales Professional

In my experience, however, the worst performance by sales professionals comes in terms of dealing with customer requests for contact. These are the most important contacts: the customer either has a problem (even if it is only some information he wants) or he wants to discuss placing more business. In either case you will want (or at least should want) to respond very promptly. Yet almost every vendor sales professional I have come across has failed to respond promptly; and many *haven't* responded at all.

It is almost as if sales professionals believe that all requests are complaints – they aren't. Some, at least from satisfied customers, are enquiries about new business (which certainly won't come your way again if you studiously avoid them). What is worse, assuming that they actually are complaints, is that sales professionals appear to believe that the best way of handling a complaint is to ignore it. Believe me, the one way of making sure that even a minor complaint rapidly grows into a major issue is steadfastly to ignore it! As we will see later in this chapter, the essence of problem handling is promptness.

If you maintain regular contact with your customers you start well ahead of your rivals in the sales game. The silliest aspect of the failure by most sales professionals to maintain contact, is that it needn't even use up much of their valuable personal resource. If you use my approach of *ad hoc* calls, just dropping in on customers between fixed appointments with other customers and prospects, the customer will feel that you are still taking an interest. You will pick up his intentions about new business at the earliest opportunity, and you will defuse the problems that your incompetent message centre has forgotten to tell you about.

I probably made three to four times as many customer calls as my colleagues; but these only took perhaps 50 per cent more of my resource, and I estimate I achieved as much as three times more repeat business than my colleagues did. In any case, I enjoyed customer calls most of all. They were rarely stressful; the relationships had already been successfully built. The customers were my friends.

Monitoring account health

Based on these regular meetings, it is sensible actively to monitor your account's health. Indeed, from time to time it is worthwhile extending your normal contacts to include user management throughout the business. The danger, otherwise, is that you may have a marvellous relationship with your prime contact which hides problems building up elsewhere in the organisation. *All* the users must be happy with your offering. Even one dissatisfied user can become the focus of discontent.

Most sales professionals make the assumption that their customer accounts are in good health, unless they are told about specific problems. I agree with Miller, Heiman and Tuleja when they say:

> ' ... many sales representatives simply end up talking to the people whom they feel comfortable with, who have approved their orders in the past, or who have the "right" titles on their doors.'

I, on the other hand, deliberately took the pessimistic view that I had to *prove* to myself that they were in good health. This meant that I never lost a customer due to major problems; indeed I never lost a major customer!

Monitoring the competition
No matter how healthy the account is, it is still dangerous to assume that your competitors are locked out. It pays dividends to track what they are up to; even if (as John Fenton suggests) you just check the visitors' book to see who's been in to see whom. If nothing else, tracking them will provide excellent information on your competition, for use in other sales situations. I found customers an invaluable source of such information, as seen (particularly valuably) from the 'prospect's' viewpoint.

But, at the same time, it makes certain that you are never taken unawares by a competitive onslaught. Even though you are the sitting tenant you are by no means invulnerable. If you are not too obviously competitive about the subject yourself, customers will happily talk about the situation; and respect and appreciate a 'humble' attitude where you take your competitors seriously.

Complacency
As far as customers are concerned, the worst enemy of a sales professional is his own complacency. As a buyer I have seen excellent sales professionals spend hard months fighting eventually to win my business, and was impressed by their skills and effort. Yet, immediately the sale was closed, their whole attitude changed. We were no longer important; they had moved on to win the next sale. I didn't know if this really was complacency on their part, or whether it was a result of a culture which sees a 'real' salesman constantly winning *new* business. Whatever the true cause, *we* saw it as

complacency; and the business was lost far faster than it was ever won, resulting in a very unproductive sales pattern for these salesmen.

Curiously, most sales professionals don't seem to notice the loss of existing business as much as that of a high profile prospect they are fighting to win, but in truth a customer lost is far more damaging.

Making the most of problems

I am surprised that sales professionals so studiously avoid dealing with problems. Needless to say, I didn't deliberately *cause* problems, but when they arose I positively welcomed them. For one thing I had no choice; I was going to have to deal with them anyway, so I determined to be positive about the process. The many sales professionals who are antagonistic about complaints (making the customer feel as if he, himself, has caused the problem) are guaranteed to exacerbate the situation.

Apologies

In practice, I found that the mandatory opening to dealing with a complaint was an apology. I have worked for managers who were unhappy about this approach, seeming to feel that it demeaned our company, and should be evaded until it was unavoidable. My own experience suggests that an immediate apology is the one, and only, guaranteed way to defuse a potentially explosive situation.

There can be only two possible outcomes. The first is that the complaint is justified, in which case you *must* apologise as soon as possible. On the other hand, if the complaint is *not* justified, an apology has done no harm. Indeed, the customer will be well aware that he has forced an apology from you; and in our society such an apology is normally not given lightly. As a result the customer usually will, somewhat guiltily, owe you a favour, which is always a worthwhile situation to cultivate. A sincere apology is worth a thousand explanations.

Heinz Goldmann's views are very similar:

> 'The customer is not always right, but it is often worth while to let him be right … Generosity usually pays for itself. It can lead to further business that will pay for your outlay in settling the claim.'

An apology also very quickly leads the way to a 'partnership' to solve the problem. You will be both sympathetic and helpful; and, more important, the customer will see you that way. It is by far the most productive environment for solving any problem.

Productive problem solving

So far we have seen how you can rapidly defuse, and then (you hope) solve, the problem. But why should you welcome it, apart from being forced to? The answer is that (always assuming that you can solve the problem) it represents one of the most potent *sales* opportunities open to you.

In the first place, your skills in problem solving (again, assuming you have them) will demonstrate that you really can provide the support that most customers and prospects rate above all other virtues of a vendor. As a 'demonstration' of your product package it will beat any other that you could offer.

Best of all, it is the one guaranteed situation where all normal barriers are down. The customer will not see it as a sales situation. As a result he will happily work alongside you to solve the problems jointly. It is an opportunity to build a partnership that you can't afford to neglect. What's more, while you are resolving the problem you can (very discreetly) talk to him about the rest of your sales campaign. The chances are that he will be more forthcoming and honest than at any other time; and will also be more receptive to your sales messages since his normal defences are down. So problems can actually be good news – just so long as you solve them, and fast!

Growing the account

The main sales activity in customers, though, should be growing the customer's business with you. This will normally be far and away the most productive use of your time; and the easiest and most enjoyable way of beating your sales targets.

Business development

If you put in the effort, the customer service to maintain a satisfied customer, you will naturally grow the business; further orders will be forthcoming without any special extra effort on your part. But if you, wisely, invest some extra effort positively to grow the business the rewards will be even greater. What is more, the customer will be even happier. Customers actually like being sold to, once the pressure is off. The customer, as much as you, will see the ongoing business in a different light from that of the 'conflict' which accompanied the original sale. In my experience the customers too come to see it as fun; well, don't you enjoy buying things – so why shouldn't a buyer? In any case, the act of selling further business generally helps to consolidate the existing business.

The volume of business will usually grow, even if you limit yourself to the existing uses. But the greatest growth is most likely to come if you actively seek out new uses.

Surveying

The best route to this new business is a survey, either formal or informal. It is also an essential part of many complex sales campaigns, being equally applicable to prospect sales. It is included in this chapter because the techniques lie close to those of account management.

It is an activity not often undertaken by sales professionals, but it is a need well recognised by customers. For example, market research showed that nearly 50 per cent of personal computer buyers looked for such an investigation, putting this requirement third in the list of support they expected – only just behind installation support and education.

Finding (new) potential

The justification (for both you and the customer) is to find new uses, and to ensure that the existing uses are being handled most effectively. The new use aspect justifies you surveying every part of the customer's business, and meeting all of his middle and senior management. Indeed, the essence of any such survey is that you visit as many parts of the customer's business as possible, and examine in some detail all aspects of his operations. Ideally, it requires many of the skills of a management consultant: you have to study, and understand in some depth, how each part of the business operates, at least in terms of the products you are offering.

For *each* department you visit you should be able to produce a comprehensive report of its requirements, together with the solutions you would propose. You may not in practice need to produce such a report, although (as we will see later) a full proposal is a very productive sales tool, but the acid test of a survey is that you *could* produce it if needed. A survey will, thus, equip you with the best possible information for any of your sales campaigns. If you actually know what you are talking about, no matter how poor your other sales skills, you must start any sales campaign as the favourite; ahead of the average sales professional who will, almost certainly, be ignorant of the customer's business.

Obviously, the exact form your survey will take will depend very much on what product or service you are selling. But in the context of what you have to offer, some of the key elements you must establish are:

1. *Existing use.* What limits the current operations? What makes them more difficult than they need be? Which of these are most important? What does the *manager* see as his worst problems?
2. *Possible needs and wants.* What does the manager need to make his operations better? What does he want, to make his life easier and more pleasant?
3. *Possible solutions.* What does he think might be the best solutions?
4. *Possible new uses.* What new operations does he believe might be possible? Which does he favour?
5. *Decision criteria.* In supporting any solution, what would his business (and personal) criteria be?

Of course, the one question you *must* ask everyone is whether you can have their support for your offering. You have to close the influencers just as aggressively (albeit in a discreet way) as the decision-makers.

Demonstrating expertise
Not least, this knowledge will enable you to demonstrate your expertise throughout the whole organisation: for example, what you learn from the production department can be used to demonstrate your understanding of the organisation, to impress the accounts department – and vice versa. But best of all, while you are carrying out the survey you will be able to demonstrate your basic business (and intellectual) expertise, simply by being able to understand each manager's own operation, together with a sympathetic appreciation of his problems and the ability to suggest some possible solutions.

Selling the influencers
Above all, though, the survey is a superb opportunity to sell *everyone* who might influence the sale, throughout the organisation. If you can convince *all* the influencers, you are in a strong position to win the sale; not least because most sales professionals will not deign to meet most of the influencers (or will not have the skills to be able to justify, and mount, a survey). Even if these sales professionals have met the influencers, it is likely that they will not have made as good an impression on them as you have, given the context of your survey and, hopefully, their commitment to support you.

A survey is one of the most productive sales techniques, if you can justify the time and effort – and, in view of its real productivity, the question should be: can you justify *not* conducting such a survey? It discovers the information needed to justify the sale, it unearths the new uses that will justify the larger sale (and will give you the competitive edge) and it will win over the influencers (and often with them the sale). Once more it is good sport, as long as you enjoy meeting people (and what sales professional would admit that he didn't!). The stresses are off – it is far removed from the hard sell – and you can just enjoy meeting interesting people.

Optimising reference potential

One aspect that should not be neglected is that of developing all of your customers so that they can be used as references. Every sales professional who uses references (as he should) is always short of these. Remembering that references need to be as close a match to the prospect's needs as possible, the more references you have the more likely you are to find a close match – one that will win you the sale.

In addition, as we saw in the previous chapter, the act of using a customer as a reference sell can in itself be a very powerful way of selling to the reference customer as well as to the prospect. Indeed, I would argue that just about the best way to develop an account is to make it a successful reference site.

Management

The essence of handling customers is not the stereotypical salesmanship, but is *management*.

Buck Rodgers describes the emphasis that IBM places on this aspect by the example of account planning, in *The IBM Way*:

> 'What IBM calls account-planning sessions are conducted annually. Here, both line and customer-support people spend from three days to a week reviewing the entire status of an account. With a major customer like Citibank or General Motors, as many as fifty IBM people could be involved. In the case of a small account, the session might include a handful of IBMers ... The customer has a well documented action plan that covers the upcoming year as well as years to come.'

Miller, Heiman and Tuleja put it succinctly: 'The question we stress in Strategic Selling is "How can I *manage this sale*?" '

As I have already stressed, I also believe that account management (in its most general sense, covering prospects as well as customers) is the essence of professional salesmanship. Customer account management, in particular, is the epitome of this. It is probably the most important single skill (apart from selling itself) required of a sales professional and yet it is almost entirely neglected by sales trainers.

If you get it right, it is also very satisfying to see your business from such an account grow; and it is almost as satisfying to see the contribution your efforts make to that customer's business as well as your own.

Managing the team

One aspect of many complex sales is the number of people involved, on *both* sides. More times than not, on your side there will be a team of personnel. In IBM, for example, a sales professional could, directly or indirectly, manage a dozen or more personnel. It has to be admitted that this is probably a much more elaborate team than most sales professionals will ever run. But many (if not most) sales professionals will at some stage have to coordinate the activities of several supporting staff, and that requires true man management.

The skills needed to run such a team are those of any man manager; and there are literally hundreds of management text books that have been written (including one by myself) to teach you these general skills. Possibly those by Peter Drucker may offer the best and most readable introduction. But, in the specific context of the sales team, the first key to success is to define clearly what each member of the team is to do.

Nothing annoys team members more than to discover that they are duplicating work; nothing except, that is, not being told what they should do, or finding that they are wasting their precious time. Having allocated the work, you will then have to charm them along. You will find that, not infrequently, you have to work harder at selling to your own supporters than to the customer. But ensuring your team is enthusiastic, and 100 per cent behind you, is essential to any team manager's success. The sale will depend on *everyone* in the team pulling his weight. There is no way you can do it alone.

I have lost count of the number of times I have encountered sales professionals totally abandoning their team management of, and even their contact with, their team members – in the forlorn hope that they could win the sale purely by their own sales techniques. They didn't stand a chance. Even if the sales professional doesn't recognise the importance of the team, the customer will. If it needs a team to sell a product, it surely will need a team to install it; and if that team is disunited the installation will be a disaster. As a result, no buyer with any sense will place an order. True partnership is as important a concept within your team as with the customer.

Not the least benefit of managing your team well is that it shows your own management what a good manager you yourself would make!

Resource management

Much as you will have people to manage, you will probably also have resources to manage. There are many management text books to guide you and, again, those of Peter Drucker may provide the most suitable introduction. In a direct sales situation, resource management is generally less critical than man management. The resources are not going to walk out on you if you treat them badly – but you can easily waste them, and your own management may not be impressed by this. Whatever these resources are, you will need to plan your budgets very seriously and ensure that you keep within them. Many sales professionals find this a bore. But if you don't want to reach the limit of your resources just when you need them most, or you don't want your management to think you are the last of the big spenders, you should acknowledge that it is an *essential* bore.

Project management

Perhaps the most important skill in handling customer accounts is that of project management. The customer sales 'business' tends to run as a series of projects. Clearly, each sales campaign can be thought of as a separate project, and managed as such. But when an order is won, this is followed by possibly the most complex project of all, the installation; and this probably requires the highest management skills of all. In addition, there are other smaller projects, such as training or the extension of use of your product into new areas, that can also benefit from project management skills.

The first, and critical, requirement is that you should produce a viable project plan. The viability of any project depends on making available the right resources (particularly people) at the right time. If you don't plan sufficient resources the project will fall apart. If you plan too many resources you waste money; and the project may still fall apart, because people with nothing to do start arguing over who is to do what!

Getting your plan right is no easy task, particularly where that plan needs to be right at every point in time; it is no use having the right resources available at the wrong time. I have, a number of times, seen a full set of personal computers delivered to a customer who was desperate to use them, only to have them lie unused for weeks; simply because the supplier didn't have the people available to install them and (in particular) train the customer's staff.

It is essential, then, to start with a meaningful project plan. This may well turn out to be complex, and may require a significant input of expert effort just to bring together all the elements of the project; particularly in terms of getting the interrelationships correct. But it is better that you have problems with the plan than with the actual project. Many (if not most) of your projects will follow similar patterns, so much of the plan can be standard and it should not be necessary to reinvent the whole project from scratch. All that will be needed will be that the existing plans should be modified to take account of the special needs of the particular customer. Even so, it is worthwhile fully documenting all aspects of the plan. This will ensure that there can be no excuse for anyone (particularly the customer) misunderstanding what is expected of them. In the process it will also provide a historical record which can, in turn, be modified to be used on future projects. Not least, it will impress the customer enormously. With modern word-processors, once the initial documents have been created, it will be no hardship to produce a full set of new plans; often it will simply be a matter of changing the customer's name in the text.

Planning charts
The conventional approach to project management is to describe the problems and, in particular, the relationship between the main elements by charts. The most popular chart is the flowchart. The classic flowchart, as shown in Figure 7.1, comprises a series of boxes (which represent the various actions needed), linked by lines which show the relationships; in particular which action follows, or precedes, any other.

The flowchart is an almost essential part of the systems design that goes into any complex computer project. To a lesser extent, it can be a great help in *any* project. It helps to visualise, in a very direct way, exactly what the key relationships are.

A much more complicated version of this technique is the critical path method (CPM). In a complex flowchart the relationships are not easy to see, particularly where the boxes are separated by different time periods. CPM simply allocates times to activities (which, rather

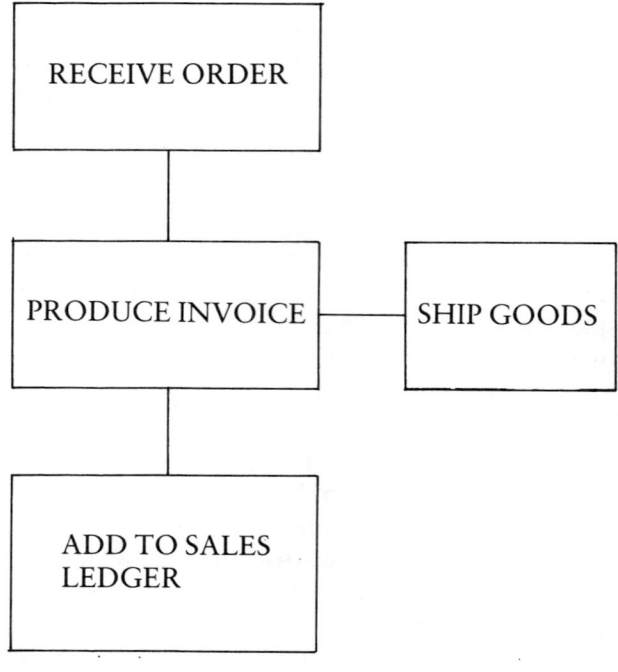

Figure 7.1

confusingly, are represented by lines, not boxes), so that you can work out which path through the various complex links between the activities is the longest. This determines the length of time the whole project will take. If an activity is not on this one critical path any slippage will not make a difference in the overall time (unless the slippage is so great that it creates a new critical path); but any delay in the activities on the critical path will result in an equal delay for the overall project.

The great advantage of this technique is that it highlights the bottlenecks that will hold back the whole project, so that attention can be focused where it will be most productive.

A later development of this technique was project evaluation and review technique (PERT). Potentially, this was *much* more complex and much more powerful. It allowed the introduction of costs as well as times, so that the trade-offs between time and cost could be evaluated. The oft-quoted origin of the technique, and still its most dramatic example, was the original Polaris missile programme for the US Navy. PERT was reported to have saved hundreds of millions of dollars, and several years of development time.

In practice, though, PERT techniques are generally only used to plan the timescales, the cost element being ignored. It does, more conveniently than CPM, assign the activities to the boxes rather than the lines joining them. All of the various forms of PERT (and of CPM) are dependent on computers (now usually personal computers) for their analysis. The problems are typically so complex that to do the calculations by hand would be unthinkable.

One method that *can* be produced by hand, but more typically is an output from a PERT system, is a GANTT chart, shown in Figure 7.2. This is merely a chart with time (typically as a calendar) along the horizontal x-axis and the various resources (or activities) as blocks grouped along the vertical y-axis. The use of these resources is then 'blocked in' for the relevant calendar periods.

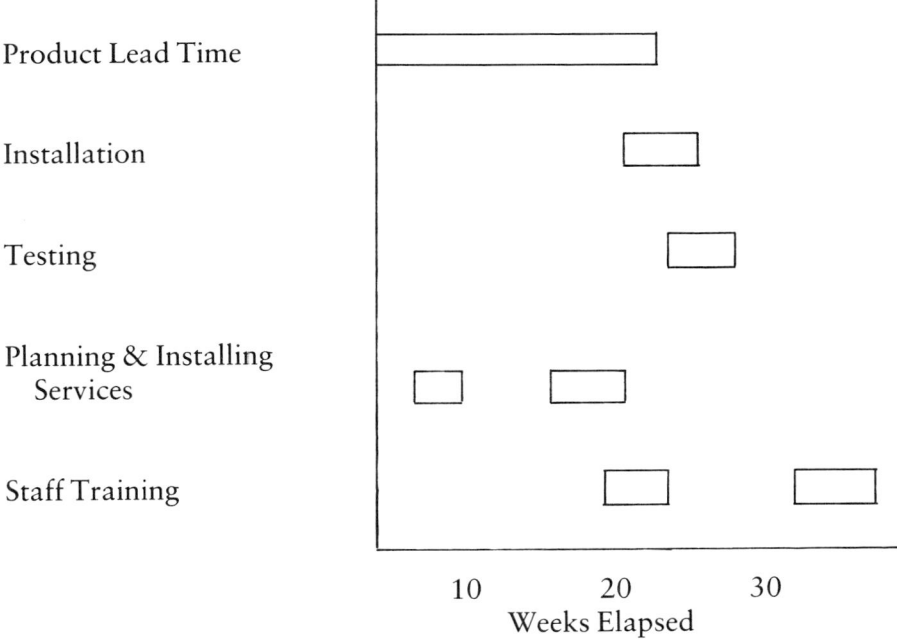

Figure 7.2

This is a useful way of showing, at a glance, where and when are the likely bottlenecks (where key resources overlap), and where there are resource exposures. If the chart demands, in any one period, more resources than you've got, you can be sure there will be problems.

All of these techniques are impressive. They will show your customers just how sophisticated you are. They can even help you to understand complex problems rather better.

On the other hand, they are *very* labour intensive. Creating the networks in the first place is time consuming and requires significant expertise. But it is the most useful part of the exercise, since it forces you to understand the problems fully, and highlights the bottlenecks. The real bother, though, is in keeping these networks up-to-date. To use them as control devices (as they were meant to be, and were used on Polaris and still are on very elaborate civil engineering projects) *all* the figures in the network must be regularly updated. The new reports are only as good as the data that is put into them. But updating is a very labour intensive process, deadly boring, and with little reward, since the reports change so little over short periods of time.

The almost inevitable result is that, even where such project control systems are initiated, they soon lapse into disuse. I have seen many brave attempts start and then, a few weeks later, disappear without trace. It is a nice idea to use them, but my advice is not to bother. As a sales professional you will not have the time or motivation to keep them updated.

With project management, KISS (keep it simple, stupid) is just as applicable as elsewhere. The simpler the system the more likely that you will use it; and, one way or another, you *must* control any such projects that you manage.

Realistic targets
The easiest way that you can make your whole project management more successful is to set realistic targets. Whatever you are selling, you are almost bound to find buyers who want a fast delivery or installation, and the temptation is to shave your normal timescales to keep the prospect happy. In practice, though, almost all customers are more interested in *predictable* delivery than in fast delivery. Customers can often manage to plan around a long delivery time, but they are thrown into chaos when the product doesn't appear when promised. There is no quicker way of alienating a new customer.

Heinz Goldmann's general advice is: 'Avoid making promises you can't fulfil ... Promise less than you can do, rather than more.'

I always traded off fast delivery for predictable delivery and never had any severe problems selling to my prospects, but I did have very satisfied customers. I *always* set pessimistic targets, in terms of costs as well as time. The customer manager who (on the basis of your promises to him) has promised his senior management that he will bring in his project at a cost of £100,000 (and within 100 days), and actually manages to keep costs down to £90,000 (and deliver the goods in 90 days) is feted. On the other hand, his colleague who (for an identical project) manages to hold his cost down to £80,000 (and delivery down to 80 days), but who has promised a cost of £60,000 (and a delivery of 60 days) will be reviled; and, in turn, will revile, if not dismiss, you as his supplier.

My advice is always to set *very* realistic, indeed pessimistic, targets for yourself. In beating them you will be a hero to your customer and you won't have to waste enormous amounts of effort and resources trying to meet impossible deadlines.

Planning meetings
The installation will not just require resources from you and your company. Typically, it will require far more resources from the customer. It is, therefore, as important to coordinate the customer's activities as it is your own.

The best way I found was to use formal meetings as the vehicle for this control. The reason for the meetings was so that I could get all the participants together and ensure that their 'promises' were public (and also avoided any conflict with the actions of the others); these promises were then duly minuted. I found it useful to run the first of these meetings, the 'systems assurance meeting' at which my technical support personnel were the main contributors from my side, just *before* the order was placed. It was very impressive for the prospective customer, and often helped to clinch the order. It also ensured that everyone knew *before* the order was signed exactly what they were committing themselves to.

In my personal computer dealership, I always tried to run an earlier internal version of this meeting, because it was my experience that many of the systems proposed were sub-optimal – and not a few were completely unworkable. With this internal meeting behind us, we went to the systems assurance meeting confident that we really knew what we were talking about (something of a rarity in the personal computer industry!).

These meetings (both internal and external) need to be repeated regularly over the life of the project. At them, every action needed must be definitively assigned as the specific responsibility of one individual who is present at the meeting, and agrees to accept that responsibility. The key to success is defined personal responsibility;

and this must also include agreed target deadline dates. Later meetings should be used to update the status of all these actions so that you develop your human equivalent of the GANTT chart (and this is reflected in the minutes).

This degree of tight control is essential on large projects. I was project manager for the first phase of IBM's relocation of its UK marketing headquarters to Basingstoke. The total project included the commissioning of an extra half a million square feet of space, bringing an extra 1500 employees on to the resulting 'campus', and providing something like 2500 terminals linked by literally thousands of miles of cable. Its cost ran into tens of millions of pounds, and it took the best part of 18 months to complete.

The only way I could exercise any degree of control of my phase was to run a day-long coordination meeting, at which the 20 or so appointed representatives (typically the managers) of all the departments involved reported progress. Even then, to complete all the coordination work in a day, these managers were only required to report significant changes, together with any problems that had emerged. If they simply reported that they were on target, their part of the meeting would be brief, but they were still *committed* to achieving their target. As they could attend in 'shifts' (only attending the parts that affected them) the amount of time that some of the participants needed to contribute was minimised but, even so, a small core of half a dozen of us had to be present all day.

One golden rule, though, was that there were *no* recriminations. If there were problems (and there often were, which was why the meeting lasted a whole day) nobody was allowed even to mention whose fault it was (although, of course, everyone already knew!); the only discussion was about how to resolve the problem.

This process worked remarkably well, and the phase came in just two weeks late against my own target (but, of course, ahead of that promised to senior management!), despite running into major difficulties in terms of installing just about the most sophisticated computer network in the world. Close control pays dividends.

Installation management

The most critical aspect of the project will be the installation phase. This is well recognised by customers. For example, market research showed that more than 60 per cent of personal computer buyers rated installation support as a key need (only being exceeded in importance by the need for training). This is one that you should manage directly yourself, although without getting too much in the hair of the technical people who will claim it as their own province.

It has been my experience that the main problems have usually been logistical rather than technical. I always ran my own check on the various items needed for the installation. Not least I checked the equipment. I almost invariably found something missing, usually because some other sales professional had taken it, since his own machine had something missing (causing a never-ending problem). Needless to say, however, I nearly always resolved this by stealing it from another machine myself! Sometimes, though, there was no such simple solution. I regularly had to use couriers across the Atlantic, and I once had to send someone by air to Sweden to pick up one special part that was missing, only to discover that it comprised a six-inch piece of wire and a single piece of paper telling us which terminals to connect it across! But I never failed to deliver the logistical goods; even if it was only beer and sandwiches to keep the installation team going into the small hours of the night.

Back-up systems
Most sales professionals, even if they do plan, assume that their equipment will not break down. That is often a vain hope; and customers are rarely more irate than when they find their whole operation brought to a lengthy halt because of a failure on the part of your equipment. It is usually the 'consequential loss' (which every vendor insists on ignoring, at least at law) which is the worst.

The impact of these problems can, however, be easily minimised; simply by planning for back-up. Such back-up should be an essential part of every plan, assuming that things *will* go wrong, even to the extent of your equipment failing totally for an extended period of time. Fall-back needs to be provided at all levels. Ultimately, you have to be able to bring in a complete alternative system (for example, a manual system to back up a computer). In many cases this ultimate back-up will be a 'mothballed' version of the previous system.

Managing yourself
The most important resource you have is yourself. Among all the problems of account management it is all too easy to overlook this fact. Many sales professionals spend their time 'fire-fighting', and can't understand why they never have the time to manage anything effectively. Most of the elements are described elsewhere, in Chapter 3 for example, and at the end of this chapter there is a particularly important section on training yourself.

I will not repeat this material, but merely stress (in the context of account management) just how important it is also to manage yourself.

Your own 'added-value'

Perhaps the biggest contribution you can make is one that is not merely undervalued by almost all sales trainers, but totally ignored by them. Your biggest contribution can be your own added-value. You are usually in a unique position to make a major personal contribution to the development of your customer's business.

If you are a true sales professional, you will have high degrees of skill and knowledge in the areas of technical and business matters in which you specialise. You will have considerable intellect to back up these skills and knowledge; intellect and awareness that will be matched by few of your customer's management. You will also have significant amounts of facts, particularly in terms of your products or services, that are far beyond anything possessed by your customer.

This point is put, with rather different phrasing, by Alan Williams in *All About Selling*:

'Salesmanship is a highly professional skill where the most ignominious failure is to sell the wrong product for the job, whether knowingly or not. In its best form it is a creative and conceptual pursuit that reaches far beyond the face-value of the client's apparent problem and pre-conceived ideas.'

The other profession that comes closest to matching this profile is that of the management consultant; and the match is, indeed, very close. The impressive, and justifiable, claim of management consultants is that they offer massive added-value to their client's businesses, for which they often charge equally massive fees. My suggestion is that in only a slightly different context (you can't charge such exorbitant fees) you can easily add similar amounts of added-value, for very similar reasons.

There is no way to define how this part of your job should operate. You just have to use all your skills and knowledge to improve your customer's business, as defined in the widest possible sense. Mainly this will relate to the best use of your products or services; here your personal contribution may be to develop new uses, or more effective ways of meeting old uses. But you may also be able to make more indirect contributions to your customer's business.

In particular, you may be able to aid information transfer, even technology transfer, from your other customers (always assuming this does not breach any confidentiality). Most managements can learn significant lessons from what other managements have done, if only they have the necessary contacts to find out – and that contact is exactly what you offer. You are in a unique position to say: 'I think I have seen the solution to that problem elsewhere.'

All of this means that as a sales professional you no longer play a largely passive role, where sales professionals are supposed to be only a communications channel and their only skill is that of persuasion. This extended role actually sees you personally adding more value than almost anyone else in the chain. As the pivot between the customer and your company (as well as your other customers), you are uniquely placed to optimise the flow of information; and to convert that into genuine added-value for the customer.

In my case, one implementation of this approach was in IBM Biomedical Group. My main task was clearly to market blood processing equipment. Yet much of my time was spent developing, in conjunction with my customers, the techniques of 'plasma exchange'; a very sophisticated medical treatment in which the equipment was used. I set up elaborate channels to distribute information (the foremost being my quarterly medical journal), I personally communicated ideas between the various research and clinical groups, and I even stimulated (and occasionally funded) development work in the field.

At least partly as a result of these efforts, the UK came to lead the world in certain areas of this medical treatment. My personal contribution added value on quite a large scale in this case; and this was rewarded by IBM obtaining a better than 90 per cent share of this business, together with a great deal of personal satisfaction for me.

As the last example illustrates, the pay-off is that you become the favoured supplier. The added-value that you generate typically comes free to the customer; it is very difficult to charge for it. But it does have *value* for the customer – and he should be aware of that. As a result he is buying not just your product, but also the added-value that you personally bring; and that may be a significant part of the sale.

Proposals

Arguably, this section should be included in the chapter on standard selling skills rather than here, but the skills are very close to those needed for project management, and (in particular) relate to those of surveying (a good survey is almost a prerequisite of a proposal).

Objectives
The first question to ask is: do I need a proposal? Often the answer will be 'no', in which case don't do one! Proposals are time and resource consuming. Much better that you confirm your agreements with a short letter and use the time saved to build your prospect base.

Occasionally, it will be necessary to produce a full proposal, particularly where you are involved in a competitive sale. A well-prepared and presented proposal is very impressive and you can be almost certain that your competitors won't have produced one, or will have produced one to a very poor standard, so it may well give you a competitive edge. If you do produce one, it is also a very useful record of all the agreements. When the prospect later complains that something is missing (as they almost always do) you can simply say, 'Let's have a look at the proposal.' As always, though, you should have clear objectives in preparing the proposal. Why do you need to produce it, and what do you intend that it should achieve?

KISS
Once more, the essence of a proposal should be brevity. A long proposal will be impressive (it shows just how much effort you have put in), but the prospect will have considerable difficulty in finding (and even more in remembering) the key sales messages buried in it. So the shorter the proposal, always assuming it covers all the material adequately, the better.

You can aid simplicity by putting all the detailed material into supporting appendices, which the prospect is not forced to read and certainly is not expected to remember (although he is expected to be duly impressed by the quantity and thoroughness of the work). The main part of the proposal is then still kept brief. So, for example, a 50-page proposal might contain less than 10 pages of true proposal, supported by 40 pages of appendices (much of which might be tailored standard material).

Even then, it would *always* begin with a one- or two-page summary. This brief summary would contain *all* the key sales points. The prospect would, therefore, have received all the essential sales messages by the time he had finished reading these initial one or two pages; and these messages would be reinforced by the later restatement in the body of the proposal. The summary also provides a useful document for the prospect to photocopy and circulate to the minor players.

Relevance

From the prospect's point of view, though, the one prerequisite is that the proposal must be *relevant*. Of the very few proposals I have received in my time, most have obviously been standard proposals, unrelated to my specific needs; and, as such, have been largely wasted. The even fewer relevant proposals I have received, on the other hand, have been winners which have typically clinched the sale.

The acid test of any proposal, therefore, is: will the prospect find it 100 per cent relevant to his needs; will it 'grab' him as soon as he opens it?

Content

The content is what is important. If you can't put in good content don't produce the proposal. In general, the content will be a direct reflection of your sales campaign. If your sales campaign has a sound structure, as it should, you will find that your proposal is also likely to have a sound structure.

Agreed material

The one rule, however, is that *all* the main material in a proposal should have been previously agreed with the prospect. None of the material should come as a surprise to him. If you want to introduce new material do this face-to-face. A proposal should in essence contain a summary of the *agreements* that have been reached in the face-to-face meetings.

Structure

To be easily readable and referenceable, a proposal should have a clear structure. John Fenton's system is:

1. The Customer's Objectives [stating what you agreed with him).
2. Your Recommendations [a condensed picture of these].
3. Summary of Additional Benefits.
4. Financial Justification.
5. Your Guarantees and After Sales Service.

My own typical format is similar, but rather more detailed:

1. Summary.
2. Prospect requirements (in summary).
3. Summary background (including a review of the problems to be solved).
4. Proposed solutions (in summary).
5. General benefits.
6. Financial justification and costs.
7. Appendices:
     A   Detailed background (survey results)
     B   Detailed solutions (including flowcharts)
     C   Product descriptions
     D   References (descriptions of similar systems with customers).

As you can see, I like to start the main body of the proposal (after the overall summary) with material (in summary form) on the general background, including the prospect's own objectives and the survey results. This establishes immediately that I have understood the prospect's business, and it makes the proposal obviously specific to him. It is in summary form (with the detail relegated to the appendices, where it appears only in 'formal' justification of the summary material) so that the customer is not too long in reaching the meat of the benefits, and my sales messages. Even then, I make certain that these are the *first* things he sees in the proposal, by highlighting them in the overall summary, which comes before anything else.

This is, however, just one of the many possible structures. As always, you must choose one that suits; that suits the prospect, the material and, above all, yourself.

Whatever the structure, I believe that it helps (me at least) to make the structure even clearer if you have a numbering system for the various sections. There are several different schemes: for example you can distinguish subsections by a full stop (for example 4.5.3), or you can use a mix of numbers and letters (for example 4E, part III). Once more, the choice is yours, just so long as you are consistent throughout the document.

Another useful technique I learned, when I worked in an advertising agency, was to provide a very brief summary at the beginning of each section; a short paragraph (underlined to highlight the fact that it was a summary). This helps to break the document into easily digestible sections; it also helps to put the sections into context.

Proposal presentation

If you submit a proposal it *must* be professionally presented. It will represent the one tangible piece of evidence in favour (or refutation) of the quality you claim to provide. If the proposal itself doesn't demonstrate that quality, then you will sow the seeds of doubt in your prospect's mind.

Writing skills

Perhaps one of the greatest 'intellectual' shortcomings of most sales professionals is that they can't write well. At one stage I insisted that I received copies of all the proposal letters that my personal computer sales professionals were sending out. It was a depressing experience. Most of the letters were, to some degree, illiterate; and not a few were almost totally incomprehensible.

The best answer, if you have problems with writing, is to spend time on the *structure*, and keep the verbiage very short indeed. The main failing of most proposals is that they are too wordy. You can make your disadvantage (finding it difficult to write many words) into a positive advantage; your proposal can be crisp and to the point – but for this to be the case, you will need to put in significant effort. On the other hand, the long verbiage put in the appendices to impress the customer can usually simply be copied from your company's standard handouts.

The secret of a good proposal is in *rewriting* it a number of times, until you get it exactly right. The more times you edit out the unnecessary material (to refine the message down to its bare essentials) and the more times you rewrite (to make the words flow more naturally) the better. If it is any consolation, despite my experience, I still rewrite at least six times. This book, for example, has seen that many rewrites!

Word-processing

The one recent advance that makes all of this editing and rewriting tolerable is that of the word-processor. You can rewrite your proposal a dozen times with minimal effort. I now actually find it quite enjoyable, where it was previously a nightmare persuading the typing pool to do *one* retype.

Best of all, though, a word-processor allows you to build up a library of 'boiler-plate': paragraphs, and whole sections, that you have used previously (and have sweated blood to get exactly right). A great deal of each new proposal can be assembled from these sections, and then tailored, in a matter of a few minutes. This way a professional-looking document can be produced in a matter of a few hours.

Desktop publishing
The latest form of word-processing is desktop publishing. The software houses would have you believe that it is a new art form, but in reality it is an extension of word-processing (although it can also include images). The great advantage is that it can result in output that looks *very* professional. But it does also need more skill, particularly if you are including images. Despite the advertisers' claims, you still need to be an artist to produce good computer graphics, although it is much easier for the less artistic to modify images that have already been drawn by an artist.

Physical presentation
There are a whole range of ways you can physically present the material. Four-ring binders are a very flexible way of collecting the contents (they could easily include brochures as well as the typed material). I have also used spiral (or comb) binders, which look very nice but are rather inflexible once the binding is in place. Simplest of all, though, for short documents is the spring spine, which simply clasps the pages. I used a textured stiff back and a transparent front sheet (actually just a blank foil) to make the presentation look more professional.

To make the separator pages (which should be a different colour) more interesting I often used blow-ups of logos (preferably the prospect's as well as my own); very easily produced on an enlarging photocopier. I also used transparent foil overlays to make the key diagrams more lively.

But no matter how slick the presentation, the one thing that really counts in a presentation (and which should be the focus of your efforts) is the content.

Customer training

The most important requirement of many customer installations, and often the worst supported, is that of educating customer staff. Most complex sales relate to products or services that involve a degree of technical complexity, which must be faced by the customer staff as well as by the sales professional. The ultimate success of your product may depend more on how well the customer staff use it than on its inherent technical excellence. A customer only sees (or chooses to see) the results, not the causes.

The significance of training or education is shown by the fact that, for example, market research showed that this was easily the most important support need of personal computer buyers, listed by more than 70 per cent of them. Yet such training is almost universally neglected.

Training plan

It should not come as a surprise to you that your customer's staff need training. Your company should have a full training package to support its products, although this may range from the mini-university that IBM runs to a single page of instructions. If your company doesn't have such a training plan you potentially have a great deal of work ahead of you.

You, yourself, need specifically to include an education plan, no matter how brief, as a part of your overall account plan. You must know, before you start your installation, exactly how you are going to provide the necessary training.

Manuals

Most training is, in practice, self-teaching by customer staff reading the manuals; 'If all else fails, read the instructions!' This may often be less than ideal, but you need to recognise that it is the reality, no matter how elaborate your own education plan.

As a result, you have to be certain that the relevant manuals contain all the necessary information, or that the system itself will provide the requisite help; for example, much of the support material for computers is now held on the systems themselves, accessible as needed by a 'help' key. If they don't, you will have to provide supplements, if necessary writing them yourselves, or arranging to have them written. Perhaps the one extra guide most often needed is a simple map as to where in all the documentation are the descriptions of the actions needed to meet the simplest user needs (especially how to start the system running!).

Not least, you should make certain that your customer has a full set of manuals. Even if your administrators succeed in getting all the various pieces of product to the customer, you can be sure that they will miss half the manuals, and the half they miss will be the ones that are needed; almost by definition, the useful manuals (and hence the popular ones) will be the ones out of stock. So personally make certain that the customer gets a full set, even if you have to photocopy them yourself (it is always worthwhile holding some spares).

In any case, even if your administrators deliver a full set, the customer's staff will soon lose some (and again, these will be the important ones). Such manuals are essential to handle emergencies; so when you visit a customer, check that they have all their documentation. Then, when an emergency hits, you won't have to be hauled out of bed (or even worse, an important prospect meeting) to handle the problems.

On-site training

Most training is conducted on the customer's premises, when the product or service is delivered; most often as an afterthought, when it becomes obvious that the staff don't even know how to open the boxes. It is undertaken by a sales professional or by a member of his support team. It is almost always poor and perfunctory. It is, belatedly, recognised that a token instruction session is needed so that, from then on, the customer can be legally abandoned! Most such training is *ad hoc*. The 'trainer' (for whom training is at best a sideline) is typically unprepared, and makes up his material as he goes along.

In fact, on-site training can be just about the most effective; if only it is done well. It has the great advantage of being face-to-face (typically with very small classes), and run in the customer's own environment (where his staff feel at home). But it should not be an excuse for second-rate training. It should be as rigorously prepared and mounted as any of the classroom sessions described in the next section. Indeed, the techniques used should be identical, it is only the location which will differ.

Classroom training

This is the classic form of training. Despite this, it is relatively infrequently used; the norm being self-education from manuals, sometimes supplemented by skimpy on-site training. I will, however, describe it in some detail, since many of the techniques and principles are transferable to on-site work.

Class size

The first parameter to take into account is that of how many 'students' you will have to teach. I have, in my time, taught classes as large as 150. With numbers as high as this I had no chance of controlling the interaction between myself and them, which is the essence of good teaching, so it was really just 'lecturing'. Indeed, I found it impossible to control (at least to the degree I wanted) classes of more than 20.

As a good teacher you need to be aware of how well *each* student is understanding what you are saying. In the larger classes you have to judge this mainly by body language (especially eye contact). I discovered that I could maintain this interaction in classes up to 20 in size; but this came with a number of years experience. Below that limit, I would immediately be aware (by a change in body posture, typically to a more 'hesitant' pose) of anyone who wasn't following. I could rephrase what I was saying, and direct it at the ones who were in difficulty (and even conduct a short dialogue with them) until I was happy that they were once more following the material. In IBM I often had to teach classes larger than 20 and, in these cases, I deliberately 'shut out' those who sat beyond the first 20. If you chose to sit at the back of such a class you denied yourself the benefits of interaction.

It is very unlikely, however, that any training you run will involve classes anywhere near this limit. In my experience, the largest classes, where customers are taught, normally will not exceed eight students. This is fortunate, since I reckoned that I could teach a class of eight just about twice as fast as one of 20, and could teach a class of four (the average size) twice as fast again.

The reason for these dramatic increases in speed of learning is that it reflects the degree to which you can give individual tuition. With a class of 20 your interaction is largely limited to registering that everyone has understood you, and to keeping everyone interested in the subject matter. With classes as low as four you can teach each person almost individually, so that there is constant interaction between the two of you. The proportion of time the class would be speaking, as opposed to me lecturing, would rise from as low as a quarter with a large class, to in excess of a half with a small class; and, of course, the amount of time the average individual in those classes was speaking would rocket from about 1 per cent to as high as 15 per cent (and that 15:1 ratio makes a dramatic difference to understanding).

Interaction
Such interaction is the key to successful teaching, particularly with smaller classes. The traditional hierarchical approach, with the

teacher lecturing (or often hectoring) his pupils, depends on authority as the means of commanding attention. Even with a very commanding teacher it is inherently wasteful. It is one-way communication; it doesn't use the talents of the pupils, only those of the teacher.

Much better, in my experience, is the participative (team) approach, where the student is totally involved and feels he is contributing as much as the teacher (and probably is). This uses the talents of all involved, and the student learns rather than is taught. As with a sale to a prospect, each piece of information that such a student discovers for himself is many times better appreciated and remembered than any one you might describe to him in your own lecture. With very small classes, of four or less, I used to concentrate on getting the students to 'instruct' me. Where possible I asked *them* for the answers, so that they were forced to deduce the answers for themselves.

Hands-on

The most effective form of training is direct experience. An hour's practical experience of using an automatic lathe is worth several days of sitting in front of a blackboard having it described. So, wherever possible, classroom teaching should take the form of workshop teaching, with the product or service actually being used.

Even if this is not possible, or is not suitable for making the points you are trying to communicate (about theory, for example), the best form of teaching constantly uses examples (worked through by the students) to reinforce the lessons; and to allow the teacher, as well as the students, to check that they really do understand.

Preparation

All of this sounds ideal. Most of the work will be done by the students themselves, and you can have a relaxing time. It is true, in my experience, that this style of teaching is much more relaxing – for students as well as teachers. But it probably requires more actual work (even if it is more pleasant) from the teacher than does lecturing. Once you have given a lecture a few times you could probably give it in your sleep; and possibly do! But if you are practising interactive teaching you will need to be constantly alert, ensuring that all the material is understood, not just delivered.

The greatest part of the extra workload, however, comes in the preparation. It takes far longer to prepare interactive material, and even longer for hands-on work. With at least a decade of high-level teaching experience, I can almost make up a 'chalk and talk' session on a subject I know well without any preparation – although the few times I have been tempted into this have been notably less successful. It takes me long hours, and days, to create good interactive training; and, in particular, the examples the students will work on.

Whatever style you choose, you must adequately prepare all your material. This is a task neglected by too many teachers. In IBM we had a rule of thumb that said the preparation of new material would take at least 10 times as long as its delivery; thus, a day's teaching would take a full two weeks to prepare.

Such an investment of effort is obviously more productive where the resultant course can be reused several times, but it is essential, whatever the number of reruns, if the teaching is to be of the high standard you will need. Although it may not look so, it is also a very productive investment for single courses; the better the student understands the material, the less support he will need in the field – and such hidden on-site tuition (disguised as problem handling) can easily eat up large amounts of resource.

Teaching techniques
In many, indeed most, respects a teaching session can be viewed as another presentation. As a result, all the techniques described in the next chapter can be applied. There is no reason to treat teaching sessions as the poor relations of prospect presentations. The only acid-test, for both, is what will best communicate ideas.

The only notable difference in technique is that the questioning of the audience, by the teacher, can (and should) be much more aggressive in the classroom situation. He has a right to know if the students have understood what he has said, whereas a prospect in a presentation has the right to keep his thoughts to himself. Otherwise, the techniques are virtually identical, although the subject matter will be very different.

With your experience as a sales professional, you are better placed than many professionally qualified teachers to provide the best form of education; at least you understand the need to *sell* your ideas, even to a class of students, where most teachers seem to expect that their pupils will absorb the material of their own volition.

Timing
One major difference from presentations is the timescale. Teaching lasts over much longer periods than presentations. As a result it is important that you carefully break the long sessions up into more

manageable blocks of time. In part this is so that the students can have a 'natural break'. Few things distract a student more than a bursting bladder – unless it is the need to have a cigarette, where smoking is banned in the classroom.

Such breaks also allow students to relax for a couple of minutes. It is conventionally reckoned that the typical span of attention of students is about 45 minutes, which is why classes are usually scheduled at this length. To help to increase attention, by reducing monotony, it is advisable to run different styles of teaching in adjacent timeslots. Thus, for example, a chalk and talk session would be followed by a hands-on workshop, followed by a video etc.

I also used deliberately to vary my style and pace *within* the 45-minute segments. There was a limit to what could be accomplished where the material was already fixed. But, for example, if I noticed attention slipping I would switch to asking more questions of the audience, or I would deliberately lift the material by making it more controversial, or just much louder.

I once attended a very dreary lecture on acoustics, which was enlivened after half an hour of sheer boredom (and just when most of the audience were on the edge of sleep) by the lecturer pulling a revolver from his pocket and firing (a blank) at the ceiling. The impact on the audience was dramatic, compounded by those who had actually gone to sleep falling off their chairs – but I have never felt it necessary to go to quite such extremes myself!

Hand-outs

An essential part of the preparation should be to produce notes and other hand-outs that the student can follow in the classroom, and can take away as reference material for later use. It is relatively unproductive if the student has to spend his time making his own notes. It is much better if he can use the framework of notes that you have prepared, only highlighting the points he finds important, and concentrating on adding his own comments. Conventionally, most students concentrate on making notes that they can refer to later, rather than on understanding. So the more you can take the task of note-taking away from them, the more of their time will be available for understanding what you are talking about.

Once again, the standard of such notes has to be high, since they are the one tangible item that students will take back with them and may show to their colleagues. As such, the standard of this material will have an impact on your image in the account.

In addition, as these notes are often passed to other people, it is worth (if you have the time) preparing summaries (and other reference material) usable by those who have not attended the course. In any case, these 'stand-alone' notes will probably be required to support those who still insist on learning only from the manuals.

Follow-up
Such courses should not be viewed in isolation. They are often part of a sequence. It is more productive to spend a day teaching a skill to a certain level, and then let the student spend some time (typically a few weeks) consolidating this with practice. When the student has consolidated his skills he then returns for the next session of classroom training, to take him up to the next level of skill, to be again followed by a period of practical consolidation; and so on, until the student finally becomes an expert.

Even if this is the only course that the student is attending, you should ensure that he takes away material that will allow him to continue, and extend, his training at leisure (and as he consolidates it by his practical experience). In addition you, as the sales professional, need to check that he really is progressing. Education is a product just like any other, and you need to check that it is a product that works.

Evaluation
After every course you, and any other members of the teaching team, need to evaluate the success of the course. The most important input to this evaluation should come from the students. Just before they leave you should ask them to fill in an assessment form. In this way you will find out what they thought of the course and how much they learned from it. Such information is invaluable in making certain that you maintain high standards.

This assessment may (and preferably should) also cover the performance of the individual teachers. Being individually assessed by your students can be stressful for any teacher, but in my experience it is the only practical way of finding out how good your teaching really is. Without such assessments you cannot easily develop your skills as a teacher. You can be sure that the students will assess you informally, and possibly destructively! But it is better to know about any problems before their management does. You would, though, be a trifle unwise to show such assessments to your management until you are sure you are consistently achieving good ratings, although you should in practice find that the ratings are quite reassuring; as a good sales professional, you are likely to be a far better teacher than any the students have come across previously.

Computer based training (CBT)

This is a specialised form of training which used to be rare but, with the widespread use of personal computers, is becoming increasingly common. It uses the computer, rather than the instructor, to interact with the student. It requires a great deal of skill and a great deal of time to prepare the material, so it must be undertaken by specialists (usually by an outside company specialising in the field), and it is expensive. But if there are large numbers of personnel to be taught it can't be beaten for productivity.

Training yourself

As mentioned earlier in this chapter, the most important resource is yourself. The means to develop that resource come most directly from training or education. This self-development should be just as central a part of your management plans as your development of your accounts.

Training its staff was one of IBM's major preoccupations, and one of the reasons for its outstanding success. It spent hundreds of millions of dollars every year on training its own staff; and it *insisted* (not just encouraged) that its field force spent at least one month a year in training. In part this was to cope with the very rapidly changing product environment within which it operated, but in the main it was to develop those personnel. Its people resource was recognised by IBM as being its most important investment.

Training objectives

Much as you must have education plans for each of your customers, you need one (and an even more sophisticated one at that) for yourself. You should carefully analyse your training needs. Training is a major investment of time and money, for you as well as your employer; you could be profitably employed earning commission in the time you will make available. As a result you need to make certain that any training will be productive. I have, many times, seen salesmen choosing courses almost entirely on the basis of the social facilities. If you want a free holiday that is fine, but don't fool yourself into thinking it is training.

Your review of your own training should look at it from three perspectives. The most obvious, certainly to your management, is the need to rectify your existing weaknesses. Even so, in some respects, this is the most difficult to plan; because, in common with most sales professionals, you will probably be somewhat loth to admit your weaknesses to your management (or even to yourself). But it is the most important: if you have basic weaknesses these will undermine your strengths.

Easier to approach is the second perspective, which seeks to build on and develop your strengths. Just because you are already strong in an area doesn't mean that you cannot be even stronger with some training.

The third perspective is that of what training you will need to be able to understand the job you want to develop into. For many ambitious sales professionals the obvious target of this training will be sales management. This area will probably be the one that you are most keen to explore, but also the one in which your management will be least willing to invest.

Once you have established your needs and agreed your objectives with your management (if you need their support and their money), you should then build your own training plan from the many resources available to you.

Knowledge

The sales professional usually has a constant thirst for knowledge. The more he knows about his products and his customers the better he can sell. The only trade-off is the productive selling time he can afford to give up to obtain the knowledge. As Buck Rodgers writes:

> 'It goes without saying that the rep should know his product line like the back of his hand. How, otherwise, can he relate his products to customers' needs? A company that sends an improperly trained salesperson into the field is insulting its customers and wasting their time.'

Product knowledge

This is one element that should be available in-house. The only problem is obtaining access to it. All too often it is locked away, not because of secrecy (although that often does play a part), but simply because nobody recognises the need to transmit the knowledge from the experts, who are typically locked away in R & D and production, to the field force. You may well have to put in some effort to dig out the knowledge, even in this area.

Obtaining copies of all the manuals and technical write-ups as they are produced is a good starting point. Apart from that (and any product training that *is* offered) it is really down to personal contact. Talking to the experts when you can is a very productive investment of your time. At conferences (and particularly at sales conferences) forget all the free booze; concentrate on chatting up the experts.

I well remember spending an afternoon walking along the beach at Travemunde, just north of Hamburg, with both the leading IBM technical expert and the world's leading medical expert in our field. I learnt an immense amount during that conversation. At times the level of scientific knowledge took off into the stratosphere, but I managed to follow most of it – and I finished that walk a much better educated sales professional. It was also a very enjoyable and painless way of learning.

Industry training
Most of the aspects of industry training were covered in Chapter 3. But if you can supplement this with specific industry courses, it is well worth taking advantage of these; not least because of the contacts you can make. On just one course, covering 'local area networks' in major corporations, I met key contacts from the largest 50 corporations, and even booked appointments with four of them. All of this was achieved on a course that lasted just one day and cost only £150, which worked out at just under £40 per appointment. I used to attend such courses regularly, and rarely found any other sales professionals there; they offered the near ideal sales environment.

Business training
Perhaps the most useful knowledge-based training in which you can invest is that of general business training. The one common factor you will have with most of your customers and prospects is business. The more you know about all aspects of business the more likely it is that you will be able to share the business interests of your contacts; and to understand their language fully.

Exactly what aspects of business you choose to study will depend upon your own specific business needs and knowledge weaknesses – and what you can persuade your management to accept! There is a wide variety of courses available, ranging from a two-year MBA at a leading business school down to one-day seminars run by management consultancies. The Open University, for example, runs some excellent short courses. It's up to you to choose; and to find the justification that will persuade your management.

It is an area that, unfortunately, sales management tend to undervalue, so you may have some difficulty in persuading your management to go along with you. But it is worth the effort because it will probably contribute more to your skills and sales performance (as well as job satisfaction) than any other training.

IBM took it so seriously that about one-third of its year-long training was dedicated to such general business training. The most spectacular element of this, which was made available to all sales professionals, was a full month of 'business school'. This took the key elements of the first year of the London Business School MBA course, and compressed them into just four weeks. The first two weeks were taken up with classroom teaching of the theory that was the backbone of the MBA course, covering accounting, marketing and production, as well as corporate strategy.

In the case of the trained sales professionals, who found it difficult to justify the time off territory, this part was covered by 'distance learning'; using text books and specially prepared notes. To make learning even easier the course was summarised (albeit with nearly six hours of material) on audio cassettes, so that the sales professionals could play these when driving.

The remaining two weeks were residential at the London Business School; covering the 20 case studies from the MBA course, and taught by the professors and lecturers there. The case studies covered the same ground as the theory, consolidating and extending this. By the end of the course the students could at least use the language of an MBA graduate, and were better qualified to handle management theory and practice than most of their customers' executives. It gave the sales professionals a distinct edge in their contacts with customers. This was reflected in the significant sales increases they achieved over the next months and years.

I give this example partly because, as the manager responsible, I believed it was by far the most productive sales training I ever ran; but mainly to indicate that there is normally *no* upper limit to the amount of business education that you can profitably absorb.

Sales training

The most controversial training, in the context of this book, is that which impinges on your primary skills; on the techniques of selling. The first rule I would offer is to be sure to put these in perspective. They are only a *part* of the training of a sales professional; even if they usually represent the whole income of sales trainers, which may explain their preoccupation with them (to the exclusion of other, equally important, matters).

Specific sales training represented only about a quarter of IBM's training programme, with three-quarters given over to knowledge training in the products, technical and business areas – but (as these were seen as the key elements of sales training) still under the supervision of, and largely taught by, the sales training staff. There was no distinction between these elements: all was sales training, with the aim of producing the well-rounded sales professional.

Even the specific sales training in IBM was not wedded to techniques. It was deliberately designed to allow each sales professional to develop his own well-rounded style – a theme that, you will have noted, pervades much of this book.

Dummy calls
The core of the IBM sales training programme was a series of dummy calls. The principle was simple: it was to simulate real calls (in every respect possible), for the trainees to learn by experience.

The practice was, inevitably, rather more complex. Some time in advance of making the dummy (or practice) call, the trainee was given a 'brief', which gave the general background to the call he was about to make. It typically gave the sort of information he could expect to have available before approaching a prospect. The trainee was expected to undertake the research he would carry out before a real call; finding out the suitable products, details of the market, and suitable references (which had to be real, since the instructors checked them out).

The instructor, who was to role-play the prospect, was given a much more detailed brief, simulating the real-life prospect situation. This instructor brief included some possible scenarios, but the skill of the instructor (for which he was carefully trained) lay in *realistically* playing the role of prospect, so that the trainee could experience the whole range of calling situations.

The dummy call itself lasted around half an hour. It took place in front of five or six other trainees and, at the end of the call, both they and the instructor commented on what had happened, although it was really only the instructor's comments that carried weight. The involvement of the other trainees was as much to ensure that they also learnt. This way each trainee made perhaps 20 to 30 calls himself, and saw another 100 or so made by his fellows.

The trainees learnt their skills by *experience*. They had the best possible opportunity to learn from the things they did wrong; and, most importantly, from the things they did right (the emphasis was always positive). The calls themselves, which were all based on real calls that IBM sales professionals had experienced, were designed to expose the trainees to the widest possible variety of call situations. They ranged from first calls on a prospect to problem handling with a customer. They were also designed to stretch the skills of the trainee. They were tough calls. Real-life calls, when the trainees qualified and went on territory, were a doddle in comparison (which was, incidentally, a great boost to morale at that critical time).

There *were* some lectures on sales techniques. The trainees were given the maximum theoretical exposure to the widest range of ideas on sales techniques, as well as the practical experience. But it was the practical experience that was at the heart of the learning process. It was this that so clearly differentiated IBM sales training from almost every other sales training course.

It was the simplest sales training technique of all: let the trainee loose to gain experience. But it was also one that, run at the level of sophistication IBM employed, required resources well beyond that of the average company. It required a team of highly trained instructors, who could convincingly role-play and at the same time analyse what the trainee was doing (both right and wrong) – and who could then use this as a basis for both individual and class teaching. It required a team of such instructors, because the trainee needed the experience of calling on a range of different people.

It also required a great deal of time from the trainee. Even without the knowledge training, the specific sales training took the best part of two months.

The technique is, though, applicable in less sophisticated environments. You can run such training even if you only have a small group of sales professionals willing to take part. At its most basic, it simply requires that each of the sales professionals in the group produces some briefs, based on interesting calls that he has made. Using these briefs, but only as a guideline (as a framework which makes role-playing easier for each side), you can then take it in turns to be the instructor (role-playing the prospect) and the student (as the salesman).

The instructor need not be the one who contributed the call (indeed, others might play the role even better, since they would be less involved in the real-life situation), so that calls can be reused (if the new instructor gives them a different slant). The bonus here is that there is as much to be learnt from playing the instructor (prospect) as from playing the salesman.

Not surprisingly, persuading busy sales professionals to write the briefs is not an easy task. So, one way of getting round this problem, I found, was to get the sales professionals to base them on the calls that they were *about* to make (not those they had already made), since they were going to have to prepare for these anyway. A dummy run of the call in advance also helped their preparation – as long as they didn't assume that the real-life call would go the same way as the dummy call did.

At first it will be a strange experience, but as you and the other sales professionals learn to play the role of prospect (and that of salesman, because – under the circumstances – there is a degree of acting required even in this role), you will gradually be able to learn from the experience. There is no great secret to role-playing the instructor (particularly where there is less need to analyse the call simultaneously, since other members of the watching team can carry out that part of the job).

Even so, it may be that you will never feel truly comfortable role-playing, on either side. Playing the role of salesman is much easier for the more glib sales professionals who rely on technique, but then so is most sales training. It is unfortunate that, even in this most sensible form of training, the best sales professionals (those who put their effort into building rapport and partnership with their customers) are 'penalised' by the artificiality of the environment, and by the brevity of the call.

Because my own style requires that I understand my prospects in some depth, and relate very strongly to their real problems, I found particular difficulty in coming to terms with the artificiality of the situation, when I was a trainee. I didn't set the world alight, only just scraping through each of the sales courses at IBM!

Despite the problems, there is so much to be gained from this form of training that it is worth suffering the 'pain'.

It is arguable, however, that you should not make your training sessions competitive, even if that does give them an edge and add to the interest. The team should be there to help each other, not to beat each other. Indeed, the only rule should be that all involved must view it as a positive exercise and, in particular, only make constructive criticisms of their colleagues. It is all too easy destructively to criticise the trivial mistakes of other sales professionals. More important, it is all too easy to want to impose your own style on others; which is a failing, I believe, far too many sales trainers are guilty of.

One crucial aspect of the IBM system was that it recognised that there were as many correct styles as there were sales professionals;

the emphasis was on allowing every trainee to develop his own style. I believe, unlike most other trainers, that this is a rule you must enforce in any training you organise or take part in.

Evaluation

How, then, do you evaluate these training calls? The usual way is to use a checklist of all the things that the sales professional is generally supposed to do in the call (close, handle objections, dress neatly etc). However, I believe that if you can manage to do without such a checklist, you will be able to concentrate better on what matters.

All you really need are two sections on your evaluation sheet. In the first of these you write the three main aspects of the call that were least well (note: *not* badly) handled, preferably in order of importance. There is no real point in putting down more than three main points, since this is about the number a student can deal with in one session; giving him more will only cause confusion (another reason why a long checklist is not helpful). The second section is even more important. It should list the three things the student did particularly well. It is essential that you build him up, not knock him down. In any case, he and his fellow students can learn just as much from what is done right – a lesson that not many sales trainers seem able to cope with.

If you must grade the call (which, in the informal environment you will probably be working in, I would advise against) then use a system such as that used by IBM. The grades were:

Excellent
Good
Satisfactory +
Satisfactory
Satisfactory −
Weak
Unsatisfactory

The virtue of this structure is that it tends to force grades into the satisfactory range, which is still informative but does not demoralise the students. Best of all, though, do not evaluate; just concentrate on learning.

Indeed, the core of the whole process is what the student *experiences*. A useful aid, allowing the student to review this later, is to record the session on a cassette recorder or, even better, videotape the session. This was done in IBM even before home video recorders made it an easy process, and there is no better way of seeing what mannerisms (good as well as bad) you are prone to.

Live calls
Perhaps the most useful extension of the dummy call is to treat every *live* call you make as a training call. That is not to say that you should risk any call by using it primarily as a training session. But real calls are, once the risk element is removed, the most productive training environment.

All it requires is that you evaluate each sales call as soon as it is finished. As well as analysing what the prospect said, and what you need to do next, take a bit of time to analyse how you performed. Treat it, afterwards, exactly as if it had been a training call; with painful honesty, list the three things you did well and the three things you did not so well – and learn the lessons these highlight.

If you have the courage, take a colleague with you and listen to his independent comments.

Calls with management
If at all possible, use the calls you make with your own management as an opportunity to learn from them. There is a good chance that they have had rather more experience than you. Their comments on your call, in terms of your sales skills and techniques, should be valuable; and their advice is usually worth having.

Of course, asking for such advice has to be done discreetly. Any manager asked for advice in this way will feel flattered, so it can be a very positive move in terms of career progression. The danger is that it may prompt him actually to watch your selling style; whereas most managers spend the call trying to be the sales professional themselves, and don't notice what the sales professional is doing (but, as such, they do not manage well).

If you are confident that your general selling style can withstand such critical appraisal, you may be on to a winner – and you can notch up another point on your personnel record. But if any of your techniques are less than classical, and particularly if you are using any of the advanced sales techniques (such as those I describe) which are not well known, you may have problems, since your manager may not recognise what you are up to. (This is why I suggest you make a great point of advertising that you are using such advanced techniques. He may still not understand, or like, them; but at least he will know they exist!)

Sales skills courses

There are almost as many sales training courses as there are sales training books; one spawns the other. If you wanted, you could probably attend a new one every day; and you could learn how to negotiate (the new buzzword for discounting!), how to close that sale and how to make a million – all in less than a week. The problem is that the great majority of such courses are delivered by presenters who are rather more interested in making a million themselves than in helping you to make one.

You may find yourself paying good money to attend a theatrical performance in the company of several hundred other aspiring salesmen. I well remember such an evening performance; attended by about 400 salesmen at a cost of £40 each, it must have brought in something like £10,000 net to the 'trainer', who was an excellent salesman of his own wares. It was meant to be an almost religious experience, 'Go out there and sell!', but the day after I couldn't remember a single point I was supposed to have learnt.

Alternatively, you may have been subjected to gimmicks that would make a TV game show host blush. Gimmickry is a major hazard of much sales training. Each trainer strives for ever more extreme and unlikely gimmicks to give his course the necessary USP, regardless of what it does for the training. You will have come across various acronyms (AIDA is probably the best known) and analogies (the sales 'funnel', for example, used to describe the prospecting process). There are even whole courses based on American football: 'Let's run with the ball, and show up those suckers in the stands!'

Miller, Heiman and Tuleja comment:

> 'Many sales-training systems actually *encourage* manipulation and deceit, by teaching salesmen "tricks" and "techniques" for getting the order in spite of what the customer really wants.'

There are some good training courses but they are in the minority, and it is difficult to find them among all the colourful claims made in the brochures. You can ask for relatively independent advice, such as that from the Institute of Marketing or from the Institute of Sales and Marketing Management, both of whom also run their own courses and programmes leading to a professional qualification.

You can also ask other sales professionals about their own experiences. Which courses did they really find useful (not just which ones did they find inspirational at the time), and why? But beware, most sales professionals are suckers for well-presented garbage!

Be yourself

Whatever training you undertake, be sure that you retain your sense of perspective and your identity, as well as your existing sales style. If you are already a successful sales professional, it is very unlikely that any totally new style will be a worthwhile investment; it may just risk what you already have. No matter how evangelical the sales trainer, be your own person.

On the other hand, don't shun new ideas, for you can always improve your performance. I don't believe that there was one genuine sales course that didn't teach me at least something (and this book contains a number of those lessons); although there *were* plenty of gimmick-ridden excuses for sales training that offered nothing. Heinz Goldmann (perhaps rather influenced by his role as a sales trainer) makes some valid criticisms:

> 'Many salesmen – especially the experienced "old hand" – are convinced that their own method is the right one ... So they automatically reject the experience of others ... Salesmen will gladly lay the blame for every lost sale on any other cause ... they never apply self-criticism, they never analyse their own work to find the true cause, and so they learn nothing from their own mistakes.'

His criticisms are largely justified, but I still reiterate my message that you should judge you own needs carefully. You may feel that I have repeated the message too frequently, but I believe it is very important. Your own unique style, the one you feel most comfortable with and most productive in using, is a very valuable asset. Treat it with care. Nurture and grow it, and as it grows so will your success.

Chapter 8

Presentations

Presentations represent a skill that many sales professionals, especially those involved in complex sales, are supposed to possess naturally. The reality is that very few sales professionals are actually called upon to make formal presentations; and very few indeed are ever trained in this skill, even among the most experienced. As a result, those sales professionals who are suddenly called on to demonstrate such skills can find it a terrifying ordeal; stage fright is a not infrequent problem.

This is a pity because presentations can be great fun, particularly for those, such as myself, who are frustrated actors at heart. More important they can be a very useful, if not essential, part of a professional sales campaign. Quite frequently decisions need to be taken by a *group* of people; often, in the complex sale, by the board of directors. It is, of course, ideal if you can obtain separate meetings with each of these decision-makers, but that is a luxury which is not often available; and even then, with a group decision, it is not possible to 'close' these individual calls separately. As soon as you meet them in a group the situation calls for the use of professional presentation skills in some form or other; and these are very different from those associated with calls (which are essentially based on *single* face-to-face contact).

Apart from sheer panic, the normal reaction of most sales professionals appears to be to treat such meetings as a variation on a call, or as an excuse for a speech. Either reaction fudges the issue, and normally means that the sales professional loses control, 'outvoted' by the greater numbers of customer personnel.

This problem of controlling numbers of decision-makers can often get totally out of hand, even from the customer's point of view. I once had a situation where the account group of a leading advertising agency decided that the way to 'win' their presentations was to outvote me. They attempted this by simply loading the audience with their own supporters. To my amazement I found that the only way that I could eventually control the final decision was to bring in three cars full of my own supporters, to vote for me; and I was the client – nominally at least the decision-maker! What hope is there, then, for the sales professional, trying to control a comparable situation?

If, on the other hand, you treat the situation from the start as a genuine presentation you will always be in control – and will make certain of presenting your case in the best possible light. Better still, if you are up against competitors, there is a good chance that your professionalism will shine out in comparison with everyone else's amateurishness.

Objectives

Even more than is necessary with a call, every presentation *must* be based on a very clear set of objectives. It is fair to say that the success of a presentation may be largely predicated on how sound and clear are its objectives.

I once had the pleasure of making an evening presentation, over dinner, to the board of Tesco. I delivered a hard hitting, hard selling presentation. But on returning to my seat next to Daisy Hyams (who was the managing director) I began to feel that it was perhaps a bit forceful for an evening's 'entertainment', so I apologised to Daisy for its directness. Her answer was to tell me a story about Jack Cohen, the legendary founder of the chain. Daisy had been with him when he too was invited to an evening meeting, in this case by one of the leading detergent manufacturers. The supplier spent a fortune on the evening, running it at the best hotel, with the best food and a superb cabaret. It must have cost thousands of pounds; and throughout the whole evening there was not even a hint of sordid commercialism – business was never mentioned. Daisy shared a taxi with Jack after the dinner, and was surprised to find that once he was in private he was livid. He had expected to do business, and thought he had wasted a whole evening when none was forthcoming. His very telling point was: 'What right have that load of cowboys to demand that I give up a whole evening of my time to entertain them?' Of course they thought they were doing him a favour by giving him the entertainment, but they weren't – and they certainly weren't doing themselves any!

The moral of the story – and it applies to any sales situation just as much as to a presentation – is that you are wasting your customer's time just as much as your own if you indulge in anything other than business; and indeed in anything other than direct selling. There is only one reason for you to be in front of a customer, and particularly in front of a group of customers, and that is to give him (or them) the information to make the best buying decision. It is common courtesy to limit yourself to this task, rather than indulge in any pleasantries that are not directly productive, and waste their valuable time.

Unlike a call, a successful presentation cannot normally be seen in isolation; it must be part of an overall sales campaign. Typically it will be part of the close of that campaign. The objectives will, therefore, be inextricably intertwined with those of the overall campaign. It also means that the presentation will not usually introduce new material, but will bring together the previously agreed material for final, formal approval.

These links to the overall sales campaign *are* important – and must be kept in mind at all stages of that campaign in general and (of course) during the presentation itself.

The objectives must also be kept simple; the complexity that you can handle in a call (with diversions resulting from questioning being followed by clarification in the form of a restatement of the perspective) is simply not possible in a presentation. As you will see later, it *is* possible (and indeed desirable) to encourage questions during a presentation, but these are qualitatively different from those used in a call.

Preparatory meetings

It is arguable that, in the type of sales campaign that leads up to a presentation, *all* earlier calls are preparatory. But the last set of calls before the presentation is certainly critical. These calls should be used to contact the key decision-makers and influencers, finally to agree the content of the presentation. This can, in its own right, be a powerful sales process, since it will be in the context of a positive partnership – with the customer's decision-makers agreeing what *they* want to see in the presentation (and hence defining, as a joint venture, what needs to be done to get the order).

It is also a useful time to make certain that you *have* got it right (and are on the way to getting the order). In this respect it is very similar to the trial close discussed earlier. If you detect any diffidence on the part of any contributor it allows you to ask why, with every justification; and 'Why?' is the most powerful question in your armoury. As with the trial close, this question (which is perfectly acceptable in this context) allows you to pursue the underlying problems until they are solved. It is acceptable because it is your job, and that of all your contacts in the company, to put together the best solution. If it has its flaws (or is unacceptable for any reason) then everyone should want to rectify them.

By the time you arrive at the presentation, therefore, everyone involved should have given you their informal support. As a result the presentation should almost be a formality, albeit a very important one. On the other hand, if you go into the presentation with significant work still left to do before achieving the close then the odds against success lengthen significantly.

In particular, if you go into the meeting with one or more of the participants openly and actively opposing you then you are unlikely to win the order. If they are less than 100 per cent supportive, but recognise that you are likely to win (and are correspondingly subdued in any opposition), you might still be able to win. But beware the situation where there is still *open* criticism. In the first place this means you have a fight on your hands; and even a partly hostile audience can destroy the fragile atmosphere of a presentation. Second, it signals that these critics probably think that the decision is still open with the rest of the decision-makers; which is bad news when you are counting on their support!

In my dealership the sales manager himself took the lead in one particularly important sale to a major corporation. It was for a large network of personal computers to replace Burroughs, minis. Somewhat to my surprise, for the situation was clearly very competitive, the sale appeared to progress well. The network solution my team proposed was workable, and half the price of the competition. Furthermore, the consultant who had been called in by the prospect, effectively to make the decision, had assured us that we would win.

As we approached the final decision there appeared to be only one fly in the ointment: we were inexplicably having difficulty obtaining technical information from the software house that had provided some of the existing programs. I suspected this might be due to Burroughs' influence, although we couldn't find any link. But, as we were just one day away from the presentation, I stumbled upon one further problem, which my team had known about but had not thought significant. Of those attending the presentation, I was proudly told, four out of the five were voting in our favour; the decision was clearly already as good as ours, by a majority verdict. At this point some very loud alarm bells began to ring in my head. Where my team saw four out of five as a massive vote to win, I saw that one out of five had some reason confidently to oppose. The outcome was that we *did* lose.

The subsequent post mortem showed that the opponent was the DP manager, whose nose had been badly put out of joint by the appointment of the consultant. He had then undermined the consultant's work; the problems with the software house had been his work. His efforts were redoubled when Burroughs, who were his first choice, were knocked out of the race; and he switched his energies totally to undermining his rival, the consultant (combined with ourselves, since he correctly saw that we were in league with him). Eventually, just before the presentation, he took all our proposal documents to one of our competitors, who simply used our specs to put in a bid that was 20 per cent cheaper. Thus we were beaten by a bid that we didn't even know existed. There are no such things as simple majority votes in the average sales campaign.

Audience selection and terms of reference

To the limited extent that it is possible, it is advantageous to influence the audience make-up for the presentation, together with the terms of reference under which it will be given. This is very similar to 'hi-jacking', the specification described in Chapter 6.

Your influence on the make-up of the audience is bound to be limited (particularly in terms of the exclusion of those members that you might wish were not there!). But you may just be able to include a few more of your supporters; and may even be able to prime them to ask positive questions of you, and negative ones of your competitors! You will also need to ensure that the 'level' of audience is consistent, even offering to run two meetings (one for the board, and one for the users) so that the message is not confused by the different requirements of the separate audiences.

What you should be able to influence more easily is the format of the presentation. If you can arrange for this to match your own style, then you have a major advantage. And it *should* be possible to influence the format significantly, as the prospect himself will have very little experience of such meetings – and your competitors probably not much more.

In this way a presentation can be productively used to act as a showcase for your sales skills; and, hopefully, for the shortcomings of your competitors.

Putting the message across

The traditional, almost infamous, IBM approach was to split a presentation into three parts. In the first you told the audience what they were about to be told. In the second you told them. In the third you told them what you had told them.

In other words, the presentation always started with a clear and concise introduction, which explained what the audience was about to be told. The main body of the material came next. Finally, it was concluded by a clear and concise summary of all the key points which had just been presented in detail.

Although the first and third parts are much shorter than the middle section, perhaps only five minutes each out of a total of 45 minutes, they are no less important. The first is necessary because it sets the perspective and does away with many of the unproductive questions which can disrupt presentations (where the majority of these, and the most disruptive, will usually relate to material to be dealt with later in the presentation). The last section is vital, because this is the true close; bringing together all the previous arguments to build an overwhelming case that can, there and then, be converted into an overall agreement (the order).

There are, of course, many other approaches; ones that can appear more exciting. Indeed, the IBM approach has often been derided as pedantic and boring. The problem is that most of the other approaches tend to gimmickry — and such gimmickry in a presenta-tion must nearly always detract from the content, which is the true key to success.

In my time I have seen seen presentations created around a variety of weird and wonderful frameworks; from acronyms that were based on the product name (I can remember the product name, but not what it did) through to very enjoyable games (which were, however, so irrelevant that I can't even remember the product name). Many were instantly memorable, but just as forgettable over the following weeks, and almost all smothered their important messages under a blanket of largely irrelevant decoration. My experience suggests that in the end simplicity usually wins the day, and the order.

I particularly well remember a presentation by a highly reputable management consultancy, to obtain my business in the area of production control. I had, foolishly, mentioned an interest in computing. The result was that we were shown a portable terminal connected via our telephone line to a mainframe. For a very enjoyable 45 minutes we took it in turns to play 'hangman'. The whole experience was fascinating, since this was in the 1960s when very few people had ever touched a computer (and just getting the service into our offices must have cost a fortune). However, when the team of presenters had finally walked out of the door my immediate reaction was to cross them off the shortlist. We were looking for solutions to our production control problems, and I couldn't see that any consultancy which had been happy to waste an hour of my hard-pressed management team's time on an irrelevant game were likely to be red-hot on improving our productivity!

KISS

Perhaps this simplicity is once more best summed up by the acronym KISS (keep it simple, stupid). It is arguable that this has now become a cliché, albeit a useful one, but it has too often been misused by sales trainers, about overall sales campaigns, as a justification for gross over-simplification; for replacing in-depth awareness of customers' needs with dangerously simplified gimmicks and clichés.

In the special case of presentations, though, it can be a particularly productive concept. There is inevitably much less interaction in a presentation, and hence less opportunity to explore more complex arguments. As a result, it is essential to keep the concepts as simple as possible, while still encapsulating what has been agreed in the previous meetings.

Accordingly, you should perhaps attempt to limit yourself to no more than half a dozen concepts or arguments at a time. Long lists might appear to be able to win the business, by swamping the customer with benefits; but in reality all they will do is confuse him, and bury the half-dozen really important points that *might* sway him.

Refine the overall structure down to these few most important points. Then refine the supporting arguments down to those that most positively and powerfully support these points; and ruthlessly cut out any material that does not fit this picture (although it is always a good idea to keep this rejected material 'under the counter', to handle any questions on these topics).

Ask for the order

It is obvious to everyone involved that, in making the presentation, you are looking for an order. It is just as obvious to the prospect as it is to you: he too will be giving up his valuable time, presumably because he too expects to do business. Yet remarkably few sales professionals are honest about why they are making their presentations. Most pussyfoot around, trying to describe it in other, more acceptable terms; but there are no other better terms – the prospect has to be there to buy, otherwise you and he are both wasting your efforts.

The most powerful approach is always to be open about your motives. Explain that you want the business, which is both flattering and reassuring to the prospect. The most frequent complaint about a poor sales professional is: 'Does he want our business or not?' How often have you heard that said, and yet how rarely have you heard any buyer *complain* that a sales professional was 'after our business'? The complaints are always about how a sales professional goes about obtaining the business, not about his wanting it. So tell them that you want it. But recognise that you will have to justify the order fully – and ask just what you have to do to to earn it.

This one simple objective, then, automatically provides the framework for the whole presentation, and allows you subsequently to check progress in the context of what really matters: are you progressing towards the order? Again, it is worth remembering that the buyer has as big an incentive to place the order as you have to win it; so honestly involve him in the process.

Media

Having decided on the overall structure of the presentation, and the audience that is to receive it, the next choice is the medium that is to be used.

In the days of my youth flipcharts were the norm, posing major problems for those of us whose artistic and graphic skills were abysmal on the small scale, degenerating into the farcical on the scale of a flipchart. These days, fortunately, the more normal (and much easier) medium is that of foils (A4 size transparencies) shown by means of an overhead projector.

Overhead projected foils (transparencies)

These have become the standard because they are probably the easiest medium of all to use, and certainly the easiest to prepare. The capital cost of the overhead projector and screen, at less than £500, is affordable by most companies; most companies of the size able to afford a sales force already have at least one.

They are easy to prepare quite simply because of their size, which is the same as the normal A4 (letter-size) sheet of paper. Thus, all the techniques (such as typing and photocopying) that you can apply to a normal sheet of paper are available for use on a foil. You should, however, remember that their use is ultimately very different from that of normal paper, so keep in mind their projected size and environment when you are designing and producing them.

Although foils can be made by drawing directly on to the acetate (using the special pens available in most stationers), probably the easiest means of producing a professional-looking foil is to create the original on ordinary paper and then copy this on to a foil. You can make this foil (copy) with an ordinary photocopier, using one of the special acetate foils designed specifically for use in such photocopiers. Alternatively, you can use one of the special thermal copiers, again using the foil material produced specially for these – ideally using a photocopy, which will often reproduce better than original material under the heat process. In addition, special materials can be obtained for the thermal copiers (usually from 3M) which reproduce in colour, and are very effective where you want to differentiate the material on overlays (but this is probably the only justification for the rather specialised capital investment, of £800 or so, for this equipment).

If you can't get access to a suitable photocopier, or simply prefer to use hand-drawn foils (possibly because you can use a multiplicity of colours on these), then make certain to use *permanent* markers, which are less generally available than the water soluble ones but don't smudge when you touch them. These pens can, in any case, be used to add colour to the black and white material produced on photocopiers. Or photocopied foils can be coloured by using coloured adhesive film available, once more, from 3M (who tend to specialise in this medium).

The main advantage of the copied foils is that you can use a variety of devices to produce them. As the main component will be words and figures, the main device will be a typewriter (or something similar). In IBM it was almost mandatory for every golfball (now daisy-wheel) typewriter to have a very large font (size) of the Orator typeface which, with its simple outlines, is designed for presentation use. But ordinary typefaces can be as effective; and if you need them to be larger, then simply enlarge the typed material in a photocopier that has an enlarging facility. In this way you can even produce a foil which has a single character filling the screen – but bear in mind that the defects in the type will, at this size, badly blur the edges (although this may even add to the 'style').

To these characters can be added other items of artwork, ranging from simple lines (and, of course, charts) to drawings (there are whole books of ready-made drawings for use on photocopiers). All of these can be pasted-up to produce your final design: you simply photocopy the design you want (enlarged or reduced to the size you want), cut it out and paste it in the desired position on a new sheet of A4 paper; then carefully photocopy (and possibly rephotocopy) the result, painting out any join lines that show with typewriter correction fluid. Perhaps the most effective addition, very easily achieved, is to add in your prospect's own logo (simply taken from his letterheading), which makes it very obvious that you have taken some trouble personalising the material for him.

In IBM one trick was to prepare a standard personalised border for each foil (containing, for example, the IBM logo together with the customer's, and the date of the presentation – a useful way, incidentally, of keeping track of such material). Once produced, this frame was copied on to a foil and then overlaid on each of the originals while they were being photocopied – so this 'frame' was only ever produced once.

If you have access to a personal computer there are a number of programs that, after some learning, are relatively easy to use (particularly if you have a tame computer aficionado on hand), and which produce excellent materials for foils. The most popular of these come from Lotus and Ashton-Tate but, whatever the source, be sure to allow plenty of time to learn how to use them. The output from these programs can be via a printer (preferably a laser, but also, at a lower quality, from a dot matrix), in which case the output is once more photocopied on to a foil. Alternatively it can be via a plotter, in which case this higher quality output may be drawn directly on to an acetate foil (and can be in a number of colours).

Finally, for special presentations it is possible (if very expensive) to have foils professionally produced. In particular it is possible to have reversed image foils produced which project a white (or coloured) image on black – which is crisper and easier to read. It is almost impossible to achieve this any other way, since the 3M thermal material which aims to achieve this usually gives somewhat blurred results.

It is also possible (again at a relatively high cost) to have slides reproduced in this foil format. These may be a good investment if you regularly need to show photographs (of your products for example), since they remove the need to mix the use of foils with that of slides; where the use of the two media can significantly add to the complexity (and cost) of the presentation.

Foils can be used in most situations. The slight disadvantages are that they need more space than flipcharts (and, of course, the correct equipment) and need somewhat dimmer lighting conditions. It is rare, though, for the ambient lighting conditions, in anything other than direct sunlight, to be too bright. I never had any problems with the visibility of foils, where I did with slides for example. In any case, it is always worth checking in advance that the environment *will* be suitable (and this applies equally to any of the media). These slight disadvantages of foils are, in my opinion, heavily outweighed by the advantages of ease of use and preparation.

Flipcharts

Just occasionally you may have no alternative but to use flipcharts as your prime medium. For example, you can carry a full-size portable flipchart stand (with a presentation already set up) in the back of your car, and be ready to present in about 30 seconds – less than one-tenth of the time it would take to set up any other form of presentation.

The problem is quite simply that of achieving the correct quality of visual material. It demands considerable practice, and not a little effort in preparation, to produce tidy, readable flipcharts. The only way (apart from having them professionally made – which is usually prohibitively expensive) is to hand draw them with magic markers. It is always preferable to outline them in pencil first, having previously drawn a layout grid. It is also preferable to use stencils to prepare these outlines. But this is so time consuming that, although I had several sets, like most of my colleagues I rarely used them, preferring to gamble on my own poor artistic ability rather than take several hours longer.

It is a great help if you make use of the generally available pads of flipcharts that are already printed with a grid of light blue lines. Although people often think these are for mathematical work, they are excellent in that they save the chore of drawing up the initial guide lines – and the light blue grid is hardly noticeable to the audience when it is overlaid with the very heavy lettering needed for the presentation. (Remember that the very heavy letters normally show through from the flipchart underneath, so it is usually advisable to leave a blank chart between each one being presented.)

These days it is more normal to use flipcharts to back up an overhead foil presentation. These flipcharts can be very effectively used to link the foils (with, for example, the agenda displayed as a flipchart throughout the presentation). One tip which can make life easier if you plan to write in material during the meeting, is to use a pencil to sketch in very lightly (in advance) the letters you propose to write in later. The audience shouldn't be able to see these, but check – if they could see them, then gently rub out the letters until they can't (but you still can!). This will help you to shape your letters better, a difficult art to achieve under the stress of presenting, and will remind you of what you plan to write in.

The main use of the flipchart, though, is as a blank sheet to draw up *ad hoc* material, when answering questions for example. It is quite possible to do this on a foil, and many lecturers do exactly that, but in a sales presentation it is preferable when answering questions to maintain eye contact – and this is difficult when the audience's eyes are on the screen rather than on you. A flipchart allows you to remain the focus of attention.

Be careful what you draw, however – it is still part of the presentation. In my days as a trainee I valiantly launched into an *ad hoc* technical explanation and (strictly following the advice of the pundits) looking at my audience rather than the chart. It involved the use of a couple of circles and some curves. It was only after the bemused looks on the faces of my audience turned into barely muffled guffaws, that I realised that the resulting picture could be viewed as somewhat pornographic.

Desktop presentation

A specialised form of the flipchart presentation is the miniaturised form used in desktop presentations. In this case the 'flipchart' is a normal A4 size of paper (although larger sizes can be used if wanted). It is held in a ring binder, usually of a special type (available from stationers) that is designed to sit neatly, like a miniature flipchart stand, on the desk. As the size is A4 (letter size), it is possible to use all the techniques used for producing foils; so such presentations are easy to produce. Indeed it is a neat trick actually to use transparent A4 foils as overlays on the basic charts (a technique that is not available on full-size flipcharts).

Such presentations are useful for very small audiences (not more than three or four people), and in particular for a single person. They are, incidentally, also ideal for a run-through with the key customer personnel prior to a full presentation; this is a very effective means of informally 'debugging' the facts to be used, and of getting those personnel on your side in advance of the main meeting.

Desktop presentations are somewhat more informal than the full-scale variety. And, of course, they are very portable – consisting only of an A4 folder that easily fits into a normal briefcase. They allow you to get a presentation in front of your prospect without forewarning him, although out of courtesy you *must* ask him if he wants to see it. But desktop presentations are, nevertheless, presentations; you should not make the mistake of treating them as calls.

Almost all the various media can be used in desktop form. Thus, there are desktop slide and film presentation systems; although, as they are usually the size of a large portable TV, you would find it diffi-cult to smuggle one into a normal call (and they do typically require that you hunt for a power socket – which is never available where you need it). I have even seen portable computers used quite effectively. But, once more, beware of the pitfalls, and only use these forms of presentation if they are strictly relevant to the message you wish to convey.

Slides

Most professionally produced company presentations, the sort that are produced centrally (usually, it seems, in New York – complete with the US version of English), are made available on slides; simply because this is the best (and cheapest) way of copying them. In addition they offer the cheapest medium for originating such material, particularly if they are produced by computer. They also offer the highest quality of visual presentation, especially where photographs are needed.

The problem is that they need a special environment, and their inflexibility means that they tend to take over the style of the presentation (and often put a straitjacket on it). They need dim lighting conditions, which are not always available. Worse, the dim lighting makes it difficult for the audience to see you. Worse still, it makes it difficult for you to see them – and a good view of them is essential if you are to control the event. In addition, slides are a particularly inflexible form of presentation; which you will find out the first time you are asked to return to a previous slide!

However, if most of your material is already on slides, and in particular if photographs are important, this medium will have been largely determined for you; as long as you can create the right physical environment. The ideal environment is a relatively dim area around the screen (so that the slides can be clearly seen, and are not bleached out by light falling directly on the screen), but with some lighting over the audience – it is ultimately more important that you can see them than that they can see you.

Slides are quite portable. A Kodak Carousel, the industry standard slide cartridge which holds 80 slides, will easily fit into a briefcase. Even the complete projector is not much bigger. I have many times happily taken one as hand baggage on planes – it is very unwise to consign it, in the hold, to the tender mercies of baggage handlers! If you are giving a whole series of identical presentations, slides also tend to last better; they become less dog-eared and grubby – and the initial investment is easier to justify.

If you are an amateur photographer, of even mediocre skills, it should be possible to make your own slides. All you need is a single lens reflex, 35mm camera together with a close-up lens (or a set of adapter rings costing less than £20) which will be able to blow up typewritten words to fill the screen. You can set up your charts in exactly the same way that you make your A4 foils, and then simply photograph them. The quality may not be outstanding, certainly not as good as professionally produced material, but it may be good enough for what you need; and it is cheap, easy and quick to produce.

If you need to copy slides then it is worth buying a slide duplicator that will plug into your single lens reflex. When on my travels, at major meetings, I always carried one with me. Then if I saw a slide I liked I copied it (with the owner's permission of course) on the spot. People will always promise to send you copies of their slides – but they never do!

In this way you can also produce your own slides to tailor presentations that you inherit from elsewhere. Every staff department is convinced that it knows exactly what is needed to show to prospects, and not a few spend a small fortune backing their judgement by producing slide sets. Needless to say, these will almost certainly *not* meet your own practical needs; but they will contain some good material which is well worth using. However, you will almost certainly need other slides to supplement this material, and to tailor it to your prospects' needs; this is where your own slides can be used. The one problem is that the slides from different sources are bound to have different styles; in particular, your own amateur efforts will suffer by comparison with the professional ones. But as a sales professional you should be able to talk your way around this shortcoming, in the few situations where you cannot escape using such mixed material.

I used slides frequently, because they were easier to carry around, and the photographic material was essential. I learnt how to set up the meeting rooms with the correct lighting conditions (and I learnt how to return quickly to any slide on the carousel – an art in itself). I also used my own slides mixed in with professional sets. I justified this by describing them as 'comments' on the professional material (and I justified the latter by its value, and rarity, as leading-edge material from the USA). The presentations were very successful and I never had any comments about my own slides. Once more, the content on them was excellent and this hid the quality of the visual.

Audio-visual
A very special form of slide presentation is where the slide projector (or in a more professional form, a pair of slide projectors, to allow

smooth dissolves between slides) is linked to a tape-recorder so that the presentation is totally recorded. This can be useful if there needs to be a regular repetition (they are most usually used to show short bursts of material repetitively at exhibitions), or if the timing or script is critical, or if the presenter just needs a rest. I used them most to provide a standard introduction to each of my business teaching sessions. The change of pace was as much of a rest for the students as it was for me.

But the equipment is much more complex, and the preparation of the material quite difficult. The biggest disadvantage is, once more, that you totally lose control of the presentation. There is just no way that you can change it to take account of audience reactions.

I suppose an even more restricted application might be audio only, perhaps verbal testimonials. But I have never come across its use – and in an essentially visual medium, which presentations are, it would probably weaken the overall impact.

Film and video

The same comments apply just as strongly to film (which is rarely used these days) or video (which is often used). They are totally non-interactive. Once you have switched on the VCR you are committed, no matter how irrelevant parts of the material may be.

Both film and video can be used, though, to show and demonstrate things that may not be possible for the customer to see by any other means. It may be the only way that a seller of large capital equipment can show his wares. It can also show how a more portable product is being used in the wider environment. I used it very successfully, for example, to show whole computer systems supporting production control in a manufacturing environment – an environment that is easy to show in a video, but otherwise impossible to reproduce in a conference room.

Alternatively, video may be needed to compress time; to show a process that would be too lengthy to illustrate otherwise. We, for example, used it particularly effectively to show the various stages of computer aided design (CAD), where the set-up of the dozen or so examples would have taken two or three minutes each if it was handled as a live demonstration – unproductive waiting time that would have been unacceptable to the audiences.

The problem with videos (and even more so with films) is that they are very expensive to have professionally produced, costing tens of thousands of pounds for just a few minutes. It is sometimes thought possible to use home video equipment to produce your own material (in much the same way that you can produce your own slides) and, if correctly used, this may be possible – although the level of skill will need to be that much higher. For example, our CAD demonstrations were simply created by shooting a series of video pictures of the computer monitor screen. The results were rather crude, but it was possible to explain this as a means of saving the prospects' time – and we found that everyone was happy to accept this.

The problems came when we wanted to make the presentation more professional. Adding 'voice-over' proved to give results that were disjointed and clearly amateurish. And there was no way that we could edit the material: even a semi-professional video editing suite would cost tens of thousands of pounds. As a result we eventually used the video in silent mode, with the presenter providing the verbal commentary and controlling the video with the VCR's remote, hand-held control (in much the same way as he would control a slide projector). As a form of moving slide it was very effective, and its amateurishness was not intrusive.

Too many companies expensively produce videos to illustrate material that could be handled better, in general presentations, by other means. No matter how slick the material appears, the wise sales professional's decision should be to consign these to the store cupboard (if it is not politically expedient to consign them immediately to the waste-basket). It is impossible to edit them effectively, and the resulting introduced irrelevancies (where specific audiences are concerned) will rapidly negate any advantage offered by slickness of presentation. Worst of all they once more remove all control from the presenter; and often allow bored audiences to go to sleep quietly in the gloom.

If the material is good, however, they can be used in short bursts to break up a long presentation. Arguably IBM's most effective use of this medium was a series of films commissioned from the Muppets (before they became famous on television – at times IBM patronises the most unlikely of arts!). These were two-minute humorous films which simply added up to to the message, 'Coffee is now being served' – a useful way of ensuring that the audience was laughing and talking as it went into that hardest of sales pitches, the coffee break.

Computerised presentations
A recent development has been the ability to use visual images directly generated by computer. These may be shown on a large monitor (typically in excess of 26 inches in size, costing more than £1000, and heavy enough to require two people to lift it – so it

does not represent a very portable set-up) or projected on to a normal screen (where a full colour video projector can cost upwards of £10,000).

A very recent development is that of a black and white system designed to work with your existing overhead projector. One of these, of the type made for example by Kodak, can be bought for just over £1000. Although the picture is somewhat grainy and the projection facilities are limited, this is cheap and portable enough (it will fit into your briefcase – but you still need a computer to drive it) to make computer presentation a possibility in many situations; for example, where the ability to interact directly with figures (say, in a spreadsheet that is being used for a cost justification) is a critical requirement. Of course it has major advantages for the growing number of firms in the computer industry who wish to show software in action.

For simplicity, you can just use a simple standard monitor for a small audience, or a number of these linked for a larger audience (although you will need special electronic equipment for this). I have successfully run meetings with up to 20 participants using just five such monitors linked together and scattered through the audience.

Whatever means of display you choose, you will need a dedicated computer system, typically costing around £3000. On top of all that you will need some suitable software to prepare, and show, the 'visuals'. The industry standard currently appears to be IBM's PC Storyboard, although there are other excellent programs around.

The end result can be thought of as a series of foils. These can be animated to a certain degree, but be aware that this will take an inordinate amount of effort. The changeover between foils can be more prettily achieved, using such film devices as wipes, fades and dissolves. But these do not of themselves justify the use of a computer. The programs can, on the other hand, take 'snapshots' of computer output (as shown on its screen), so it is possible to introduce real examples of such material, interspersed with the foils. Where there is a requirement to show real-time computer output these systems can win hands down.

For the average sales professional, however, such systems are as yet too specialised. They are difficult to prepare: before you can produce your own material you need to learn the software package and, as these are relatively complex, you should allow a couple of days just dedicated to learning how to use them. They are not that easily portable, even though the newest system will sit in you briefcase and you could in theory couple this to an IBM compatible portable PC (which is not much bigger). But together with the necessary extension leads and your other material, you will end up with quite an armful – and then you will have all the hassle of setting up such sensitive electronic equipment in a strange environment. Finally, they are not necessarily that easy to use in practice. Although you can in theory move backwards and forwards through the various foils, in reality you need to be computer literate to do this; and you must accordingly assume that they are as inflexible as projected slides.

In practice they are, as yet, mainly used to produce 'rolling demonstrations', unattended demonstrations of computer software that keep on repeating for hour after hour.

Other media

The other item most usually included in presentations is a demonstration of some form or other; this can be a particularly productive highlight, just so long as it is relevant. Demonstrations are discussed at some length in the next chapter.

Another medium sometimes used is a model. Architects, for obvious reasons, often use a model as the focus for their presentations. But it can also be used to illustrate large-scale capital equipment; as it was during the hearings into introducing pressurised water reactors into the UK's nuclear energy industry. It was possible to show a detailed model where the reactor obviously had not yet been built. Although the cost of several millions of pounds quoted for the production of this model was ludicrously extreme, it does indicate that all such models will tend to be expensive.

A specialised, two-dimensional form of model is the 'magnetic'. In this case the elements of a large 'flipchart' are broken down into separate pieces, each of which is mounted on card backed by magnets. These can then be magnetically attached to a steel-backed board. It is a very effective device for building up a picture, and for highlighting changes to this (I have also used them effectively to build up flowcharts, and even very theatrically to build up lists of benefits), but it is limited by the availability of the suitable steel-backed boards – although on a small scale some portable flipchart stands and writing boards with magnetic backing are available.

I have seen presentations that included dramatised scenes or 'sketches', but I have never seen this technique used successfully as part of a normal presentation. Even in the very theatrical atmosphere of a large convention it has been my experience that, while being entertaining (which, to be fair, is usually their sole function in such events), they are rarely successful in getting across serious messages.

My most recent experience was that of a 45 minute presentation laid on by a leading software company. Of that time, the product received marginally over five minutes. The remaining 40 minutes were given over to embarrassingly amateur comedy sketches based on a TV series, backed by a girl singer, who did at least have the good grace to look embarrassed by the fact that she was singing off key! An American sitting in the seat next to me succinctly characterised it as, 'The biggest turkey I've seen since Thanksgiving'; and I lost any interest I might have had in the product.

Multi-media

I have briefly touched on the more complex techniques used in very large, theatrical presentations; but they are in a different world altogether, which (fortunately, for it can be a logistical nightmare) you are unlikely to be invited to enter.

IBM, along with other large companies, uses them for major product launches. It also uses them on its very lavish sales conventions. The sky is the limit for such events, and they can out-dazzle any West End show. IBM regularly uses troupes of singers and dancers in spectacular sets, hosted by world-class entertainers. Laser light shows and special effects are also almost standard. I was involved in mounting one launch where a full size mock-up of a jet airliner was rolled on to the stage – just to provide a dramatic entrance for the national sales manager! But the cost of these high jinks was phenomenal; often running into hundreds of thousands of pounds.

The basic standby was almost always the multi-screen audio-visual, employing dozens of computer-linked slide projectors to cover a screen perhaps 50 feet wide. They *were* spectacular, but were typically used in all their glory for as few as five or six sessions of five minutes each (less than half an hour out of a two-day meeting) – and at a total cost approaching £100,000. They were intended to be uplifting centrepieces (in theory they had a message), but more usually they were instantly forgettable as any message was swamped by the spectacular medium.

In practice, the real heart of even these meetings was the simple presentation that is described in this chapter. The real meat consisted of IBM managers talking at single slide presentations. It was the content of these simple presentations that enthralled the audience (otherwise that speaker had to review his future career!).

It was, I believe, symptomatic that the two highlights of the IBM conventions over the years, as remembered by the popular culture, were on the one hand the spectacular on-stage firework show that just as spectacularly went wrong and set fire to the set (with panic among the organisers as the audience had to be evacuated, and the theatre nearly burnt down), and on the other hand the performances of Frank Cummiskey (one of IBM's star performers and a US vice-president) simply sitting on the edge of the stage, with only a hand mike as support, informally chatting with an enthralled audience of hundreds.

Content

Despite what many of the more flamboyant practitioners might aspire to, it is inevitably the *content* that is the driving force of a professional presentation. It certainly was so for Frank Cummiskey, whose staff worked hard and long to provide the few elegantly simple thoughts he so superbly presented. The medium is only relevant in terms of the extent to which it gets in the way of communicating this content.

The pyrotechnics of presentation may be immediately impressive but they are usually just as instantly forgettable; ask any sales professional just two days later what the real message was and I bet he gets it wrong, if he remembers at all.

The danger of such pyrotechnics covering poor content was, for me, epitomised by the very high profile launch of IBM's replacement for its personal computer; the PS/2. The audience, of some hundreds of dealer principals, including myself, was clearly rooting for IBM; it desperately needed something totally new to lift the whole industry out of the rut it was in. I believed then, as I still do now, that the PS/2 range had hidden under its covers all the revolutionary advances that the dealers wanted. What we got though was one of IBM's fabulous multi-media extravaganzas. Illustrated by specially made videos and excellent visuals we were entertained to a series of lectures on IBM quality, as the products themselves were revealed; to the constant repetition, duly interleaved with comedy interludes in case anyone was getting bored, of the theme that it was IBM's biggest announcement ever.

As we made our way out of the theatre everyone was saying that it had been a marvellous presentation – and it had been. Yet less than three weeks later the industry was saying that the product range was a damp squib, and IBM was desperately trying to reassure Wall Street that nothing was wrong; fulfilling a prediction that I had made as I left the presentation.

The problem was that there really was no meat in the content. Half the presentation was taken up with pitches on quality, which was largely irrelevant in the specific context of the new products. All we were told about the four new products themselves was their box identification numbers (ranging from 30 to 80, hardly inspiring stuff), and their bare specifications (which fell some way short of those of IBM's competitors already out in the market). This was backed up by dramatic references to the really revolutionary material, the operating system (OS/2) and the new 'micro-channel'; but apart from the repeated use of superlatives (it *really* was IBM's *biggest* announcement *ever*) no details were given.

Over the next few weeks the competition, understandably, set out to rubbish the new range (gladly pointing out for example that the key operating system, which was the justification for the new products, would not be available for nearly a year); and they succeeded, for the audience had no knowledge, no meaty content, to rebut these stories.

Thus, IBM wasted a unique opportunity of offering an audience clamouring for its product a true understanding of the really powerful and revolutionary developments it had come up with. Instead it brought to bear all the skills of its multi-media specialists; and made an eagle look just like any old turkey, a delicious meal for the vultures that immediately descended on it!

If you haven't got the content don't make the presentation. If you *have* got the content make certain that you communicate it. The following sections make some suggestions as to how this communication might be achieved.

Category of presentation
I would argue that, at least for a sales professional, *every* presentation should be a sales presentation. Indeed, almost *any* presentation is likely to contain a sales element. Even a teacher, if he is a good one, will be trying to sell the ideas he is presenting. But there are, nevertheless, significant gradations of style.

These range from the hard-hitting, and directly selling, sales presentation that may be the highlight of the sales campaign – the real test of a sales professional and the main category of presentation described in this chapter – through to the largely educational presentation. The latter is ostensibly only to inform the audience; but if you, as a sales professional, are involved there must be some sales elements and, in my experience, such 'educational' presentations are often the most powerful sales tools of all. In between are a wide range of different categories of presentation, including those called to agree plans for future projects and those seminars designed to introduce larger mixed audiences to your products.

All of these are discussed in other chapters, but they all revolve around the techniques addressed in this present chapter. For the sake of simplicity and clarity, however, I will assume for the present that we are considering the pure sales presentation.

Overall content

Where inexperienced sales professionals concentrate on the mechanics of a presentation, more experienced presenters will recognise that most of the time in the preparation of a presentation needs to be directed to establishing the correct overall *content*. Brilliant style can rarely carry poor content; at least not for the duration of a sales campaign.

I do, however, remember the sales professional from one computer manufacturer who made a superb job of selling to us. We stocked his product largely on the basis of his sales presentation which, against my earlier strictures, was his first contact and was a presentation to the whole group. Unfortunately, the product and its support did not in reality live up to his claims. It simply did not, after all, meet our needs, and three months later we discontinued the line.

Some would argue that his slick, but not wholly truthful, presentation at least bought his company the possibility of sales through our outlet. But I believe he wasted his, and his company's, considerable investment in appointing us as dealers. He certainly wasted *our* time and money, and for this reason we subsequently dissuaded others from becoming their dealers, so his actions might actually have been, in the longer term, quite counter-productive. Perhaps my earlier strictures *aren't* totally disproved by this case!

Within IBM it was a rule of thumb that largely new material required a ratio of between five and 10 times as long in the preparation as in the presentation, and totally new material a ratio of up to 20:1. Thus, a 45-minute presentation could take up to 15 hours of concentrated work (probably spread over at least three days), and would take at least five hours to rework for a different audience.

Preparation of the *content* of a presentation is, therefore, no trivial matter but, all the same, is usually neglected by most sales professionals. Even with my experience I must admit that I have made a few presentations that were real turkeys. In each of these cases the subsequent post mortem concluded that the key factor in the failure was simply that I had not spent sufficient time on preparation. Now I *always* make sure to prepare and rehearse thoroughly all presentations I give.

Above all the content has to be carefully selected to be relevant to the *audience*. I well remember attending an IBM evening presentation to 50 or so dealer principals. The 30 minutes or so about new financing arrangements went down well, as did the 30 minutes of questions. On the other hand the other two hours (in a hot sticky basement room, where IBM had switched the air-conditioning off at 5.00 pm to economise) was given over to listening to a detailed presentation of IBM's new internal management structures. As might be expected, this was tedious for the audience, although of considerable interest to the IBMers making the presentation. But their undoubted enthusiasm was insufficient to dull the mind-blowing boredom they inflicted on their very captive audience.

Level

Having decided the outline of the overall content (which will inevitably vary with the sales situation), and having chosen the key messages to convey, the next exercise is to pitch the presentation at the correct *level* for the audience. Every audience is, to some degree, different, and allowance needs to made for its special characteristics. (This diversity is one of the fascinations of selling, and may be the only thing that keeps you reasonably fresh when you are making essentially the same presentation to a number of audiences.)

The categorisation that is normally most important is that of level within the organisation. To get the level right you have to see the world with the eyes of the audience: you have to understand just what is important to them, what interests them, and from what perspective they would want to see it. Thus a DP manager will probably be primarily concerned with the technical solution, because that is what his performance will be judged on. He may also have an interest in the strategic implications but will assume, with some justification, that the board will call the tune in such matters. The managing director, on the other hand, will assume that all the boring technical details will have been thoroughly vetted by his DP staff, but will be very concerned to establish what benefits (and costs) will accrue to the firm *overall*. Hence the two presentations will typically be very different, probably only overlapping to a limited extent.

More generally, there will probably be quite distinct differences of interest between the main categories of users, technical advisers, buyers and board members. Any sales professional ignores these differences at his peril. Too many sales professionals have one all-encompassing presentation, delivering it regardless of the audience – and are surprised at their lack of success. Getting the level right is the acid test of any presentation, a test that the audience themselves will have made within the first few minutes.

Verbal content

This highlights the fact, common to all sales situations, that you should use the right 'language'. As Tom Hopkins says in his book:

'The Champion learns to speak many of these special languages because it's the most efficient way to establish rapport with many different groups of people.'

I would add that it's also the only way that they will fully understand you, or as he says:

'You say it in words they want to hear.'

He also goes on to suggest that you actually enliven the verbal content of a presentation:

'Look for words that are charming, eloquent, picturesque, exciting, creative. Add sparkle to your speech by using common words in unexpected new ways.'

Visual content

One key factor of a presentation is its visual content. Where the sales call is almost entirely verbal (at least in terms of its overt messages, although the hidden visual messages conveyed by body language should not be ignored), the presentation is primarily visual. All eyes should be fixed on a common focus – and the sales professional's voice then becomes secondary. A human being's prime source of information on the environment is vision, followed some way behind by sound. Thus, any verbal information from the sales professional will instantly be swamped by visual stimuli (from a new foil, for example).

It is inevitable, therefore, that in a presentation what a customer will remember most clearly is what he sees rather than what he hears. As a result the organisation of the visual messages is a critical task if these are to do the selling job you want. This is perhaps the most difficult new skill of all (and the most important to learn) for sales professionals whose previous experience has been almost totally verbal.

It is quite amazing how many sales professionals, who otherwise have a sound (and convincing) sales style, fail to make good use of visuals, even when they have taken the trouble to have all the equipment to hand.

Many of the *ad hoc* presentations (that have not been mounted by professional audio-visual companies) that I have seen have consisted of perhaps one (or at most two) obligatory visuals, which the speaker dutifully unveiled, before he thankfully (and usually hurriedly) moved on to the rest of his otherwise totally verbal presentation. These sales professionals obviously preferred to talk. This almost inevitably means that the audience's attention will eventually wander; there are usually just too many visual distractions unless the speaker is spellbindingly good. By omitting the visual material they are wasting something over half the messages (and the most memorable ones at that) that they could get through to their audience.

The mistakes made by the inexperienced tend to fall at either end of the spectrum. The classic mistake is to show too much information. I have, on a number of occasions, been presented with a foil of a fully typed sheet of A4 paper, containing perhaps a thousand words. There is no way that any audience can quickly absorb such visual complexity. The result is that they spend the next two to three minutes desperately trying to read it; and in the process ignore every word the sales professional is uttering. Almost inevitably, this is the time the inexperienced sales professional launches into his most important pitch, unnoticed by his distracted audience.

I have never yet seen such complex visuals work effectively. On just a few occasions I have deliberately tried to use this very visual complexity to illustrate theatrically the complexity of a product situation; usually in a jokey manner – removing the foil after just a few seconds, when the complexity has become obvious to the audience. But despite my experience I still felt that my use, even in such a specialised manner, was probably counter-productive. I was inevitably left with at least one member of the audience who had started reading, and felt cheated that he wasn't allowed to read it all.

The next mistake is usually made by those sales professionals who have recognised the folly of over-complexity, but who react against this with over-simplicity. The resulting foil typically contains just a few very general words. These certainly do not interfere with the verbal material, but neither do they significantly add to it, which misses the benefit of the very powerful visual stimulus. A typical visual in this mould would state, for example, 'cost effective'; in itself a laudable objective. But where the 10-minute accompanying verbal pitch would develop the supporting arguments, so that the case was proved, this visual would never be updated. The audience would have to carry these extra arguments solely in their head, without any visual reminder.

The ideal lies somewhere between these extremes. The visuals do need to be kept simple, with perhaps no more than five items of information on each. But they also need to be informative; the words, or visuals, have to be very carefully chosen most powerfully to encapsulate the messages you want to put across. This persuasive brevity is the lifeblood of advertising agencies. We all believe that 'Coke is the real thing' and that 'Avis tries harder'. The sales professional has to try to adopt some of these 'shorthand' skills. At the same time he has to ensure that the resulting visuals will be truly integrated with the verbal presentation, referring to them regularly, perhaps at least once a minute. It is surprising how many sales professionals move on to a new subject in their verbal pitch but leave the old visual on show – with an audience wondering what the talk of 'this season's fashion colour' has to do with a visual still showing 'cost effective'.

There is some argument as to how many foils you can present before you confuse the audience by presenting too much information – but a rule of thumb says that you should think twice before using more than 10 to 15 foils (or flipcharts) in a 45-minute presentation. You can, though, usually present more slides, since these will typically contain less information each. Thus, where you would reveal further information on a foil (by sliding down a piece of paper covering the lower part of the chart) you could show another slide. Even so, if you use more than 80 slides in a 45-minute show you will probably make the audience's heads ache.

Again, the inexperienced often gravitate to the extremes. The totally inexperienced tend to use very few foils indeed (perhaps only two or three, but crammed with complexity), and talk a great deal; thus losing most of the vitally important visual impact and leaving the audience wondering why the projection equipment was needed at all. The slightly more experienced tend, once more, to recognise their initial mistakes, and react by producing too many visuals. Getting the balance exactly right needs a great deal of experience, and then considerable effort in the preparation.

The visual content of each foil should be kept as simple as possible – only the direct messages must remain. There is a temptation to gild the picture by adding 'artistic' effects or irrelevant illustrations. Beware: these embellishments can only detract from the messages you should really be trying to put across. They add nothing to the basic message, unless you are very lucky and find an illustration that exactly matches your needs, and they can very easily confuse. What is more they will almost certainly demonstrate your own lack of artistic skill, as laying out such illustrations demands genuine artistic abilities – one reason why advertising agencies can still make a living. So KISS: keep it absolutely as simple as possible, and you can't go wrong.

Pruning

Once you have the content and are happy with it, get out your pruning shears and set to work with a certain degree of savagery. It really hurts to cut out material which has taken hours of sweat and tears to create, but which turns out on inspection not to be central to your theme. It is a necessary sacrifice if you want to produce the most powerful argument – in the best films more scenes end up on the cutting room floor than get on to the screen.

You have to force yourself to prune and then prune again. Try to see the material from the viewpoint of the audience; judge which pieces really earn their keep and which merely serve to dilute the overall impact. It is worth getting, even at this early stage, a second opinion. Asking a colleague, whose opinion you respect, to review the material may catch the more obvious flaws (to which constant exposure has created a blindspot); and if you do ask, then listen.

The aim is to strip the whole presentation down to its bare essentials, so that nothing gets in the way of the key messages being communicated.

One of the best presentations I was ever given by trainees in IBM lasted just five minutes. It was a presentation to the 'board' which was the climax of a series of calls and presentations. The message was delivered on just one flipchart, containing only two points. The first point was quite simply that the problems had been investigated in depth and a sound solution developed, which the whole management team had approved. The second was that the solution provided all the benefits I wanted and exceeded the cost savings that I had asked for. The third point, made verbally, was, 'So why waste everyone's time; let's sign the order' – which I did! There was no need to add any more, as most other sales professionals would have been tempted to do. I should point out, however, that as an excellent team of sales professionals they had a further 20 flipcharts ready to conduct a more conventional presentation if their initial close failed –

but it didn't. Although it was simple, it contained everything I needed to hear.

Quality of material

The next stage will be the preparation of the material itself, in particular the production of the visuals. The previous sections have concentrated on making the material as simple as possible. But this is not to say that the presentation should not be of the highest quality. Indeed, flaws are more obvious the simpler the material – elegance is usually simple, and expensive!

Amateurish, crude visuals will not hide good content, but they will distract from the message – and will counter any message of quality that you will probably wish to convey. Not long ago I was at a meeting where a number of vendors of networking software presented their wares to the leading 50 or so UK corporations. There was little to choose between the material. Some was elegant, some rather florid; but overall their messages came through clearly.

The one exception was, paradoxically, the one vendor chosen by the organisers to be the star turn. To be brutally honest, his visuals were a disgrace. He even made the classic beginner's mistake of using some foils that were far too complex; they were very obviously made from crude photocopies of the pages of technical manuals, and the typeface was so small that they were not readable beyond the front row of the audience. He had taken his material from a number of sources, to save effort I presume, and had not even made the effort to remove the references that made it obvious that they were all photocopies of other people's work. As a result there was no consistency of style. There were at least half a dozen typefaces, and as many styles of layout. To add insult to injury, there was duplication of information and a considerable amount of material that was clearly irrelevant.

The resulting impression, which was (in view of the clear lack of effort) not surprisingly compounded by a less than competent (and poorly rehearsed) verbal presentation, was of gross amateurishness and abysmal quality. Worse, it gave the impression that the presenter did not care and did not value his audience. Indeed, his attitude was almost insulting when compared with the obvious effort his competitors had put in.

Thus, a presenter who had started with the invaluable advantage (in a very competitive market) of being rated by the organisers as the star attraction, managed – largely by the poor quality of his visuals –

to alienate his audience with his poor quality message and incompetent delivery; to the extent that he was not even invited to the rerun of the meeting for a different audience. But above all, what made me (and the rest of the audience) really angry was not his lack of skill, but his obvious lack of effort.

One aspect of quality which emerges from the above example is consistency of style. Using the same typeface across all the visuals, with a standard layout, is all that is required to make this happen. It is, incidentally, well worth keeping such a style consistent across *all* your presentations; so that when you need to borrow a foil from another presentation it isn't an obvious afterthought.

Occasionally it may be necessary to mix in material from other sources, producing an obvious conflict of styles. I have done so myself. But in this case the answer is, once more, to be honest in declaring the sources of the material. Using such material from US sources, supplemented by my own (clearly different) material, I used its exotic origins to give it an added cachet.

To ensure good quality almost certainly means using typeset foils (or similar material). Yet this is not too onerous; it just means you need access to a typewriter and perhaps also to an enlarging photocopier, and can manage to draw a straight line (with the aid of a ruler). But I would stress that care is still needed. The characters must be correctly spaced, and the lines really must be straight and parallel. Slipshod work looks bad on an A4 page; on a six-foot square screen it screams amateurishness.

The touchstone for quality, though, should not be elegance or any aesthetic design sense, but clarity. Such presentations are not artistic exercises, but are about hard-nosed selling. The aim of the exercise is to get the various messages across to the audience in the most powerful way. (It was for this reason that IBM presenters tended to use the Orator typeface. It is not a very elegant type, but being simple it is one of the easiest to read at a distance.)

The quality of the presentation should extend to the less obvious aspects. Mount the acetate foils in cardboard mounts so that they won't blow away, slip around or simply stick together. This has the added benefit that the mount's locating slots ensure that the foil is instantly aligned (with none of the fiddling to get it central and level, that accompanies many presentations). These mounts also allow overlays to be taped in place so that they can be hinged to register exactly (again removing one of the potential sources of annoyance). If you are using slides then mount them in glass so that they don't pop in and out of focus, requiring you constantly to adjust the focus, once more to the annoyance and distraction of your audience.

Finally, it is necessary to apply the same criteria of quality to the handouts you plan to give to your audience. After all, they will be the only permanent examples of your quality standards.

Quality *is* important in a presentation; not just because it demonstrates your overall commitment to quality, but also because it demonstrates your commitment to the customer. If you have clearly taken pains over the presentation he will be impressed that you take him seriously – and that you will take similar pains to support him later as a customer.

Style

Once more, style is a contentious issue. Many of the pundits try to lay down exact rules although, typically, they never seem to recommend the *same* set of rules. Once more, as you will by now expect, I beg to differ. For style is an individual matter; it is what works for you as an individual – it is what you, and your audience, are comfortable with.

Having made that disclaimer, it has to be admitted that there is less flexibility in a presentation, and hence less room for developing idiosyncratic styles. However, let me reassure you that quite dramatic variations are still possible, by describing one very extraordinary situation I was involved with.

We were due to run a series of computerised accounting seminars at quite a sophisticated level, for which in-depth expertise was essential. Fortunately we had a consultant sales professional who knew the subjects inside out. Less fortunately, we discovered only two days before the highly publicised seminars were due to start that he had the worst case of stage fright I have ever come across. He simply could not stand up in front of an audience; being in front of an audience, in any capacity, made him physically ill.

The solution turned out to be having him present from *behind* the audience. For it emerged that he could happily present just so long as the audience couldn't look at him all the time! So, with considerable trepidation, we built a presentation based on a disembodied voice floating from the rear of the conference room. Visuals were not a problem since we were mainly using linked television monitor screens; and the few foils were easily handled by myself at the front. This latter aspect was eventually the key to success, for clearly there was no way that an effective presentation could be built where there was no interaction (and particularly no eye contact) with the audience, so I provided that contact by proxy. As the presentation rumbled on from the back of the room, I acted as the visual focus and the channel for audience participation, interjecting the further explanations that questions (and visual symptoms) demanded.

We gave a very flimsy excuse (related to the computer equipment) as to why the real presenter was at the back, but this was never challenged. And, I must admit, to my great surprise and even greater relief, these 'double-headed' seminars went remarkably well, despite a handicap that at first seemed insuperable.

The moral is not that this is a style to be recommended, but that it illustrates just how idiosyncratic your style can be – if you handle it well. (As a footnote, I should mention that the sales professional never did manage to emerge from the back, but his confidence did grow to the extent that he became quite critical of my contribution, fearing that it might be dragging down his own!)

In general, however, there are a number of main categories of style, described in the following sections.

Formal or informal?

There is a tendency for inexperienced presenters to make presentations very formal affairs. This is understandable where they are new to the techniques, and want to keep the complexities under control by the use of a rigid, formal structure. This tendency is often compounded by their previous experience, on the receiving end, in the form of public meetings or lectures; which tend also to be very formal – although, I would argue, less effective for being so.

The formal style takes the term 'presentation' almost literally and looks mainly for one-way communication from the presenter to the audience, although (hopefully) there will still be some feedback.

My own preference, where it is possible, is for a more informal style, with significantly more feedback from the audience – and ideally with interactive involvement of that audience. This is now to a large extent ruled out in public meetings. Indeed, modern political meetings, with the television cameras rather than the audience in mind, have their audiences carefully screened so that there will be no (unwanted) interaction – apart from the obligatory eight-minute standing ovation at the end! Perhaps this protects the weaker speakers from the dangers of interruption (which, wrongly, worry every inexperienced speaker), but it deprives the best speakers of an invaluable stimulus. In previous decades the most memorable parts of the speeches of Harold Wilson, for example, were those where he dealt brilliantly with the interruptions of hecklers; and those meetings were 10 times livelier than the modern, stage-managed media events.

But we are, here, talking of small groups where it *is* quite possible to make presentations interactive. Remember what I am describing is a *sales* presentation, and the customer's contribution is always more important than yours. In a call, listening rather than talking is the most important skill. In a presentation the balance shifts somewhat, where your talking and the visuals become the focus of the event, but listening (and watching) is still the secret of success.

I believe that the success of a presentation can often be directly proportional to the degree to which the key participants are *actively* involved. As a result I will do almost anything to wake up my audience and make them react to me.

Room layout

The traditional formal layout is 'theatre' style, with the audience in rows of chairs facing the presenter (who is sometimes even on a raised stage). It allows the audience the best possible view of the proceedings. Sometimes it is supplemented by providing tables (still in rows) to make it easier for the audience to make notes. These tables create a physical barrier, but this is no greater than the psychological barrier that is created by the formal separation of the presenter from the audience in any theatre-style meeting.

The layout that I prefer, if the group is small enough, is 'conference' style – seated *around* a table (or, for rather larger meetings around a horseshoe of tables). This confers the ambience of a 'discussion' meeting, anticipating such discussion and providing the best psychological environment for interaction. It is true that the sightlines for the audience are worse, and their comfort may not be as great (having to twist to see the screen, for example), but I believe the psychological benefits of integrating the presenter with the group far outweigh the disadvantages.

At the London Business School, where the audience often sits in tiers of seats in the shape of a raked horseshoe, the lecturer is very clearly the physical focus of the group. However, in the case study discussions the group itself has to be the focus (otherwise too many difficult decisions, from which the students are supposed to learn, default to the lecturer). To compensate for this, some of the most effective presenters there conduct such sessions from *behind* the students. This works remarkably well, generating the best interaction between members of the group. I have used this technique myself, deliberately retreating to a position where I was out of the direct line of the group, when I wanted to force the group to work out ideas among themselves – equivalent to the pregnant silence used in a call to force the prospect to comment.

Sitting or standing?

It may come as a surprise to some that you can give a presentation sitting down. But this style enjoyed quite a vogue at IBM, and is still the normal style for many internal meetings there. For, with the overhead projector alongside your seat (and pointing *on* it rather than to the screen) you can comfortably remain seated, and integrated with the group. It is an effective style for very informal presentations, although it can come across as somewhat affected where the relationships are more formal (and the other participants are expecting a more formal style). But, as it removes him from the focus, it can be much less nerve-wracking for an inexperienced presenter.

Most presenters, of course, do it standing up! This is the traditional style, and it has the advantage of making certain that the presenter is the clear focus of the meeting. It also integrates him with his visuals, if not with his audience.

I use both techniques, often combining them in the same presentation. But I suppose, as I enjoy larger than life theatrical gestures, I tend to conduct most of my presentations standing. Even then, however, where possible I do intersperse my periods of standing with periods sitting at the table as part of the group; when the meeting shifts into discussion mode, which are often the most fruitful parts of the meeting.

Notes

How do you remember your script? The extremes vary from actually reading the script word by word to situations where the presenter has only the broadest idea of where he is going, and plans to develop the rest of his material from his audience's comments. Both of these extremes have their dangers.

The use of a verbatim script is widespread; it is the staple diet of most political speeches. By itself it is relatively foolproof, just so long as you don't lose your place or mislay a page. Otherwise, the first major problem comes when you try to integrate visuals, which are an essential part of most presentations, public speeches excluded (even there, although it is totally counter to tradition, I believe these would be more understandable and memorable with such visuals). It is impossible both to point to the visuals and read your script at the same time. The only thing guaranteed is that you will not be able to point effectively with a wadge of paper in your fist. So you will almost certainly choose to make a speech where the visuals look after themselves (and handling them is usually delegated to a projectionist). This loses some of the impact and creates the danger of the speech and visuals getting out of step, as an increasingly panic-stricken projectionist loses his way, even if you don't.

An even worse problem than losing the link between the presenter and his visuals is losing the link between him and his audience. Hunched over his script, his eyes are always downcast. The audience inevitably loses eye contact (he becomes remote from them) and he loses control since he cannot observe their reactions.

The problem of eye contact has been partly alleviated, at least from the audience side, by the invention of the teleprompter (now more often called an autocue). Originally developed for television (it's what newscasters rely on), a television monitor relaying a script on a roll manually fed by an assistant behind the scenes is reflected by one or more angled glass screens just in front of the presenter's face. It makes it seem as if the speaker has no notes and is looking directly at the audience (particularly if two screens are used so that the presenter can alternately look at different parts of the audience) and it has rapidly become the essential prop of almost all modern political speakers. It is a fudge, though, if it is used in true presentations, because the presenter *isn't* really looking at the audience. He is really still looking at the script, and he is still in danger of missing the visual signals coming back from the audience and so losing control.

Sometimes verbatim scripts are inevitable, particularly where the facts are complex and must be delivered exactly right. The scripts of all major IBM public presentations are closely examined by its lawyers, word by word, to ensure that they contain nothing that might offend (or might be the least bit monopolistic; anti-trust in the US jargon). These speeches *have* to be given verbatim, and the teleprompters came as a great relief to the beleaguered IBM senior managers who did not have actors' memories.

But otherwise, using verbatim scripts can be less than fully productive in the true presentation environment; and once you are addicted to them they can become a psychological prop that is almost impossible to discard. To 'detoxify' my partner, who was by training an architect, not a sales professional, I eventually had to resort to the subterfuge of telling him (just five minutes before his presentation, which he had already given several times, and knew backwards) that his script had been accidentally destroyed. It hadn't been, of course, and I kept it ready to prompt him, but the result, fortunately for our friendship, was that for the first time he gave a really fluent performance – and enjoyed it.

The opposite extreme (of having no notes at all) is fraught with just as many dangers. Just occasionally I have been trapped by over-confidence into giving an 'off-the-cuff' pitch (without any notes) about something I knew very well. The result has almost invariably been a disaster; even though my style deliberately looks as if I am doing it off-the-cuff and the subject matter was second nature to me. Quite simply, it is well nigh impossible (at least for me, and I suspect for the great majority of sales professionals) to give a good presentation that is genuinely *ad hoc* that is without *any* previous consideration of what is to be said.

So the happy mean lies somewhere between these extremes. The conventional wisdom holds that presenters should use brief notes – essentially subject headings. It is normally recommended that these are put on cards, usually 5 by 3 inches. How these notes are organised depends on the individual. Some people just write down a simple list of the topics to be covered. Others go to great lengths, adding symbols and colour coding, and verbatim quotes where these are particularly important. Once again, it is up to you to decide just what suits your style; only experience will tell you just how little you can get away with. Even so, you should always aim to reduce the quantity of notes, simply because fewer notes are easier to handle and get in the way of true flexibility less. But don't begrudge the time spent in getting your notes to the standard you need; it is a key part of your preparation.

One useful technique, if you are using foils, is to write the notes on their cardboard mounts. This also removes the one remaining pitfall, that of getting your notes out of step with the visuals; and it removes them from your hands which allows you to become more involved, in terms of gestures, with the visuals. It is a technique that I have used very effectively, although it does mean that you may have to remount the foils if you want to use them again.

Mainly, though, I cheat! I use the visuals themselves as my prompts. If the visuals are closely integrated into your presentation, as they should be, they will closely match your verbal pitch. With foils this is particularly easy, because you can easily see what is coming next (and you can add extra notes to the frame if necessary). With slides it is more problematic, since if you do forget what is coming next it can sometimes catch you by surprise. But that is not really a great problem: it adds to the spontaneity and is perfectly acceptable to audiences as long as you have the confidence and experience to carry it off. It is even acceptable to return to the previous slide to complete that pitch if you have moved on by mistake. Just be honest and explain your mistake – the audience will be sympathetic.

The greatest problem is that of disobeying the oft-quoted dictum that you must look at the audience, not the screen. In general, this is true – you cannot control the audience and they certainly cannot hear you if you don't look at them most of the time. But that doesn't prohibit you from looking at the screen occasionally. Indeed, your audience will almost certainly be looking there as you put up new material, so it is only natural for you to do the same. In any case, without looking at the screen occasionally (and preferably with each slide), you run the risk of getting out of step with your visuals – you never know what the projectionist may have done with your precious material.

The main danger of using your visuals as prompts is that, probably subconsciously, this aspect may take over the priorities. The visuals are no longer designed for the audience, but are reduced to being prompts for the presenter. You must guard against this danger if you use this approach.

Personal presentation

I have talked at length about the material you will be using, but ultimately the main instrument you will use, the real focus for most of the time, will be yourself.

Physical projection

As I have already indicated, a presentation usually requires a larger than life performance; indeed, at times it may get close to a stage performance. The gestures, for example pointing to the visuals (and, if you need to use one, do make certain you have a pointer that will reach!), do need to be slightly theatrical.

Most of the texts on presentation comment, at length, that you should remove annoying personal habits. It goes without saying that if you consistently pick your nose as you make the presentation it will not impress your audience. But most personal habits are only noticed if the presentation is not succeeding in conveying content that the audience finds interesting. If you, as a member of the audience, find the messages fascinating you will not notice, let alone worry about, the fact that the presenter sways backwards and forwards, as many presenters do. Perhaps you should ask your colleagues if you do have any *really* annoying habits, but otherwise don't worry – concentrate on making the material fascinating.

A specialised aspect of personal habits is whether you should move or not. The received wisdom is that you should not; indeed, it is often recommended that a lectern is used, and firmly gripped to avoid such a habit. My own view is that this is probably rubbish. It creates, in my view, the far worse sin of totally immobilising yourself, and of removing the natural gestures (problematic or not) that normally enliven a person's performance. I, and many other excellent speakers I have seen, have happily bounced all over the stage, and this has posed no problems – just so long as it was compatible with the material. But once again the decision is yours; whatever is more natural for you.

Vocal projection
This too needs to be somewhat larger than life. You will have to speak louder than normal and always towards the audience; if you talk with your back to them they certainly will not be able to hear. Always, when you present in a strange environment, get your colleagues to check that you can be heard clearly in all parts of the room. Have them sit at the back during the presentation ready to warn you if you get too quiet, as your audience will usually be too polite to tell you. Maintain your voice level, being too loud rather than too soft; it is all too easy in the stress of the situation to drop your voice to the normal level.

One problem that sometimes afflicts speakers is a monotonous delivery; in its worst form (which I have had) the voice can literally become a monotone. It is most obvious with speakers reading verbatim from a script. The solution to this is not, in my experience, voice training (although I have no doubt that this can be a great help), but is simply to get enthusiastic about the subject matter. If you are enthusiastic this will normally be communicated in your voice. My partner reading his script was monotonous. Without it, his enthusiasm became infectious, and there was not a trace of monotony.

If, due to the size of the room, you need to use microphones and amplification equipment you will need professional assistance. Do not try to do this yourself – it is a skilled art just balancing the sound, and you will already have enough on your plate.

Finally in this vocal section, what about accents? It used to be required that speakers took voice training to acquire the perfect 'King's English', which was in those days based on the Oxford accent and later superseded by the BBC standard accent. Fortunately, such days are past, and accents are now acceptable and largely unnoticed.

The one exception is if your accent is so thick that your audience has problems understanding you. I once attended an oil industry meeting in a Scottish city where, at the ceremonial dinner, the provost spoke. The main problem was that he had such a thick Scottish accent, and dialect, that nobody could understand him. I eventually found that the best source of enlightenment was my neighbour at the table who, being a Norwegian, seemed to be able to translate more than I could!

Humour, anecdotes and references

It is often thought that it is wise to open a speech with a joke, to break the ice. I will later in this chapter suggest how you should break the ice – and I would now suggest that you don't try to do this with a joke. It is possible, and I have heard some marvellous speakers who have got away with it, but for every one who succeeds I would estimate there are a hundred who fail. Being a successful comedian is a very rare talent; if you are successful then get in front of the TV cameras, but otherwise refrain from even trying.

Using an anecdote is, however, a much safer ploy, particularly if it is from your own (or your company's) background. I used a fund of amusing anecdotes about IBM to break up the long sections of more stodgy material, but I always used one that was relevant to the issues at hand. This is the ideal use of an anecdote; lightening the presentation but being totally relevant to the main material – advancing it, not distracting from it.

A safer idea, and one that you generally cannot make too much use of, is references (discussed in Chapter 5.) In a presentation they both lighten the material and personalise it, while adding authority to your claims.

Mistakes

The greatest fear of many inexperienced presenters is that they might make a mistake. They should not worry. I actually welcomed mistakes (although I did not go out looking for them). As long as you don't allow your terror to destroy your presentation, mistakes are useful for breaking down the barriers between you and the audience. Audiences like to find out that presenters are only human after all; it brings the presenter down to their own level – which should be the aim of the presenter. It actually makes audiences more sympathetic towards you; perfection is always seen as a very cold virtue.

This presupposes, however, that you admit your mistake and join in (even encourage) the laughter. If you try to hide your mistake you are in danger of losing their sympathy, and merely looking a fool. If you accept it, and see the funny side of it with the audience, then you are on to a winner.

Mistakes can actually be used to very productive effect. One of my most successful presentations was to the board of Gallahers , when I was a brand manager there. I was asking for a doubling of the promotional budget, another million pounds, for my main brand (which was Condor pipe tobacco). Although I did have a good case, it is never easy to persuade a board to accept such a radical step, particularly where the brand had previously been seen as a loser.

The presentation was the first that I had ever made with overhead foils, and in my enthusiasm I wrote a comment on the screen rather than on the foil. At this the whole board fell apart laughing, and continued to do so every so often thereafter, as the comment remained on the screen. But that was the turning point of the presentation; the laughter released the tension (that was clearly there before) and diverted much of their potential criticism – and they gave me the money!

Confidence

The most difficult thing for any sales trainer is to instil confidence in his charges. The worst possible advice is to 'be confident', because that reduces those lacking confidence (and well knowing they lack it) to the state of quaking jellyfish. But by now you should have the basic confidence, and the remaining confidence will come from the knowledge that, just so long as your material is good, presentations cannot go very badly wrong (and in any case mistakes needn't be a disaster). With time and experience you will relax and enjoy them, and give an even better performance.

It is said that all the greatest actors suffer from nerves before each performance; and they believe that this is almost necessary, since it means that they are taking their work, and the audience, seriously. Once in front of the audience the actor's adrenalin takes over; and it will do the same for you – all good sales professionals love an attentive audience.

Beware, however, the perils of alcohol in such a situation; normally alcohol should be shunned. It impairs your reflexes and distorts your perceptions. While you may think you have given a good performance your audience may not, and will think even less of you when you breathe alcohol fumes over them.

I once made a presentation to the sales force of Cussons (where I was marketing manager). I felt that the audience was rather more attentive than usual, but it was only after I had finished that I was told what had befallen my predecessor the year before. He was, like many inexperienced presenters, very nervous, so his friends had helped him by providing a goodly supply of alcohol. When his turn came, he managed to climb the stairs to the platform, but seemed to have some trouble seeing the slide. With long pointer outstretched he gradually inched backwards from the screen, until very elegantly he fell backwards off the edge of the stage, dead to the world. I was grateful that I had not been warned about this, as I could not have hoped to have matched that performance for drama!

Rehearsals

If the content is what will convince the audience, rehearsal is what will ensure that this content is communicated, and does convince. Such rehearsals fulfil a number of functions, all of which are essential to the professional presentation.

As Tom Hopkins says:

> 'To become a Champion, you have to polish your performance and practice it against the clock until you can do an effective presentation or demonstration within the seventeen-minute limit of maximum client concentration. It may be a stiff challenge, but meeting it will do wonders for your closing ability.'

I am not certain where he gets his 17-minute limit from – most others seem to agree on 45 minutes as the normal span of attention, and this has seemed to work in my own experience – but otherwise I would totally agree with him.

In the first instance rehearsals will help to reveal whether the messages are correct, powerful and can be communicated. It is only when you put them to an audience, even if that audience is only yourself (although it is preferable if that trial audience also includes some of your colleagues), that you can really judge their effectiveness. The overall content should not need to change dramatically, for it should be the result of extended, in-depth work which has already been agreed with the members of the audience. But the detail of how this content is communicated, by the various specific messages in the presentation, may change significantly.

It has been my experience that almost all of the presentations to which I have devoted significant rehearsal time (arguably I should have devoted such attention to all my presentations) *have* been subject to extensive reworking, to their great benefit.

Second, rehearsal allows you to get the dynamics of the presentation right. What looks good on paper often needs rebalancing in practice. The time and weighting given to each section will need to be adjusted. And the process of ruthlessly pruning out the ineffective, to leave a taut and powerful skeleton, should continue.

Finally, it allows you to learn the material. Whichever 'notes' you use, you must rehearse until you are word perfect. If you rehearse time and time again, until you absorb the material almost by osmosis, you will not be exposed (at least, not for long) to the vicissitudes of drying up, or being thrown off course by unexpected events. This can be a long, time consuming process, for very few people are word-perfect after only two or three read-throughs. Knowing the material backwards also helps to build that all-important confidence; in the material and, in particular, in yourself.

For the last few, 'dress' rehearsals bring in your colleagues (or at least those of them whose judgement you trust) to try out the material on them; and listen to what they say. If you are brave, bring in your management. I found that the manager to whom I reported for most of my time at IBM had an uncanny knack for putting his finger on the weak points, and for generally toning up the presentation.

Rehearsing for hour after hour was what made IBM's top managers so good at presentations. For example, I have described Frank Cummiskey's easy, informal style, sitting on the edge of the stage 'chatting' with his audience. What I have not described was the hours of rehearsal needed to get the material just right, and to allow him the confidence to take such an easy-going approach. Any time you see someone doing something difficult 'effortlessly' you can be sure that an immense amount of practice lies behind it.

Once you have rehearsed to the necessary level, stop. Allow a period of rest, preferably 24 hours, between the last rehearsal and the presentation. The danger is that otherwise your presentation will become jaded and stale, due to over-rehearsing. If you have a rest, and go fresh into the actual presentation, the result will be that much more stimulating – both to you and the audience.

Having said that, it was my usual experience with major senior management presentations in IBM that the last rehearsal finished, with everyone in a state of collapse, at 3am. But just seven hours later everyone would be on stage, giving the performance of their lives. If you are a true sales professional, the adrenalin of getting in front of an audience will pick you up, no matter how jaded you may think you are.

Preparing the room and facilities

Before you even begin to develop your final presentation you should ideally survey the room where it is to be given, since the whole shape of the presentation may depend upon the facilities available. In my time I have given speeches and presentations in venues ranging from superbly equipped lecture halls through to a waxworks' chamber of horrors (I was the one that moved!) – and each of them had its own particular character that influenced the shape of the presentation.

I found out the value of such investigation at the first major speech I ever made, while still at university. I was proposing the formation of a new society to the Social Committee of the University of London Union. I had painstakingly prepared a fairly intimate speech for what I imagined would be its eight to 10 members. As I was politely ushered into their presence I was horrified to discover that there were in reality perhaps 100 of them, stretching out into the distance. Fortunately I was able to change the style in flight to handle the problem. It was the classic example of 'in at the deep end', that probably made later speeches that much easier. But I also learnt to avoid such stress by checking out the facilities first.

When it comes to physically preparing for the presentation try to obtain access to the room as early as possible. This will allow plenty of time to set up, and time also to carry out a short rehearsal. You may find that the dynamics of the room, and the set-up, are quite different from those you have rehearsed with, and you may need to make changes (in voice projection, for example) to allow for this.

The main benefit of setting up early is that it allows you to get everything out of the way and relax, confident in the knowledge that the worst problems are behind you. There is nothing worse for your self-confidence than having to rush, hot and flushed, into the beginning of the presentation because the set-up was not ready on time.

As part of the set-up, you must also check all the ancillary arrangements. Does the receptionist know where to send the audience, and are the direction signs in place? Will coffee be ready for them when they arrive, and is lunch booked? These 'household' arrangements are often overlooked, but even something as trivial as the absence of ashtrays can cause a problem if there is a heavy smoker in the audience. Always make certain that there is a pad of paper and pencil at each place; you will be amazed how many of the audience will have forgotten to bring their own – and how much disruption they will cause in the middle of the presentation when they try to borrow materials to make notes.

Depending on the circumstances, the set-up may have to begin weeks before; if you have to hire or book special equipment and facilities, for example. If you are involved in a lavish set-up (with staging, lighting and sound) you will have to allow at least half a day for the crews to do their work, and another half-day to rehearse in this strange new environment. If you are involved in an even more lavish show you needn't worry; you will have hired a specialist production company (if you have any sense) and they will run your life totally for the period of the meeting; but even then you will probably be constantly behind schedule!

Prior to the meeting you will normally need to check (and recheck) that all the equipment will be there; and then again that it actually *is*. The sort of equipment used for presentations appears to have a fatal attraction for sales professionals, and regularly 'walks', to the dismay and despair of the sales professional who next needs it for his own meeting.

Always have back-up for the main items of mechanical and electrical equipment, particularly for the projection equipment which will be at the heart of the presentation. These days both overhead projectors and slide projectors may have replacement bulbs (the most usual item to fail), which just slide into place – although even then always make a point of checking that the replacement works, as sales professionals have an annoying habit of not replacing such spares. But you should note that other things can go wrong – a fuse can blow, a lens can crack – so, if possible, have another complete unit available as back-up. Rest assured that if it can go wrong it will!

The potential problems of such equipment failure were brought home to me early in my career. I was conducting the annual presentation of a range of cleaning products to the board of one of the largest supermarket chains. We were one of the few companies privileged to be given just one two-hour session every year to get our message across. With a well-prepared slide show, I was confident that we would do well; until two-thirds of the way through my presentation when the light from the projector flickered out. I was not unduly worried, for I had brought a back-up, and I happily ad-libbed while this was put in place. After just a couple of minutes I was given the thumbs-up sign, only to be followed almost immediately by the thumbs-down – and an aide sidled up to let me know that the second projector had also failed!

Fortunately, as it was a very important (and lavish) presentation, I had provided each member of the audience with a folder which contained a full colour copy of each slide – and I had persuaded them to follow these (so that they could make notes on them). So, without a break, I switched them to looking at these instead. I lost a degree of control, with them looking at the folders not at me; but I survived – and we got the business we wanted.

This story is a good introduction to the final aspect of the set-up; the handouts. In this case, handouts saved the day. But in any case, I am a great believer in providing handouts to an audience, although I have to admit that just as many pundits advise against. I believe that handouts ensure that the notes that the audience take are in the context of your own message; otherwise the audience may end up with only a list of their objections written on their pads, and forget your carefully presented benefits.

They should, however, be brief – a series of headings or reminders (with plenty of space for the audience to write notes). The most usual format is to prepare copies of the key foils. As in a call, the handing out of more detailed material (unless it is a necessary specification or reference) is normally dangerous. It allows the audience, at their leisure (and not infrequently, actually during the presentation – distracting them from your message), to ponder on points that you did not bring out; points which are irrelevant, but which may still cause potential objections just when the sale should have been closed.

On the other hand, one detailed handout that might be productive is a list of the criteria you need to meet in order to win the sale, which you can get the audience to tick off as your story progresses. If you are in a competitive situation and are making your presentation before the others, give each of the audience several copies of this checklist; hopefully they will also tick it off at your competitors presentations as well. (If your competitors are presenting before you, watch out for their equivalent lists being used; or play safe by handing out your own lists when you agree the material in advance with the participants.)

A number of other presenters make the point of providing handouts *after* the meeting, although they usually explain at the beginning of the meeting that the audience will be given such handouts and need not make notes. This gets round the problem of distraction (and of showing your hand to those members of the audience who will read ahead to see what is coming next).

On balance, though, I believe that the availability of copies of the foils for the audience to make notes on outweighs the disadvantages, since it ensures that these notes (which they almost inevitably will make, whatever your wishes) are at least in the context you want. But once more it is a matter of personal judgement and experience. The only question is: does it work for you and your customers?

Incidentally, it is usually good manners at least to give each attendee a copy of the agenda. This also answers the problem of those prospects who spend the whole of the meeting on the edge of their seats, distracted by the (probably unnecessary) worry of whether their own favourite topic will eventually be covered.

Opening the presentation

Apart from the final part of closing the presentation (with its trauma of asking for the order), I find that opening the presentation is the most difficult part of all. You need very rapidly to put the audience into the right, receptive mood. Just occasionally they may already be in such a mood; thirsting for information and wanting to buy – and a joy to present to. But more often they will be the presenter's nightmare; a sullen, morose group of individuals who don't want to attend because they know that you are going to try to sell to them (and that, conversely, it is their job to stop you!)

I find that the key to the opening often lies in what goes before. I usually offer my audiences (certainly if they are small ones) coffee when they arrive, before I launch into my pitch. It is this session that is often the key to the whole meeting. I have often attended meetings where at this time the presenter was closeted in some back room (I presume), having his fevered brow mopped before he launched into the fray. I believe this is normally a mistake, since it is in the presenter's best interests to use this time to mingle with the audience and build the right atmosphere for the presentation. Of course, if you are following a very formal style you may deliberately separate this coffee break from the main presentation, and will probably run it in a separate room.

If on the other hand, like me, you prefer the informal environment, you will find it is advantageous to integrate the two. The coffee break will naturally be informal; and you can use this to help to establish the informal atmosphere you want to see at the beginning of the presentation (where otherwise it takes precious time for the audience to relax). It is thus preferable if the coffee is provided in the meeting room, so that the audience can get acclimatised to their surroundings and their hosts (instead of using the critical first few minutes of the presentation to do this, so distracting them from your messages).

This coffee break can also be used to start to establish personal relationships with the key members of the audience (which will be rolled over into the presentation); and it can be used to start conversations which can be brought out in the presentation, to personalise it. You should find that most prospects will open up, warmed by the informal atmosphere over a cup of coffee, far more than in the presentation itself. Having opened up, they will remain in this happy mood; the ideal start to the presentation. There is also a good chance that you can quickly establish their key questions (where these may perhaps have changed after seeing your competitors' presentations), and later impress them (both with your knowledge and with your personal interest) by answering these questions in the context of the presentation itself.

I was so addicted to this informal, coffee break start that I used to deliberately slide from it into the presentation proper, almost unnoticed, while the audience's defences were still down. Having got the audience seated, usually just by sitting down myself, and suggesting that they made themselves comfortable too, I would eventually start to develop a discussion across the whole group (assuming it was small enough, say less than eight) – effectively starting an informal, but conventional meeting. Then at a convenient moment I would start to introduce the presentation proper, and switch on the projector.

In this way the audience would be primed to be part of the presentation, to be integrated in a participative meeting. In many important respects such a presentation becomes more akin to an extended call – which is exactly what I was aiming for.

Handling questions

For many sales professionals, questions during a presentation are as worrying as objections during a call. This is understandable where these sales professionals are inexperienced and desperately trying to retain control of a script that constantly threatens to run away from them. With experience, however, they will learn to welcome questions; at least they show that the audience is still listening.

The basic decision is quite simply: do I allow questions or not? Many presenters, if they remember to mention it at all, ask their audience to hold their questions until the end. I suppose this may be necessary where the timing is critical and may be spoilt by interjections, or the subject is very complex so that offbeat questions might tend to confuse. But in general, I believe a silent audience in a presentation is as bad as a silent prospect in a call. It can cause the prospects to bottle up their objections (at this late stage usually caused by misunderstandings) so that you have no opportunity to answer them – or even to know that they exist.

As you might expect, therefore, I positively encourage questions. I always state formally, at the beginning, that I will be happy to take questions at any time. But that in itself is not enough – members of an audience are usually nervous about being the first to ask a question. So, to break the ice I deliberately try to provoke the first few questions, and after this there are normally no problems. If necessary, and they won't ask me, I ask *them* questions (which is, in any case, a useful approach to closing) just to get a conversation going.

Just occasionally questions can be a problem. If the question is at the wrong level for most of the audience it may be a distraction. But even then, if it can be quickly answered (in a minute or two), I believe it is still worth answering there and then. If it is at too technically sophisticated a level it will be over the heads of most of the audience. But they will still sense that you are answering it correctly (always assuming that you can) and will be impressed by your expertise – and by your courage in answering such a difficult question in mid-flight.

I remember finding that a technical (computer) consultant had insinuated himself into one of my seminars on accounts. His first question, to try to test me, was on a very esoteric aspect of computer networking, to which I fortunately knew the answer. Having reassured the rest of the audience that they did not need to understand this, I allowed myself to be cross-examined on a very high technical level for just two or three minutes.

This achieved a number of things. First of all, it broke the ice with the first question (something I will usually go to almost any lengths to achieve) and there was then no shortage of questions from the rest of the audience. Second, it established my technical credentials beyond doubt – although the audience would not have understood the conversation, they sensed that the consultant (who clearly knew his stuff) was testing me out, and I passed with flying colours.

Even if the level is too low, it is likely that the audience will still appreciate your sensitivity in handling it. But if the question is irrelevant to the main theme, and will take an inordinate time to answer, persuade the questioner to allow you to answer it 'off-line' at the end of the meeting; but make a point of doing just that. No matter how much fun you are having answering such questions, remember that the rest of the audience will be turned off. If, however, it is the final presentation and the question is relevant then you *will* have to answer it; and you will need all your sales skills to get the questioner to accept the briefest possible reply.

Of course, there may be questions that you cannot answer, simply because you don't know the answer. Here you *must* admit that you do not know the answer; the audience will respect your honesty. It will add to your stature, as most sales professionals will bluster rather than admit their lack of knowledge. You must promise to get back with the answer later, and must do just that.

Incidentally, if it is not the final presentation it may be a good idea deliberately to arrange to answer a number of such questions later (perhaps even if you already know the answer), since it gives you an excuse to have further individual meetings with the questioners, if you want this.

But in general, questions are relevant and usually a valuable contribution to the overall presentation. If nothing else, your ability in dealing with them will ensure that the audience does not feel it is being manipulated into a standard solution; an all too familiar feeling after being on the receiving end of a very slick, but non-interactive presentation. At the same time, questions are an excellent barometer of audience opinion.

Closing

Let us not forget that the whole purpose of this very elaborate charade is to ask for the order. If you can, by some miracle, persuade them to sign the order over coffee before you start, then tear up your presentation and take them for a celebratory meal (or more realistically use the meeting as the first 'installation' planning session). Even as you go through the presentation, be constantly aware of the possibility of closing; and test, with questions. If it is possible to do it, do it there and then (abandoning the rest of the presentation). Remember that you can only go downhill from the point at which the prospect is first willing to sign.

In reality, of course, the close will most usually come naturally with the end of the presentation. But even then it takes courage for the presenter to ask *unequivocally* for the order, or an agreed course of action towards that order. No presentation should finish without an agreement to some critical action, or series of actions, that will ultimately lead to the order; and the opportunity to ask for the order itself should never be shirked (no matter how much 'safer' it will be to ask next time). No prospect who is genuinely interested will be offended by being asked just where he stands.

The presenter must set himself such a positive objective *in advance*; and must make sure he achieves it. It is all very well to end a presentation with a warm glow, knowing that it went well. But it is not good salesmanship if this success has not been converted into real, positive agreements and actions. The presenter is not there to receive critical acclaim. He is there simply and brutally to get the order.

This process starts even before the presentation. The objectives of the presentation, agreed with the participants in advance, must include a commitment (assuming they find the presentation acceptable) to action. Then, as the presentation unfolds, the presenter must seek agreement at every stage that it meets these objectives (which will ultimately justify the action). This is clearly more difficult to achieve in a formal presentation, where there is no two-way communication with the audience.

If the objectives lay themselves open to it, a neat trick is to build up the case (typically on a flipchart) as you go along. You may have the objectives already listed, or (if your handwriting is good enough) you may write them up as you go along. Then you put a tick beside each item (or write in figures if cost savings, for example, are important) as you obtain their agreement that you have met that objective. But you *must* get a genuine agreement; glibly saying, 'That's all right then' and adding a tick fools nobody.

At the end of the presentation you should have a full set of ticks and you can justifiably ask for the order. It may be wise, though, to leave some space at the bottom of the list, just in case the order is not forthcoming. In which case you can ask that most powerful of questions, 'Why?', and establish what further is needed – and proceed to answer that too, until you win the order.

Of course, do have the order ready to sign. I have, on a number of occasions, closed the business only to realise that I had, very foolishly, not anticipated this and didn't have an order made out. On at least one occasion I have been forced to change an order document prepared for another company, and for different equipment, so that the customer could sign. It meant him initialling dozens of amendments on a very messy document (full of crossings out and substitutions); but it also meant I had a cast-iron order – and that was certainly worth all the effort. But better that I had had the right contract in the first place.

The key message, then, is to ask for the order. When I was still a trainee I had to take over a presentation and demonstration from a sales professional who was ill. It was not clear just why the customer had asked for this, since he had recently ordered a small system, and the presentation was about a much larger system, costing four to five times as much. I, however, accepted the sales professional's bed-ridden explanation that it was just curiosity about the new equipment that prompted this – after all, any presentation was valuable experience for me, and it went well.

It so happened that I gave him a lift back to his offices, since this was not too far out of my way. In the intimacy of the car, among the social chit-chat, I went on to ask him some more questions. Eventually it dawned on me that his interest was rather more than everyone was allowing for. So very daringly, remembering that I was a trainee, I asked him just *why* he wanted to see the new equipment. His answer was, for the first time, forthright: 'because we are reorganising our business and have decided we need a much larger computer system to cope with this'. I then closed an order, for the first UK System/3 mainframe to be used for teleprocessing, within the next five minutes.

Out of interest, I asked him why he hadn't mentioned this before. His answer was blunt, but illuminating: 'It's for you, as the salesman, to find out!' I have never forgotten that lesson, and now I always do find out.

After the event

Whatever happens, success or failure, it is worth having a post mortem. Your colleagues in the audience will have seen things that you have overlooked. It is valuable to bring all this information together as soon as possible. Don't be afraid of asking for criticisms of your style – you may learn something from them. So be grateful for them; if nothing else they may shed a new light on your techniques. On the other hand, don't take them too much to heart (unless you recognise that they are obviously correct, and important). Most sales professionals have little idea of what makes a successful style, and assume their own style is the ideal; and they tend to want you to conform to these, their own, shortcomings too!

Take the opportunity to thank everyone involved. You will need their services again, and they will be that much more willing if they know their efforts are appreciated. You would be surprised just how few sales professionals, flushed by success, have time for the team that really made the success possible.

Finally, carefully file away all the material. You never know when you will need it next. I regularly plundered presentation sets going back five years or more; and, since I used a standard format, it saved me reinventing the wheel every time.

Chapter 9
Demonstrations and Seminars

Demonstrations

As with presentations, demonstrations are an activity at which the sales professional is expected naturally to excel; and one that he is even less prepared for. In my experience, many sales professionals will do almost anything rather than undertake a complex demonstration. This is a pity, since a good demonstration is one of the most productive of sales tools, at least where complex products are concerned. Demonstrations are, though, probably the toughest test of a sales professional, since they stretch (often to breaking point) all his skills. To succeed in giving an excellent demonstration you need to be expert in almost all areas of salesmanship.

It is doubly a pity as many prospects *expect* to see a demonstration. According to market research, no less than three-quarters of personal computer buyers expected to see a demonstration before buying; and nearly half of all the buyers rated such a demonstration as being the most influential marketing factor affecting their decision (twice the level of any other factor). This may be a market which is more susceptible to demonstrations but, in view of the atrocious standard of demonstration skills shown by the average personal computer salesman, I very much doubt it!

When to give a demonstration
Many complex sales campaigns can benefit from a demonstration; just so long as it is well handled. Such a demonstration is often a clincher in persuading your prospect of the viability of your system. If he can see it working, he has many of his doubts removed; albeit, as we will see later, demonstrations rarely prove anything about technical competence – but the prospect thinks they do, and that is what counts.

There are a number of times in a sales campaign when a demonstration is likely to be most relevant, and you may even successfully run several demonstrations (each covering a different aspect) as the campaign progresses. The main excuses for a demonstration are:

Exhibitions
A demonstration is one excellent way of stimulating interest in your product. If the prospect sees your product doing things he likes but cannot do with his existing product, you may have made a convert.

Clearly, this type of demonstration will be in a standard mould. It will also be given to a relatively large audience, not to an individual; since the cost of giving demonstrations (at least on a complex product) usually makes them inappropriate for single prospects. The classic form of such introductory demonstrations is that employed on exhibition stands. It is also the most abused. Many such stands have products that stand idle most of the time because the staff don't see the real need for demonstrations or, more likely are, terrified by the thought of having to give them. That terror is often justified, because the other great failing of exhibition demonstrations is that they are often of poor quality; badly thought out, ill-prepared and even worse rehearsed.

To be fair, exhibition demonstrations are particularly difficult to mount. The audience is constantly coming and going and swirling around the product on the stand, so prospects arrive randomly during the demonstration and ruin the best endeavours of any designer. Even so, the very busy atmosphere surrounding it will attract people to the stand and interest them in your product. But, as a result of the comings and goings, such demonstrations need to be short and very simple. In this sort of environment I used to run demonstrations lasting no more than three minutes, with something happening all the time. If you have any lulls, with nothing apparently happening, the audience will melt away.

The best alternative to this approach is to run longer demonstrations at fixed intervals, usually in a 'theatre'. This can be a very effective way of showcasing your product, and is used by many of the major manufacturers, but it can be prohibitively expensive.

Seminars
I often used seminars featuring demonstrations to open campaigns, but (depending on the exact subject matter) they can be used throughout the earlier stages of any campaign. In demonstration terms you have the advantage of a captive audience, although this will usually be relatively small – I found eight an ideal number. It is still, though, a general audience, and the demonstration will need to be equally general. With such a small audience, however, it becomes possible to introduce special features in response to questions.

As the audience is captive, typically for half a day in total, the demonstration can be much longer. In these circumstances I frequently used to run a half-hour demonstration, with an extra half-hour (overlapping a coffee break) to allow for additional 'specials' in answer to specific questions. This also meant that a larger than expected audience could be split in half by running two half-hour sessions.

Pre-closing

The classic demonstration, however, is given for a single prospect; one who has been qualified as being worth all the effort. It is normally given in the closing stages of the campaign, as a final 'working' proof of the viability of a proposal.

It should be carefully tailored to meet the prospect's needs. This is usually only in terms of the content, so it is not as major an investment as it first sounds. The demonstration itself will change direction depending on the prospect's questions and requests; it is a very interactive art form. As such, it requires a significant amount of preparation and should not be embarked on too lightly. Its length can be anything upwards of half an hour. In my experience it is rarely less, although there is no theoretical reason why it should last more than 30 seconds if you can make all the essential points in that time. It will be unlikely to last much more than an hour, since, by that time, the prospect's attention will be beginning to wander. But I have seen successful demonstrations that have lasted three hours or more, although I suspect that they were an unnecessary overkill.

Who gives the demonstration

Most sales professionals would say, and pray, 'Anyone but me!'; but, as we will see, they would be wrong. There are, however, a range of alternatives:

1. *Demonstration by support personnel.* In this case the sales professional is only at the demonstration as a spectator. His support personnel do everything; running the demonstration and describing it. Sometimes the sales professional does not even bother to attend. This is the easiest demonstration for the sales professional, but it is also the least productive – why does the account need any sales professionals at all, if the support personnel are fully capable of making the sale?
2. *Support personnel demonstration, described by the sales professional.* This is the most usual form of demonstration. The hard work is still done by the support staff, but the sales professional does the talking – and claims all the credit! It is a

more productive form; at least the sales professional does the verbal selling. It is favoured because the sales professional (wrongly) thinks he doesn't need to know much about the demonstration and can pass any awkward questions, or problems with the demonstration itself, to his 'experts'; but in the process he inevitably loses some credibility – if he can't handle it how can the customer be expected to do so?

3. *Demonstration by the sales professional.* This is nearer the ideal, because the sales professional himself is totally in control. It demonstrates significant competence; justifiably so, since the sales professional has to know what he is doing. Indeed, the fact that the sales professional must know all aspects of the demonstration and must be technically at least competent, is probably the major reason why it is so frequently avoided.

4. *Demonstration by the prospect.* By far the most effective method, and my favourite, is to let the prospect demonstrate to himself. Unfortunately, it is also the most difficult for the sales professional, and requires the most preparation. It is, though, the one I would recommend, because it is so productive.

Designing the demonstration

A demonstration is not about showing how your product works. It is about proving that it works. Above all, it is about selling your product by showing it off to its best advantage. This is not always an easy process. To get the best effect you have to work at it. Many companies produce superb products, but put very little effort into highlighting their selling points, which really is the proverbial 'hiding your light under the bushel'. Nobody is going to see that light, let alone buy it, unless you bring it out into the open.

The general design of the demonstration, therefore, has to bring out the product's selling points. It also has to do this interestingly, understandably (but not patronisingly), and even entertainingly. Ideally, a demonstration should be a 'theatrical' performance, although not intrusively so. The demonstration, as theatre, has to tell a story, building to a climax, and with variations in pace to make it more interesting – very like a stage play.

In specific terms, of course, it has to be designed (or redesigned from the standard company demonstration) to meet the specific needs of the prospect. I have, unfortunately, been the victim of too many demonstrations where the product features shown (at great length) were superb, but were also totally irrelevant to my needs.

In the next few sections I will describe some of the design features that you may need to consider in setting up the longer pre-closing demonstration. The requirements will be rather different, less complex, for the more general introductory (group) demonstrations, but even then these suggested guidelines may be a useful starting point:

Demonstrate the basic needs
In the rush to show all the goodies, there is a temptation to avoid showing the prospect the basic features that are essential to his needs. The basic needs will probably not be 'sexy', and may not be the factors that decide the sale; but if they are omitted they may lose it! A demonstration, at least one late in the campaign, needs to *prove* that your offering will work. It needs to demonstrate the major features that are essential to the prospect's needs.

Be realistic
In this context, the demonstration needs to be realistic and believable. In meeting the prospect's needs, it has to do this in a way that simulates (at least) the real-life situation. He has to be able to visualise it working in his own environment. It will fail in its purpose of proving your product's viability (and will not impress the prospect) if it is seen as a 'toy' demonstration. I have always felt that demonstrations of industrial robots, for example, moving little boxes aimlessly around (the typical exhibition fare) was no real indication of how they would work in the real environment.

In the field of computerised accounting packages, one of the most complex 'products' to demonstrate, I always used the complete production package itself, with all the facilities and data that you would find in a real-life situation. The prospect was never in any doubt that it was a real and viable product.

Be brief
You should make these routine, mundane and potentially boring tasks as brief as possible; as long as you do demonstrate them. Typically they will be actions *en route* to the more interesting activities but they need to be included for the sake of completeness – the prospect will want to see a complete solution, not a partial one. In the case of machining, for example, the prospect will want to see the work actually put into the jig. With computers he will want to see some input of the basic data.

The best advice is to do it just once, and as fast as possible (without, that is, doing it so fast that the prospect thinks it is sleight of hand). The first rule is to have all the parameters set up and ready to roll. With machine tools the jig needs to be set up, ready for the work to be locked into it.

With computer input there is typically a need to specify exactly how this should be handled. This is most obvious where the first 'screen' of most application packages asks you for all these parameters. It is a trap most personal computer salesmen fall into; they spend anything up to half an hour explaining what size of lettering you can print, where you can put the margins, and a dozen other trifles that the prospect would never normally consider. Have all this set up as 'standard defaults'. When that first complex screen appears, simply say, 'All you need to do here is press ENTER'; and skip the whole set-up procedure. The prospect will never miss it. On the other hand, he will definitely not thank you for wasting his time as you painstakingly (and very boringly) set up all these basic parameters.

The second rule is to move very briskly through all these mundane procedures (but always checking that the prospect is happy with this breakneck pace) to reach those that will be particularly interesting to him.

Highlight the selling points
The other objective of any demonstration is to *sell* your product. It is important, therefore, that your demonstration clearly highlights those aspects that are crucial to the main sales messages. Such highlighting is best achieved by making it the focus of a logical structure, however, the demonstration should develop towards each of these points. Equally, these highlights can be brief. There is no need to repeat these points *ad nauseam*; indeed, there is no value in repeating them once the prospect has accepted them, often by the end of the first example. Least of all do you need fanfares to accompany these highlights. If they won't work without fanfares then they shouldn't be highlights. Such hype only tends to distract the prospect, usually into disbelieving the claim, where in a demonstration such points should be made self-evident.

Make them attractive and interesting
It is almost always possible to make a demonstration attractive. In machining, it may be more impressive, and aesthetically pleasing quickly to mill sweeping curves (rather than spend long minutes milling out a square). In computing, the 'pictures' on the screen can always be made much more attractive; for whatever reason, most

computer programmers seem to be visually illiterate and produce screens that are boring to the point of offensiveness.

It is usually a simple matter (if often time consuming) to tart up these aspects of the demonstration so that they look attractive. The element of theatre can profitably also include theatre 'design'.

Make them comprehensive
This is the most difficult aspect for sales professionals to justify (particularly to themselves). If a feature is not to be included as one of the main items in a standard demonstration, it would appear inherently wasteful to spend time developing it as part of that demonstration, just in case someone asks for it. There does, of course, have to be a balance. There is no point in spending large sums of money developing a feature that will be asked for by one prospect in a thousand – there will always be easier, and more productive, ways of addressing such problems.

But few things impress a prospect more than his question being answered by: 'Well, let's see it.' There are often many secondary features that could be easily included, but which are better kept (fully working) as back-up to answer such questions.

KISS
Once more, though, the emphasis should be on keeping the demonstration *simple*. As with a presentation, there have to be just a few clear points that you want to make. You will need to pare down your demonstration to its basic essentials, so that those key points are *clear*. There is always a temptation to add 'decoration', irrelevant features added just to win with numbers. The aim may be to swamp your prospect with benefits (in reality with features), but it is usually the sale that will sink, with the main points lost in a sea of trivia.

Structure
To give the greatest clarity, the structure of the demonstration needs to be simple, clear and logical (to the extent that it should become self-evident to the prospect). This structure should be evident from the demonstration itself, but it is also helpful to keep returning to reiterate where each part of the demonstration fits in the context of the overall objectives.

Invulnerability
One key aspect of any demonstration is that it must be, as far as possible, idiot-proof. If pressing the wrong button at the wrong time

can ruin your demonstration, you can be certain that some idiot will push it (either accidentally or in an exhibition, where the 'idiot' may be a wily competitor, deliberately) with monotonous regularity. Recovery will almost always take an inordinate length of time (and will cause highly visible panic among your entourage), which will allow plenty of time for your prospect to decide which of the competitors' systems he will order!

Idiot-proofing means that you will have to test for all eventualities. You can avoid some, perhaps by simply putting a guard over the offending button. Some, though, will be unavoidable, in which case you will have to devise a very rapid back-up which returns you to where you were – and which, if skilful enough, can actually impress the prospect with your technical abilities (not to say your sang-froid).

Simplicity of use
In addition to keeping the overall design simple, the actual use should be kept as simple as possible. This is so that even the proverbial idiot (in this case you, as the sales professional) can run the demonstration. Ideally, it should be simple enough for the prospect, who you have to assume will have no previous experience, to run. This usually involves most of the more complex activities being set prior to the demonstration, so that there are a few, relatively easy steps to follow. The complex elements are, in any case, unnecessary complications to introduce into most demonstrations.

Even if you are technically competent it is a good discipline to keep the demonstration as simple as possible. It will be that much easier for the prospect to follow and perhaps even run, with a little judicious help, and will allow you more time and effort to concentrate on him rather than on the technicalities of the demonstration itself.

Documentation
Standard demonstrations are usually developed to cover a number of expected events. Typically, they are then tailored to produce individual presentations. It is very rare for a totally new demonstration to be produced just for one occasion – it is usually very unproductive, unless the prospect is expected to bring in a great deal of business.

To be usable by a wide range of demonstrators, however, standard demonstrations must be well documented. This is generally the area where demonstration designers fail. After the excitement of producing the demonstration itself, followed by the long boring slog of making it idiot-proof, they lose interest and cannot face the further chore of fully documenting how it should be run. Yet such documentation is essential. If the demonstrator cannot immediately find out how to run all the various facilities (including the back-up features), and (most importantly) how to handle problems, he is crippled. In the unlikely event that he has the technical skills, he can spend unproductive hours plodding through all the various alternatives to find out what is available. More likely is that he will abandon the demonstration, or give such a cut-down version that it is markedly less productive.

The only disastrous demonstrations I have ever given have occurred when I have had to rush in to rescue a sales professional who was floundering; but where I, too, was unprepared. That alone might not have caused the disaster (my experience usually enables me to flannel my way through the difficulties), but what *did* wreck my rescue attempts was that there was no documentation to which I could refer when I got into trouble.

Documentation is the most important final act of designing any demonstration.

Preparation

The one prerequisite for a successful demonstration is adequate preparation; and adequacy, here, is a matter of putting in some considerable effort. Demonstrations are usually inherently complex affairs, at least where complex sales are concerned, and a great deal of effort needs to be expended on learning them, tailoring them and ensuring that the environment is exactly right.

Learning

It is essential that you learn the demonstration. Even if you are not running it yourself, you still need to know your way around all parts of it. You must be prepared to meet all the prospect's questions. If you can justify the time (and, as most demonstrations are repeated a number of times, you should be able to), you should even try to understand the theory behind it, as well as knowing the various back-up elements that are available to meet more complicated requests.

If you plan to give the demonstration yourself, as ideally you should, you will need to understand it in some depth. When a demonstration runs smoothly there is no need for this level of expertise. But as soon as it wanders off that straight and narrow (as you can be sure it will do) you will be lost. Even if you have prepared well, it is still worth having a technical expert at hand during the demonstration, just in case you really get out of your depth.

To learn, you have to run and rerun the demonstration until it comes almost automatically. Only if you are 100 per cent confident with it will you be able to ignore it, and get on with the most important matter – selling to the prospect.

The examples

The major problem with most demonstrations is that they have nothing to work on. Prospects want to see something actually happen. They want to see your product or service being productive.

This means that you must provide examples for the products to work on. In the case of computing, this meant that we had to spend long hours pounding in data, to create the mythical companies that our accounts detailed. For particularly important prospects, it also meant spending almost as long recreating these accounts in the form that most closely simulated their own accounts, as opposed to the less intensive changes (typically only company names and 'top level' tailoring) implemented for other prospects.

In general, a demonstration is only as good as its examples. The more effort you put into these the better and more realistic they will be.

The environment

Just as with a presentation, you need to ensure that the environment is suitable for the demonstration. Most of the same rules apply. But it is particularly important that there are no distractions; with the complexity of your own role in the demonsration, *you* as well as the prospect need no diversions.

All the other activities, described in Chapter 8 on presentations, will also need to be allowed for in the case of demonstrations.

Visuals

A demonstration may directly incorporate many of the presentational devices. For larger audiences, at an exhibition or a seminar, overhead or slide projectors or (in particular) a flipchart may be used to add to, or explain, the material being demonstrated. In the case of those to smaller groups, the desktop presentation is perhaps a more suitable (and less formal) medium.

These visuals can be used to link together the various elements of the demonstration and put them into context. They can be used to explain the theory behind what is happening. They can also be used as shortcuts to cover parts of the demonstration that would take too long to show live.

Such visuals can play a particularly important role in a demonstration, but they are sadly neglected by the majority of those few sales professionals who dare to try giving one. A demonstration seems to be a cue for the removal of everything but the product itself; an exercise in minimalism. It is true that nothing must unnecessarily intrude on what the product or service is doing, but relevant visuals can significantly enhance what is being said and shown, explaining and highlighting the main points.

The 'equipment'
The product or service has to be the focus of the demonstration, and the related equipment must be in perfect condition. It must look pristine, or at least well looked after (a well-worn but impeccably maintained piece of equipment can show that the product is viable even towards the end of its working life). Grubby tattered equipment impresses no prospects but, as demonstration equipment inevitably takes a battering, keeping it presentable will not be an easy task. Not least, the equipment needs to be working and able to support all the features you need. This requires advance planning to make certain the equipment will be available, and then some chasing to check that the promises are actually being kept.

One aspect of equipment that should not be forgotten is that of allowing people to see the details. For many demonstrations, particularly for larger audiences, it is necessary to use closed circuit television (CCTV) to show these details on a large screen or television monitor. This is even the case with computer demonstrations, where the small letters on the VDU screen are not easily visible by more than the two or three people closest to it; and extension monitors (or even the newest, very simple, projection equipment) are needed. Such equipment need not be too expensive or difficult to use, but it does take some time to set up properly and the sheer logistics of hiring it can be daunting.

Set-up
As with the presentation, it is important to set up the demonstration with plenty of time to spare. It has far more elements that can go wrong (and which will go wrong if you are rushing), so you need that much more leeway. I cannot overemphasise the importance of having just a few minutes to relax, knowing that everything is set up correctly, before the prospect arrives. A relaxed demonstration is a

much more productive demonstration.

Demonstration styles

I believe that a very relaxed and informal approach to a demonstration is by far the most productive style. Of all the sales devices, apart from the call, in my experience the demonstration is the one that benefits most from interaction with the audience. This is even true of the larger audiences at exhibitions and seminars.

I have attended many *totally* scripted demonstrations, typically opening with the request, 'Could you please leave questions to the end.' Some of these were quite effective; as with presentations, interaction is not the only style and you may feel more comfortable with something more formal. But interaction is often the most productive approach; avoiding it can be somewhat akin to putting a sign on your equipment saying, 'Don't touch.'

The demonstration is the ideal opportunity to involve prospects. They love well-run demonstrations precisely because they can be involved. They can make things happen, to check their understanding and to see if your product is as good as you say it is – and have fun at the same time! If there is no interaction they might almost as well be watching a film of the product (this form of demonstration is in fact sometimes used – and it certainly removes the technical uncertainties that many sales professionals fear).

Where does the audience stand?

It is important to keep the audience down to the size where everyone can have a clear view of everything that is happening. Depending on the layout, 10 'viewers' is generally the maximum, although less is preferable. If necessary, and possible, bringing the equipment up to shoulder height will probably double the number you can accommodate; perhaps up to 20 (rather cramped) viewers. The prospects will typically group themselves into a pattern that will allow them best to see, in the way that they personally want. Many prospects really do feel more comfortable hiding anonymously away at the back.

If you have small details that are difficult to see, however, it is important that you deliberately rotate the audience (bringing those from the back to the front) so that nobody misses these.

For a longer demonstration you may take pity on an audience and let them sit (although again it is best to let them arrange their own chairs to suit their needs). But you will have to reduce the numbers even further, and you lose some of the flexibility that a standing audience allows.

Where do you stand?

The only requirements are that you do not obstruct the view of what is happening, and that you can easily be seen. If possible, this means you should stand behind the product (then you definitely do not obstruct it, and you are always facing your audience). But most frequently you will have to stand in front, because that is where the controls are, so the audience will have to spend part of the time looking at your back.

In computer demonstrations, where I didn't have an operator running the system, I got around this by sitting on the table alongside the terminal, facing the audience; although it did mean that I had to enter everything upside down. It had the great advantage that it was much more relaxed, obviously so, and this helped to relax the audience as well. It also allowed me to maintain almost constant eye contact with them.

Where I did have an operator (which sometimes happened if there was a lot of data to be entered) there was no problem. But what I really liked to do was to persuade one of the prospects to be my operator; this gave me the best of all worlds, although it did require by far the greatest skill on my part.

Demonstrations run by support personnel

I will gloss over those demonstrations run totally by support personnel, since then you do not have to worry about any techniques; although, as you will have gathered, I believe that in so doing a sales professional abdicates some degree of control over his account. I have watched too many sales professionals, in that situation, hover around the edge of the group like a wallflower at a dance; eventually drifting away to get on with some other work — having lost control, and often also lost morale.

Most demonstrations are, though, run by support personnel, with the sales professional giving the accompanying sales pitch.

The first thing to be recognised is that it is not really the easy option: it is still the sales professional who is giving the demonstration. It may not be his fingers on the controls, but it is his voice that guides the actions. Once you let the support personnel appear to dictate where the demonstration is going you have, once more, lost control. Of course, to maintain that control you too must know the demonstration well; indeed, so well that you could give it yourself, where the operator is merely standing in for you as a matter of convenience.

The second point, however, is that you need to recognise that it is a double act. As with all great double acts, both partners contribute equally to the 'show'. The teamwork approach adds significantly to the impact: it demonstrates that you are a team operation (which is always good news for a buyer), it uses your operator's strengths (his technical competence is likely to be significantly greater) as well as your own, and it adds variety – boredom is the worst enemy of any presentation.

Despite this, the essence of such demonstrations is that *you* give them.

Running the demonstration yourself

The better solution is that you run the demonstration yourself. This allows you to be totally in control; as much as you would be in a call. It also clearly establishes you as an expert.

Even so, the best approach is apparently to let the audience control the demonstration; asking questions to determine what they want to do. This is, however, a skill that needs some development, since you have to persuade them to ask for what you want to show!

The essence of the best demonstrations is that they are interactive in exactly the same way that a call is interactive. The direction that they take should, within limits, follow the direction in which the prospect's logic propels him. If a prospect wants to see a word-processing program and you are in the middle of a spreadsheet, then throw that out and move immediately to the word-processor; just as long as he is the only member of the audience, or the only one that counts.

What you show, how much you show and how you show it should be judged by the audience's responses. Demonstrations rarely follow the same pattern, and that is part of the fun – it also stops you falling victim to boredom, which will surely communicate itself to your audience.

Such flexibility, though, does need considerable skill. Partly this is technical skill, since you really do need to know every bit of the whole if you are to follow where the prospect points. But partly it is sales skill and the ability to think very fast on your feet; which is why the two-man (support personnel driven) approach cannot give the same degree of flexibility – and is ultimately that much less powerful.

Letting the prospect demonstrate

The ideal in demonstrations is to let the prospect get his hands on the product and operate it himself. Once he feels it is under his control, his confidence in it will soar.

This approach, however, requires considerable skill and knowledge on the part of the sales professional, for it is constantly courting disaster. This demonstration really does have to be *very* simple to run, although not simplistic; a prospect does not want to feel he is being patronised.

The prospect has just a minute or two to learn the skills that you may need a week or more to teach an operator. It should, therefore, be self-steering; apparently offering plenty of choice, but actually (under your guidance) following some very easy (and predictable) choices. It *must* be idiot-proof. You can bet that the prospect will hit almost as many wrong buttons as right ones. And, as a result, you must be superb at handling the resulting problems.

One demonstration program I saw offered an interesting solution to the problem. *Whatever* key was hit it acted as if the right one had been hit. This is great, just as long as the prospect doesn't catch on. (Having recognised what was going on, I caused chaos by 'innocently' asking why the cursor was moving down when I was hitting the up key!)

Rehearsing

As I have already said, the success of a demonstration is largely dependent on the preparation; on how well you know it and, accordingly, how comfortable you feel with it. Whatever your style, the most important preparation is to rehearse (particularly if you are using an operator) until you are totally comfortable with it. Even after I became very expert at demonstrating, I would aim to rehearse a specific demonstration at least four or five times, and would also spend some time checking out just how idiot-proof it was.

The pitfalls

Perhaps the reason why so many sales professionals avoid demonstrations is that there are so many potential pitfalls. This is, on the other hand, why I enjoy them so much; they are a constantly varying challenge with a whiff of danger thrown in.

Demonstrating incompetence

The real danger is that, if you don't know what you are doing, you can all too easily (and all too publicly) demonstrate incompetence.

When you fall off the 'expert' tightrope you can do a considerable amount of harm to your sale. You can very easily demonstrate that your solution won't work.

Demonstrating is, I believe, the highest skill that a sales professional (at least one involved in a complex sale, with a complex product) can aspire to. But the number of things that can go wrong is 10 times as many as in almost any other sales activity. If you can't cope with the problems you are lost. So, it is perhaps the acid test of the sales professional.

Problem handling
The first golden rule of problem handling is to be prepared for it. Most potential problems should be known, and the solution documented. Even the unexpected problems should be capable of being 'trapped', and a back-up brought into play. If nothing else, you should be able to abort and reboot the demonstration discreetly at the point at which it went wrong. If you are prepared, problems can easily be taken in your stride, to the extent that the prospect needn't even notice them.

I learnt my demonstrating skills in the early 1970s at the receiving end of an unusually unreliable IBM bureau system, called Terminal Business System (TBS). This was run on a large central mainframe, but the customer had a (typewriter) terminal. The system was almost totally unpredictable; you never knew when you would be able to get through to the mainframe, or when it would stop talking to you. Demonstrations were a nightmare.

The eventual solution, I found, lay in combining the demonstration with a presentation, and walking a lot. When the system died on me, as it did once or twice during almost every demonstration, the golfball on the typewriter terminal would stop chattering. At this point I used to suggest quickly, 'I think we should now have a look at some of the theory', and transfer to the presentation. The walking was necessary because to check if the system was up again you had to hit a key on the terminal. As I walked backwards and forwards in front of the terminal, while giving the presentation, I would surreptitiously hit the key. If the golfball chattered into life I would rapidly say: 'Now is a suitable time to have another look at the demonstration.' Very few of the prospects ever realised that there were any problems; and very few of them even appeared to wonder why there were such peculiar switches between demonstration and presentation. It was superb experience in demonstration techniques and, after learning to cope, it was also great fun.

The Sales Professional

Making the most of problems

As long as you can cope with them, problems can actually enhance a demonstration. At the most basic level, I always found that making even the simplest mistake helped to enliven the demonstration. Prospects are happy to discover that you are only human, and will laugh along with you if you have the confidence to treat it as a joke.

But the main benefit of a problem is that you can show the customer how to recover from it. 'All systems have problems; it is how easy it is to recover from them that is the acid test' is a superb point to make in a demonstration. Thereafter, you should smoothly recover, explaining (in terms that the prospect can understand) exactly what you are doing.

Correctly played, this can be the most effective part of the demonstration. The prospect will believe what is happening, where he may suspect (often with justification) that the rest could be simulated; and, indeed, you need to emphasise (albeit jokingly) that it is a 'clanger'. He will appreciate the true level of your expertise, especially if you emphasise that this *is* the acid test. He will also be able to compare your abilities with those of the competition (if they dare to demonstrate). Indeed, it is a good idea to coach him; teach him to test the others by causing a problem: 'What you should do is ever so accidentally switch the machine off, and see what happens.' With any luck the competitor's demonstration will disintegrate into total chaos.

I always found that the discussion with the prospects, as I handled problems, became markedly more positive. It was almost as if, being involved in solving the problem, they became part of my team. That partnership is the key to the most successful selling.

Sleight of hand

As I indicated at the beginning of this chapter, with some practice you can persuade a prospect of almost anything. You can use almost all the techniques of the stage magician, particularly that of diverting attention away from embarrassing faults. I will not expand on these techniques, since I believe that they should not be necessary. They *are* very dangerous, because if the prospect finds out what is happening (or your competitors tell him) you will instantly lose any chance of winning the business.

I mention it because you should be aware that your competitors may use such techniques. You need to be on the lookout for such 'magic' so that you can explain the tricks of the trade to your prospect.

I once had an almost unbeatable USP. My computer was one of the first to be able to run without air conditioning, where my competitor's couldn't; and the prospect couldn't get planning consent to put air conditioning in the listed building where he had his offices. However, the competitor still ran a demonstration, and the prospect came back enthusiastically proclaiming (to my initial mystification) that the competitor's machine didn't really need air conditioning.

At the demonstration, he explained, all the windows had been wide open, and the machine was still clearly working. The printer was pounding away at a stupendous speed. It was only when I asked what was being printed out, to receive the reply, 'Oh, some computer work; it was not normal printing', that I began to see the light. The competitor had tried to run the machine without the air conditioning, and it had crashed. He had, however, been able to print out the diagnostics which told the engineers why it had crashed; and it was these that the prospect had seen being printed. It was a brilliant sleight of hand, and it nearly worked; it took all my sales skills discreetly to persuade the prospect what had really happened!

Closing
Just because you are running a demonstration there is no reason to forget your normal sales skills and objectives. The aim, even here, is to *close*. Get agreement to move positively to the next, higher level of the campaign, even if you don't close the order itself. In practice, I have obtained almost as many orders at demonstrations as in any other situation.

Demonstrations at customer sites
The best demonstrations of all are those given by customers, as part of a reference visit. There can be no doubt that this really is 'live' running. It is the best possible proof that your system works.

You should prepare just as much as for your own demonstrations, although, obviously, in the customer environment you will have that much less control. As a result, it does once more require even greater skills on your part. You *must* let the customer staff make the presentation (even if they do it poorly); but at the same time you must, *very* discreetly, support and complement this – remembering that, if this is not your own customer, it may be a totally alien demonstration.

There are, of course, risks; perhaps more so than when under your control. On the other hand, there should be less technical problems, particularly as the prospect will not usually be allowed 'hands-on', because it is production work (which is exactly what he will have come to see).

I took one important prospect several hundred miles to see a demonstration of a very sophisticated application at a customer site in the West Country. My heart sank when we were ushered into the computer room, to be faced by the computer in pieces; there were mounds of its innards distributed around the room as it had been *completely* dismantled! Fortunately, the customer went on to explain that it had worked so well, and was so important to his business, that he had decided to move it from the computer room (where nobody could see it) to the centre of the main office (where it was to be a feature of the business). He also went on to explain that it was so trouble-free that it didn't need to be molly-coddled in a special computer room like most computers.

We then took the opportunity of a very extended lunch. For three hours solid the customer management enthused about our offering and went in detail through every one of the prospect's requirements, proving (by their own experience) that they would work. It won the business, and was one of the most successful demonstrations I ever ran!

Taking the demonstration to the prospect

It is often, of course, possible to take the demonstration to the prospect. This has the advantage that he, and all his staff, can see it working in their own environment.

On the other hand, it does often take significantly more resource (as complex products are often not very portable). I once had to arrange for a 200-lb machine to be shipped to Glasgow, where I picked it up and drove it in a hired van the 200 miles to Aberdeen. The prospect had been adamant that all he wanted was a demonstration on site, and he would place the order there and then. Of course, no such thing happened. He spent about 15 minutes cursorily looking at the machine and I never sold anything to him, even though it took two very gruelling days of my time.

This example encapsulates the major problem. If the prospect won't put in the effort to come and see the demonstration at your offices he can hardly be thought of as a hot prospect. It is debatable whether it is worth running any demonstration for him, let alone all the hassle of taking it to him. I regret to say that I very rarely closed a prospect who insisted that I took the demonstration to him, and I eventually stopped doing this. There may have been a flaw in my selling style in this area, but I suspect it was much more an indication of the value of such prospects.

This is not to say that you should not demonstrate on site, if this does not pose problems for you. I have happily bought a number of products under such circumstances, although I would just as happily have gone to demonstrations elsewhere. It is to suggest you think twice about this where the logistics become problematic.

Post-demonstration
One thing most sales professionals fail to do is to clear up afterwards; or to arrange for someone else to clear up (as the sales professional usually needs to continue the meeting elsewhere). The one sure way of endearing yourself to your support team is to make certain that you break this rule and *do* clear up. In terms of obtaining future support it pays good dividends.

Seminars

The one activity that brings together all these sales activities is the seminar. In my opinion, this represents the pinnacle of the sales professional's art. He is likely to be personally involved in presentations and demonstrations, he will control reference presentations, and he will coordinate the expert speakers.

As a result, seminars demand a wide range of sales skills if they are to run well. But they are a very powerful sales device, just about the most effective way of snaring prospects in your net. The market research undertaken on personal computer buyers, for example, showed that 70 per cent of them found an invitation to a seminar an acceptable approach from a sales professional, which was more than double that for any other sales activity (for example, only just over 30 per cent would have found acceptable a direct approach, asking for an appointment, from a sales professional).

If the seminar content is targeted correctly, prospects expect to learn something from the event, and in the company of others feel less threatened by sales pressures. Having captured your audience, it is also a very positive way of introducing your company's products; and showing your own, and your company's, expertise. Seminars can be so effective as an introductory device, that in them I often took 'cold' prospects from their first contact through to a *close*; all in a group of up to eight prospects.

Even if I couldn't close, I could 'qualify', and very accurately determine which prospects to concentrate on (before ever meeting them individually, in a face-to-face call). It was just about the most productive selling I ever did.

Recruiting the participants

The preparation of seminars requires an investment of effort if they are to be successful. As such, they become most productive if you can run a series of them. I rarely ran less than four and often more than 20 in a series, by which time they were becoming very productive investments.

This means, however, that you will need to recruit numbers of prospects to attend them. You will need to use mailings and teleselling to attract them. On the other hand, seminars are often used (very productively) as the bait to evoke a positive response from such mailings and teleselling; so the two sorts of activities can happily work hand in hand.

The one caveat with seminars is that you should allow for a relatively high drop-out rate. In my experience, even after the prospects had been contacted again the day before, we were actually lucky to achieve 50 per cent of those promising to come.

You should also take notice of the lead time. It will usually take at least six weeks to complete all the arrangements; and a further six weeks if you are using a mailing to recruit the participants. With such a long lead time, it is also worth checking that it doesn't clash with another event, such as a major exhibition.

Audience size

Many people look for audiences in the range of 20 to 30 people. I liked to aim for a much *smaller* audience, typically six to 10, and ideally eight. In view of the likely drop-out rate, I planned to issue (confirmed) invitations to 12 to 14 prospects. The reason for the small size was that with these numbers I could interact with the prospects almost on an individual basis (much as with teaching small classes).

As a result, I always preferred to run two eight-man seminars rather than one 16-man seminar. On paper the latter might look more productive, but in reality it won't be – at least in terms of the business eventually closed. I found it more difficult to justify the productivity when the attendance fell to four; but the personal interaction was even more powerful, and the closing ratio higher – so it was a fine decision. However, below four became unproductive, since there were not enough prospects to stimulate each other.

One further reason for such small audience sizes is that this is also important to the prospects. Having a small group, with opportunities for questions and the chance to discuss matters with other businessmen, is (rather than content, somewhat surprisingly) the main requirement for seminars, as shown by the market research on personal computer buyers.

Where I have had special speakers, or have had special difficulties in limiting attendances, I have run seminars with more than 20 participants; although I did have some difficulty in controlling them as productively. Other sales professionals would, though, probably see 20 to 30 as the norm for such seminars; but they would be satisfied with a distinctly one-way communication.

The location

I always tried to run my seminars in locations which reinforced my sales messages. Ideally, I ran them at my customers' premises; I was fortunate that many of these had excellent conference rooms, as well as good demonstration facilities. Some care is needed to ensure that the meeting facilities are good enough, but given some effort it is possible to use almost anywhere.

In its excellent kit supporting dealer 'accounts' seminars, IBM includes a very comprehensive list of considerations to be taken into account when selecting a seminar location (where this would typically be a local hotel):

Proximity to you target market.
The image you are trying to project.
Adequate space provisions: is there a separate room for coffee and buffet lunch?
Electrical power provision: are there enough power points?
Are there enough catering staff for the buffet lunch/coffee?
Is there adequate car parking? Is a map available?
How easy is access by public transport?
How good are the acoustics?
Equipment: most locations offering seminar facilities can provide items such as overhead projectors, carousels and screens.
Access for your equipment.
Telephones: are they disconnected during the day? Are there separate facilities for urgent messages?
Lighting: are there dimmers, easy controls, and black out for films?
Heating/air conditioning.
Seating: check the quantity and comfort.

Noise: are there any other functions running at the same time? Is there any building work in progress?

Displays: do you need any floral displays or table covers?

Stage: do you need one?

Toilets: are they adequate and convenient?

Is there a separate area for reserve equipment/staff?

Are the lifts adequate?

Are there telex, photocopying facilities, and typing services?

Communications: can you have a separate, dedicated telephone line?

Can you arrange access to the location for set-up?

Is there a conference/seminar manager and will he be on duty?

Book your choice in writing: get written confirmation and be clear on any cancellations.

Check your seminar location is clearly signposted.

Is there a special registration or reception area?

To this very comprehensive list I would add just one item: safety precautions – particularly fire precautions. IBM unfortunately lost a number of senior sales management in the USA, when one conference centre caught fire.

The environment

I surrounded the participants with my sales messages. I used portable exhibition stands to display relevant material and, for once, I made a full range of brochures available to take away, as well as having samples of all the products (even those not described in the seminar) and manuals. My intention was to inundate the prospect visually, as he arrived, with examples of our expertise and commitment.

The environment must be particularly carefully prepared to meet all the presentational needs. The facilities for visuals need to be good; for example the projectors need to work (I always brought my own, as I never trusted other people's for such an important role). The facilities for demonstrations need to be equally good.

Again as part of its seminar kit for dealers, IBM also provided a very comprehensive equipment checklist (much of which will not, however, be needed for the normal small seminar):

Lectern	Speaker's console	Blackboard
Flipchart	Microphones	Tape-recorder
Record player	Overhead projector	16mm projector
Screen(s)	Slide projector	Monitors

Televisions	Video	Spotlights
Staging	Wiring	Extension leads
Power points	Agendas	Seating plans
Pens	Pencils	Pads
Foil pens	Flipchart markers	Adhesive tape
Badges	Scissors	Films
Handouts	Brochures	

The programme

I found that a half-day was the most productive length for my seminars. Beyond that many prospects began to lose concentration, and I found it difficult to sustain the interest and the entertainment value. This half-day format fairly naturally broke down into four 45-minute sessions, running from 9.30am to 1.00pm, or from 1.30pm to 5.00pm.

The format I found most successful was:

9.15	Coffee
9.30-10.15	*Product introduction*
10.15-11.00	*'Industry/topical' lecture*
11.00-11.30	Coffee break
11.30-12.15	*Product demonstration*
12.15-1.00	*Visiting/reference speaker*
1.00-2.00	Buffet lunch

There are many other formats possible and, once more, you should carefully choose one that suits your own style, but I found this format almost universally effective for such introductory seminars. In more detail the sections were:

Product introduction. This was a general introduction, in my role as 'host'. It was also my opportunity to make the sales pitch that was expected of me. It was a straightforward presentation.

'Industry/topical' lecture. This was an almost totally technical lecture. It could be given by a visiting speaker, but more often it was given by my technical support staff. Most often, though, I gave it. It was important, however, to differentiate this clearly from the earlier sales pitch, emphasising the technical element (although still, very discreetly, incorporating some sales messages). The exact topic depended on the theme of the day but, for example, we ran a number on the theme of the use of CAD in architects' offices (where the overall seminar was about CAD, and the audience was exclusively composed of architects).

Product demonstration. This was a standard demonstration; sometimes run twice, splitting the eight participants into two groups of four (for better control).

Visiting/reference speaker. This was the advertised 'highlight' of the seminar. According to market research, nearly half of personal computer buyers, for example, wanted to see an expert speaker, with topics of general interest, at a seminar; in practice, though, it was usually the earlier sessions that most interested the audience. The speaker was chosen to meet the specific needs of the seminar content and audience. Thus, for architects we usually brought in one of the leading exponents of CAD who also ran an architectural practice.

Ideally, the speaker should be a customer, and hence double (*very* productively) as a reference. He should be a good speaker. But, even though I have experienced some disappointments in the standard of presentation, these were rarely fatal (for, despite the fact that they were not good speakers, I had chosen them to be experts – which still carried weight).

Coffee and lunch breaks

It is necessary to have these, but they do not have to be very elaborate. The only rule I made was that they should normally be in the form of buffets, so that everyone could circulate (and, of course, they are much easier to provide).

Even if they hadn't been strictly necessary, I would have used them; because they contained the most powerful sales pitches of the whole seminar. I always loaded these sessions with my colleagues, who mysteriously appeared from the wings at such times. No doubt the prospects thought it was the attraction of the free food that drew them (and in part it was), but the reality was that they were there (having been very carefully briefed in advance) to *sell*. I aimed at a ratio of one of my staff to every two prospects; about the ratio that they could handle easily, but which didn't obviously swamp the group. At the same time I circulated (together with my most trusted henchmen), so that I spoke, or rather sold, to every prospect.

Self-persuasion

Perhaps the most important reason for running at a ratio of 2:1 was that it allowed the prospects to talk to each other; and usually, in my experience, to sell to each other. This was, indeed, at the heart of my seminar style. From the beginning of the first session, I deliberately worked to get all the participants personally involved. I found that I was then able to build their enthusiasm (remembering that they were attending, whatever their reservations, because they had effectively classed themselves as prospects) to the extent that they started, with my help, to sell to each other. This was where I most often used negative selling; appearing to be trying to damp down the excesses of over-enthusiasm, but in the process, of course, stimulating it further – and, at the same time, building my image as an honest broker, very early in the sales campaign.

Qualification

One key function of such seminars was to qualify prospects *en masse*; and very productively. At the end of the seminar the whole team (including those who had attended the breaks) would get together in a debriefing session. We then decided who were the potential winners, and who were the tyre-kickers who were to be discarded. In practice I nearly always found that at least half the participants came into the 'winners' category. Less than a quarter were tyre-kickers, but these were unceremoniously, albeit discreetly, dropped. In just half a day it allowed me to qualify up to 10 prospects, which might otherwise have involved several weeks' work.

Follow-up

The hot prospects, typically numbering four or five from each seminar, have to be followed up as a matter of urgency, before the enthusiasm wanes. It astounded me how many of my sales professionals took their time following up these prospects, who had very clearly demonstrated their potential. I even had some such prospects eventually ring me and ask if I could *send* a salesman.

Timetable of events

My last quotation from IBM's excellent seminar package for its dealers is the suggested timetable of events. Once more, it is comprehensive:

Six Weeks Prior	*Four Weeks Prior*
Announce seminar plans	Confirm seminar date(s), time
Discuss objectives:	Prepare agenda
attendance/sales	Prepare presentation
Delegate support	(Invite guest speakers)
responsibilities	Prepare demonstration
Book venue	Develop invitation list
	Prepare invitation/letter

Prepare attendance letter
Prepare follow-up letters
Check administrative support
Check availability of
demonstration machines
Arrange engineering support
Prepare handout material

Three Weeks Prior
Begin invitation/letter/phone
Review seminar plan/agenda
(Arrange local advertising)
(Confirm guest speaker)

Two Weeks Prior
Mail accept response letter
Mail 'Sorry you can't make it'
letter
Reserve necessary equipment
Review progress with staff

One Week Prior
Begin attendance assurance:
(telephone)
Practise presentations
Practise demonstrations
Assemble visuals
Assemble handouts
Organise reception/
registration material
Order refreshments (quantity)
Coordinator checks acceptances

Two Days Prior
List confirmed attendees
Prepare name badges/tags
Emphasise attendee's goal to
staff
Assemble total presentation,
handouts and demonstration

One Day Prior
Full rehearsal
(Set up facilities)
Check equipment
Check direction signs
Confirm refreshments
(Reconfirm guest speakers)
Contingency plan

Seminar Day
Personnel arrive at least
one hour early
Review agenda with personnel
Ensure refreshments are set up
Check facilities and equipment
Set up attendees':
handouts/reception
Check seminar direction signs
Register attendees
Remove seminar direction signs

Seminar Performance
Seminar host/overview
Welcome/mood setting

One Day After
Start follow-up campaign
Telephone for appointments

Seminar presentations
Demonstrations
Q & A
Evaluation forms
Conclusion
Seminar 'break-down'

Send follow-up letters
Evaluate success/failure of
seminar
Tracking system for attendees

Symposia and conferences

As your ambition grows, so may the size of your meetings. But, in practice, the character of the meeting changes dramatically as a result. Once there are more than, say, 20 attendees the meeting ceases to be interactive in any way. Even in the coffee breaks the majority of prospects will be talking to each other rather than to one of the staff. Long demonstrations are usually ruled out, unless you put in substantial effort. Indeed, the only interaction I was able to include in such events was to erect an exhibition stand (usually in the coffee area), so that those prospects who did want to come and talk, or see a short demonstration, could easily do so.

The main change is that the content of the presentations must carry the whole event. As a result, you will have to select your speakers very carefully; for it is their quality, and that alone, that delegates will remember and judge you by. The sales messages become very indirect; unless it is a product launch meeting, which is a separate type of event. To a degree it is the style of the meeting, which is often set almost as much by the details as by the overall importance of the subject matter, which is seen as your contribution.

As such, the setting may become important. I ran one very successful seminar at the Royal Society; but if you plan to do the same you should be aware that the logistics will have to include persuading a Fellow of that august institution to sponsor you!

It may be the context that matters. I ran another symposium as an extension of an international conference, and was successful in persuading most of the delegates attending that to stay on for mine; including, very impressively for my prospects who also attended, the *world's* top oncologist (cancer specialist).

The details are important and influential, where they are not in seminars. So the logistics can be quite horrifying.

You may not be involved in organising events on such a scale; fortunate since they absorb massive resources for relatively little short-term gain. My own involvement in them was because my strategy called for the long-term expansion of the whole market, and they were ideal for this.

To give an idea of some of the complexities, though, I organised several learned symposia. Each lasted a full day with a dozen or more speakers, presenting papers that were at the leading edge of medical research (identifying who were the most important researchers in the forefront of medicine was no easy task in itself). I brought these speakers in from around the world, flying them from the USA as well as from Europe, at a cost of several thousand pounds in air fares alone. The audience, typically of around 600, had to be housed; and there are relatively few venues capable of handling this number and providing the atmosphere needed. They had to be seated, and had to be able to see and hear what was going on (which required full, professional, lighting/projection and sound teams – with up to half a dozen outside staff just for this). Of course, they also required feeding; and, where the details now counted, this had to be well done. It was a monumental task, and cost the best part of £10,000 each time; together with a number of weeks' work on my part.

As you can see from the above example, the logistics of this sort of event can be horrendous. Of course, you can run much smaller meetings with much less effort; but the logistics will still dominate, and make them debatable (in terms of productivity) for even the most ambitious sales professional.

Factory visits

Another special event, which can combine several areas of sales activity (including presentations, demonstrations and references – albeit internal), is a visit to your manufacturing facility or laboratory (or even your head office). The intention is to impress your prospect with the technology, quality and expertise that goes into the product; and to prove that you can also provide it in the field of support.

Factory visits have to be at least as carefully organised as seminars. Nothing can be left to chance. They will normally require all the usual presentation and demonstration facilities. These can usually be found (or can be created), as long as you have the support of your factory management. You cannot, though, just drift through the factory; it needs to be highly organised – although it shouldn't appear so to the prospect (and that casual informality needs an even higher degree of organisation!). The management will, understandably, not want you to disrupt production, and neither will you; there is nothing worse than the prospect finding a production line coming to a halt while all the workers gawk at him.

You should carefully plan the route to cover all the highlights, and to avoid the demolition areas which seem to afflict all factories. It also needs to be safe. Safety is an essential item whatever you are involved in. It is easy to forget to check the fire-exits before a meeting; but losing a prospect himself to an accident is much more embarrassing than just losing his business!

You should carefully choose the departments you want to visit. John Fenton suggests quality control as one essential stop *en route*. You will also want to be sure that everyone *is* working, and working as they should, so you will need to send runners ahead to alert the management (who should, in any case, have been well briefed in advance). You will, of course, need production managers as your guides.

Such a visit can have many of the benefits of a good reference visit and, once again, the opportunity to spend an extended period with the prospect away from distractions should not be ignored. But it will often require a disproportionate amount of organising. As a result, it is better to organise such factory visits for groups of prospects; since the organisation, and disruption, is almost the same for a hundred as for one.

IBM, almost inevitably, used to undertake these on the grand scale; but an example can illustrate what might be involved. I was part of a team of no less than six organisers that used to take groups of 150 customers and prospects at a time to our Vimercarte plant in Italy. Three of us went on ahead several days in advance to prepare the ground in Italy. The other three oversaw the travel arrangements which, as they involved chartering an airliner, were not insubstantial. A further 30 IBMers also travelled with the party as 'hosts' looking after the 150 customers and prospects. This part of the event was somewhat similar to organising a package holiday; and absorbed similar resources.

In Italy there were the logistics of housing 180+ persons for the night, and giving them two lunches, a dinner and breakfast, almost all at different locations (which was one of the reasons for the advance party); as well as arranging the six coaches to carry everyone around the Italian countryside. At the plant itself we needed speakers to run the various presentations, and something like 10 guides for the various groups touring the factory. We eased the problem by splitting the overall group into two parts, each of which had a different itinerary and each of which was further split into groups of six for the plant tour.

Most factory visits are much less spectacular. But, as the above example shows, it is the incidental logistics which (once more) dominate and absorb significant resources.

Entertaining

In all of the events described in this chapter, you are likely to be involved in providing food for your prospects. In general the food need not be that extravagant; a finger-buffet is usually quite sufficient. It is the quality of conversation that is much more important than the quality of the food.

Sometimes, though, more elaborate entertaining is called for. John Fenton suggests that the highlight of a factory visit should be lunch in the boardroom. The 'detail' of food *is* important in those events, such as symposia, where the details count.

For one group of seminars (where food would not normally be important) I also used very good restaurants. This was not as a bribe, it was simply an excellent way of painlessly extending the seminar for another three hours. This gave extra time to talk to the prospects and (in particular) to allow them to sell themselves. The wine, flowing freely, certainly helped to promote the very informal, friendly atmosphere that made these very productive events.

In general, though, such entertaining is unnecessarily lavish. It requires special justification to your own management and, not least, to the prospects who will suspect your motives.

A beer and a sandwich

I have found lunchtime a particularly useful time to catch my busiest prospects. Taking them out for a beer and a sandwich (hardly the height of expense account entertaining, but usually quite acceptable to the prospect) has the benefit of getting them away from the inevitable distractions. It also breaks down the barriers, relaxes the prospect and makes for a much friendlier atmosphere.

I also used the 'social conversation' during such sessions for a particularly hard sell of IBM; which was what the customers were buying as much as the product. I used to explain how the company affected me personally and by extension I also sold the benefits to him; if IBM was so good to me, a mere employee, just think what it did for its customers! Furthermore, they didn't see it as a sales message, although it was a very strong one, and that made it that much more effective.

Chapter 10
The Profession of Selling

Many salesmen, and almost all of the rest of the population, will think I am mad even to talk about the 'profession' of selling. A salesman is too often seen as some form of second-class citizen. The archetypal salesman for too many of us has been Willy Loman, from Arthur Miller's *Death of a Salesman*. William Davis refers to Willy Loman in his book, as does Buck Rodgers where he says: 'Today's salesperson has to be a lot more to the customer than a genial, back-slapping, joke-telling Willy Loman type, who drops in each season to entertain and show his wares.' But the stereotype is all pervasive; the salesman, in this perspective, is to be despised or pitied.

Thomas J Watson, at the beginning of the century, summed the problem up for me when he said: 'I want the IBM salesmen to be looked up to. Admired. I want their wives and children to be proud of them. I don't want their mothers to feel that they have to apologise for them when asked what their sons are doing.' Regrettably, things have not moved on a great deal since. Miller, Heiman and Tuleja tell the story: ' ... when we asked a senior vice-president if "sales" was considered a dirty word by his people. "Oh, no" he assured us. "Everybody is really on board with the importance of selling. But" he went on without batting an eye "we call it marketing".'

Even sales professionals themselves recognise dominance of the stereotype. In a recent survey of its members, the Institute of Sales and Marketing Management found that only 4 per cent (just one member in every 25) believed that, 'there is now a widespread public acceptance of selling as a good career opportunity and a very worthwhile business function'.

I hope that this book shows that the stereotype could not be farther from the truth; at least as far as sales professionals are concerned. The problem is persuading the world at large of this.

What should make a good sales professional?

In Chapter 2 I spent some time defining, very broadly, what makes a good sales professional. In this last chapter I want to look ahead somewhat; to see where the sales profession may be going – to see what, in the future or perhaps just in the ideal world, should make a sales professional.

In the past century the role of the salesman has changed dramatically. As the century opened, the salesman *was* the stereotypical traveller, a middle-man hawking his wares around those remote locations not fortunate enough to have good access to large business or shopping centres. But, in truth, that was only half the story. For the real predecessor of many modern salesmen, and certainly of most sales professionals, was the individual entrepreneur; the owner of the small company, who was also its only salesman (a role, though, that he probably didn't recognise as different from any other).

Since then there have been dramatic changes. Most of the 'middle-men' salesmen have disappeared. Self-service has decimated retail salesmen, who have been replaced by shelf fillers and checkout operators. During this time the salesman selling to retailers has emerged, taking over the stereotype, to return once more to the shadows; as more specialised and routine skills, such as merchandising, took over — and the group buyers for the new retail chains became the prey of a new 'professional', the negotiator, for whom so many books on pricing actions have recently been written.

Perhaps the main change, and the one that most concerns us as sales professionals, has been the emergence of the 'industrial salesman'; the expert in the complex sale. At the turn of the century, as I have already indicated, this role was typically just one of many handled by the owner himself. The average enterprise was small, as were most organisations at that time.

The time since has seen the growth of the giant corporations; to the extent that more than half of all business worldwide is now handled by less than 500 corporations. Clearly, there is no way that the individual 'owners' of these giants could get around all their customers; in any case, the other major trend has been that owners have progressively been succeeded by professional managers. The sales content of the owner's role was, accordingly, taken over by the industrial salesman; the precursor of the sales professional, the eponymous hero of this book.

En route, however, they also (quite unnecessarily) took on board the stereotype of the existing salesmen. Industrial salesmen, too, learned how to 'persuade'. As the century progressed, the sales techniques developed became more sophisticated and more complex; until the modern creation of the sales trainers is a walking encyclopaedia of devious tricks that would have astounded Machiavelli.

Owner to sales professional

The problem has been that this simplified role did precious little justice to the model it replaced. That model should have been the owner, but in practice the travelling salesman was chosen. Unfortunately, apart from the superficial similarities (that they both visited customers and took orders) they are totally different animals.

What most companies have signally missed in the translation are the elements of professionalism and management. IBM is almost unique, at least in my experience, in recognising the true range of skills needed by its sales professionals; and it is willing to spend up to £100,000 each on training to make certain that its sales professionals really do possess these skills. However, the indications from IBM's success over the years are that this was a sound investment. In their own way the personal computer dealers, who would blanch at the thought of spending £100 on the whole of their staff training, have also confirmed the importance of this training – by their own abject failure!

Professionalism

There has, it is true, been much talk of professionalism; this is, indeed, a favourite topic of sales trainers. But much of this has been a diversion. What they, in the main, mean by 'professionalism' is the ever slicker presentation of ever more complex techniques to 'persuade' the prospect.

My own view of professionalism is far removed from this. I believe that persuasion is only a small part of the salesman's role; and ultimately one that is generally wrongly described. The skills that the market place, the customers and prospects, demand of a sales professional cover a much wider range.

Professionalism in my terms means being able to offer the whole range of skills that the customer or prospect needs; and preferably having a sound level of expertise in each of them. In the ultimate it could mean being an expert in all the many skills described in this book.

I will not list even the main skills, since this would only repeat the earlier sections. But I would stress that the most important area of such skills is that of knowledge, technical (product) knowledge and in particular business knowledge; far outweighing sales skills (or, more accurately, sales techniques).

The original owner, when he went to meet a customer, went equipped with a whole armoury of knowledge about his own (and his customer's) business. The modern sales professional needs a similar range of skills.

Management

Clearly, the owner was a manager. He made his money by expertly managing the resources at his command; and he brought that same expertise (albeit often unknowingly) to his management of the interface with his customers.

Management, in its true sense, is a key aspect of the sales professional's role, as evidenced by the large sections devoted to it in this book. Again, I will not list these different management skills; they will have become very evident from the earlier chapters.

Account management, which is the aggregate of all these management skills, is a much underrated talent. Indeed, almost all the sales trainers totally ignore it. Yet account management lies at the heart of the sales professional's role.

I suspect that few sales professionals really have any idea of the true importance of their role; and I am fairly certain that most of their managements will have even less understanding. I am positive that very few members of the general public will!

I was fortunate to be part of the 'brand management' movement that took many of the larger consumer goods companies by storm in the 1960s and 1970s. With their portfolios of different (branded) products, these companies had begun to experience major problems of coordination. Their answer was to superimpose on the conventional, functional (vertical) hierarchy a totally horizontal management structure; the brand management. This was very successful, to the extent that in a number of these companies this brand management became the dominant management team, and effectively captured control of these companies.

There is a good definition of a brand manager: he is supposed to be to his brand what his managing director is to the whole company. This is a particularly useful and powerful definition.

I have included this aside because I believe that this analogy can be very directly transferred to the sales professional. In their own special areas, there are significant parallels between the brand manager handling the mass consumer good and the sales professional dealing with the complex sale. The sales professional also provides the horizontal management that coordinates the company's vertical, functional structures; as applied to his customers. It should be fair to say that he is to each of his customers (and prospects) what the managing director is to the customer set of the whole company. He truly should be the inheritor of the original owner salesman.

It is a concept that may seem very strange to many salesmen, even more so to sales trainers; and the general public would have considerable difficulties trying to match it to the stereotype. But I believe it is already valid for the top sales professionals, and could become so for a great many more. It is a valid concept because it encompasses the true scope of the real sales professional's role. It is not to put the sales professional on a par with his managing director; the managing director must carry a great deal more responsibility – and will very quickly disabuse any sales professional who has such ideas above his station! The main justification for the concept, though, is that it challenges the sales professional to expand his horizons; to look beyond the conventional limitations of his role – to see what could, and should, be possible.

Communicator

A sales professional should, however, never lose sight of his basic function, which must still be to obtain the order. Most sales trainers would emphasise, in this context, the need for persuasion.

I feel that the term 'persuasion' is somewhat loaded. Most of all it is redolent of selling refrigerators to Eskimos. It challenges the salesman to sell the unwanted, when the sales professional should be looking for the want he can satisfy. It also, once more, limits a sales professional's role. I prefer the term 'communication'; not least because it can, and should, be two-way. My comments in the earlier chapters should amply expand my views in this area.

Communications can also encompass the role of facilitating communication between customers and your company, and with other customers, regardless of whether an order is involved. You become the interface between all these groups; funnelling ideas between them. It is a very powerful position, and one in which you can make a great personal contribution; a contribution that few others are capable of. As such it can be a very satisfying role.

What is the sales professional's value?

To some this may seem a strange question, particularly where society has very clearly placed such a negative value on the role as played by the salesman stereotype. Such an individual has been viewed as something of a waste of society's valuable resources. He can only win by making the buyer the loser; and the net effect is a loss to society overall. In some ways he is a thief, taking away from others; only to be tolerated because, in some inexplicable way, he is a necessary evil.

The Sales Professional

It is not surprising that society rates the salesman as only slightly more acceptable than the politician!

Indeed, over the years salesmen as a group have largely *earned* this opprobrium, by amply living up to the stereotype. Many of them have been patently dishonest and untrustworthy. They have sold the wrong product, regardless of the customer's needs. They *have* won at the expense of their customers, and at the expense of society. So let's not shed any crocodile tears for them.

But history need not repeat itself. The sales professional of the future can, and should, be a useful member of society.

So what does society really want? I have touched on this in the previous chapters, but I will now be more explicit. These ideas are partly derived from my own observations, but mainly from various pieces of market research carried out in the early days of personal computer marketing. These questions related to the purchase of personal computers, but I believe that they are probably fairly typical of complex sales in general. In any case, they represent what commonsense might lead us to expect.

Expertise

Not unexpectedly, the buyers want their sales professionals to be expert in what they are selling. The purchase of new equipment, or of a new service, can be a fraught experience for a buyer. He is very exposed, because he usually lacks expertise in the product – and he is well aware of this. What he desperately wants and needs is someone who can expertly advise him. Were it an ideal world, the sales professional would be just such an expert. For, if he lives up to my advice, nobody should have more expertise in the products than he.

Honesty

The problem is: how can a customer trust the sales professional's advice? He would certainly be very foolish to accept that given by the stereotypical salesman. This is why customers rate honesty as being almost as important as expertise. It is also why, of course, they recognise that there is almost no hope of this ideal ever being attained.

But the ideal should not merely be attainable; for the sales professional it should be essential. In a win-win sale there should be no incentive for dishonesty.

Perhaps this quality would be better described as integrity. Honesty is in many ways just reactive, where integrity can go rather further and incorporate a positive attitude; in this context a clear commitment to customer service.

But these two virtues, albeit essential (and difficult enough for most sales professionals to live up to), are only the tip of the iceberg in terms of what the sales professional potentially has to offer society.

Manager of the group interface

Our society increasingly revolves around information. Indeed, it is argued that perhaps two-thirds of all employees are now information workers. The flow of such information has become a torrent but, despite what many of the pundits would have you believe, most of this communication is not yet handled by computers. To that extent, the telephone rather than the computer should still be the symbol of our age. Computers *will* increasingly take over the more mundane tasks, but the more important ones will still be handled by human beings for the foreseeable future.

This information flow is most problematical at the various group interfaces. Within a single company the flow can be positively managed; but even there the boundaries between different groups, typically between different departments, need very careful handling. The boundaries with groups outside the organisation pose major problems. The information flow simply cannot be managed in a tidy way. It is at this interface that the company can, and often does, develop partial blindness. It is where it most needs help, and should be most appreciative of that help.

As a result the people who *can* manage the interface are becoming increasingly important to society; although society has, as yet, scarcely registered this fact.

The sales professional is the one individual ideally suited to manage that interface. He is ideally placed. His job requires him to spend almost all of his time in that 'no-man's land' and to devote all his energies at that interface. He has the ideal knowledge and skills which bracket the interface, with bases in the camps on either side. Most of all, he is (or should be) an expert communicator; trained to carry complex messages, and to deliver them in an intelligible form.

As a result, he should become one of the pivotal figures in the next stage of society's evolution; into the information revolution.

Added-value

Once more, though, the 'manager of the interface' implies a somewhat passive role; not in terms of managing (that can hardly be passive), but in terms of the information managed – where the sales professional might appear to be a very sophisticated messenger boy.

In truth, the sales professional can contribute very positively to that information flow himself; creating more added-value than anyone else in the chain.

Marketing agent

The creation of wealth in our society now largely comes from marketing, rather than manufacturing, activities. It is the discovery of the customer's true needs, and the matching of these with the best solution, that generates the most wealth. The sales professional is not merely ideally placed to handle this, but (for once) this is recognised to be his function.

Change agent

Our society is changing ever faster; the pace of change is accelerating. Once more, managing that change will be of critical importance.

Much of this management of change will, of course, be internal to the various organisations; to the companies. Again, perhaps the most crucial and least controllable element of change will lie at the interface. And again, the sales professional is ideally placed to manage the change that is occurring, and ensure that it is as painless as possible. If nothing else, his own role is the epitome of change; so he, more than almost anyone else, has the experience as well as the skills to manage it.

But the sales professional can go much further than this. He can actually promote change himself; he can stimulate new ideas. This is already much of the role of the best sales professionals: they sell far more by finding new uses for their product than by limiting themselves to fighting their competitors for the existing uses. It is even arguable that the accelerating pace of society is mainly due to the emergence of the powerful influence of marketing, in its most general sense.

Much of the stimulus for change now is provided by 'communication'. The manager typically reads about (or now, increasingly, sees on television) what someone else is doing in the same (or similar) field; and tries it himself. As communications have rapidly expanded the pace of change has accelerated.

The sales professional has a very direct role to play in this communication process. If he is doing his job well, he will be steeped in all the (relevant) aspects of his customer's business; and will be aware of the developments taking place. He will also be aware of these across a number of customers, and can communicate these ideas (always assuming that this will not breach any confidentiality) to his other customers. What is more, most of these developments will not have been written up, even by the most esoteric of trade publications. So the sales professional can be a very powerful facilitator of change. He can lubricate the wheels of progress.

Wealth creator

Bringing together all these roles, the sales professional can now have more influence on the development of the business community than almost any other individual. His expertise and advice can very positively influence just how well his customers' businesses run. More important, he can see, and suggest, new ideas that can sometimes dramatically influence the future of those businesses. His 'vision', backed by his business experience, offers a considerable contribution to the creation of wealth. Arguably, in our modern society, the sales professional (as the pivotal member of the marketing team, where complex sales are concerned) has now become the main individual wealth creator.

Society can ill afford to neglect him; let alone disparage him.

How to change the stereotype?

The problem remains that pitifully few people recognise the importance of his role. Indeed, as the survey results at the beginning of this chapter showed, perhaps as few as 4 per cent of sales professionals themselves believe that society has any faith in the importance of the role. This ignorance is an unnecessary limitation on what the sales professional can offer to society, as well as what he is entitled to take from it (in terms of personal satisfaction).

Society's responsibilities

The sales professional's role in society is becoming so pivotal that society must take a positive stance. It is no longer productive to look the other way, or to see the sales professional as a member of a caste of untouchables.

First of all, society must be more demanding of sales professionals. While it goes on expecting nothing of them, too many of them will be quite happy to *offer* nothing. Society, and in particular all its buyers, should go on record that it at least expects the sales professional to have the requisite expertise, backed by a suitable degree of honesty; and it should go on demanding that sales professionals live up to these requirements. It should also strive for the ideal, where the sales professional is reasonably expected to provide significant added-value.

It is ludicrous that society sets high standards for many of its less influential members, such as taxi-drivers and even insurance salesmen, but has no comment to make about sales professionals; who could contribute so much, and yet so often detract even more. Both the Institute of Sales and Marketing Management and the Institute of Marketing have valiantly tried to set some standards. But they have been largely voices crying in the wilderness. It is imperative that the role of the salesman (at least at the professional level) should be seen as a true profession. Society should demand that the whole range of professional standards applied to the more traditional professions are brought into being – and implemented in practice.

Second, society must reappraise and revalue the salesman's role. While it deprecates the whole profession it cannot expect the flower of its youth to join the profession. Equally, it can hardly expect existing salesmen to give a damn, when nobody gives a damn about them. Society needs, instead, to show that it values the truly professional salesman. This is essential, if society wants salesmen to make the significant contribution of which they are ultimately capable.

Third, society should demand that salesmen are adequately trained; and should itself put in place programmes to ensure that this happens. Almost every job has its training programmes. Many on the shop floor still serve long apprenticeships. Typists and clerical assistants are carefully taught their skills. Almost alone, the salesman is left out in the cold. There is almost no awareness, even among those most closely involved, of a need for sales training. Just read the job advertisements. *None* ask for any form of sales qualification, and some even state (with a perverse pride), 'no experience necessary'.

What is more, the sales training that is available is all too often a disgrace. There are good sales trainers, but there are more charlatans. *Anyone* can set up as a sales trainer, and often does. Both the Institute of Sales and Marketing Management and the Institute of Marketing run excellent training programmes leading to qualifications including those of the City and Guilds and the Open University. But very few study for them; understandably so, where these paper qualifications (for which their holders have studied hard and long) are unrecognised by most employers, and certainly ignored by the world at large. Society, in the form of government, needs to put some teeth into these qualifications. Until it does salesmen will always have the excuse that, 'There is no way I can learn to do it better.'

The final action of society might be to discriminate. For a long time to come there will be salesmen who fail to measure up to any professional standards; some because they can't, some because they won't, but most because they don't see the need. Society should differentiate between these salesmen and the sales professionals who are the subject of this book. I can have no criticism if society continues to deprecate and shun *bad* salesmen, just as long as it encourages and admires good sales professionals.

There are precedents for such a significant change in status. Less than two centuries ago it was the barber who often acted as surgeon; with standards that make the average modern salesman look something of a paragon. Yet now the surgeon is just about the highest valued member of society. I believe that there is good justification for applying a similar transformation to the sales professional; and the lesser salesman can go the same way as the ordinary barber.

What are the sales professional's own responsibilities?

The sales professional can scarcely complain of society's unfair treatment as long as he lives up to most of what society complains about. There are large numbers of salesmen who come perilously close to the stereotype in the way that they sell. There are many more who are happy to accept at least some of the stereotype's limitations. On the other hand, there are as yet very few indeed who live up to all the ideals I describe in this book; those who can truly describe themselves as sales professionals. For example, the whole sales professional membership of the Institute of Sales and Marketing Management is probably less than 10,000; out of the total of millions of salesmen, of one kind or another, in the UK.

Professionalism
A sales professional, as an individual, cannot hope to be thought of as a professional unless he behaves like one. The first requirement, therefore, is quite simply that each sales professional decides that he *will* become genuinely professional; and earn the title, not just assume it.

Education
The second requirement is that this sales professional becomes educated, so that he can live up to his role. Letters behind your name, be they MInstSMM (from the Institute of Sales and Marketing

Management) or MInstM (from the Institute of Marketing) or even BA (from the Open University), mean little by themselves; but at least they show you are trying – and can offer your customers that much more.

Lobbying

The final requirement is that these sales professionals band together, most practically by joining one of the two institutes, and put political pressure on the key elements in society (notably the government) to recognise their demands.

The sales profession fully deserves to be recognised as a true profession. But before that can happen, all its members – the sales professionals – will have to earn that right!

Even if you don't succeed in changing the world, I am certain you will find that being a true sales professsional will be much more satisfying (even fulfilling), as well as being more enjoyable; and that is what, at least for me, selling is all about.

Bibliography

There are too many books about selling even to begin to list all of them, or even to list the useful ones. Instead, listed below in strictly alphabetical sequence, are the few that I have found useful enough (at least in part) to quote in this book.

The Secret of Successful Selling Tony Adams, Heinemann, 1985

The Principles and Practice of Management edited by E F L Brech, Longman, 1975

How to Win Friends and Influence People Dale Carnegie, Cedar Books, 1953

The Supersalesman's Handbook William Davis, Sidgwick & Jackson, 1986

How to Sell Against Competition John Fenton, William Heinemann, 1984

The Principle and Practice of Selling Alan Gillam, Heinemann, 1982; on behalf of the Institute of Marketing

How to Win Customers Heinz M Goldmann, Staples Press, 1958

How to Master the Art of Selling Tom Hopkins, Champion Press, 1982

Negotiate to Close Gary Karass, Collins, 1985

IBM: How the World's Most Successful Corporation is Managed David Mercer, Kogan Page, 1987

Strategic Selling Robert B Miller, Stephen E Heiman and Tad Tuleja, William Morrow, 1985

The Dartnell Sales Promotion Handbook edited by Ovid Riso, The Dartnell Corporation, 1979

The IBM Way Buck Rodgers, with Robert L Shock, Harper & Row, 1986

Getting Sales Richard B Smith and Ginger Dick, International Self-Counsel Press, 1981

How to Succeed in Selling Alfred Tack, The Windmill Press

The Gentle Art of Salesmanship Harry Turner, Fontana, 1985

All About Selling Alan Williams, Mcgraw Hill, 1983

Appendix 1: Sales organisations

There are just two well-known organisations in the UK that work on behalf of sales professionals:

The Institute of Sales and Marketing Management, Georgian House, 31 Upper Street, Luton, Bedfordshire LU1 2RD. Tel: 0582 456767

Institute of Marketing, Moor Hall, Cookham, Berkshire SL6 9QH. Tel: 06285 24922

Rather perversely, in view of their names, it is the Institute of Sales and Marketing Management (ISMM) that mainly caters for sales professionals rather than management. The Institute of Marketing (IM) tends to concentrate more on 'pure' marketing.

Both institutes emphasise the importance of education and have extensive education programmes. Both have programmes that lead to recognised qualifications. The IM will, though, generally only admit as members (or associates) those who have such a qualification (or are studying for it). The ISMM, on the other-hand, has some grades of membership which only require some degree of relevant experience; the Associate (AInstSMM) level, for example, only requires two years in a selling or marketing role.

Both institutes represent their members, and the rest of the sales profession, to government and the general public; they are both expert lobbyists on our behalf. Both provide excellent facilities: the IM has probably the best marketing training facility in Europe and the ISMM's magazine offers good information about opportunities for new business.

Index